FUNDAMENTALS of English Grammar

FIFTH EDITION

with **MyEnglishLab**
access code inside

Betty S. Azar
Stacy A. Hagen

**Fundamentals of English Grammar, Fifth Edition
with MyEnglishLab**

Copyright © 2020, 2011, 2003, 1992, 1985 by Betty Schrampfer Azar
All rights reserved.

No part of this publication may be reproduced, stored in a retrieval system, or transmitted in any form or by any means, electronic, mechanical, photocopying, recording, or otherwise, without the prior permission of the publisher.

Azar Associates: Sue Van Etten, Manager

Pearson Education, 221 River Street, Hoboken, NJ 07030

Staff credits: The people who made up the *Fundamentals of English Grammar Fifth Edition* team, representing content development, design, multimedia, project management, publishing, and rights management, are Pietro Alongi, Sheila Ameri, Jennifer Castro, Tracey Cataldo, Dave Dickey, Gina DiLillo, Warren Fischbach, Sarah Henrich, Niki Lee, Stefan Machura, Amy McCormick, Robert Ruvo, Katarzyna Starzynska-Kosciuszko, Paula Van Ells, Joseph Vella, and Marcin Wozniak.

Contributing Editors: Barbara Lyons, Janice L. Baillie
Text composition: Aptara

Disclaimer: This work is produced by Pearson Education and is not endorsed by any trademark owner referenced in this publication.

Library of Congress Cataloging-in-Publication Data

A catalog record for the print edition is available from the Library of Congress.

Printed in Malaysia by Vivar Printing/02 (2024)

ISBN 13: 978-0-13-499882-4
ISBN 10: 0-13-499882-0

ISBN 13: 978-0-13-653445-7 (International Edition)
ISBN 10: 0-13-653445-7 (International Edition)

ScoutAutomatedPrintCode

To
Shelley Hartle and Sue Van Etten
B.S.A.

To the students and teachers at Edmonds Community College, from whom I learned so much
S.A.H.

Contents

Preface to the Fifth Edition x
Acknowledgments xii
Getting Started xiii

Chapter 1	PRESENT TIME 1		
	1-1	Simple Present and Present Progressive 2	
	1-2	Forms of the Simple Present and the Present Progressive 2	
	1-3	Singular/Plural 9	
	1-4	Spelling of Simple Present Verbs: Final *-s/-es* 11	
	1-5	Frequency Adverbs 14	
	1-6	Verbs Not Usually Used in the Progressive 18	
	1-7	Present Verbs: Short Answers to *Yes/No* Questions 21	
Chapter 2	PAST TIME 30		
	2-1	The Simple Past: Regular Verbs 31	
	2-2	Expressing Past Time: The Simple Past, Irregular Verbs 32	
	2-3	Common Irregular Verbs: A Reference List 33	
	2-4	Recognizing Verb Endings and Questions with *Did* 40	
	2-5	Spelling of *-ing* and *-ed* Forms 43	
	2-6	The Past Progressive 46	
	2-7	Simple Past vs. Past Progressive 50	
	2-8	Expressing Past Time: Using Time Clauses 57	
	2-9	Expressing Past Habit: *Used To* 60	
Chapter 3	FUTURE TIME 64		
	3-1	Expressing Future Time: *Be Going To* and *Will* 65	
	3-2	Forms with *Be Going To* 66	
	3-3	Forms with *Will* 69	
	3-4	*Be Going To* and *Will* in Spoken English 71	
	3-5	*Be Going To* vs. *Will* 73	
	3-6	Certainty About the Future 77	
	3-7	Expressing the Future in Time Clauses and *If*-Clauses 80	
	3-8	Using the Present Progressive to Express Future Time 83	
	3-9	Using the Simple Present to Express Future Time 85	
	3-10	Immediate Future: Using *Be About To* 86	
	3-11	Parallel Verbs 87	

Chapter 4	PRESENT PERFECT AND PAST PERFECT	91
	4-1 Past Participle	92
	4-2 Introduction to the Present Perfect: Unspecified Time with *Ever* and *Never*	94
	4-3 The Present Perfect with Unspecified Time: *Already, Yet, Just, Recently*	96
	4-4 Present Perfect with *Since* and *For*	99
	4-5 Simple Past vs. Present Perfect	104
	4-6 Present Perfect Progressive	108
	4-7 Present Perfect Progressive vs. Present Perfect	110
	4-8 Past Perfect	116
Chapter 5	ASKING QUESTIONS	121
	5-1 *Yes/No* Questions and Short Answers	122
	5-2 *Where, Why, When, What Time, How Come, What … For*	125
	5-3 Questions With *Who, Whom,* and *What*	128
	5-4 Using *What* + a Form of *Do*	131
	5-5 *Which* vs. *What* and *What Kind Of*	133
	5-6 Using *How*	135
	5-7 Using *How Often / How Many Times*	138
	5-8 Talking About Distance	140
	5-9 Length of Time: *It + Take* and *How Long; How Many*	141
	5-10 Spoken and Written Contractions with Question Words	143
	5-11 More Questions with *How*	146
	5-12 Using *How About* and *What About*	147
	5-13 Tag Questions	149
Chapter 6	NOUNS AND PRONOUNS	157
	6-1 Plural Forms of Nouns	158
	6-2 Pronunciation of Final *-s/-es*	160
	6-3 Subjects, Verbs, and Objects	162
	6-4 Objects of Prepositions	164
	6-5 Prepositions of Time	167
	6-6 Word Order: Place and Time	168
	6-7 Subject-Verb Agreement	169
	6-8 Using Adjectives to Describe Nouns	171
	6-9 Using Nouns as Adjectives	173
	6-10 Personal Pronouns: Subjects and Objects	175
	6-11 Possessive Nouns	178
	6-12 Using *Whose*	180
	6-13 Possessive Pronouns and Adjectives	181
	6-14 Reflexive Pronouns	183
	6-15 Singular Forms of *Other: Another* vs. *The Other*	184
	6-16 Plural Forms of *Other: Other(s)* vs. *The Other(s)*	186
	6-17 Summary: Forms of *Other*	188

Chapter 7	MODAL AUXILIARIES, THE IMPERATIVE, MAKING SUGGESTIONS, STATING PREFERENCES 193
7-1	Introduction to Modal Auxiliaries 194
7-2	Expressing Ability: *Can, Could, Be Able To* 195
7-3	Expressing Possibility: *May, Might,* and *Maybe;* Expressing Permission: *May* and *Can* 198
7-4	Using *Could* to Express Possibility 200
7-5	Polite Requests with *I*: *May, Could, Can* 202
7-6	Polite Requests with *You*: *Would, Could, Will, Can* 205
7-7	Expressing Advice: *Should* and *Ought To* 207
7-8	Expressing Advice: *Had Better* 209
7-9	Expressing Necessity: *Have To, Have Got To, Must* 210
7-10	Expressing Lack of Necessity: *Do Not Have To;* Expressing Prohibition: *Must Not* 214
7-11	Making Logical Conclusions: *Must* 215
7-12	Tag Questions with Modal Auxiliaries 218
7-13	Imperative Sentences: Giving Instructions 219
7-14	Making Suggestions: *Let's* and *Why Don't* 221
7-15	Stating Preferences: *Prefer, Like ... Better, Would Rather* 222
7-16	Summary: Modal Auxiliaries Taught in Chapter 7 224

Chapter 8	CONNECTING IDEAS: PUNCTUATION AND MEANING 228
8-1	Connecting Ideas with *And* 229
8-2	Connecting Ideas with *But* and *Or* 231
8-3	Connecting Ideas with *So* 232
8-4	Using Auxiliary Verbs After *But* 234
8-5	Using *And* + *Too, So, Either, Neither* 236
8-6	Connecting Ideas with *Because* 241
8-7	Connecting Ideas with *Even Though/Although* 244

Chapter 9	COMPARISONS 250
9-1	Introduction to Comparative Forms of Adjectives 251
9-2	Introduction to Superlative Forms of Adjectives 255
9-3	Completing Comparatives and Superlatives 258
9-4	Making Comparisons with Adverbs 262
9-5	Repeating a Comparative; Using Double Comparatives 264
9-6	Modifying Comparatives with Adjectives and Adverbs 266
9-7	Negative Comparisons 267
9-8	Using *As ... As* to Make Comparisons 268
9-9	Using *Less ... Than* and *Not As ... As* 272
9-10	Using *More* with Nouns 274
9-11	Using *The Same, Similar, Different, Like, Alike* 276

Chapter 10	THE PASSIVE	282
	10-1 Active and Passive Sentences	283
	10-2 Forming the Passive	283
	10-3 Progressive Forms of the Passive	287
	10-4 Transitive and Intransitive Verbs	290
	10-5 Using the *by*-Phrase	292
	10-6 Passive Modal Auxiliaries	296
	10-7 Past Participles as Adjectives (Stative or Non-Progressive Passive)	298
	10-8 Participial Adjectives: *-ed* vs. *-ing*	302
	10-9 *Get* + Adjective; *Get* + Past Participle	305
	10-10 Using *Be Used/Accustomed To* and *Get Used/Accustomed To*	308
	10-11 *Used To* vs. *Be Used To*	310
	10-12 Using *Be Supposed To*	312

Chapter 11	COUNT/NONCOUNT NOUNS AND ARTICLES	315
	11-1 *A* vs. *An*	316
	11-2 Count and Noncount Nouns	317
	11-3 Noncount Nouns	318
	11-4 More Noncount Nouns	320
	11-5 Using *A Lot Of, Some, Several, Many/Much,* and *A Few/A Little*	322
	11-6 Nouns That Can Be Count or Noncount	325
	11-7 Using Units of Measure with Noncount Nouns	328
	11-8 Articles with Count and Noncount Nouns: *A/An, The,* Ø	330
	11-9 More About Articles	332
	11-10 Using *The* or Ø with People and Places	337
	11-11 Capitalization	339

Chapter 12	ADJECTIVE CLAUSES	344
	12-1 Adjective Clauses: Introduction	345
	12-2 Using *Who* and *That* in Adjective Clauses to Describe People	346
	12-3 Using Object Pronouns in Adjective Clauses to Describe People	349
	12-4 Using Pronouns in Adjective Clauses to Describe Things	353
	12-5 Singular and Plural Verbs in Adjective Clauses	358
	12-6 Using Prepositions in Adjective Clauses	359
	12-7 Using *Whose* in Adjective Clauses	362

Chapter 13	GERUNDS AND INFINITIVES	369
	13-1 Verb + Gerund	370
	13-2 *Go* + *-ing*	372
	13-3 Verb + Infinitive	374
	13-4 Verb + Gerund or Infinitive	375
	13-5 Preposition + Gerund	380
	13-6 Using *By* and *With* to Express How Something Is Done	383
	13-7 Using Gerunds as Subjects; Using *It* + Infinitive	386
	13-8 *It* + Infinitive: Using *For* (*Someone*)	388
	13-9 Expressing Purpose with *In Order To* and *For*	391
	13-10 Using Infinitives with *Too* and *Enough*	394

Chapter 14	NOUN CLAUSES	400
	14-1 Noun Clauses: Introduction	401
	14-2 Noun Clauses That Begin with a Question Word	402
	14-3 Noun Clauses That Begin with *If* or *Whether*	406
	14-4 Noun Clauses That Begin with *That*	410
	14-5 Other Uses of *That*-Clauses	411
	14-6 Substituting *So* for a *That*-Clause in Conversational Responses	414
	14-7 Quoted Speech	416
	14-8 Quoted Speech vs. Reported Speech	418
	14-9 Verb Forms in Reported Speech	419
	14-10 Common Reporting Verbs: *Tell, Ask, Answer/Reply*	421

Appendix	SUPPLEMENTARY GRAMMAR CHARTS	429
Unit A:	A-1 The Principal Parts of a Verb	429
	A-2 Common Irregular Verbs: A Reference List	430
	A-3 The Present Perfect vs. The Past Perfect	431
	A-4 The Past Progressive vs. The Past Perfect	431
	A-5 Regular Verbs: Pronunciation of *-ed* Endings	432
	A-6 Pronunciation of Final *-s/-es* for Verbs and Nouns	432
	A-7 Review: Subject and Object Pronouns, Possessive Pronouns, and Possessive Adjectives	433
	A-8 Comparison of *Yes/No* and Information Question Forms	433
Unit B:	B-1 Phrasal Verbs	434
	B-2 Phrasal Verbs: A Reference List	435
Unit C:	C-1 Preposition Combinations: Introduction	437
	C-2 Preposition Combinations: A Reference List	437

Listening Script 439
Trivia Answers 449
Index 451
Credits 462

Preface to the Fifth Edition

Fundamentals of English Grammar is an intermediate skills text for English language learners. It functions principally as a classroom teaching text but also serves as a comprehensive reference for students and teachers.

Using a time-tested approach that has helped millions of students around the world, *Fundamentals of English Grammar* blends direct grammar instruction with carefully sequenced practice to develop speaking, writing, listening, and reading skills. Grammar is not a mere collection of rules; rather, it is presented as a framework for organizing English. Students have a natural, logical way to help make sense of the language they see and hear.

This edition has been extensively revised to keep pace with advances in theory and practice, particularly from cognitive science. We are excited to introduce important new features and updates.

- **A pretest at the start of each chapter** allows learners to assess what they already know and orient themselves to the chapter material. Research indicates that taking a pretest may enhance learning even if a student gets every answer wrong.
- **Practice, spaced out over time**, helps students learn better. Numerous exercises have been added to provide more incremental practice.
- **New charts and exercises show patterns** to help learners make sense of the information. This reflects research showing that the adult brain is wired to look for patterns.
- **Meaning-based practice** is introduced at the sentence level. Students do not have to wait for longer passages to work with meaning, as is the case with many textbooks.
- **Frequent oral exercises** encourage students to speak more naturally and fluidly, in other words, with more automaticity—an important marker of fluency.
- **Step-by-step writing activities** promote written fluency. All end-of-chapter tasks include writing tips and editing checklists.
- **A wide range of contextualized exercises,** with an emphasis on life-skills vocabulary, encourages authentic language use.
- **Updated grammar charts** based on corpus research reflect current usage and highlight the differences between written and spoken English in formal and informal contexts.
- The **BlackBookBlog,** new to this edition, focuses on student success, cultural differences, and life-skills strategies.
- **End-of-chapter Learning Checks** help students assess their learning.

Now more than ever, teachers will find an extensive range of presentations, activities, and tasks to meet the specific needs of their classes.

Components of *Fundamentals of English Grammar,* Fifth Edition

- **Online Resources**
  - For the teacher: **Teacher's Guide** and front-of-classroom **PowerPoint** presentations
  - For the student: A Pearson Practice English **App** (with diagnostic tests, end-of-chapter Learning Checks, review tests, Student Book audio, and guided **PowerPoint** videos)
- A comprehensive **Workbook** that consists of self-study exercises for independent work
- A **Teacher's Guide** that features step-by-step teaching instructions for each chart, notes on key grammar structures, vocabulary lists, and expansion activities
- A revised **Test Bank** with quizzes, chapter tests, and mid-term and final exams
- A **Chartbook**, a reference book that consists of only the grammar charts

MyEnglishLab

MyEnglishLab for *Fundamentals of English Grammar,* Fifth Edition has been thoroughly revised and includes

- Rich online practice for all skill areas: grammar, reading, writing, speaking, listening, and pronunciation
- Robust assessments that include diagnostic tests, chapter review tests, mid- and end-of-term review tests, and final exams
- Instant feedback on incorrect answers
- Remediation activities
- Gradebook and diagnostic tools that allow teachers to monitor student progress and analyze data to determine steps for remediation and support
- Guided PowerPoint video for reinforcement/self-study

The Azar-Hagen Grammar Series consists of

- *Understanding and Using English Grammar* (blue cover), for upper-level students.
- *Fundamentals of English Grammar* (black cover), for mid-level students.
- *Basic English Grammar* (red cover), for lower or beginning levels.

Acknowledgments

We are indebted to the reviewers and other outstanding teachers who contributed to this edition by giving us extensive feedback on the Fourth edition and helping us shape the new Fifth edition.

In particular, we would like to thank Tammy Adams, University of Missouri-Kansas City; Maureen S. Andrade, Utah Valley University; Dorothy Avondstondt, Miami Dade College; Judith Campbell, University of Montreal; Shirlaine B. Castellino, Spring International Language Center, CO; Holly Cin, Houston Community College; Eileen M. Cotter, Montgomery College, MD; Yecsenia Delgado, Monrovia Adult School, CA; Andrew Donlan, International Language Institute, Washington, D.C.; Gillian L. Durham, Tidewater Community College; Jill M. Fox, University of Nebraska; Frank Grandits, City College of San Francisco; William Hennessey IV, Florida International University; Clay Hindman, Sierra Community College; Zoe Isaacson, Queens College; Barbara Jaccarino, Brooklyn College; Sharla Jones, San Antonio College; Balynda Kelly Foster, Spring International Language Center, CO; Noga Laor, Long Island University; Ann Larios, Queens College; Sara Miller, Queens College; June Ohrnberger, Suffolk County Community College, NY; Deniz Ozgorgulu, Bogazici University, Turkey; Jan Peterson, Edmonds Community College; Miriam Pollack, Grossmont College; Ray Schiel, College of English Language, Santa Monica, CA; Malek Shawareb, Houston Community College; Carol Siegel, Community College of Baltimore County; Elizabeth Marie Van Amerongen, Community College of Baltimore County; Laura Vance, Spring International Language Center, CO; Melissa Villamil, Houston Community College; Daniela C. Wagner-Loera, University of Maryland, College Park; Summer Webb, University of Colorado-Boulder; Kirsten Windahl, Cuyahoga Community College; Katarina Zorkic, Rosemead College of English.

We thank the teachers of the focus group at Edmonds Community College for their invaluable feedback: Linda Carlson, Jan Peterson, Patrick Rolland, Ruth Voetmann, and Kelly Roberts Weibel.

We once again had a stellar management and editorial team every step of the way. Product Manager Amy McCormick oversaw the project with insight and vision. We were fortunate to once again have Senior Content Producer Robert Ruvo, who deftly juggled the many components of this revision and kept us on track. Barbara Lyons, our development editor, shaped the charts, exercises, and layout with precision and care. Janice Baillie, our production editor, lent her eagle eye to every detail on every page. We are grateful as always to Sue Van Etten for her expert business management of Azar Associates.

We'd also like to thank our talented supplement writers: Geneva Tesh, Houston Community College, for the revised Workbook, MyEnglishLab, and PowerPoint material; Kelly Roberts Weibel, Edmonds Community College, for the updated Test Bank, and Ruth Voetmann, Edmonds Community College, for the reworked Teacher's Guide.

Once again, we are grateful for the Pearson design team of Tracey Cataldo and Warren Fischbach for their suggestions and expertise.

Our gratitude also goes to Pietro Alongi, Portfolio Director, and Paula Van Els, Content Development Director at Pearson. They were with the series for many years, and we appreciate the support they brought to each new edition.

Our thanks also to our illustrators Chris Pavely and Don Martinetti for their engaging artwork.

Finally, we are grateful for the support of our families as they continue to cheer us on.

Betty S. Azar
Stacy A. Hagen

Getting Started

EXERCISE 1 ▶ Listening and reading.
Part I. Listen to the conversation between Daniel and Sofia. They are at a college orientation. They are interviewing each other.

It's Nice to Meet You

DANIEL: Hi. My name is Daniel.
SOFIA: Hi. I'm Sofia. It's nice to meet you.
DANIEL: Nice to meet you too. Where are you from?
SOFIA: I'm from Montreal. How about you?
DANIEL: I'm from Miami.
SOFIA: Are you a new student?
DANIEL: Yes and no. This is my third year of college, but I'm new here.
SOFIA: This is my second year here. I'm in the business school. I really like it.
DANIEL: Oh, my major is economics! Maybe we'll have a class together. So, tell me a little more about yourself. What do you like to do in your free time?
SOFIA: I love the outdoors. I spend a lot of time in the mountains. I hike on weekends. I write about it on social media.
DANIEL: I spend a lot of time outdoors too. I like the beach. In the summer, I swim every day.
SOFIA: This town has a great beach.
DANIEL: Yeah, I want to go there! Now, when I introduce you to the group, I have to write your full name on the board. What's your last name, and how do you spell it?
SOFIA: It's Sanchez. S-A-N-C-H-E-Z.
DANIEL: My last name is Willson — with two "l"s: W-I-L-L-S-O-N.
SOFIA: Oh, it looks like our time is up. I enjoyed our conversation.
DANIEL: Thanks. I enjoyed it too.

Part II. Use the information in the conversation to complete Daniel's introduction of Sofia to the class.

DANIEL: I would like to introduce Sofia Sanchez. Sofia is from Montreal. This is her second year of college. In her free time, she ...

_____
_____
_____
_____

Part III. Now it is Sofia's turn to introduce Daniel. Write her introduction. Begin with *I would like to introduce Daniel Willson*.

_____
_____
_____

EXERCISE 2 ▶ Let's talk: interview.

Part I. Interview a partner.

Find out your partner's:

name (and spelling of name)
native country or hometown
free-time activities or hobbies
reason for being here

Part II. Introduce your partner to the class. After you learn each student's name, write it down.

EXERCISE 3 ▶ Writing.

Write answers to the questions. Then, with your teacher, decide what to do with your writing. See the list of suggestions at the end of the exercise.

1. What is your name?
2. Where are you from?
3. Where are you living?
4. Why are you here (in this city)?
    a. Are you a student? If so, what are you studying?
    b. Do you work? If yes, what is your job?
    c. Do you have another reason for being here?
5. What do you like to do in your free time?
6. What is your favorite season of the year? Why?
7. What are your three favorite TV programs or movies? Why do you like them?
8. Describe your first day in this class.

Suggestions for your writing:

a. Give it to a classmate to read. Your classmate can then summarize the information in a spoken report to a small group.
b. Work with a partner and correct errors in each other's writing.
c. Read your composition aloud in a small group and answer any questions about it.
d. Hand it in to your teacher, who will correct the errors and return it to you.
e. Hand it in to your teacher, who will return it at the end of the term when your English has gotten better, so you can correct your own errors.

CHAPTER 1
Present Time

PRETEST: What do I already know?
Choose the correct verb form in each sentence.

1. My alarm ____ at 7:00 every morning. (Chart 1-1)
   a. ring   b. is ringing   c. rings

2. We ____ late. (Chart 1-2)
   a. don't be   b. aren't   c. isn't

3. ____ right now? (Chart 1-2)
   a. Are you waiting   b. You wait   c. Do you wait

4. The train ____ at 5:00 every evening. (Chart 1-3)
   a. it arrives   b. arrive   c. arrives

5. My friend ____ several languages. (Chart 1-4)
   a. speak   b. speakes   c. speaks

6. ____ homework on weekends. (Chart 1-5)
   a. I have always b. I always have   c. Always I have

7. I ____ the answer to your question. (Chart 1-6)
   a. am knowing   b. know   c. am know

8. A: Do you need more time for the test? (Chart 1-7)
   B: Yes, I ____.
   a. do   b. am   c. need

EXERCISE 1 ▶ Warm-up. (Charts 1-1 and 1-2)
Read the statements, and choose *yes* or *no*. Make the answers true for you. Share your answers with a partner (e.g., *I use a computer every day.* OR *I don't use a computer every day.*).

1. I use a computer or tablet every day.   yes   no
2. I am holding a tablet right now.   yes   no
3. I check emails every day.   yes   no
4. I send text messages all day long.   yes   no
5. I am sending a text message now.   yes   no

1-1 Simple Present and Present Progressive

SIMPLE PRESENT		
past — now — future XXXXXXXXXXX	(a) Ann *takes* a shower *every day*. (b) I *usually read* the newspaper in the morning. (c) Babies *cry*. Birds *fly*. (d) NEGATIVE: It *doesn't snow* in Bangkok. (e) QUESTION: *Does* the teacher *speak* slowly?	The SIMPLE PRESENT expresses *daily habits* or *usual activities*, as in (a) and (b). The simple present expresses *general statements of fact*, as in (c). In general, the simple present is used for events or situations that exist always, usually, or habitually in the past, present, and future.
PRESENT PROGRESSIVE start — now — finish? in progress	(f) Ann can't come to the phone *right now* because she *is taking* a shower. (g) I *am reading* my grammar book *right now*. (h) Jimmy and Susie are babies. They *are crying right now*. Maybe they are hungry. (i) NEGATIVE: It *isn't snowing right now*. (j) QUESTION: *Is* the teacher *speaking* right now?	The PRESENT PROGRESSIVE expresses *an activity that is in progress (is occurring, is happening)* right now. The event is in progress at the time the speaker is saying the sentence. The event began in the past, is in progress now, and will probably continue into the future. FORM: ***am***, ***is***, ***are*** + ***-ing***

1-2 Forms of the Simple Present and the Present Progressive

	Simple Present	Present Progressive
STATEMENT	I *work*. You *work*. He, She, It *works*. We *work*. They *work*.	I *am working*. You *are working*. He, She, It *is working*. We *are working*. They *are working*.
NEGATIVE	I *do not work*. You *do not work*. He, She, It *does not work*. We *do not work*. They *do not work*.	I *am not working*. You *are not working*. He, She, It *is not working*. We *are not working*. They *are not working*.
QUESTION	*Do* I *work*? *Do* you *work*? *Does* he, she, it *work*? *Do* we *work*? *Do* they *work*?	*Am* I *working*? *Are* you *working*? *Is* he, she, it *working*? *Are* we *working*? *Are* they *working*?

Contractions		
pronoun + be	I + am = **I'm** working. you, we, they + are = **You're**, **We're**, **They're** working. he, she, it + is = **He's**, **She's**, **It's** working.	
do + not	does + not = **doesn't** She **doesn't** work. do + not = **don't** I **don't** work.	
be + not	is + not = **isn't** He **isn't** working. are + not = **aren't** They **aren't** working. (am + not = am not* I am not working.)	

*NOTE: *am* and *not* are not contracted.

EXERCISE 2 ▶ Looking at grammar. (Charts 1-1 and 1-2)
Read the paragraph. Is the activity of each verb in green a usual activity or happening right now (an activity in progress)? Write the verb in the correct column.

Lunchtime at the Café

It's noon at the café. Many students **come** here every day. They **bring** their books or laptops. They **do** their homework at tables. Right now some people **are standing** in line. A man **is ordering** lunch. He usually **orders** just coffee, but today he is hungry. Two women **are talking**. They **are waiting** to order. They **meet** here once a week for a study group. A man in front of them **is asking** questions about the food. He **is taking** a long time. Many people **are eating** at the café today. It is very busy.

USUAL ACTIVITY	RIGHT NOW
come	are standing
_____	_____
_____	_____
_____	_____
_____	_____
_____	_____

EXERCISE 3 ▶ Let's talk: pairwork. (Charts 1-1 and 1-2)

Work with a partner. Take turns completing each statement and asking a follow-up question for your partner to answer. You can look at your sentence before you speak. When you speak, look at your partner.

PARTNER A	PARTNER B
1. I usually wake up at _____ (*time*). How about you?	1. I write with my _____ (*left/right*) hand. How about you?
2. I drink _____ every morning. How about you?	2. I am living in _____ (*a dorm/an apartment/a house, etc.*) How about you?
3. I usually eat dinner at _____ (*time*). How about you?	3. I buy a lot of _____ every week. How about you?
4. I go to bed at _____ (*time*). How about you?	4. I usually do my homework _____ (*in the morning/in the afternoon/in the evening*). How about you?
5. I'm speaking _____ (*quickly/slowly*) right now. How about you?	5. I'm looking at _____ right now. How about you?

EXERCISE 4 ▶ Reading and grammar. (Charts 1-1 and 1-2)

Choose the correct verbs.

Commuting on the Train

Lisa   **takes / is taking**₁   the train to school every day. She always   **meets / is meeting**₂   her friend Ari at the station, and they   **sit / are sitting**₃   together. Lisa usually   **works / is working**₄   on her laptop. She generally   **does / is doing**₅   her homework at the last minute. Ari often   **looks / is looking**₆   at social media on her phone and   **posts / is posting**₇   messages. Right now she   **doesn't post / isn't posting**₈   anything. She   **deletes / is deleting**₉   photos because the memory is full.

EXERCISE 5 ▶ Let's talk: pairwork. (Charts 1-1 and 1-2)

Work with a partner. Take turns describing your photos to each other and finding the differences. Use the present progressive.

PARTNER A: Cover Partner B's photos in your book.
PARTNER B: Cover Partner A's photos in your book.

Example:

PARTNER A

PARTNER B

PARTNER A: In my picture, a soccer player is throwing a ball.
PARTNER B: In my picture, a soccer player is kicking a ball.

PARTNER A

1
2
3
4
5
6

PARTNER B

1
2
3
4
5
6

EXERCISE 6 ▶ Game: trivia. (Charts 1-1 and 1-2)
Work in small groups. Complete each sentence with the correct form of the verb in parentheses. Then choose "T" for true or "F" for false. The group with the most correct answers wins.*

1. In one soccer game, a player (*run*) _____ 7 miles (11.3 km) on average. T F
2. In one soccer game, players (*run*) _____ 7 miles (11.3 km) on average. T F
3. Right-handed people (*live*) _____ 10 years longer than left-handed people. T F
4. Mountains (*cover*) _____ 3% of Africa and 25% of Europe. T F
5. The Eiffel Tower (*have*) _____ 3,000 steps. T F
6. Honey (*spoil*) _____ after one year. T F
7. The letter "e" (*be*) _____ the most common letter in English. T F
8. It (*take*) _____ about 7 seconds for food to get from our mouths to our stomachs. T F
9. A man's heart (*beat*) _____ faster than a woman's heart. T F
10. About 145,000 people in the world (*die*) _____ every 24 hours. T F

EXERCISE 7 ▶ Looking at grammar. (Charts 1-1 and 1-2)
Complete the sentences. Use the simple present or the present progressive form of the verbs in parentheses.

At Home

1. Shhh. The baby (*sleep*) __is sleeping__. The baby (*sleep*) __sleeps__ for 10 hours every night.
2. Thomas (*take*) _____ a nap on the couch right now. He (*snore*) _____ loudly. He usually (*snore*) _____ when he _____ (*sleep*).
3. Right now I'm in the kitchen. I (*sit*) _____ at the counter. I usually (*sit*) _____ at the counter every morning for breakfast.
4. My husband (*speak*) _____ Arabic. Arabic is his native language, but right now he (*speak*) _____ English on the phone to my sister.
5. A: Look outside. (*it, rain*) _____?
   B: It (*start*) _____ to sprinkle.**
   A: (*it, rain*) _____ a lot in this area?
   B: No. The weather (*be*) _____ usually warm and sunny.

---

*See *Trivia Answers*, p. 449.

**sprinkle = rain lightly

6. A: There's my neighbor Akiko. She (*leave*) _____ her house. She (*walk*) _____ to work. Akiko (*walk*) _____ to work every day.

   B: (*you, walk*) _____ to work too?

   A: Sometimes.

   B: (*your husband, walk*) _____ with you?

   A: No, he (*leave*) _____ for work before me.

EXERCISE 8 ▶ Let's talk. (Charts 1-1 and 1-2)

Your teacher will ask one student to perform an action and another student to describe it using the present progressive.

Example: stand next to your desk
To STUDENT A: Would you please stand next to your desk? (*Student A stands up.*)
To STUDENT B: Who is standing next to his/her desk? OR What is (Student A) doing?
  STUDENT B: (Student A) is standing next to his/her desk.

1. stand up
2. open your book
3. look at the ceiling
4. give your book to another student
5. shake your head "no"
6. hold your pen in your left hand
7. read the title of your book
8. count aloud the number of people in the classroom

EXERCISE 9 ▶ Listening. (Charts 1-1 and 1-2)

Listen to the statements about Irene and her job. Decide if the activity of each verb is a usual activity or happening right now. Choose the correct answer.

Example: You will hear: Irene works for a video game company.
  You will choose: (usual activity)   happening right now

1. usual activity   happening right now
2. usual activity   happening right now
3. usual activity   happening right now
4. usual activity   happening right now
5. usual activity   happening right now

EXERCISE 10 ▶ Listening. (Charts 1-1 and 1-2)
Listen to the questions. Write the words you hear.

A Problem with the Printer

Example: You will hear: Is the printer working?
You will write: _Is_ the printer working?

1. _____ need more paper?
2. _____ have enough ink?
3. _____ fixing it yourself?
4. _____ know how to fix it?
5. _____ have another printer in the office?
6. Hmmm. Is it my imagination, or _____ making a strange noise?

EXERCISE 11 ▶ Reading and writing. (Charts 1-1 and 1-2)
Part I. Read the paragraph and answer the questions.

Do you know these words?
- scalp
- strand of hair

HAIR FACTS

Here are some interesting facts about our hair. Human hair grows about one-half inch per month or 15 centimeters a year. The hair on our scalp is dead. That's why it doesn't hurt when we get a haircut. The average person has about 100,000 strands of hair. Every day we lose 75 to 150 strands of hair. One strand of hair grows for two to seven years. After it stops growing, it rests for a while and then falls out. Hair grows faster in warmer weather, and women's hair grows faster than men's hair.

1. How fast does hair grow?
2. Why don't haircuts hurt?
3. About how many strands of hair does an eighteen-year-old have on his/her head?
4. Name a good place to live if you want your hair to grow faster.

Part II. Choose one part of the body, for example: fingernails, skin, eyebrows, eyes, heart, lungs. Make a list of interesting facts about this part of the body. Organize the facts into a paragraph. Begin with the topic sentence below. NOTE: If you are researching information on the internet, search this topic: "interesting ____ facts" (e.g., interesting hair facts).

Topic sentence: Here are some interesting facts about our ____.

EXERCISE 12 ▸ Warm-up. (Chart 1-3)

Make sentences. Add **-s** where necessary. Do not add any other words.

1. One diver \ dive _____
2. Two diver \ dive _____

1-3 Singular / Plural

(a) SINGULAR: *one bird*	SINGULAR = one, not two or more
(b) PLURAL: *two birds, three birds, many birds, all birds,* etc.	PLURAL = two, three, or more
(c) A bird sings.	*A third person singular verb* ends in **-s**, as in (c).
(d) Birds sing.	*A plural noun* ends in **-s**, as in (d).*
(e) A *bird sings* outside my window. *It sings* loudly. *Ann sings* beautifully. *She sings* songs to her children. *Tom sings* very well. *He sings* professionally.	A singular verb follows a singular subject. Add **-s** to the simple present verb if the subject is (1) a singular noun (e.g., *a bird, Ann, Tom*) or (2) *he, she,* or *it.*** Note that the noun is not followed by a pronoun: INCORRECT: *Tom he sings very well.*

*For more information, see Chart 6-7, p. 169.

**He, she,* and *it* are third person singular personal pronouns. See Chart 6-10, p. 175, for more information about personal pronouns.

EXERCISE 13 ▸ Looking at grammar. (Chart 1-3)

Look at each word in green. Is it a noun or verb? Is it singular or plural?

ANIMAL SOUNDS	NOUN	VERB	SING.	PLURAL
1. **Cows** say moo.	x			x
2. A cat **meows** when it's hungry.		x	x	
3. **Cats** meow when they are hungry.				
4. Dogs **bark** at squirrels.				
5. A bee **buzzes** in a hive.				
6. **Wolves** howl at night.				
7. A **snake** hisses when it's angry.				
8. A bat **makes** sounds, but people don't hear them.				

 EXERCISE 14 ▶ Grammar and listening. (Chart 1-3)
Add **-s** where necessary. Write Ø if no **-s** is needed. You can check your answers by listening to the audio.

Natural Disasters: A Flood

1. The weather _Ø_ cause_s_ some natural disaster_s_ .
2. Heavy rains sometimes create____ flood____ .
3. A big flood____ cause____ a lot of damage.
4. In town____, flood____ can damage building____, home____, and road____ .
5. After a flood____, a town____ need____ a lot of financial help for repair____ .

EXERCISE 15 ▶ Let's talk: pairwork. (Chart 1-3)
Work with a partner. One partner says the first sentence. The other completes it with a contrasting idea. Begin with *My roommate*. More than one answer may be correct. Pay attention to the third person **-s** in the completion.

Differences

1. I work in the morning.
   → My roommate works in the evening.
2. I exercise alone.
3. I love Italian food.
4. I drive a small car.
5. I wake up early on weekends.
6. I drink coffee every day.
7. I enjoy math.
8. I dream in English.

EXERCISE 16 ▶ Warm-up. (Chart 1-4)
Write the third person form of each verb under the correct heading. Can you figure out the rules for when to add **-s**, **-es**, and **-ies**?

drive	mix	speak	stay	study	take	try	wish

Add **-s** only.	Add **-es**.	Add **-ies**.

1-4 Spelling of Simple Present Verbs: Final -s/-es

(a)	visit → visits speak → speaks	Final **-s**, not **-es**, is added to most third person singular verbs. INCORRECT: *visites, speakes*	
(b)	ride → rides write → writes	Many verbs end in **-e**. Final **-s** is simply added.	
(c)	catch → catches wash → washes miss → misses fix → fixes buzz → buzzes	Final **-es** is added to verbs that end in **-ch, -sh, -s, -x,** and **-z**. PRONUNCIATION NOTE: Final **-es** is pronounced /əz/ and adds a syllable.	
(d)	fly → flies	If a verbs ends in a consonant + **-y**, change the **-y** to **-i** and add **-es**, as in (d). INCORRECT: *flys*	
(e)	pay → pays	If a verb ends in a vowel + **-y**, simply add **-s**,* as in (e). INCORRECT: *paies* or *payes*	
(f)	go → goes do → does have → has	The third person singular forms of the verbs **go**, **do**, and **have** are irregular.	

*Vowels = a, e, i, o, u. Consonants = all other letters in the alphabet.

EXERCISE 17 ▶ Grammar and speaking. (Chart 1-4)

Part I. <u>Underline</u> the verb(s) in each sentence. Add a final **-s/-es** if necessary. Do not change any other words.

What is the best way to fall asleep at night?

1. I <u>count</u> backwards from 500.

2. My wife <u>count</u>^s sheep.

3. Some people listen to white noise, like ocean waves or the sound of rain.

4. My doctor drinks warm milk before bedtime.

5. Yoga relax some people before they go to bed.

6. My grandmother think about a relaxing place, like the beach. This work well for her.

7. My best friend use a meditation technique: she breathe in and out. The in-breath take two seconds and the out-breath take four seconds.

Part II. Ask three people what they do to fall asleep. Tell the class their answers.

EXERCISE 18 ▶ Grammar and listening. (Chart 1-4)

Add *-s/-es/-ies* to the verbs. Check your answers with a partner. Listen to the pronunciation of the verbs.

1. talk _s_
2. fish _es_
3. hope ____
4. teach ____
5. move ____
6. kiss ____
7. push ____
8. wait ____
9. mix ____
10. watch ____
11. study ____
12. buy ____
13. enjoy ____
14. try ____
15. carry ____

EXERCISE 19 ▶ Let's talk: pairwork. (Chart 1-4)

Work with a partner. Look at the photos and make conversations. Take turns being Partner A and Partner B. Follow the model. Use *he*, *she*, or *they* as appropriate. You can look at the model before you speak. When you speak, look at your partner.

Example:
PARTNER A: What is he doing?
PARTNER B: He ____ .
PARTNER A: Does he ____ often?
PARTNER B: Yes, he does. He ____ several times a week.

1

2

3

4

5

6

EXERCISE 20 ▶ Game. (Chart 1-4)

Work in groups of three to four students. Combine a phrase on the left with one on the right. Use each phrase once. Add *-s/-es/-ies* to the verb as necessary. Choose one person to write the sentences. The group with the most correct answers wins.

Jobs

Example: 1. A plumber
h. fix problems with sinks and toilets
→ *A plumber fixes problems with sinks and toilets.*

1. A plumber __h__.
2. Security guards _____.
3. A hospital orderly _____.
4. Do bank tellers _____?
5. Auto mechanics _____.
6. An accountant _____.
7. A barber _____.
8. Does a dental hygienist _____?
9. A janitor _____.
10. Farmers _____.

a. work with deposits and withdrawals of money
b. fix cars
c. grow crops
d. help doctors and nurses with nonmedical tasks
e. cut hair, usually for men
f. study and prepare financial information
g. clean buildings
✓ h. fix problems with sinks and toilets
i. protect people and property
j. clean teeth

EXERCISE 21 ▶ Warm-up. (Chart 1-5)

How often do you do each activity? Give the percentage (0% → 100%). Your teacher will ask which activities you never do, sometimes do, or always do.

1. _____ I take the bus to school.
2. _____ I go to bed late.
3. _____ I skip breakfast.
4. _____ I eat vegetables at lunchtime.
5. _____ I cook my own dinner.
6. _____ I am an early riser.*
7. _____ I sleep with my phone.
8. _____ I look at social media when I wake up.
9. _____ I check the news in the middle of the night.
10. _____ I fall asleep to music.

---

*early riser = a person who gets up early in the morning

1-5 Frequency Adverbs

100% — always / almost always / **usually** / **often** / **frequently** / generally / **sometimes** / **occasionally** (positive)
50%
seldom / rarely / hardly ever / almost never / not ever, never (negative)
0%
	Frequency adverbs usually occur in the middle of a sentence and have special positions, as shown in examples (a) through (e) below.
	
	The adverbs in **boldface** may also occur at the beginning or the end of a sentence.
	
	   I sometimes get up at 6:30.
	   Sometimes I get up at 6:30.
	   I get up at 6:30 sometimes.
	
	The other adverbs in the list (not in boldface) rarely occur at the beginning or the end of a sentence. Their usual position is in the middle of a sentence.

S + FREQ ADV + V (a) Karen *always* *tells* the truth.	Except with the main verb *be,* frequency adverbs usually come between the subject and the simple present verb. INCORRECT: *Always Karen tells the truth.*
S + BE + FREQ ADV (b) Karen *is* *always* on time.	Frequency adverbs follow *be* in the simple present (*am, is, are*) and simple past (*was, were*).
(c) Do *you always* eat breakfast?	In a question, frequency adverbs come directly after the subject.
(d) Ann *usually doesn't* eat breakfast.	In a negative sentence, most frequency adverbs come in front of a negative verb (except *always* and *ever*).
(e) Sue *doesn't always* eat breakfast.	***Always*** follows a negative helping verb, as in (e), or a negative form of *be.*
(f) CORRECT: Anna *never eats* meat. INCORRECT: Anna *doesn't never eat* meat.	Negative adverbs (*seldom, rarely, hardly ever, never*) are NOT used with a negative verb.

(g) — Do you *ever take* the bus to work?
    — Yes, I do. I often take the bus.
(h) I *don't ever walk* to work.
    INCORRECT: *I ever walk to work.*
	Ever is used in questions about frequency, as in (g). It means "at any time."
	
	Ever is also used with ***not***, as in (h).
	Ever is NOT used in affirmative statements.

EXERCISE 22 ▸ Grammar and speaking. (Chart 1-5)

Part I. Look at your answers in Exercise 21. Make complete sentences using the appropriate frequency word from Chart 1-5.

Examples: 1. 0% = I **never** take the bus to school.
              50% = I **often** take the bus to school.

Part II. Walk around the room and ask people about their habits.

Example: STUDENT A: I **always** take the bus to school. Do you **always** take the bus to school?
         STUDENT B: No, I don't. I **often** take the bus to school. Do you **usually** go to bed late?
         STUDENT A: Yes, I do. I **usually** go to bed late.

EXERCISE 23 ▶ Let's talk. (Chart 1-5)

Work in pairs, small groups, or as a class. Take turns asking and answering the questions. Discuss the meaning of the frequency adverbs.

What is something that …
1. you seldom do?
2. a polite person in your country often does?
3. a polite person in your country never does?
4. our teacher frequently does in class?
5. you never do in class?
6. you rarely eat?
7. you occasionally do after class?
8. drivers generally do?
9. people in your country always or usually do to celebrate the New Year?
10. people in your country sometimes do to celebrate an important birthday?

EXERCISE 24 ▶ Looking at grammar. (Chart 1-5)

Complete the sentences using the information in the chart. Use a frequency adverb in each sentence to describe Mia's weekly activities.

MIA'S WEEK	S	M	TU	W	TH	F	S
1. wake up early				x			
2. make breakfast		x	x		x		
3. go to the gym	x	x		x		x	x
4. be late for the bus		x	x	x	x		
5. cook dinner	x	x	x	x	x	x	x
6. read a book	x	x	x	x		x	x
7. do homework			x			x	
8. go to bed early							

1. Mia ___seldom / rarely wakes___ up early.
2. She _____ breakfast.
3. She _____ to the gym.
4. She _____ late for the bus.
5. She _____ dinner.
6. She _____ a book.
7. She _____ her homework.
8. She _____ to bed early.

EXERCISE 25 ▸ **Let's talk: pairwork.** (Charts 1-1 → 1-5)

Work with a partner. Use frequency adverbs to talk about yourself and to ask your partner questions.

Example: walk to school
PARTNER A (*book open*): I usually walk to school. How about you? Do you usually walk to school?
PARTNER B (*book closed*): I usually walk to school too. OR
                            I seldom walk to school. I usually take the bus.

PARTNER A	PARTNER B
1. wear exercise clothes to class	1. wear a hat to class
2. go to sleep before 11:00 P.M.	2. believe the things I hear in the news
3. check text messages during class	3. get up before nine o'clock in the morning
4. read in bed before I go to sleep	4. call my family or a friend if I feel homesick or lonely
5. speak to people who sit next to me on an airplane	5. have ice cream for dessert

EXERCISE 26 ▸ **Grammar and speaking.** (Charts 1-1 → 1-5)

Part I. Complete the sentences with the correct simple present or present progressive form of the verbs in parentheses. Use the given frequency adverbs where necessary.

Filling out Forms

1. A: Hi, Mia. What are you doing?

   B: I (*apply*) _____ for a part-time job. I (*fill*) _____ _____ out the application, but it (*be*) _____ difficult. I don't understand some of the language.

   A: I can help you.

2. You (*need, always*) _____ to use your legal name on a form.

   Your legal name (*be*) _____ on your passport or visa.

3. The phrases *last name* and *family name* (be) _____ the same.

4. What (be) _____ your middle initial?

5. For your marital status, (be) _____ you married, single, divorced, or widowed?

6. In the U.S., a form (ask) _____ for your zip code. A Canadian form (use) _____ the phrase *postal code*.

7. In the U.S., people (write) _____ "1" for the number one. In Europe, they (do) _____ it like this: "1". To Americans, this (look) _____ like the number seven. People (write, sometimes) _____ "7" for "7."

8. The abbreviation *DOB* (mean) _____ "date of birth."

9. For your DOB on U.S. forms, the month *mm* (come, usually) _____ first, the day *dd* (be) _____ second, and the year *yyyy* (come) _____ last.

10. Phone numbers (have) _____ an area code first. Some forms (use) _____ a hyphen, *360-555-1212*, and some forms (use) _____ parentheses, *(360) 555-1212*, for the area code.

Part II. With a partner, take turns finishing each sentence.

My first name is …
My last name is …
My middle name is …
My middle initial is …
My legal name is …
My marital status is …
My zip code/postal code is …

EXERCISE 27 ▶ Warm-up. (Chart 1-6)
Choose the correct completions.

CHARLIE: Shhh! I _____ something on our roof.
    a. hear   b. am hearing

I _____ there is a person up there.
    a. think   b. am thinking

DAD: I _____.
    a. don't know   b. am not knowing

It _____ more like a small animal, maybe a cat or squirrel.
    a. sounds   b. is sounding

1-6 Verbs Not Usually Used in the Progressive

(a) I **know** Ms. Chen. INCORRECT: *I am knowing Ms. Chen.* (b) This book **belongs** to Mikhail. INCORRECT: *This book is belonging to Mikhail.*	Some verbs express a state or situation, not an action in progress. These verbs are called "non-action," "non-progressive," or "stative" verbs. They are generally not used in progressive tenses.*

Common Verbs That Are Generally Non-Progressive

believe	like	hear	remember	agree	own
know	need	sound	forget	disagree	belong
understand	want				
	prefer				

(c) I **think** that grammar is easy. (d) I **am thinking** about grammar right now.	Some verbs can have both progressive and non-progressive meanings. In (c): When **think** means "believe," it is non-progressive. In (d): When **think** expresses thoughts that are going through a person's mind, it can be progressive.

Common Verbs with Both Non-Progressive and Progressive Meanings

	NON-PROGRESSIVE	PROGRESSIVE
be	My grandma *is* very kind.	My grandpa *is being* difficult right now.
feel	I *feel* that you are right.	Jae *is feeling* sick today.
have	Tom *has* a car.	I *am having* a good time right now.
look	You *look* happy!	Are you *looking* for something?
love	Mia *loves* her husband.	Mia *is loving* retirement. She's really enjoying it.
see	Do you *see* the moon?	I *am seeing* my parents today.
smell	Mmmm. The soup *smells* good.	The dog *is smelling* my clothes.

*In everyday conversation, you may hear some verbs (for example, *want, like, need, hear, think*) used in the present progressive to express a state or situation: *I am wanting a sandwich. We're liking that idea.* However, the simple present is grammatically correct and more common: *I want a sandwich. We like that idea.*

EXERCISE 28 ▶ Looking at grammar. (Chart 1-6)
Choose the correct answers.

1. A: What do you like better: coffee or tea?
   B: I _____ tea.
   a. am preferring   (b.) prefer

2. A: Can you help me set the table for dinner?
   B: In a minute. I _____ my report.
   a. am finishing   b. finish

3. A: Are you busy?
   B: I _____ a few minutes.
   a. am having   b. have

4. A: _____ a good time?
   a. Are you having   b. Do you have
   B: Yes, I _____ myself.
   a. am enjoying   b. enjoy

5. A: There goes Salma on her new racing bike.
   B: Yeah, she really _____ bikes.
   a. is loving   b. loves
   A: That's for sure! She _____ several.
   a. is owning   b. owns

EXERCISE 29 ▶ Looking at grammar. (Chart 1-6)
Complete the sentences with the simple present or present progressive form of **think** and **have**.

1. A: How is your new job going?
   B: Pretty good. I (think) ___think___ I am doing OK.

2. A: You look upset. What's on your mind?
   B: I'm worried about my daughter. I (think) _____ she's in trouble.

3. A: You look far away.* What's on your mind?
   B: I (think) _____ about my vacation next week. I can't wait!

4. A: Hey, how is the party going?
   B: Great! We (have) _____ fun right now.

5. A: Could I borrow some money?
   B: Sorry, I only (have) _____ a little change** on me.

EXERCISE 30 ▶ Looking at grammar. (Chart 1-6)
Complete the sentences. Use the simple present or present progressive form of the verbs in parentheses.

1. Right now I (look) ___am looking___ out the window. I (see) ___see___ a window washer on a ladder.

2. A: (you, need) _____ some help, Mrs. Bernini? (you, want) _____ me to carry that box for you?
   B: Yes, thank you. That's very nice of you.

3. A: Who is that man? I (think) _____ that I (know) _____ him, but I (forget) _____ his name.
   B: That's Mr. Martinez.
   A: That's right! I (remember) _____ him now.

---

*look far away = look like you are thinking about other things; daydream

**change = coins

4. A: (*you, believe*) _____ in ghosts?

   B: No. In my opinion, ghosts (*be*) _____ only in people's imaginations.

   What (*you, think*) _____?

   A: I'm not sure. Maybe they (*be*) _____ real and maybe they (*be, not*)

   _____.

EXERCISE 31 ▶ Reading and grammar. (Charts 1-1 → 1-3, 1-6)
Choose the correct completions.

Shopping at a Clothing Store

It's Saturday at the clothing store. Many people **are shopping / shop** (1) there today. A woman **is looking / looks** (2) at jeans. She **is seeing / sees** (3) several cute styles. She **is checking / checks** (4) the sizes. Another woman **is waiting / waits** (5) for a dressing room. A man **is returning / returns** (6) a jacket at the counter. It is too big. A teenager **is checking / checks** (7) the sales rack. Every week, the store **is having / has** (8) new items on sale. A salesperson **is folding / folds** (9) shirts. Often customers **aren't folding / don't fold** (10) them after they **are picking / pick** (11) them up. The salesperson **is folding / folds** (12) the clothes on the display tables several times a day. The tables **are looking / look** (13) neat and tidy.

EXERCISE 32 ▶ Warm-up. (Chart 1-7)
Choose the correct answer for each question.

1. Does Janet eat fish?
   a. Yes, she does.   b. Yes, she is.   c. Yes, she eats.

2. Do you eat fish?
   a. No, I don't.   b. No, I am not.   c. No, I don't eat.

3. Are you vegetarian?
   a. Yes, I do.   b. Yes, I am.   c. Yes, I like.

4. Is vegetarian food popular in your country?
   a. Yes, it does.   b. Yes, it is.   c. Yes, people like.

1-7 Present Verbs: Short Answers to Yes / No Questions

	Question	Short Answer	Long Answer
QUESTIONS WITH DO/DOES	*Does* Bob *like* tea?	Yes, he **does**.* No, he **doesn't**.	Yes, he likes tea.* No, he doesn't like tea.*
	Do you *like* tea?	Yes, I **do**. No, I **don't**.	Yes, I like tea. No, I don't like tea.
QUESTIONS WITH BE	*Are* you *studying*?	Yes, I **am**.** No, I**'m not**.	Yes, I am (I'm) studying. No, I'm not studying.
	Is Yoko a student?	Yes, she **is**.* No, she**'s not**. OR No, she **isn't**.	Yes, she is (she's) a student. No, she's not a student. OR No, she isn't a student.
	Are they *studying*?	Yes, they **are**.* No, they**'re not**. OR No, they **aren't**.	Yes, they are (they're) studying. No, they're not studying. OR No, they aren't studying.

*In the simple present, short answers do not include the main verb: INCORRECT: *Yes, he likes. No, he doesn't like.*

**Contractions are common in spoken English, but *am, is,* and *are* are NOT contracted with pronouns in short answers. INCORRECT SHORT ANSWERS: *Yes, I'm. Yes, she's. Yes, they're.*

EXERCISE 33 ▶ Reading and grammar. (Chart 1-7)
Part I. Read the paragraph.

   Roger is 21 years old. He rides a bike every day. He lives in an area with a bicycle helmet law. The law says that helmets are necessary for everyone under 18. Roger wants to be safe. He has a new helmet, and he wears it every time he rides. Right now he is riding in the countryside. He is wearing his helmet. His brother Tom is riding his motorcycle on the highway. He is also wearing a helmet. The law requires all motorcycle riders to wear helmets.

Part II. Choose the <u>expected</u> short answers.

1. Does Roger ride a bike every day?
   a. Yes, he ride.
   b. No, he doesn't.
   c. Yes, he does.
   d. No, he isn't.

2. Does his area have a bicycle helmet law?
   a. Yes, it have.
   b. Yes, it does.
   c. No, it doesn't.
   d. No, it isn't.

3. Is Tom riding with Roger?
   a. No, he isn't.
   b. No, he doesn't.
   c. Yes, he is.
   d. Yes, he does.

4. Do Roger and Tom always wear their helmets?
   a. Yes, they wear.
   b. Yes, they do.
   c. No, they aren't.
   d. No, they don't.

EXERCISE 34 ▶ Looking at grammar. (Chart 1-7)

Complete the conversations. Use the simple present or present progressive form of the verbs in parentheses. Give short answers to the questions as necessary.

Family

1. A: (*Lillian, have*) __Does Lillian have__ siblings?

   B: Yes, __she does__. She (*have*) __has__ two sisters. Lillian and her siblings (*be*) _____ triplets!

2. A: (*they, look*) _____ the same?

   B: No, _____. They (*look*) _____ different.

3. A: (*they/spend*) _____ time together during the school year?

   B: No, _____. They (*attend*) _____ different universities.

4. A: (*they, spend*) _____ time together right now?

   B: Yes, _____. I mean, I (*think*) _____ so because it's summer.

5. A: (*you, have*) _____ siblings?

   B: No, _____. I (*be*) _____ an only child. But I (*have*) _____ many first cousins about my age. My mom (*come*) _____ from a big family. She (*have*) _____ 11 siblings, with two sets of twins!

6. A: (*they, visit*) _____ much?

   B: Yes, right now two sisters and their kids (*stay*) _____ with us for the holidays.

7. A: Oh, (*you, live*) _____ at home right now?

   B: Yes, _____, but I (*pay*) _____ my parents rent every month because now I (*work*) _____.

22 CHAPTER 1

EXERCISE 35 ▸ Let's talk: pairwork. (Chart 1-7)
With a partner, complete the conversation. Practice it and then perform it for the class. You can look at your sentences before you speak. When you speak, look at your partner.

A: Do you translate from (*your language*) _____ to English when you speak?

B: (Yes/No/Sometimes) I _____.

A: Are you translating from your language right now?

B: (Yes/No) _____.

A: Do you dream in English?

B: (Yes/No/Sometimes) I _____.

A: What about you? Do you dream _____?

B: _____.

EXERCISE 36 ▸ Reading and speaking. (Chart 1-7)
Part I. Read the blog entry by co-author Stacy Hagen.

> # BlackBookBlog
>
> *Do you know these words?*
> - strategy
> - study session
>
> ## A Technique for Remembering Information
>
>
>
> When you study, do you study for a long time and then take a break? Or do you take breaks more frequently? For many students, an hour or two seems like a good amount of time. However, studies show that your brain remembers information best at the beginning and end of your study time. The middle is actually hard to remember. If you study for an hour, you have a lot of information in the middle to remember.
>
> Here's a strategy to help you remember more. Study for 25 minutes, and then take a 5-minute break. During this time, maybe you can check social media or get a quick snack. Then begin another 25-minute study session. When you do this, you create a new beginning, and when you finish, you create a new end. Also, the middle time is shorter, so you don't have so much information to remember. Do this a third time. If you study for 90 minutes and take these breaks, you have three beginnings and three ends. This is a better way to remember information.

Part II. Work with a partner. Answer the questions, first with a short answer and then with a long answer. Tell the class a few of your partner's answers.

1. Do you take breaks when you study?
2. Are your breaks long or short?
3. Do you look at social media during your break?

4. Is it easy for you to take just a 5-minute break? If not, why?
5. Is the technique in the blog a good technique for you? Why or why not?

EXERCISE 37 ▶ Listening. (Chart 1-7)

Part I. Listen to these examples. Notice the reduced pronunciation of the phrases in *italics*.

At the Doctor's Office

1. Do you   → *Dyou*   *Do you* have an appointment?
2. Does he   → *Dze*   *Does he* have an appointment?
3. Does she   → *Duh-she*   *Does she* have an appointment?
4. Do we   → *Duh-we*   *Do we* have an appointment?
5. Do they   → *Duh-they*   *Do they* have an appointment?
6. Am I   → *Mi*   *Am I* late for my appointment?
7. Is it   → *Zit*   *Is it* time for my appointment?*
8. Does it   → *Zit*   *Does it* hurt?

Part II. Complete each question with the non-reduced form of the words you hear.

Example: You will hear: *Dyou* want to tell me what the problem is?
You will write: _____Do you_____ want to tell me what the problem is?

1. _____ have pain anywhere?
2. _____ hurt anywhere else?
3. _____ have a cough or sore throat?
4. _____ have a fever?
5. _____ need lab tests?
6. _____ very sick?
7. _____ serious?
8. _____ need to make another appointment?
9. _____ want to wait in the waiting room?
10. _____ pay now or later?

*See Chapter 5 for more examples of questions with *be* in spoken English.

EXERCISE 38 ▶ Let's talk: interview. (Chart 1-7)

Make questions. Then walk around the room and ask and answer questions. Give both a short and long answer.

Example: be \ gorillas \ intelligent?
STUDENT A: Are gorillas intelligent?
STUDENT B: Yes, they are. They are intelligent.

1. gorillas \ eat \ leaves?
2. your country \ have \ gorillas in the wild?
3. mosquitoes \ carry \ diseases?
4. the earth \ revolve \ around the sun \ right now?
5. the moon \ revolve \ around the earth \ every 28 days?
6. be \ the sun and moon planets?
7. be \ Toronto in western Canada?
8. be \ Texas \ in South America?
9. you \ know \ the names of the seven continents?
10. be \ our teacher \ from Australia?
11. it \ rain \ outside \ right now?
12. be \ you \ tired of this interview?

a mosquito

a gorilla in the wild

EXERCISE 39 ▶ Listening. (Chart 1-7)
Choose the correct answers.

Getting Ready to Leave

Example: You will hear: You're holding your keys. Are you ready to leave?
You will choose: (a.) Yes, I am.
b. Yes, I do.

1. a. Yes, I want.
   b. Yes, I do.

2. a. Yes, I need.
   b. Yes, I do.

3. a. Yes, it is.
   b. Yes, it does.

4. a. Yes, we need.
   b. Yes, we do.

5. a. Yes, he does.
   b. Yes, he is.

6. a. Yes, they are.
   b. Yes, they do.

Present Time 25

EXERCISE 40 ▶ Check your knowledge. (Chapter 1 Review)
Correct the verb errors.

Omar's Visit

1. My friend Omar is owning his own car now. It's brand new.* *(owns)*

2. Today he driving to a small town north of the city to visit his aunt.

3. He love to listen to music, so he is stream music from his phone — loudly.

4. Omar is very happy: he is drive his own car and listen to loud music.

5. Omar is visiting his aunt once a week.

6. She elderly and live alone.

7. She is thinking Omar a wonderful nephew.

8. She love his visits.

9. He try to be helpful and considerate in every way.

10. His aunt don't hearing well, so Omar is speaks loudly and clearly when he's with her.

11. When he's there, he fix things for her around her apartment and help her with her shopping.

12. He isn't staying with her overnight.

13. He usually is staying for a few hours and then is heading back to the city.

14. He kiss his aunt good-bye and give her a hug before he is leaving.

15. Omar a very good nephew.

---
*brand new = completely new

EXERCISE 41 ▸ Reading, grammar, and listening. (Chapter 1)

Part I. Read the passage.

Aerobic Exercise

Jeremy and Nancy believe exercise is important. They go to an exercise class three times a week. They like aerobic exercise.

Aerobic exercise is a special type of exercise. It increases a person's heart rate. Fast walking, running, and dancing are examples of aerobic exercise. During aerobic exercise, a person's heart beats fast. This brings more oxygen to the muscles. Muscles work longer when they have more oxygen.

Right now Jeremy and Nancy are listening to some lively music. They are doing special dance steps. They are exercising different parts of their body.

How about you? Do you like to exercise? Do your muscles get exercise every day? Do you do some type of aerobic exercise?

Do you know these words?
- *oxygen*
- *muscles*
- *lively*

Part II. Choose the correct verbs.

1. Jeremy and Nancy   (think) / are thinking   exercise is good for them.
2. They   prefer / are preferring   aerobic exercise.
3. Aerobic exercise   makes / is making   a person's heart beat fast.
4. Muscles   need / are needing   oxygen.
5. With more oxygen, muscles   work / are working   longer.
6. Right now Jeremy and Nancy   do / are doing   a special kind of dance.
7. Do you exercise / Are you exercising   every week?
8. Do you exercise / Are you exercising   right now?

Present Time 27

Part III. Listen to the passage and complete the sentences with the words you hear.

Many people _____(1)_____ aerobic exercise. It _____(2)_____ a special type of exercise. Aerobic exercise _____(3)_____ the heart beat fast. Running, fast walking, and dancing _____(4)_____ some examples of this exercise.

Right now some people _____(5)_____ in an exercise class. They _____(6)_____ to music, and they _____(7)_____. Their hearts _____(8)_____ fast. Many parts of their body _____(9)_____ exercise.

How about you? _____(10)_____ you exercise every day? _____(11)_____ you _____(12)_____ aerobic exercise?

EXERCISE 42 ▶ Reading and writing. (Chapter 1)

Part I. Read the paragraph. Discuss the questions that follow with a partner or in small groups.

INTERESTING WAYS TO STAY FIT

Alexi doesn't have a lot of time to exercise, but he has interesting ways to stay fit. At work, he never takes the elevator. His office is on the fifth floor, and he always uses the stairs. Once a day, he walks up to the top floor of the building and then back down. When he goes home, he gets off the subway one or two stops early and walks the rest of the way home. Also, he walks very quickly. When he drives to a store, he chooses a parking space far away from the entrance. Inside the store, he balances on one leg when he waits in line to pay. He also stands on one foot when he brushes his teeth. Sometimes he watches movies at home to relax. But he doesn't relax completely. He stretches or does yoga during the movie. Alexi moves a lot during the day, and this helps keep him healthy.

1. What verb tense does the writer use? Why?
2. The main idea of the paragraph is in bold. What examples talk about interesting ways to stay fit?

Part II. Write about a healthy person you know. What does this person do to stay healthy? Does he or she exercise? Follow a special diet? Other things? Follow these steps:

1. Begin with a sentence about the person you know, and make a general statement about his/her healthy habits (main idea).
2. Give examples of the healthy habits.
3. Finish with a summary sentence: Say the main idea in different words from step 1.

WRITING TIP

When you write a paragraph, make sure to start with a topic sentence that states the main idea. Then include examples to support the topic sentence. Finish with a short summary sentence. Look at how the paragraph does this:

Topic sentence: Alexi doesn't have a lot of time to exercise, but he has interesting ways to stay fit.

Examples:
- uses stairs instead of the elevator
- walks to the top floor of the building
- gets off the subway early and walks
- walks quickly
- parks far away from the store entrance
- balances on one leg in line
- stands on one foot when he brushes his teeth
- stretches or does yoga when he watches a movie

Summary sentence: Alexi moves a lot during the day, and this helps keep him healthy.

Part III. Edit your writing. Check for the following:
1. ☐ use of the simple present to describe habits
2. ☐ correct placement of frequency adverbs
3. ☐ correct use of final *-s*/*-es*/*-ies* on singular verbs
4. ☐ topic sentence, examples, and summary sentence
5. ☐ correct spelling (use a dictionary or spell-check)

CHAPTER 1 Learning Check

Choose <u>all</u> the correct sentences.

1. a. My sister is owning a new car.
   b. My sister owns a new car.
   c. Do you own a car?
   d. Are you owning a car?
   e. You owning a car?

2. a. Hello! Does anyone hear me?
   b. Hello! Is anyone hearing me?
   c. Hello! Are you listening to me?
   d. Hello! Do you listen to me?

3. a. Hey, Jon. Are you downstairs?
   b. Hey, Jon. Do you downstairs?
   c. Hey, Jon. Do you here?
   d. Hey, Jon. Are you here?
   e. Hey, Jon. Are you be here?

4. a. My friend Eva a wonderful friend.
   b. My friend Eva is a wonderful friend.
   c. Always Eva has time for me.
   d. Eva always has time for me.

5. a. Irene flys for a major airline.
   b. Irene flies for a major airline.
   c. Irene is flying to Tokyo today.
   d. Irene is flieing to Tokyo today.

6. A: Do you want a snack?
   B: a. Yes, I do.
   b. Yes, I want.
   c. I no have time for a snack.
   d. I don't have time for a snack.

▪▪▪▪▪ For digital resources, go to MyEnglishLab on the Pearson English Portal (see inside front cover). You can also download the Pearson Practice English app for mobile practice. Beginning with Chapter 2, all Learning Checks are available on the app.

CHAPTER 2
Past Time

PRETEST: What do I already know?
Choose the correct answer for each sentence.

1. Our cousins ____ with us last month. (Chart 2-1)
   a. was stay   b. staying   c. stayed
2. Did you ____ last weekend? (Chart 2-1)
   a. work   b. worked   c. working
3. I ____ hungry all day yesterday. (Charts 2-2 and 2-3)
   a. felt   b. feel   c. fell
4. ____ on time for school yesterday? (Charts 2-2 and 2-3)
   a. Did you be   b. Were you   c. Are you
5. I ____ dinner last night. (Charts 2-2 and 2-3)
   a. no eat   b. didn't eat   c. didn't ate
6. My two roommates ____ last week. (Charts 2-2 and 2-3)
   a. were sick   b. sick   c. was sick
7. A car ____ suddenly in the middle of the road. (Chart 2-5)
   a. stoped   b. stopped   c. stopping
8. During the movie, the person next to me ____ the whole time. (Chart 2-6)
   a. was whispered   b. whisper   c. was whispering
9. While I ____ dinner, I heard the news about the president. (Chart 2-7)
   a. was cooking   b. cook   c. was cooked
10. ____ me a grade, my teacher read my essay. (Chart 2-8)
    a. After she gave   b. Before she gave   c. When she gave
11. Richard ____ late for class a lot, but now he comes on time. (Chart 2-9)
    a. is used to   b. used to   c. used to be

EXERCISE 1 ▶ Warm-up. (Chart 2-1)
Check (✓) the statements that are true for you. Share your answers with a partner.

1. ____ I cooked dinner last night.
2. ____ I invited my friends to join me for dinner.
3. ____ I didn't wash the dinner dishes.

2-1 The Simple Past: Regular Verbs

(a) Mary **walked** downtown *yesterday*. (b) I **stayed** home *last weekend*.	The SIMPLE PAST is used to talk about activities or situations that began and ended in the past (e.g., *yesterday, last night, two days ago, in 2015*).
(c) Bob **played** tennis yesterday evening. (d) Our plane **landed** on time last night.	The simple past tense of most regular verbs is formed by adding **-ed** to a verb, as in (a)–(d).*

Simple Past: Regular Verb Forms

STATEMENT	NEGATIVE	QUESTION	SHORT ANSWER
I / You / He / She / It / We / They **walked**.	I / You / He / She / It / We / They **did not** (**didn't**) **walk**.	**Did** I / you / he / she / it / we / they **walk**?	Yes, I / you / he / she / it / we / they **did**. No, I / you / he / she / it / we / they **did not** (**didn't**).

*Some verbs ending in **-y** add **-ied**, for example: *studied, worried*. See Chart 2-5. For information about pronouncing *-ed* endings, see Appendix A-5.

EXERCISE 2 ▶ Looking at grammar. (Chart 2-1)
Create your own chart by writing the negative and question forms of the words in *italics*.

At the Computer

	NEGATIVE	QUESTION
1. *He searched* a website.	He didn't search	Did he search
2. *They streamed* a movie.		
3. *She created* a password.		
4. *I deleted* a file.		
5. *He clicked* on a page.		
6. *She uploaded* a video.		
7. *Her computer crashed*.		
8. *It downloaded* a virus.		

EXERCISE 3 ▶ Game. (Chart 2-1)
Work with a partner or in small groups. All of the sentences contain incorrect information. Make true statements by making a negative statement and then a true statement. You can use the internet. The first team to have correct answers wins.

1. Edison invented the radio.   <u>Edison didn't invent the radio. Edison invented the telephone.</u>
   OR <u>Edison didn't invent the radio. Marconi invented the radio.</u>

2. Steve Jobs started a clothing company. _____

Past Time 31

3. Princess Diana died in a boating accident. _____
_____

4. *Apollo 1* landed on the moon. _____
_____

5. Malala Yousafzai received the Nobel Peace Prize at the age of 20. _____
_____

6. The *Titanic* crashed into a boat. _____
_____

an iceberg

EXERCISE 4 ▶ Warm-up. (Charts 2-2 and 2-3)
Check (✓) the statements that are true for you.

1. _____ I slept for eight hours last night.
2. _____ I came to school on time.
3. _____ I was busy yesterday.
4. _____ I had fun last weekend.

2-2 Expressing Past Time: The Simple Past, Irregular Verbs

(a) I **ate** breakfast this morning. (b) Sue **took** a taxi to the airport yesterday.	Some verbs have irregular past forms, as in (a) and (b). See Chart 2-3.
(c) I **was** sick yesterday. (d) They **were** at home last night.	The simple past forms of **be** are **was** and **were**.

Irregular Verb Forms

STATEMENT	NEGATIVE	QUESTION	SHORT ANSWER
I / You / He / She / It / We / They **left**.	I / You / He / She / It / We / They **did not** (**didn't**) **leave**.	**Did** I / you / he / she / it / we / they **leave**?	Yes, I / you / he / she / it / we / they **did**. No, I / you / he / she / it / we / they **did not** (**didn't**).

Be Verb Forms

STATEMENT	NEGATIVE	QUESTION	SHORT ANSWER
I **was** / He **was** / She **was** / It **was** nice.	I / He / She / It **was not** (**wasn't**) nice.	**Was** I / he / she / it nice?	Yes, I, he, she, it **was**. No, I, he, she, it **was not** (**wasn't**).
You **were** / We **were** / They **were** nice.	You / We / They **were not** (**weren't**) nice.	**Were** you / we / they nice?	Yes, you, we, they **were**. No, you, we, they **were not** (**weren't**).

32 CHAPTER 2

2-3 Common Irregular Verbs: A Reference List

SIMPLE FORM	SIMPLE PAST	SIMPLE FORM	SIMPLE PAST	SIMPLE FORM	SIMPLE PAST
be	was, were	forgive	forgave	say	said
beat	beat	freeze	froze	see	saw
become	became	get	got	sell	sold
begin	began	give	gave	send	sent
bend	bent	go	went	set	set
bite	bit	grow	grew	shake	shook
blow	blew	hang	hung	shoot	shot
break	broke	have	had	shut	shut
bring	brought	hear	heard	sing	sang
build	built	hide	hid	sink	sank
burn	burned/burnt	hit	hit	sit	sat
buy	bought	hold	held	sleep	slept
catch	caught	hurt	hurt	slide	slid
choose	chose	keep	kept	speak	spoke
come	came	know	knew	spend	spent
cost	cost	leave	left	spread	spread
cut	cut	lend	lent	stand	stood
dig	dug	let	let	steal	stole
do	did	lie	lay	stick	stuck
draw	drew	light	lit/lighted	swim	swam
dream	dreamed/dreamt	lose	lost	take	took
drink	drank	make	made	teach	taught
drive	drove	mean	meant	tear	tore
eat	ate	meet	met	tell	told
fall	fell	pay	paid	think	thought
feed	fed	put	put	throw	threw
feel	felt	quit	quit	understand	understood
fight	fought	read	read	upset	upset
find	found	ride	rode	wake	woke/waked
fit	fit	ring	ring	wear	wore
fly	flew	rise	rose	win	won
forget	forgot	run	ran	write	wrote

EXERCISE 5 ▶ Grammar and vocabulary. (Charts 2-2 and 2-3)

Complete each sentence with the correct form of the verb in parentheses. Write the words in green under the correct photos.

At the Grocery Store

1. Daniel and Lara (*go*) _____ to the grocery store yesterday.
2. They (*walk*) _____ down the meat aisle, the produce aisle, and the dairy aisle.
3. Daniel (*push*) _____ the shopping cart.
4. Their baby (*sleep*) _____ in her car seat.
5. Lara (*hold*) _____ a shopping basket.
6. They (*see*) _____ many products on the shelves.
7. Lara (*read*) _____ the nutritional information on the packages.
8. They (*find*) _____ some good bargains.
9. Lara (*pay*) _____ the cashier at the checkout counter.
10. She (*put*) _____ the receipt in her wallet.

1. _____

2. _____

3. _____

4. _____

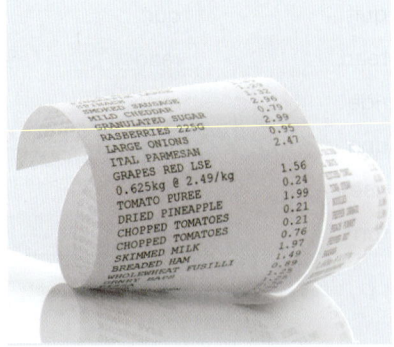

5. _____

6. _____

EXERCISE 6 ▸ Let's talk: pairwork. (Charts 2-2 and 2-3)

Make true statements for you. Write the affirmative or negative past tense form of the verb. Then tell a partner some of the things that are true for you.

1. I (*make*) _made / didn't make_ a delicious dinner last night.
2. I (*speak*) _____ English with a native English speaker yesterday.
3. I (*think*) _____ about my family this morning.
4. I (*drink*) _____ coffee or tea this morning.
5. I (*ride*) _____ the bus to school today.
6. I (*send*) _____ a text message this morning.
7. I (*forget*) _____ a website password recently.
8. I (*buy*) _____ an airline ticket last year.
9. I (*swim*) _____ in a swimming pool last weekend.
10. I (*win*) _____ a sports competition when I was in school.

EXERCISE 7 ▸ Let's talk. (Charts 2-2 and 2-3)

Answer the questions. Work in pairs, small groups, or as a class.

1. What time does school begin every day? What time did your class begin today?
2. What does your teacher often tell you to do? What did he/she tell you to do today?
3. What time do you leave your home every day? What time did you leave today?
4. What do you sometimes eat for dinner? What did you eat last night?
5. What do you frequently buy at the store? What did you buy yesterday?
6. Do you get sick very often? When did you last get sick?
7. Do you take public transportation very often? When did you last take public transportation? What did it cost? How much did you pay?

EXERCISE 8 ▸ Let's talk: pairwork. (Charts 2-1 → 2-3)

Work with a partner. Ask and answer the questions with *Yes* and a complete sentence. You can look at your book before you speak. When you speak, look at your partner.

A Broken Arm

Imagine that you came to class today with a big cast on your arm. You slipped on some ice yesterday and fell down.

Example: PARTNER A: Did you have a bad day yesterday?
    PARTNER B: Yes, I had a bad day yesterday.

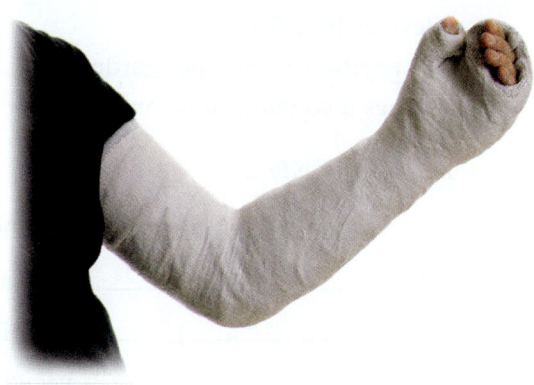

Partner A	Partner B
1. Did you fall down? 2. Did you hurt yourself when you fell down? 3. Did you break your arm? 4. Did you go to the ER (emergency room)? 5. Did you wait in the waiting room for a long time?	6. Did you speak with a nurse? 7. Did you see a doctor? 8. Did the doctor put a cast on your arm? 9. Did you get a prescription for the pain? 10. Did you pay a lot of money?

EXERCISE 9 ▶ Looking at grammar. (Charts 2-2 and 2-3)
Complete the sentences with a simple past form of a verb in the box.

| bite | break | dream | eat | feel | fly | go | shake | steal |

Oh, no!

1. Someone _____ my ID. Who took it?
2. I just _____ an earthquake. The house _____.
3. My sister fell on a hike and _____ her ankle.
4. We _____ on a small airplane over the mountains, and the ride was bumpy.
5. I _____ about a wolf last night. It _____ me for dinner.
6. The dog _____ our mail carrier. She _____ to an urgent care for stitches.

EXERCISE 10 ▶ Looking at grammar. (Charts 2-1 → 2-3)
Read the facts about each person. Complete the sentences with the correct form of the given verbs.

SITUATION 1: Whirlwind Wendy is energetic and does everything very quickly. Here are her typical morning activities:

wakes up at 4:00 A.M.
cleans her apartment
rides her bike five miles
gets vegetables from her garden
watches a cooking show on TV

makes soup for dinner
brings her elderly mother a meal
answers email messages
fixes herself lunch

Yesterday, Wendy …

1. ____woke up____ at 4:00 A.M.
2. ____didn't clean____ her car.
3. _____ her bike ten miles.
4. _____ vegetables from her garden.

5. _____ a comedy show on TV.

6. _____ soup for dinner.

7. _____ her elderly mother a meal.

8. _____ email messages.

9. _____ herself a snack.

SITUATION 2: Sluggish Sam doesn't get much done in a day. Here are his typical activities:

sleeps for 12 hours   comes home
wakes up at noon   lies on the couch
takes two hours to eat breakfast thinks about his busy life
goes fishing   begins dinner at 8:00
falls asleep on his boat   finishes dinner at 11:00

Yesterday, Sam …

1. ____*slept*____ for 12 hours.
2. ____*didn't wake*____ up at 5:00 A.M.
3. _____ two hours to eat breakfast.
4. _____ hiking.
5. _____ asleep on his boat.
6. _____ home.
7. _____ on his bed.
8. _____ about his busy life.
9. _____ dinner at 5:00.
10. _____ dinner at 11:00.

EXERCISE 11 ▶ Looking at grammar. (Chart 2-3)
Complete the sentences. Use the simple past of any irregular verb that makes sense. More than one answer may be possible.

My Roommates

1. Lita walked to her job today. Rebecca ____*drove*____ her car. Jada _____ her bike. Yoko _____ the bus.

2. Jada had a choice between a job in finance or a job in management. She _____ the one in management.

3. Rebecca doesn't have any money right now. She _____ it all last month.

4. Rebecca's parents _____ her a check, but she didn't get it. She's flat broke.*

5. Jada wears interesting clothes. She _____ a tuxedo to her brother's wedding last week.

6. Last night around midnight, Jada _____ some toast. She burned it, and the smoke alarm went off. It _____ everyone up.

7. Yoko's dog _____ several holes in the backyard. The grass looks terrible.

8. Lita grew up near the equator. She is enjoying the long summer days here. The sun _____ around 5:00 this morning. It _____ at 9:00 last night.

9. Lita _____ kindergarten for two years, but now she's teaching 2nd grade.

10. Yoko received a painting for her birthday. She _____ it in our living room.

EXERCISE 12 ▶ Let's talk: pairwork. (Charts 2-1 → 2-3)

With a partner, take turns asking each other to perform an action. Partner A tells Partner B to do something. Then A will ask B a question in the past tense.

Example: Open your book.
PARTNER A: Open your book.
PARTNER B: (*opens his/her book*)
PARTNER A: What did you do?
PARTNER B: I opened my book.

1. Shut your book.
2. Stand up.
3. Hide your pen.
4. Turn to page 10 in your book.
5. Put your book under your desk.
6. Write your name on a piece of paper.
Change roles.
7. Draw a bird.
8. Read a sentence from your grammar book.
9. Wave "good-bye."
10. Point to the board.
11. Spell the past tense of *speak*.
12. Repeat this question: "Which came first: the chicken or the egg?"

EXERCISE 13 ▶ Looking at grammar. (Charts 2-1 → 2-3)

Complete the conversations with the correct form of the words in parentheses.

Travel Questions

1. A: (*your plane, arrive*) <u>Did your plane arrive</u> on time yesterday?
   B: Yes, <u>it did</u>. It (*get*) _____ in at exactly 6:05.

2. A: (*you, sleep*) _____ on the flight?
   B: Yes, _____. I (*sleep*) _____ for four hours.

---

flat broke = completely out of money

3. A: (you, take) _____ a tour of Paris during your trip?

   B: No, _____. I (miss) _____ the tour because

   I (oversleep) _____.

   A: Why did you oversleep?

   B: I (hear, not) _____ my alarm.

4. A: (you, eat) _____ at a fancy restaurant?

   B: No, we _____. We (have, not) _____ enough money.

   We (buy) _____ food in grocery stores or small cafés.

5. A: (you, visit) _____ the Louvre Museum?

   B: Yes, we _____. We (see) _____ the *Mona Lisa*.

   A: (Da Vinci, paint) _____ the *Mona Lisa*?

   B: Yes, _____. He also (paint) _____ many other pictures.

EXERCISE 14 ▶ Let's talk: pairwork. (Charts 2-1 → 2-3)

Work with a partner. Complete the conversation. Then practice with your partner and perform it for the class. You can look at your book before you speak. When you speak, look at your partner.

Small Talk

A: Hi, how's it going?

B: Good. How was your weekend?

A: _____. I _____.

   How about you? What did you do?

B: I _____.

A: That sounds _____.

B: It was.

EXERCISE 15 ▶ Let's talk: pairwork. (Charts 2-1 → 2-3)

Choose one of the company names in the box. Find out about the name on the internet. Talk to a student who has a different company name. Follow the model. Explain vocabulary if necessary.

Al-Jazeera®	Amazon®	CNN®	Ikea®	Samsung®
Alibaba®	Boeing®	Google®	LEGO®	Skype®

Example: A: What company did you choose? (Adobe®)

   B: I chose ___Adobe.___

   A: Where did the name ___Adobe___ come from?

   B: ___John Warnock was a co-founder of the company. He lived in Silicon Valley. The___
   ___Adobe Creek ran behind his house. Warnock named the company after the creek.___
   ___A creek is a small river. Here is a photo of a creek.___

EXERCISE 16 ▸ Reading and grammar. (Charts 2-1 → 2-3)
Read the paragraph, and rewrite it in the past tense. Begin your new paragraph with *Yesterday morning*.

The Daily News

Every morning, David checks his Twitter feed. He wants to get the latest sports news. He also looks at the national news and reads several stories. His wife, Milana, checks her favorite newspapers online. She looks only at the headlines. She doesn't have a lot of time. She finishes articles later in the day. Both David and Milana know a lot about the day's events.

EXERCISE 17 ▸ Warm-up: listening. (Chart 2-4)
Listen to each pair of verbs. Decide if the verb endings have the same sound or a different sound.

Example: You will hear: plays   played

   You will choose: same   (different)

1. same   different
2. same   different
3. same   different
4. same   different

2-4 Recognizing Verb Endings and Questions with *Did*

(a) I *agreed* with you. (b) I *agree* with you. (c) She *agrees* with you. (d) We *worked* today. (e) We *work* today. (f) He *works* today.	The *-ed* ending can be hard to hear. It can blend with the next word. For the third person simple present, you will hear an *-s* on the verb.
(g) I *was* in a hurry. (h) I *wasn't* in a hurry. (i) They *were* on time. (j) They *weren't* on time.	The "t" in an "n't" contraction can also be hard to hear. The "t" sound is not released, and you may hear just the "n."
(k) Did she → *Dih-she* (l) Did we → *Dih-we* (m) Did they → *Dih-they* (n) Did you → *Did-ja* OR *Did-ya* (o) Did I → *Dih-di* OR *Di* (p) Did he → *Dih-de* OR *De*	Note the pronunciation for questions beginning with *did*. The "d" may be dropped, as in (k)–(m). Or, the sounds may change, as in (n)–(p). At this stage of your learning, it is more important to focus on hearing the differences rather than pronouncing these words.

EXERCISE 18 ▶ Listening. (Chart 2-4)
Listen to each sentence. Choose the correct completion(s).

In the Classroom

Example: You will hear: We worked in small groups …
You will choose: a. right now (b.) yesterday (c.) on our project

1. a. clearly   b. every day   c. yesterday
2. a. right now   b. last week   c. to the class
3. a. almost every day   b. yesterday   c. before every test
4. a. now   b. earlier today   c. with a quiz
5. a. with native speakers b. every day   c. yesterday
6. a. in biology   b. now   c. every day
7. a. last week   b. last month   c. about fish
8. a. every week   b. last week   c. once a week

EXERCISE 19 ▶ Listening. (Chart 2-4)
Part I. Listen to the reduced pronunciations with *did*.

1. Did you   → *Did-ja*   Did you forget something?
                Did-ya   Did you forget something?
2. Did I   → *Dih-di*   Did I forget something?
                Di   Did I forget something?
3. Did he   → *Dih-de*   Did he forget something?
                De   Did he forget something?
4. Did she   → *Dih-she*   Did she forget something?
5. Did we   → *Dih-we*   Did we forget something?
6. Did they → *Dih-they* Did they forget something?

Part II. You will hear questions. Complete each answer with the pronoun and the non-reduced form of the verb you hear.

1. Yes, he ____*did*____ . He ____*cut*____ it with a knife.
2. Yes, she _____ . She _____ it all yesterday.
3. Yes, I _____ . I _____ them yesterday.
4. Yes, they _____ . They _____ it.
5. Yes, you _____ . You _____ it.
6. Yes, she _____ . She _____ them.

7. Yes, he _____. He _____ it to him.

8. Yes, I _____. I _____ them.

9. Yes, he _____. He _____ it.

10. Yes, you _____. You _____ her.

EXERCISE 20 ▸ Listening. (Chart 2-4)
Part I. The differences between *was/wasn't* and *were/weren't* can be hard to hear in spoken English. The "t" in the negative contraction is often dropped, and you may only hear an /n/ sound. Listen to these examples.

1. It was a big wedding. It wasn't a big wedding.
2. We were early. We weren't early.

Part II. Listen to these sentences about a wedding. Circle the words you hear.

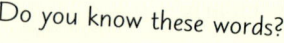
Do you know these words?
- nervous
- excited
- ceremony
- reception

At a Wedding

1. was	wasn't	6. was	wasn't
2. was	wasn't	7. was	wasn't
3. were	weren't	8. was	wasn't
4. were	weren't	9. were	weren't
5. was	wasn't	10. were	weren't

the groom and bride

EXERCISE 21 ▸ Warm-up. (Chart 2-5)
Do you know the spelling rules for these verbs?

Part I. Write the *-ing* form of each verb under the correct heading.

die	give	hit	try

Drop final *-e*. Add *-ing*.

Double final consonant. Add *-ing*.

Change *-ie* to *-y*. Add *-ing*.

Just add *-ing*.

_____   _____   _____   _____

Part II. Write the *-ed* form of each verb under the correct heading.

enjoy	tie	stop	study

Double final consonant. Add *-ed*.

Change *-y* to *-i*. Add *-ed*.

Just add *-ed*.

Just add *-d*.

_____   _____   _____   _____

2-5 Spelling of -ing and -ed Forms

End of Verb	Double the Consonant?	Simple Form	-ing	-ed	
-e	NO	(a) smi**le** ho**pe**	smi**l**ing ho**p**ing	smi**l**ed ho**p**ed	**-ing** form: Drop the **-e**, add **-ing**. **-ed** form: Just add **-d**.
Two Consonants	NO	(b) he**lp** lea**rn**	he**lp**ing lea**rn**ing	he**lp**ed lea**rn**ed	If the verb ends in two consonants, just add **-ing** or **-ed**.
Two Vowels + One Consonant	NO	(c) ra**in** he**at**	ra**in**ing he**at**ing	ra**in**ed he**at**ed	If the verb ends in two vowels + a consonant, just add **-ing** or **-ed**.
One Vowel + One Consonant	YES	ONE-SYLLABLE VERBS			If the verb has one syllable and ends in one vowel + one consonant, double the consonant to make the **-ing** or **-ed** form.*
		(d) sto**p** pla**n**	sto**pp**ing pla**nn**ing	sto**pp**ed pla**nn**ed	
	NO	TWO-SYLLABLE VERBS			If the first syllable of a two-syllable verb is stressed, do not double the consonant.
		(e) vís**it** óff**er**	vis**it**ing off**er**ing	vis**it**ed off**er**ed	
	YES	(f) prefé**r** admí**t**	prefe**rr**ing admi**tt**ing	prefe**rr**ed admi**tt**ed	If the second syllable of a two-syllable verb is stressed, double the consonant.
-y	NO	(g) pl**ay** enj**oy**	pl**ay**ing enj**oy**ing	pl**ay**ed enj**oy**ed	If the verb ends in a vowel + **-y**, keep the **-y**. Do not change the **-y** to **-i**.
		(h) wor**ry** stu**dy**	wor**ry**ing stu**dy**ing	wor**ri**ed stu**di**ed	If the verb ends in a consonant + **-y**, keep the **-y** for the **-ing** form, but change the **-y** to **-i** to make the **-ed** form.
-ie		(i) d**ie** t**ie**	d**y**ing t**y**ing	d**ie**d t**ie**d	**-ing** form: Change the **-ie** to **-y** and add **-ing**. **-ed** form: Just add **-d**.

*EXCEPTIONS: Do not double "w" or "x": *snow, snowing, snowed, fix, fixing, fixed.*

EXERCISE 22 ▶ Looking at spelling. (Chart 2-5)
Write the **-ing** and **-ed** forms of these verbs.

	-ING	**-ED**
1. wait	_____	_____
2. clean	_____	_____
3. plant	_____	_____
4. plan	_____	_____

	-ING	*-ED*
5. hope	_____	_____
6. hop	_____	_____
7. play	_____	_____
8. study	_____	_____
9. cry	_____	_____
10. die	_____	_____
11. sleep	_____	*slept (no -ed)*
12. run	_____	*ran (no -ed)*

EXERCISE 23 ▶ Spelling and grammar. (Chart 2-5)

Part I. Write the correct forms.

1. begin + *ing* _____
2. close + *ing* _____
3. hurry + *ed* _____
4. enjoy + *ed* _____
5. happen + *ed* _____

6. lie + *ing* _____
7. listen + *ing* _____
8. open + *ing* _____
9. shop + *ing* _____
10. try + *ed* _____

Part II. Complete the sentences with the correct verb from Part I. Some are present and some are past.

At the Mall

1. We are _____ for clothes today.

2. We _____ to the mall. We wanted to be there early for the sales.

3. You look upset. What _____ ?

4. This is the wrong size. I _____ on a medium and bought a large.

5. Oh, no. The elevator door is stuck. It isn't _____ .

6. Shhh. The movie is _____ .

7. I'm _____ to an announcement. It's 9:50. The mall is _____ at 10:00 P.M.

8. The dressing rooms are messy. Clothes are _____ on the floor.

9. I _____ our shopping trip. It was fun.

EXERCISE 24 ▶ Reading and grammar. (Charts 2-1 → 2-5)
Complete the sentences with the correct form of the verbs in parentheses.

> Do you know these words?
> - lemonade
> - positive
> - partner with
> - app
> - stock

FROM LEMONS TO LEMONADE

There is a common saying in English: "When life gives you lemons, make lemonade." Do you understand the meaning? Lemons are sour, but lemonade is sweet. If something bad happens to you, try to make a good situation out of it.

In 2009, software engineer Brian Acton (*have*) _____(1)_____ a bad experience. He (*need*) _____(2)_____ a job. He (*apply*) _____(3)_____ at Twitter and Facebook. But the two famous companies (*want, not*) _____(4)_____ to hire him, and both (*say*) _____(5)_____ "no." Acton was disappointed, but he (*stay*) _____(6)_____ positive. He (*write*) _____(7)_____ after the interview: "It (*be*) _____(8)_____ a great opportunity to connect with some fantastic people. Looking forward to life's next adventure."

That same year, Acton partnered with Jan Koum, a former co-worker, and together they (*build*) _____(9)_____ WhatsApp®, a social network messaging app. Five years later, in 2014, Facebook (*buy*) _____(10)_____ WhatsApp for $19 billion in stock and cash. Some people (*call*) _____(11)_____ it a multi-billion dollar mistake, but not for Acton and Koum. The company that said "no" to Acton made him an instant billionaire.

Do you know someone who made lemonade from lemons? Who? What did he or she do?

EXERCISE 25 ▶ Listening and speaking. (Charts 2-1 → 2-5)
Part I. Listen to the conversation between two friends about their weekend and answer the questions.

1. One person had a good weekend. Why?
   _____
   _____

2. His friend didn't have a good weekend. Why not?
   _____
   _____

Part II. Complete the conversation with your partner. Use past tense verbs. Practice saying it until you can do it without looking at your book. Then change roles and create a new conversation. Practice it until you don't need your book. Perform one of the conversations for the class.

A: Did you have a good weekend?

B: Yeah, I _____.

A: Really? That sounds like fun!

B: It _____ great! I _____.

How about you? How was your weekend?

A: I _____.

B: Did you have a good time?

A: Yes. / No. / Not really. _____.

EXERCISE 26 ▶ Warm-up. (Chart 2-6)
Check (✓) all the activities you were doing at midnight last night.

1. _____ I was sleeping.
2. _____ I was eating.
3. _____ I was texting.
4. _____ I was checking social media.
5. _____ I was watching a movie.
6. _____ I was having good dreams.

2-6 The Past Progressive

PAST PROGRESSIVE		
	(a) I sat down at the dinner table at 6:00 P.M. yesterday. I finished my meal at 6:30 P.M. I *was eating* dinner between 6:00 and 6:30. (b) I *was sleeping* at 9:00 last night. (c) During dinner, Sam *was checking* social media.	The PAST PROGRESSIVE expresses *an activity that was in progress (was occurring, was happening)* at a particular time in the past, as in (a)–(c). In (b), sleeping began before 9:00, was in progress at that time, and probably continued. In (c), the simple past is also correct: *During dinner, Sam checked social media.* (Meaning: He didn't continually check it.) Use of the progressive emphasizes that the activity is continuing in the past.
	(d) — Where is Jon this week? — He *is traveling* on business. (e) — Jon didn't come to the party last week. I wonder why. — He *was traveling* on business.	Compare the present progressive, as in (d), with the past progressive, as in (e).

Forms of the Past Progressive

STATEMENT		I, She, He, It You, We, They	*was working.* *were working.*
NEGATIVE		I, She, He, It You, We, They	*was not (wasn't) working.* *were not (weren't) working.*
QUESTION	**Was** **Were**	I, she, he, it you, we, they	*working?* *working?*
SHORT ANSWER	Yes, No, Yes, No,	I, she, he, it I, she, he, it you, we, they you, we, they	*was.* *wasn't.* *were.* *weren't.*

EXERCISE 27 ▶ Looking at grammar. (Chart 2-6)
Complete the sentences with a form of the verb in *italics*.

1. Our teacher *is helping* us get ready for the final exam. Yesterday at this time, he
   _____*was helping*_____ us get ready for the final exam.

2. Many students *are studying* in the library today. Yesterday, many students
   _____ in the library.

3. The registration office *is accepting* schedule changes this week. Last week the registration office
   _____ schedule changes.

4. I *am texting* my friends right now. Yesterday at this time, I _____

   my friends.

5. My roommates *are working* together on a project this afternoon. They
   _____ together yesterday afternoon too.

EXERCISE 28 ▶ Let's talk: pairwork. (Chart 2-6)
Work with a partner. Take turns asking and answering the questions. Share some of your partner's answers with the class.

1. Were you eating breakfast at 8:00 A.M. today?
2. Were you sleeping at 11:00 P.M. yesterday?
3. What were you doing at 3:00 P.M. yesterday?
4. What were you doing between 8:00 P.M. and 9:00 P.M. last night?
5. Where were you studying six months ago?
6. Where were you living one year ago?

EXERCISE 29 ▶ Vocabulary and grammar. (Chart 2-6)
Complete the sentences with a verb in the box.

| clear off | ✓ heat up | put | rinse | set | serve | sweep |

Dinnertime

1. What were you doing at 6:00 last night?

    I _____was heating up_____ cold soup in the microwave.

2. What were you doing at 6:10?

    I _____ the table with spoons and napkins.

3. What were you doing at 6:15?

    I _____ dinner to my family.

4. What were you doing at 6:45?

    I _____ the table.

5. What were you doing at 6:50?

    I _____ the dishes and _____ them in the dishwasher.

6. What were you doing at 7:00?

    I _____ the floor.

EXERCISE 30 ▶ Vocabulary, reading, and grammar. (Chart 2-6)
Part I. Write the words under the correct photos.

| an outdoor faucet | a dripping faucet | a leaking pipe | a kitchen faucet |

1. _____ 2. _____ 3. _____ 4. _____

Part II. Read the passage.

An Expensive Surprise

The Santis had a problem. They opened their water bill and were in for an expensive surprise. Their bill was much more than usual. Instead of $100 for the month, their bill was $1,100. They checked inside their house for problems. Their bathroom sinks weren't leaking. The kitchen faucet wasn't dripping. The toilets weren't leaking. The pipes weren't broken. Then they checked outside. A water faucet was running slightly. But no one used the outdoor faucet. Then they found the answer. Their dog knew how to turn it on. The weather was unusually hot that summer. While the Santis were staying indoors with air-conditioning, he was turning on cold water to cool off. The story was funny, but the ending was not. The Santis were responsible for the entire bill. But they were glad to know they had a very smart dog.

Part III. Complete the sentences about the reading. Some verbs are negative.

1. The sinks inside the house (*cause*) _____*weren't causing*_____ problems.
2. The bathroom sinks (*drip*) _____.
3. The toilets (*work*) _____.
4. Indoor faucets (*run*) _____.
5. The outdoor faucet (*run*) _____.
6. Their dog (*use*) _____ the faucet.
7. He (*turn*) _____ on hot water.
8. He (*cool*) _____ off with cold water.

EXERCISE 31 ▸ Looking at grammar. (Charts 1-1 and 2-6)

Underline the progressive verbs in the following conversations. Which are present and which are past? Discuss the way they are used. What are the similarities between the two tenses?

1. A: Where are Jan and Mark? Are they on vacation?

    B: Yes, they're traveling in Kenya for a few weeks.

2. A: I invited Jan and Mark to my birthday party, but they didn't come.

    B: Why not?

    A: They were on vacation. They were traveling in Kenya.

3. A: What was I talking about when the phone interrupted me? I forget!

    B: You were describing the website you found on the internet yesterday.

4. A: I missed the beginning of the news report. What's the announcer talking about?

    B: She's describing damage from the rainstorms in Pakistan.

EXERCISE 32 ▸ Warm-up. (Chart 2-7)

Underline the verbs in each sentence. Which action is longer? Which one is shorter?

1. I was driving when the earthquake hit.
2. The road cracked open while I was driving.
3. While the ground was shaking, my car was moving from side to side.

2-7 Simple Past vs. Past Progressive

SIMPLE PAST	(a) Maria **walked** downtown yesterday. (b) I **slept** for eight hours last night.		The simple past is used to talk about *an activity or situation that began and ended at a particular time in the past* (e.g., *yesterday, last night, two days ago, in 2014*), as in (a) and (b).
PAST PROGRESSIVE	(c) During the flight, the person next to me **was snoring** loudly.		The past progressive is used to emphasize *the duration of an activity in progress in the past*. In (c): The person was snoring from the beginning of the flight until the end.
	(d) Maria **was walking** downtown yesterday when she **saw** an old friend from high school. (e) I **was sleeping** when a loud noise **woke** me up.		The past progressive is used to talk about *an activity in progress (that was occurring, was happening) when another action occurred*. In (d): First: *Maria was walking.* Then: *She saw an old friend.* In (e): First: *I was sleeping.* Then: *A loud noise woke me up.*
	(f) You **were working** when I **was sleeping**. (g) While I **was doing** my homework, my roommate **was watching** a movie.		In (f) and (g): When two actions are in progress at the same time, the past progressive can be used in both parts of the sentence.
(h) **When** the phone rang, I was sleeping. (i) The phone rang **while** I was sleeping.		**when** = at that time **while** = during that time Examples (h) and (i) have the same meaning.	

EXERCISE 33 ▶ Looking at grammar. (Chart 2-7)
Read the sentences in the box and answer the questions that follow.

> a. Liza was looking at the limousine. The movie star was waving at her.
> b. Liza was looking at the limousine. The movie star waved at her.
> c. Liza looked at the limousine. The movie star was waving at her.
> d. Liza looked at the limousine. The movie star waved at her.

1. Which sentences have one longer action and one shorter action? _____ and _____.

2. Which sentence has two longer actions? _____

3. Which sentence has two short actions? _____

4. In Sentence b, what happened first? _____
5. In Sentence c, what happened first? _____
6. In Sentence d, what happened first? _____

EXERCISE 34 ▶ Looking at grammar. (Chart 2-7)
Complete the sentences with the simple past or past progressive form of the verbs in parentheses.

1. At 6:00 P.M. Robert sat down at the table and began to eat. At 6:05, Robert (*eat*)
   _____*was eating*_____ dinner.

2. While Robert (*eat*) _____ dinner, Ann (*come*) _____
   through the door.

3. In other words, when Ann (*come*) _____ through the door, Robert
   (*eat*) _____ dinner.

4. Robert went to bed at 10:30. At 11:00, Robert (*sleep*) _____.

5. While Robert (*sleep*) _____, his cell phone (*ring*) _____.

6. In other words, when his cell phone (*ring*) _____, Robert (*sleep*)
   _____.

7. Robert left his house at 8:00 A.M. and (*begin*) _____ to walk to class.

8. While he (*walk*) _____ to class, he (*see*) _____ Mr. Ito.

9. When Robert (*see*) _____ Mr. Ito, he (*stand*) _____
   in his driveway. He (*hold*) _____ a broom.

10. Mr. Ito (*wave*) _____ once to Robert when he (*see*) _____ him.

EXERCISE 35 ▶ Looking at grammar. (Chart 2-7)

Complete the sentences, orally or in writing, using the information in the chart. Use the simple past for the shorter activity and the past progressive for the longer one.

ACTIVITY IN PROGRESS	BETH	DAVID	LILY
sit in a café	order a salad	pay a few bills	spill coffee on her lap
stand in an elevator	send a text message	run into an old friend	drop her glasses
dive in the ocean	swim past a shark	see a dolphin	find a shipwreck

1. While Beth ____was sitting____ in a café, she ____ordered____ a salad.
2. David ____paid____ a few bills while he ____was sitting____ in a café.
3. Lily _____ coffee on her lap while she _____ in a café.
4. While Beth _____ in an elevator, she _____ a text message to a friend.
5. David _____ an old friend while he _____ in an elevator.
6. Lily _____ her glasses while she _____ in an elevator.
7. Beth _____ past a shark while she _____ in the ocean.
8. While David _____ in the ocean, he _____ a dolphin.
9. While Lily _____ in the ocean, she _____ a shipwreck.

a shipwreck

EXERCISE 36 ▶ Let's talk: pairwork. (Charts 2-6 and 2-7)

Work with a partner. Take turns asking and answering the questions. You can look at your book before you speak. When you speak, look at your partner.

PARTNER A	PARTNER B
1. What were you doing at 11:00 last night?	1. What were you doing at 5:00 this morning?
2. What were you doing when the sun came up this morning?	2. What were you doing when the sun set last night?
3. What were other students doing when you walked into the classroom?	3. What were you doing when this class began?
4. What were you thinking about when you got ready for school this morning?	4. What were you thinking about when you came to school today?
5. What were you thinking when you first spoke English?	5. What were you thinking when you started this exercise?

52 CHAPTER 2

EXERCISE 37 ▸ Reading and speaking. (Charts 2-6 and 2-7)

Your teacher will assign story A to half the class and story B to the other half of the class. Read your story several times so that you know it without looking at your book. Then tell your story to three students who have the other story. Take four minutes to tell the first person your story. Then take three minutes to tell your story to the second student. Finally, take two minutes to tell your story to the third student. The last time you speak, you should feel more comfortable than the first time.

Story A

The Ant and the Bird

Do you know these words?
- float
- leaf
- hunter
- rock
- scream

An ant was very thirsty and went to a river to drink. While he was drinking, he fell into the water. A bird was sitting in a tree and saw the ant float down the river. The ant tried to swim to safety but was unsuccessful.

The bird flew to the ant and put a leaf close to him. The ant climbed onto the leaf and floated to the shore. While the ant was resting, a hunter came to the river. He had a rock and planned to kill the bird. The ant knew this and bit the hunter in the foot. The hunter screamed, and while he was screaming, the bird flew to safety.

Moral of the story: Kind acts lead to more kind acts.

Story B

The Lion and the Mouse

Do you know these words?
- snore
- accidentally
- angrily
- hunter
- net
- roar
- escape
- hole

A mouse was running through the forest. He ran past a big lion. The lion was sleeping and snoring loudly. The mouse accidentally stepped on the lion's nose. The lion woke up and looked at the mouse angrily. "Please don't hurt me," the mouse cried. "Maybe I can help you one day." The lion laughed and put the mouse down.

A week later, a hunter's net caught the lion. The lion roared and tried to escape. While he was trying to escape, the mouse came to help him. He cut a hole in the net with his teeth. Soon the lion was free.

Moral of the story: Kindness brings more kindness.

EXERCISE 38 ▶ Looking at grammar. (Charts 2-6 and 2-7)
Read each pair of sentences and answer the question orally. Explain your answer.

1. a. Julia was eating breakfast. She heard the breaking news* report.
   b. Sara heard the breaking news report. She ate breakfast.
      QUESTION: Who heard the news report during breakfast? _____

2. a. Carlo was fishing at the lake. A fish was jumping out of the water.
   b. James was fishing at the lake. A fish jumped out of the water.
      QUESTION: Who saw a fish jump just one time? _____

3. a. When the sun came out, Paul walked home.
   b. When the sun came out, Vicky was walking home.
      QUESTION: Who walked home after the sun came out? _____

4. a. Joe looked at an email during class.
   b. Sam was looking at an email during class.
      QUESTION: Who probably spent more time looking at an email? _____

5. a. Pierre shouted and left the room.
   b. Olaf was shouting when he left the room.
      QUESTION: Who left after he shouted? _____

6. a. Erika was walking her dog, Hank. Hank was barking.
   b. Kate was walking her dog, Belle. Belle barked.
      QUESTION: Which dog barked more? _____

EXERCISE 39 ▶ Looking at grammar. (Chapter 1 and Charts 2-1 → 2-7)
Complete the sentences. Use the simple present, present progressive, simple past, or past progressive form of the verbs in parentheses.

Part I.

Right now Toshi and Oscar (*sit*) ___are sitting___ in the library. Toshi (*do*)
                                         1
_____ his homework, but Oscar (*study, not*) _____.
         2   3
He (*stare*) _____ out the window. Toshi (*want*) _____ to know
               4   5
what Oscar (*look*) _____ at.
                       6
TOSHI: Oscar, what (*you, look*) _____ at?
                                        7
OSCAR: I (*watch*) _____ the skateboarder. Look at that guy over there.
                         8
He (*turn*) _____ around in circles on his back wheels. He's amazing!
                   9

---

*breaking news = a special news report on the TV or radio

Toshi: It (be) _____10_____ easier than it (look) _____11_____.
I can teach you some skateboarding basics if you'd like.

Oscar: Great! Thanks!

Part II.

Yesterday Toshi and Oscar (sit) __were sitting__12 in the library. Toshi (do) _____13_____ his homework, but Oscar (study, not) _____14_____. He (stare) _____15_____ out the window. Toshi (want) _____16_____ to know what Oscar (look) _____17_____ at. Oscar (point) _____18_____ to the skateboarder. He (say) _____19_____ that he was amazing. Toshi (offer) _____20_____ to teach him some skateboarding basics.

EXERCISE 40 ▶ Grammar and listening. (Chapter 1 and Charts 2-1 → 2-7)
Choose the correct completions. You can check your answers by listening to the audio.

Jennifer's Problem

Jennifer **work / works**₁ for an insurance company. When people **need / are needing**₂ help with their car insurance, they **call / are calling**₃ her. Right now it is 9:05 A.M., and Jennifer **works / is working**₄ at her desk.

She **came / was coming**₅ to work on time this morning. Yesterday Jennifer **was / is**₆ late to work because she **had / was having**₇ a car accident. While she **is driving / was driving**₈ to work, her cell phone **ring / rang**₉. She **reached / was reaching**₁₀ for it. While she **is reaching / was reaching**₁₁ for her phone, Jennifer **lost / was losing**₁₂ control of the car. It **hit / was hitting**₁₃ a telephone pole.

Jennifer **is / was**₁₄ OK now, but her car **isn't / doesn't**₁₅. She **feel / feels**₁₆ very embarrassed. She **made / was making**₁₇ a bad decision, especially since it is illegal to talk on a cell phone and drive at the same time in her city.

EXERCISE 41 ▶ Listening. (Charts 2-1 → 2-7)
Listen to each conversation. Then listen again and complete the sentences with the words you hear.

At a Checkout Stand in a Grocery Store

1. CASHIER: Hi. _____ what you needed?

   CUSTOMER: Almost everything. I _____ for sticky rice, but I _____ it.

   CASHIER: _____ on aisle 10, in the Asian food section.

2. CASHIER: This is the express lane. Ten items only. It _____ like you have more than ten. _____ count them?

   CUSTOMER: I _____ I _____ ten. Oh, I _____ I have more. Sorry.

   CASHIER: The checkout stand next to me is open.

3. CASHIER: _____ any coupons you wanted to use?

   CUSTOMER: I _____ a couple in my purse, but I can't find them now.

   CASHIER: What _____ they for? I might have some extras here.

   CUSTOMER: One _____ for eggs, and the other _____ for ice cream.

   CASHIER: I think I have those.

EXERCISE 42 ▶ Warm-up. (Chart 2-8)
Check (✓) the sentences that have this meaning:

First action: We gathered our bags.
Second action: The train arrived at the station.

1. _____ We gathered our bags before the train arrived at the station.

2. _____ Before the train arrived at the station, we gathered our bags.

3. _____ After we gathered our bags, the train arrived at the station.

4. _____ As soon as the train arrived at the station, we gathered our bags.

5. _____ We didn't gather our bags until the train arrived at the station.

2-8 Expressing Past Time: Using Time Clauses

(a) **TIME CLAUSE** *After I finished my work,* **MAIN CLAUSE** *I went to bed.* (b) **MAIN CLAUSE** *I went to bed* **TIME CLAUSE** *after I finished my work.*	**After I finished my work** = a time clause* **I went to bed** = a main clause Examples (a) and (b) have the same meaning. A time clause can (1) come in front of a main clause, as in (a). (2) follow a main clause, as in (b).
(c) I went to bed *after* I finished my work. (d) *Before* I went to bed, I finished my work. (e) I stayed up *until* I finished my work. (f) *As soon as* I finished my work, I went to bed. (g) The phone rang *while* I was watching TV. (h) *When* the phone rang, I was watching TV.	These words introduce time clauses: after before until } + subject and verb = a time clause as soon as while when
	In (e): *until* = to that time and then no longer** In (f): *as soon as* = immediately after

	PUNCTUATION: Put a comma at the end of a time clause when the time clause comes first in a sentence (comes in front of the main clause):
	
	      time clause + comma + main clause
	      main clause + **no** comma + time clause

(i) When the phone *rang*, I *answered* it.	In a sentence with a time clause introduced by **when**, both the time clause verb and the main verb can be simple past. In this case, the action in the **when**-clause happened first. In (i): First: *The phone rang.* Then: *I answered it.*

*A clause is a structure that has a subject and a verb.

****Until** can also be used to say that something does NOT happen before a particular time: *I **didn't** go to bed **until** I finished my work.*

EXERCISE 43 ▶ Looking at grammar. (Chart 2-8)

Check (✓) all the clauses. Remember: A clause must have a subject and a complete verb.

1. ____ applying for a visa
2. ____ while the woman was applying for a visa
3. ____ the man took passport photos
4. ____ when the man took passport photos
5. ____ as soon as he finished
6. ____ he needed to finish
7. ____ after she sent her application
8. ____ sending her application

EXERCISE 44 ▶ Looking at grammar. (Chart 2-8)
Write "1" before the action that started first. Write "2" before the action that started second.

Taking a Taxi

1. After the taxi dropped me off, I remembered my coat in the backseat.

    a. _____ The taxi dropped me off.

    b. _____ I remembered my coat in the backseat.

2. I remembered my coat in the backseat after the taxi dropped me off.

    a. _____ I remembered my coat in the backseat.

    b. _____ The taxi dropped me off.

3. I double-checked the address before I got out of the taxi.

    a. _____ I double-checked the address.

    b. _____ I got out of the taxi.

4. Before I paid the driver, I asked for a receipt.

    a. _____ I paid the driver.

    b. _____ I asked for a receipt.

5. After I tipped the driver, he helped me with my luggage.

    a. _____ The driver helped me with my luggage.

    b. _____ I tipped the driver.

6. I tipped the driver after he helped me with my luggage.

    a. _____ I tipped the driver.

    b. _____ The driver helped me with my luggage.

EXERCISE 45 ▶ Grammar and speaking. (Chart 2-8)
Part I. Combine each set of sentences into one sentence by using a time clause. Discuss correct punctuation.

My Day

1. *First:* I cleaned up the kitchen.

    Then: I left my apartment this morning.

    Before *I left my apartment this morning, I cleaned up the kitchen.*

    I cleaned up the kitchen before *I left my apartment this morning.*

2. *First:* It began to rain.

    Then: I took out my umbrella.

    When _____

    _____ when _____

3. *First:* I worked all day.

   Then: I went home.

   After _____

   _____ after _____

4. *First:* I heard the doorbell.

   Then: I opened the door.

   As soon as _____

   _____ as soon as _____

5. *First:* I chatted with my neighbor.

   Then: I needed to go to bed.

   Until _____

   _____ until _____

6. *At the same time:* My neighbor was talking.

   I was thinking about my job.

   While _____

   _____ while _____

Part II. Work with a partner. One partner says the two sentences + the time word. The other partner, with book closed, combines the sentences. Take turns.

EXERCISE 46 ▶ Looking at grammar. (Charts 2-1 → 2-8)
Complete the sentences. Use the simple past or the past progressive form of the verbs in parentheses.

First Aid

1. I (*cut*) _____ my thumb while I (*use*)

   _____ a knife. It hurt and I

   (*yell*) _____ "Ouch." My girlfriend

   (*bring*) _____ the first-aid kit.

   bandages, tape, gauze, tablets, scissors

   She (*take*) _____ out a bandage because my thumb (*bleed*)

   _____. She (*clean*) _____ it, but the bandage (*be*)

   _____ too small, so she (*wrap*) _____ my thumb with gauze and tape.

2. A bee (*sting*) _____ Mr. Romeo on the leg when he (*plant*)

   _____ flowers. He is slightly allergic to bees. His wife (*give*)

   _____ him some medicine to help with the allergic reaction.

Past Time   59

3. While my son (*work*) _____ at a construction site, he (*fall*) _____ off a ladder and (*break*) _____ his ankle. He (*lie*) _____ on the ground when some co-workers (*find*) _____ him. They (*call*) _____ 911. They (*put*) _____ ice on his ankle and (*keep*) _____ him warm until the medics (*arrive*) _____.

EXERCISE 47 ▸ Warm-up. (Chart 2-9)

Part I. Think about your experiences when you were a beginning learner of English. Check (✓) the statements that are true for you.

When I was a beginning learner of English, …

1. _____ I felt nervous when someone asked me a question.
2. _____ I checked my dictionary frequently.
3. _____ I asked people to speak very, very slowly.
4. _____ I translated sentences into my language a lot.

Part II. Look at the sentences you checked. Are some of these statements no longer true? If the answer is "yes," you can express your ideas with **used to**. Check (✓) the statements that are true for you.

1. _____ I used to feel nervous when someone asked me a question.
2. _____ I used to check my dictionary frequently.
3. _____ I used to ask people to speak very, very slowly.
4. _____ I used to translate sentences into my language a lot.

2-9 Expressing Past Habit: *Used To*

(a) I **used to live** with my parents. Now I live in my own apartment.	***Used to*** expresses a past situation or habit that no longer exists at present.
(b) Ann **used to be** afraid of dogs, but now she likes dogs.	FORM: ***used to*** + *the simple form of a verb*
(c) Al **used to smoke,** but he doesn't anymore.	
(d) **Did** you **use to** live in Paris?	QUESTION FORM: **did** + *subject* + **use to***
(e) I **didn't use to drink** coffee at breakfast, but now I always have coffee in the morning.	NEGATIVE FORM: **didn't use to**
(f) I **never used to** drink coffee at breakfast, but now I always have coffee in the morning.	*Never* can also be used to express a negative idea with *used to,* as in (f).

*Both forms **use to** and **used to** are possible in questions and negatives: **Did** you **used to** *live* in Paris? I **didn't used to** *drink* coffee. English language authorities do not agree on which is preferable.

EXERCISE 48 ▸ Looking at grammar. (Chart 2-9)

Make sentences with a similar meaning by using **used to**. Some of the sentences are negative, and some of them are questions.

1. When I was a child, I was shy. Now I'm not shy.

   I ___used to be___ shy, but now I'm not.

2. When I was young, I thought that people over 40 were old.

   I _____ that people over 40 were old. Now I'm 40, and I don't feel old!

3. Now you live in this city. Where did you live before you came here?

   Where _____ ?

4. Did you work for the phone company at some time in the past?

   _____ for the phone company?

5. When I was younger, I slept through the night. I never woke up in the middle of the night. Now I wake up a lot.

   I _____ through the night, but now I don't.

   I _____ in the middle of the night, but now I do.

6. When I was a child, I watched cartoons on TV. I don't watch cartoons anymore. Now I stream movies.

   I _____ cartoons on TV, but I don't anymore.

   I _____ movies, but now I do.

7. How about you?

   What _____ on TV when you were little?

EXERCISE 49 ▸ Let's talk: interview. (Chart 2-9)

Walk around the classroom. Make a question with **used to** for each item. When you find a person who says "*yes*," write down his/her name and go on to the next question. Share a few of your answers with the class.

Childhood Fun

Find someone who used to ...

1. play in the mud. → *Did you use to play in the mud?*
2. play with dolls or toy soldiers.
3. believe in monsters.
4. catch frogs or snakes.
5. play jokes on the teacher at school.
6. watch cartoons.
7. swing on a rope swing.

a rope swing

EXERCISE 50 ▶ Check your knowledge. (Chapter 2 Review)
Correct the errors in verb tense usage.

1. Alex used to ~~living~~ *live* in Cairo.

2. Did you be sick last week?

3. Rico catched a cold after he plaied outside for several hours.

4. My grandma lose her keys at the mall last week.

5. Junko used to worked for an investment company.

6. We didn't no have fun when we went to the party.

7. Was your plane arrived on time last night?

8. While my mom shopping, someone took her credit cards.

9. All the students checking their phones during the class break.

10. My family used to going to the beach every weekend, but now we don't.

EXERCISE 51 ▶ Reading and writing. (Chapter 2)
Part I. Read the passage. <u>Underline</u> the time words.

Do you know these words?
- journey
- fame
- unexpected
- single mother
- take a nap
- publisher
- rejection letter
- wealthy

J. K. ROWLING

J. K. Rowling used to be an English language teacher before she became famous as the author of the *Harry Potter* series. From 1991 to 1994, she spent time in Portugal. While she was living there, she taught English. She was also working on her first *Harry Potter* book. Her journey from teacher to worldwide fame is an unexpected story.

After Rowling taught in Portugal, she went back to Scotland. By then she was a single mother with a young daughter. She didn't have much money, but she didn't want to return to teaching until she completed her book. Rowling did a lot of writing in a café. Her apartment was cold, and she enjoyed drinking coffee. While her daughter was taking naps beside her, Rowling worked on her book. She wrote quickly, and when her daughter was three, Rowling finished *Harry Potter and the Philosopher's Stone*.*

Many publishers were not interested in her book. She doesn't remember how many rejection letters she got — maybe twelve. Finally, a small publishing company, Bloomsbury, accepted it. Shortly after its publication, the book began to sell quickly, and Rowling soon became famous. Now there are several *Harry Potter* books, and Rowling is one of the wealthiest and most successful women in the world.

*In the United States and India, this title was changed to *Harry Potter and the Sorcerer's Stone*.

Part II. Choose a famous person you are interested in. Find information about the person's life. Make a list of important or interesting events. Then write one or more paragraphs to share this information. Use appropriate time words and expressions to help your readers follow your ideas, and edit your verbs carefully.

> **WRITING TIP**
>
> When you are writing about the past, it is helpful to use time words to connect some of your sentences:
>
> | Before | When | Soon | Finally |
> |---|---|---|---|
> | After | While | By then | Shortly after |
> | Now | | | |
>
> Time words and expressions make it easier for the reader to follow your ideas. Look at what happens to the beginning of the second paragraph in the passage without time words:
>
> Rowling taught in Portugal. She went back to Scotland. She was a single mother with a young daughter.
>
> It is difficult for the reader to understand exactly what happened and when. Also, the writing is "choppy" — it is not clear how the ideas connect to each other.

Part III. Edit your writing. Check for the following:

1. ☐ correct use of the simple past (a finished event)
2. ☐ correct use of the past progressive (a past event in progress)
3. ☐ use of some time words to connect ideas
4. ☐ correct spelling (use a dictionary or spell-check)

■■■■ For digital resources, go to MyEnglishLab on the Pearson English Portal. You can also go to the Pearson Practice English app for mobile practice.

CHAPTER 3
Future Time

PRETEST: What do I already know?
Choose the correct answers. More than one answer may be possible.

1. Thomas _____ this afternoon. (Chart 3-1)
   a. work   b. will works   c. is going to work

2. I _____ visit my parents this evening. (Chart 3-2)
   a. going to   b. am going to   c. am going

3. The plane will _____ at midnight. (Chart 3-3)
   a. leave   b. leaves   c. leaving

4. It _____ all next week. (Chart 3-5)
   a. will rain   b. is going to rain   c. rains

5. Alice _____ help us with our project. (Chart 3-6)
   a. maybe   b. may be   c. may

6. Before you _____ work, you will need to speak with the manager. (Chart 3-7)
   a. are leaving   b. will leave   c. leave

7. I _____ up Tom as soon as he calls. (Chart 3-7)
   a. am going to pick   b. will pick   c. pick

8. Janelle _____ to the party tomorrow. (Chart 3-8)
   a. comes   b. is going to come   c. is coming

9. The train _____ at 7:00 A.M. tomorrow. (Chart 3-9)
   a. arrives   b. it arrives   c. will arrive

10. Shhh. The show _____ begin. (Chart 3-10)
    a. about to   b. about   c. is about to

11. I am going to go to bed early and _____ in late. (Chart 3-11)
    a. sleep   b. sleeping   c. I sleep

EXERCISE 1 ▸ Warm-up. (Chart 3-1)
Which sentences express future meaning? Do the future sentences have the same meaning or a different meaning?

1. It is going to snow today.
2. It snowed today.
3. It will snow today.

3-1 Expressing Future Time: *Be Going To* and *Will*

FUTURE

(a) I *am going to leave* at nine tomorrow morning.

(b) I *will leave* at nine tomorrow morning.

Be going to and *will* are used to express future time.

Examples (a) and (b) have the same meaning.

NOTE: Sometimes *will* and *be going to* express different meanings. See Chart 3-5.

(c) Sam *is* in his office *this morning*.

(d) Ann *was* in her office *this morning* at eight, but now she's at a meeting.

(e) Bob *is going to be* in his office *this morning* after his dentist appointment.

Today, *tonight*, and *this* + *morning*, *afternoon*, *evening*, *week*, etc., can express present, past, or future time, as in (c) through (e).

NOTE: The use of *shall* (with *I* or *we*) to express future time is possible but is infrequent and quite formal; for example: *I shall* leave at nine tomorrow morning. *We shall* leave at ten tomorrow morning.

EXERCISE 2 ▶ Looking at grammar. (Chart 3-1)
Check (✓) the sentences that express future time.

At the Airport

1. ____ The security line will take about a half hour.
2. ____ The plane is going to arrive at Gate 10.
3. ____ Your flight is already an hour late.
4. ____ Your flight will be here soon.
5. ____ Did you print your boarding pass?
6. ____ Are you printing my boarding pass too?
7. ____ Are we going to have a snack on our flight?
8. ____ We will need to buy snacks on the flight.

EXERCISE 3 ▶ Looking at grammar. (Chart 3-1)
Choose all the correct completions.

At Work

1. My vacation will start — (at noon.) / (next week.) / (tonight.)
2. The project will be ready — this afternoon. / last night. / today.
3. Our manager is going to retire — tomorrow. / this week. / yesterday.
4. The new manager arrived — today. / this morning. / last week.
5. She spoke with us — this morning. / tonight. / today.
6. The office is going to close early — this evening. / next week. / yesterday.

EXERCISE 4 ▸ Let's talk: interview. (Chapters 1 and 2; Chart 3-1)

Make questions. Begin with the words in the box. Then walk around the room and take turns asking and answering questions. Share some of your classmates' answers with the class.

Past:	What did you do … ?
Present:	What are you doing … ?
	What do you do … ?
Future:	What are you going to do … ?

Example: yesterday → *What did you do yesterday?*

1. right now _____
2. tomorrow _____
3. every day _____
4. this month _____
5. a week from now _____
6. the day before yesterday _____
7. the day after tomorrow _____
8. last week _____
9. every week _____
10. this weekend _____

EXERCISE 5 ▸ Warm-up. (Chart 3-2)
Choose the verb in each sentence to make true statements.

1. I   **am going to / am not going to**   sleep in* tomorrow morning.
2. Our teacher   **is going to / is not going to**   retire next month.
3. We   **are going to / are not going to**   have a class party next week.

3-2 Forms with *Be Going To*

(a) We *are going to be* late. (b) She*'s going to come* tomorrow. INCORRECT: She's going to comes tomorrow.	***Be going to*** is followed by the simple form of the verb, as in (a) and (b).

(c) **Am** I
    Is he, she, it } *going to be* late?
    Are they, we, you
	QUESTION FORM: ***be*** + *subject* + ***going to***

(d)   I **am not**
    He, She, It **is not** } *going to be* late.
    They, We, You **are not**
	NEGATIVE FORM: ***be*** + ***not*** + ***going to***

*****sleep in** = sleep late; not wake up early in the morning

EXERCISE 6 ▶ Looking at grammar. (Charts 3-1 and 3-2)
Complete the sentences with a form of *be going to* and the words in parentheses.

Errands

1. A: Where (*Alex, go*) ___is Alex going to go___ after work?

   B: He (*stop*) _____ at the movie theater and run some other errands.

   A: Why (*he, stop*) _____ at the movie theater?

   B: He left his credit card there. He (*get*) _____ it.

2. A: What (*you, do*) _____ after work?

   B: I (*pick up*) _____ a prescription at the pharmacy and get something for dinner.

3. A: What (*you, make*) _____ for dinner?

   B: I (*cook, not*) _____.

   I (*get*) _____ takeout.

4. A: (*you, finish*) _____ your errands soon?

   B: Yes, I (*finish*) _____ them in the next hour.

EXERCISE 7 ▶ Let's talk: pairwork. (Charts 3-1 and 3-2)
Work with a partner. Take turns asking and answering questions with *be going to*.

Examples: what \ you \ do \ after class?
PARTNER A: What are you going to do after class?
PARTNER B: I'm going to get a bite to eat* after class.

you \ watch TV \ tonight?
PARTNER A: Are you going to watch TV tonight?
PARTNER B: Yes, I'm going to watch TV tonight. OR No, I'm not going to watch TV tonight.

1. where \ you \ go \ after your last class \ today?
2. what time \ you \ wake up \ tomorrow?
3. what \ you \ have \ for breakfast \ tomorrow?
4. you \ be \ home \ this evening?
5. where \ you \ be \ next year?
6. you \ become \ famous \ some day?
7. you \ take \ a trip \ sometime next year?
8. you \ do \ something unusual \ in the near future?

*get a bite to eat = get something to eat

EXERCISE 8 ▸ Let's talk: pairwork. (Chapters 1 and 2; Charts 3-1 and 3-2)

Work with a partner. Complete the conversation with your own words. Be creative! Practice your conversation and then present it to the class.

Example:

PARTNER A: I rode a skateboard to school yesterday.
PARTNER B: Really? Wow! Do you ride a skateboard to school often?
PARTNER A: Yes, I do. I ride a skateboard to school almost every day.
　　　　　　Did you ride a skateboard to school yesterday?
PARTNER B: No, I didn't. I came by helicopter.
PARTNER A: Are you going to come to school by helicopter tomorrow?
PARTNER B: No, I'm not. I'm going to ride a motorcycle to school tomorrow.

A: I _____ yesterday.

B: Really? Wow! _____ you _____ often?

A: Yes, I _____ . I _____ almost every day.

　　_____ you _____ yesterday?

B: No, I _____ . I _____ .

A: Are you _____ tomorrow?

B: No, I _____ . I _____ tomorrow.

EXERCISE 9 ▸ Warm-up. (Chart 3-3)

Complete the sentences with *will* or *won't*.

1. It _____ rain tomorrow.

2. We _____ study Chart 3-3 next.

3. I _____ teach the class next week.

4. *To your teacher:* You _____ need to assign homework for tonight.

3-3 Forms with *Will*

STATEMENT	I, You, She, He, It, We, They **will come** tomorrow.
NEGATIVE	I, You, She, He, It, We, They **will not (won't) come** tomorrow.
QUESTION	**Will** I, you, she, he, it, we, they **come** tomorrow?
SHORT ANSWER	Yes, / No, } I, you, she, he, it, we, they { **will**.* / **won't**.
CONTRACTIONS	I'll she'll we'll / you'll he'll they'll / it'll — ***Will*** is usually contracted with pronouns in both speech and informal writing.

*Pronouns are NOT contracted with helping verbs in short answers.
   CORRECT: *Yes, I will.*
   INCORRECT: *Yes, I'll.*

EXERCISE 10 ▶ Looking at grammar. (Chart 3-3)
Complete the sentences with ***will*** and the verbs in parentheses.

Around Town

1. A new restaurant (*open*) _____ Friday night.
2. The mall (*offer*) _____ free child care tomorrow.
3. The parking garage (*close*) _____ at midnight.
4. The appliance store (*have*) _____ a sale this weekend.
5. The elementary school (*show*) _____ a family movie Friday night.
6. A band (*play*) _____ music in the park this weekend.
7. Food carts (*sell*) _____ snacks.
8. Traffic (*be*) _____ heavy in the area all weekend.

a food cart

EXERCISE 11 ▶ Let's talk: interview. (Chart 3-3)
Make complete questions with ***will***. Then walk around the room and take turns asking and answering questions.

1. you \ answer my interview questions → *Will you answer my interview questions?*
2. we \ have class tomorrow?
3. it \ rain tonight?
4. the weather \ be hot next week?
5. you \ lend me some money?
6. you \ dream in English tonight?
7. we \ need our grammar books tomorrow?
8. our teacher \ give us homework today?

EXERCISE 12 ▸ **Reading, grammar, and speaking.** (Chart 3-3)
Part I. Read the passage.

An Old Apartment

Ted and Amy live in an old, run-down apartment and want to move. The building has a lot of problems. The ceiling leaks when it rains. The faucets drip. The toilet doesn't always flush properly. The windows don't close tightly, and heat escapes from the rooms in the winter. In the summer, it is very hot because there is no air conditioner.

Their apartment is in an unsafe part of town. Ted and Amy both take the bus to work and need to walk a long distance to the bus stop. Their apartment building doesn't have a laundry room, so they also have to walk to a laundromat to wash their clothes. They are planning to have children in the near future, so they want a park or play area nearby for their children. A safe neighborhood is very important to them.

Do you know these words?
- run-down - flush
- ceiling   - escapes
- leak   - air conditioner
- faucets   - laundromat
- drip

Part II. Ted and Amy are thinking about their next apartment and are making a list of what they want and don't want. Complete their sentences with *will* or *won't*.

Our Next Apartment

1. It _____won't_____ have leaky faucets.
2. The toilet _____ flush properly.
3. It _____ have windows that close tightly.
4. There _____ be air-conditioning for hot days.
5. It _____ be in a dangerous part of town.
6. It _____ be near a bus stop.
7. There _____ be a laundry room in the building.
8. We _____ need to walk to a laundromat.
9. A play area _____ be nearby.

Part III. Imagine you are moving to a new home. Decide the six most important things you want your home to have (*It will have … / It won't have …*). You can brainstorm ideas in small groups and then discuss your ideas with the class.

EXERCISE 13 ▸ **Warm-up: listening.** (Chart 3-4)
Listen to the conversation. You will hear reduced speech. Choose the correct (non-reduced) form.

A: Are you ____ come with us to the meeting?   a. going   b. going to
B: No, ____ study. I have a test tomorrow.   a. I am going to b. I am going
A: I understand. ____ you know what happens.   a. I let   b. I will let

3-4 Be Going To and Will in Spoken English

(a) You're *going to* (*gonna*) need help. (b) We're *going to* (*gonna*) be late. (c) He's *going to* (*gonna*) take the bus. (d) It's *going to* (*gonna*) rain.	In spoken English, it is common to hear *gonna* for *going to*.
(e) I*'ll* (*ahl*) help you. (f) You*'ll* (*yul*) help. (g) He*'ll* (*hill*) help you. (h) She*'ll* (*shill*) help you. (i) We*'ll* (*wul*) help you.	*Will* in contractions can be difficult to hear. The vowels can change, and the contractions may sound very fast.
(j) **Dad'll** be here soon. (k) The **test'll** take an hour. (l) **Sam'll** leave before us.	In spoken English, **will** is often contracted with nouns, as in (j)–(l).

EXERCISE 14 ▶ Listening. (Chart 3-4)

Part I. Listen to the pronunciation of the reduced forms of *going to* in the conversation.

Apartment Hunting

A: We're going to look for an apartment to rent this weekend.
B: Are you going to look in this area?
A: No, we're going to search in an area closer to our jobs.
B: Is the rent going to be cheaper in that area?
A: Yes, apartment rents are definitely going to be cheaper.
B: Are you going to need to pay a deposit?
A: I'm sure we're going to need to pay the first and last month's rent.

Part II. Listen to the conversation and write the non-reduced form of the words you hear.

A: Where ___are you going to___(1) move to?

B: We _____(2) look for something outside the city.

We _____(3) spend the weekend apartment hunting.

A: What fees _____(4) need to pay?

B: I think we _____(5) need to pay the first and last month's rent.

A: _____(6) there _____(7) be other fees?

B: There _____(8) probably _____(9) be an application fee and a cleaning fee. Also, the landlord _____(10) probably _____(11) check our credit, so we _____(12) need to pay for that.

Future Time 71

EXERCISE 15 ▸ Listening. (Chart 3-4)
Complete the sentences with the words you hear.

Before the Party
1. We'll need to get the house ready for the party tomorrow, but _____ be gone in the morning.
2. _____ need to fold the laundry and dust the furniture.
3. I talked to your sister. _____ clean the kitchen.
4. Your dad will be home. _____ vacuum the carpets.
5. Your brothers won't be home. _____ do the cleanup.
6. Some of the guests are going to come early. _____ need to be ready by 5:00.

EXERCISE 16 ▸ Listening. (Chart 3-4)
Part I. Listen to the sentences. Notice the pronunciation of the contractions with nouns.

At the Doctor's Office
1. The doctor'll be with you in a few minutes.
2. Your appointment'll take about an hour.
3. Your fever'll be gone in a few days.
4. Your stitches'll disappear over the next two weeks.
5. The nurse'll schedule your tests.
6. The lab'll have the results next week.
7. The receptionist at the front desk'll set up* your next appointment.

Part II. Listen to the sentences and write the words you hear. Write the full form of the contractions.

At the Pharmacy
1. Your prescription ___*will be*___ ready in ten minutes.
2. The medicine _____ you feel a little tired.
3. The pharmacist _____ your doctor's office.
4. This cough syrup _____ your cough.
5. Two aspirin _____ enough.
6. The generic** drug _____ less.
7. This information _____ all the side effects*** for this medicine.

---

*set up = schedule

**generic = medicine with no brand name

***side effects = reactions, often negative, that a patient can have from a medicine

EXERCISE 17 ▶ Warm-up. (Chart 3-5)

In which conversation does Speaker B have a prior plan (a plan made before the moment of speaking)?

1. A: Oh, are you leaving?
   B: Yes. I'm going to pick up my kids at school. They have dentist appointments.

2. A: Excuse me, Mrs. Jones. The nurse from your son's school is on the phone. She said he has a fever and needs to go home.
   B: OK. Please tell her I'll be there in 20 minutes.

3-5 Be Going To vs. Will

(a)	She *is going to succeed* because she works hard.	*Be going to* and *will* mean the same when they are used to make predictions about the future.
(b)	She *will succeed* because she works hard.	Examples (a) and (b) have the same meaning.
(c)	I bought some wood because I *am going to build* a bookcase for my apartment.	*Be going to* (but not *will*) is used to express a prior plan (i.e., a plan made before the moment of speaking). In (c): The speaker plans to build a bookcase.
(d)	This chair is too heavy for you to carry alone. I*'ll help* you.	*Will* (but not *be going to*) is used to express a decision the speaker makes at the moment of speaking. In (d): The speaker decides or volunteers to help at the immediate present moment; he did not have a prior plan or intention to help.

EXERCISE 18 ▶ Looking at grammar. (Chart 3-5)

Look at the verbs in green. Is the speaker expressing plans made before the moment of speaking (prior plans)? If so, circle *yes*. If not, circle *no*.

PRIOR PLAN?

1. A: Did you return Carmen's phone call?
   B: No, I forgot. Thanks for reminding me. I*'ll call* her right away.   yes   no

2. A: I*'m going to call* Martha later this evening. Do you want to talk to her too?   yes   no
   B: No, I don't think so.

3. A: Jakob is in town for a few days.
   B: Really? Great! I*'ll give* him a call. Is he staying at his Aunt Lara's?   yes   no

4. A: Alex is in town for a few days.
   B: I know. He called me yesterday. We*'re going to get* together for dinner after I get off work tonight.   yes   no

5. A: I need some fresh air. I'm going for a short walk.
   B: I*'ll come* with you.   yes   no

			PRIOR PLAN?	

6. A: **I'm going to take** Hamid to the airport tomorrow morning.
   Do you want to come along?   yes   no
   B: Sure.

7. A: We're **going to go** to Uncle Scott's over the break.   yes   no
   Are you interested in coming with us?
   B: I'm not sure. **I'll think** about it. When do you need to know?   yes   no

EXERCISE 19 ▶ Looking at grammar. (Chart 3-5)
Restate the sentences. Use **be going to** because they are prior plans.

My Trip to Thailand
1. I'm planning to be away for three weeks.
   → *I'm going to be away for three weeks.*
2. My husband and I are planning to stay in small towns and camp on the beach.
3. We're planning to bring a tent.
4. We're planning to celebrate our wedding anniversary there.
5. My father, who was born in Thailand, is planning to join us, but he's planning to stay in a hotel.
6. He's planning to show us his favorite sights.

EXERCISE 20 ▶ Looking at grammar. (Chart 3-5)
Complete the sentences with **be going to** or **will**. Use **be going to** to express a prior plan.

1. A: Are you going by the post office today? I need to mail this letter.
   B: Yeah, I <u>'ll</u> mail it for you.
   A: Thanks.

2. A: Why are you carrying that package?
   B: It's for my sister. I <u>'m going to</u> mail it to her.

3. A: Why did you buy so many eggs?
   B: I _____ make a special dessert.

4. A: I have a book for Joe from Rachel. I'm not going to see him today.
   B: Let me have it. I _____ give it to him. He's in my algebra class.

5. A: Did you apply for the job you told me about?
   B: No, I _____ take a few more classes and get more experience.

6. A: Did you know that I found an apartment on 45th Street? I _____ move soon.
   B: That's a nice area. I _____ help you move if you like.
   A: Great! I'd really appreciate that.

7. A: Why can't you come to the party?

    B: We _____ be with my husband's family that weekend.

8. A: I have to leave. I don't have time to finish the dishes.

    B: No problem. I _____ do them for you.

9. A: Do you want to go to the meeting together?

    B: Sure. I _____ meet you by the elevator in ten minutes.

EXERCISE 21 ▸ Grammar, speaking, and writing. (Chart 3-5)

Part I. <u>Underline</u> the future verbs. Then in groups, discuss the questions on page 76.

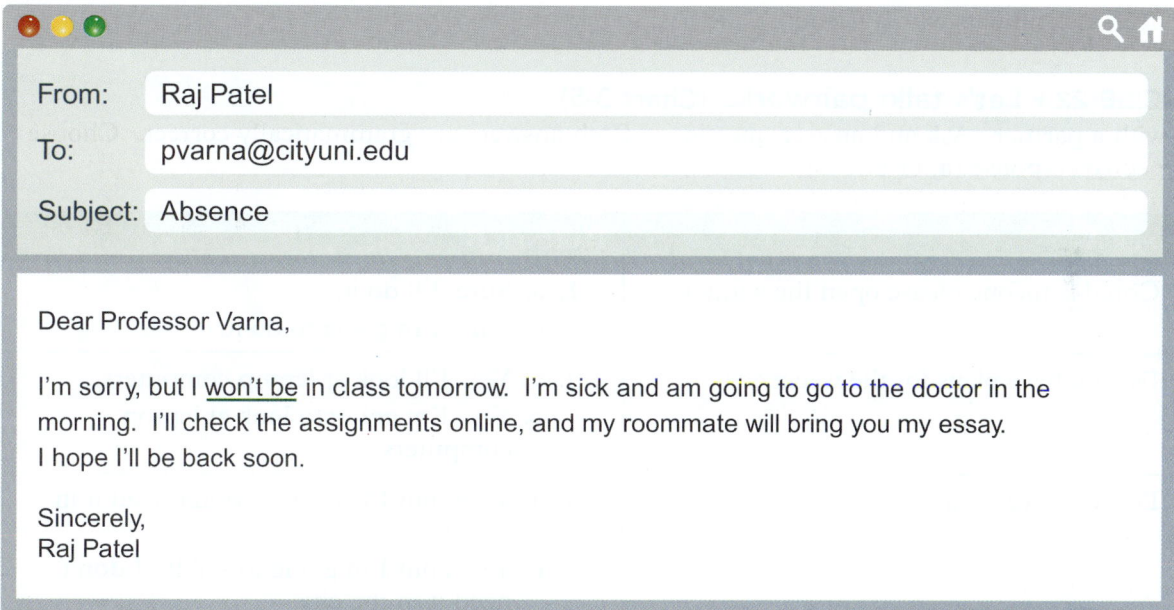

From: Raj Patel
To: pvarna@cityuni.edu
Subject: Absence

Dear Professor Varna,

I'm sorry, but I <u>won't be</u> in class tomorrow. I'm sick and am going to go to the doctor in the morning. I'll check the assignments online, and my roommate will bring you my essay.
I hope I'll be back soon.

Sincerely,
Raj Patel

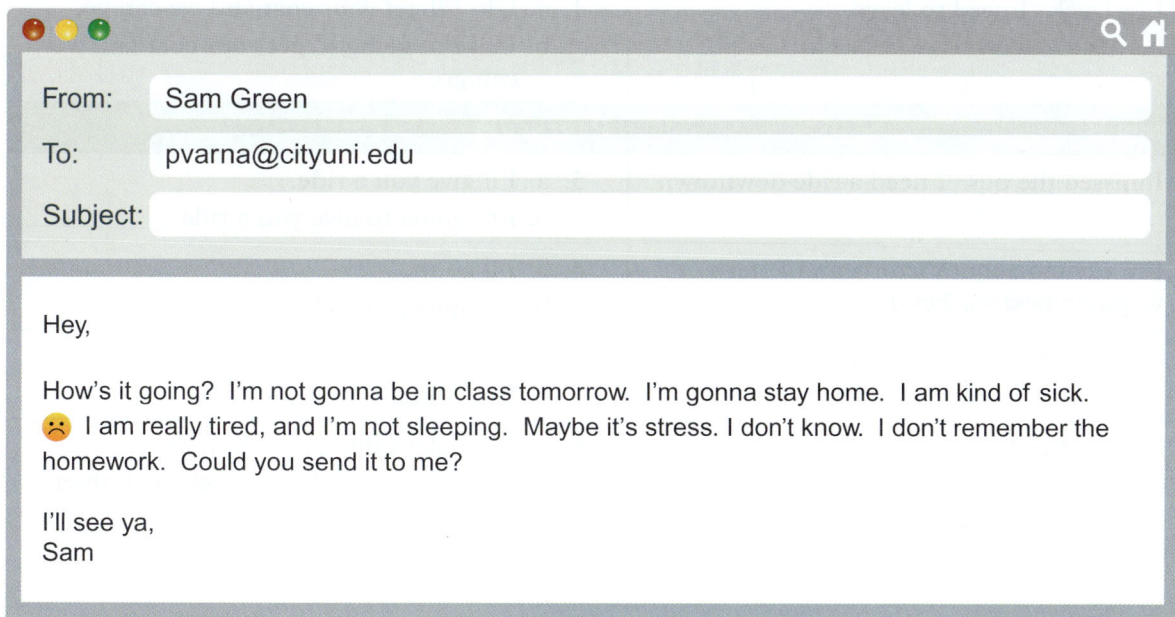

From: Sam Green
To: pvarna@cityuni.edu
Subject:

Hey,

How's it going? I'm not gonna be in class tomorrow. I'm gonna stay home. I am kind of sick. ☹ I am really tired, and I'm not sleeping. Maybe it's stress. I don't know. I don't remember the homework. Could you send it to me?

I'll see ya,
Sam

1. What differences do you notice between the two emails?
2. Which email do you think is better to send to a teacher?
3. Are there things in the second email that a teacher might not like?
4. What do you think are some features of an appropriate email? What are not? Make a list.
5. *Dear Professor* … is a form of address. Not all teachers are professors. What other forms of address are possible for writing to a teacher?
6. How much information do you think a teacher needs to have about an illness?

Part II. Write a formal email to your English teacher about missing class next week. Include these details.

- miss class on Monday
- sick
- check assignments with a friend

EXERCISE 22 ▶ Let's talk: pairwork. (Chart 3-5)

Work with a partner. Ask and answer questions. Both answers are grammatically correct. Choose the <u>expected</u> response (a. or b.).

Partner A	Partner B
1. Could someone please open the window?	1. a. Sure, I'll do it. b. Sure, I'm going to do it.
2. Do you have plans for the weekend?	2. a. Yes. I'll look at laptop computers. b. Yes. I'm going to look at laptop computers.
3. Do you have a car?	3. a. Yeah, but I'll sell it. I don't need it in the city. b. Yeah, but I'm going to sell it. I don't need it in the city.
4. I feel sick. I need to leave.	4. a. Uh, I'll get your coat and we can go. b. Uh, I'm going to get your coat and we can go.

Partner B	Partner A
5. I missed the bus. I need a ride downtown.	5. a. I'll give you a ride. b. I'm going to give you a ride.
6. I'm excited about Victoria and Peter's wedding next weekend.	6. a. I'll go too. b. I'm going to go too.
7. Oh, no! My contact just fell out of my eye.	7. a. I'll look for it. b. I'm going to look for it.
8. Why did you buy so many apples?	8. a. I'll make a dessert with them. b. I'm going to make a dessert with them.

EXERCISE 23 ▶ Warm-up. (Chart 3-6)

How certain is the speaker in each sentence? Write the percentage next to each sentence: 100%, 90%, or 50%.

What is going to happen to gasoline prices?

1. _____ Gas prices may rise.
2. _____ Maybe gas prices will rise.
3. _____ Gas prices will rise.
4. _____ Gas prices will probably rise.
5. _____ Gas prices are going to rise.
6. _____ Gas prices won't rise.

3-6 Certainty About the Future

100% sure	(a) I **will be** in class tomorrow. OR I **am going to be** in class tomorrow.	In (a): The speaker uses **will** or **be going to** because he feels sure about his future activity. He is stating a fact about the future.

90% sure	(b) Po **will probably be** in class tomorrow.
	OR
	Po **is probably going to be** in class tomorrow.
	(c) Anna **probably won't be** in class tomorrow.
	OR
	Anna **probably isn't going to be** in class tomorrow.
		In (b): The speaker uses **probably** to say that he expects Po to be in class tomorrow, but he is not 100% sure. He's almost sure, but not completely sure.
		
		Word order with **probably**:*
		(1) in a statement, as in (b):
		    helping verb + **probably**
		(2) with a negative verb, as in (c):
		    probably + *helping verb*

50% sure	(d) Ali **may come** to class tomorrow. OR Ali **may not come** to class tomorrow. I don't know what he's going to do.	**May** expresses a future possibility: maybe something will happen, and maybe it won't happen.** In (d): The speaker is saying that maybe Ali will come to class, or maybe he won't come to class. The speaker is guessing.
	(e) **Maybe** Ali **will come** to class, and **maybe** he **won't**. OR **Maybe** Ali **is going to come** to class, and **maybe** he **isn't**.	**Maybe** + **will/be going to** gives the same meaning as **may**. Examples (d) and (e) have the same meaning. **Maybe** comes at the beginning of a sentence.

*__Probably__ is a midsentence adverb. See Chart 1-5, p. 14, for more information about the placement of midsentence adverbs.
See Chart 7-3, p. 198, for more information about **may.

EXERCISE 24 ▶ Grammar and speaking. (Chart 3-6)
For each situation, predict what probably will happen and what probably won't happen. Use either **will** or **be going to**. Include **probably** in your prediction.

1. Antonio is late to class almost every day. (be on time tomorrow? be late again?)
   → *Antonio probably won't be on time tomorrow. He'll probably be late again.* OR
     Antonio probably isn't going to be on time tomorrow. He's probably going to be late again.
2. Rosa has a terrible cold. She feels miserable.
   (go to work tomorrow? stay home and rest?)
3. Sami didn't sleep at all last night. He stayed up with his friends.
   (go to bed early tonight? stay up all night again tonight?)
4. Gina loves to run, but right now she has sore knees and a sore ankle.
   (run in the marathon race this week? skip the race?)

EXERCISE 25 ▶ Listening. (Chart 3-6)
Listen to the sentences. Decide the certainty for each one: 100%, 90%, or 50%.

My Day Tomorrow

Example: You will hear: The weather will be cold tomorrow.
   You will write: __100%__

1. _____   3. _____   5. _____
2. _____   4. _____   6. _____

EXERCISE 26 ▶ Looking at grammar. (Chart 3-6)
Rewrite the sentences using the words in parentheses.

1. I may be late. (*maybe*) __Maybe I will be late.__
2. Lisa may not get here. (*maybe*) _____
3. Maybe you will win the contest. (*may*) _____
4. The plane may land early. (*maybe*) _____
5. Maybe Sergio won't pass the class. (*may*) _____

EXERCISE 27 ▶ Let's talk: interview. (Chart 3-6)
Walk around the room. Take turns asking and answering the questions. Ask two students each question. Answer with **will**, **be going to**, or **may**. Use **probably** or **maybe** as appropriate.

Example: What will you do after class tomorrow?
   → *I'll probably go back to my apartment.* OR *I'm not sure. I may go to the bookstore.*

1. Where will you be tomorrow afternoon?
2. Where will you be next year?
3. What are you going to do on your next vacation?
4. Who will be the most famous celebrity next year?
5. What will a phone look like ten years from now?
6. What do you think will be the next big discovery in medicine?

EXERCISE 28 ▸ Reading, grammar, and speaking. (Charts 3-1 → 3-6)

Part I. Read the blog entry by co-author Stacy Hagen. Then answer the questions that follow.

> Do you know these words?
> - discount
> - insurance company
> - brand
> - advertising
> - encourage

BlackBookBlog

Money-Saving Tips for Students

If you are a student and do not live at home, the cost of living may surprise you. Life can be very expensive! Fortunately there are many ways to save money. If you search the phrase "students save money" on the internet, for example, you will find lots of useful tips. I'd like to share a few of my favorites with you.

1. **Ask about student discounts.**
   Many businesses offer discounts to students. It is always a good idea to ask, "Do you have a student discount?" At the beginning of the school year, you will frequently find discounts from stores that sell clothes, computers, and housewares. In general, movie theaters offer a student discount year-round. Buses and trains usually give students a lower price. If you get good grades, some insurance companies will even give you a discount on your car insurance. Be sure you carry your student ID with you when you shop.

2. **Buy generic.**
   When you walk down a grocery store aisle, you will see a lot of different brands. Which one are you going to buy? How will you decide? One solution is to buy a generic brand. For example, let's say you like soft drinks. You can buy one that says *cola*. It doesn't have a special name. This is the generic product. Generics don't have advertising, so they will usually be cheaper.

3. **Don't shop when you are hungry!**
   This is a very simple tip. Research shows that if you shop when you are hungry, you will spend more money. Food looks much better on an empty stomach. It also helps to have a shopping list with you. If you get hungry when you are shopping, tell yourself that you will only buy the food on your list.

4. **Take care of your needs, not your wants.**
   It is important to separate needs from wants. Many things seem like needs, but they are actually just things you would like to have. Do you need to buy a cup of coffee from a coffee shop? You will save more money if you make it at home. Do you need to go to a sports event, or can you watch it on TV? Wants are nice, but they are also expensive.

   If you find these tips useful, I encourage you to look for more on the internet. You will probably find many more ways to save money. Good luck!

Part II. Discuss these questions in small groups.

1. What kind of student discounts are you already getting? What kind of discounts will you look for the next time you shop?
2. If you are at the store and see a cheaper brand that you don't know anything about and a more expensive brand that you already like, what are you going to buy and why?
3. Make a list of some of your wants and needs.
4. Do you have any shopping habits that you will change? List some things that you will and won't do to save money when you shop.
5. What do you, as a group, feel are the best ways to save money? Present a few of your suggestions to the class.

EXERCISE 29 ▶ Warm-up. (Chart 3-7)
Complete the sentences with your own words. What do you notice about the verb tenses and the words in green?

1. **After** I **leave** school today, **I'm going to** _____ .
2. **Before** I **come** to school tomorrow, I **will** _____ .
3. **If** I **have** time this weekend, I **will** _____ .

3-7 Expressing the Future in Time Clauses and *If*-Clauses

(a) *TIME CLAUSE* **Before I go** to class tomorrow, I'm going to eat breakfast. (b) I'm going to eat breakfast *TIME CLAUSE* **before I go** to class tomorrow.	In (a) and (b): *before I go to class tomorrow* is a future time clause. **before** **after** **when** + subject and verb = a time clause **as soon as** **until** **while**
(c) **Before I go** home tonight, I'm going to stop at the market. (d) I'm going to eat dinner at 6:00 tonight. **After I eat dinner**, I'm going to study in my room. (e) I'll give Rita your message **when I see** her. (f) It's raining right now. **As soon as the rain stops**, I'm going to walk downtown. (g) I'll stay home **until the rain stops**. (h) **While you're** at school tomorrow, I'll be at work.	The simple present is used in a future time clause. **Will** and **be going to** are NOT used in a future time clause. INCORRECT: *Before I will go to class, I'm going to eat breakfast.* INCORRECT: *Before I am going to go to class tomorrow, I'm going to eat breakfast.* All of the example sentences (c) through (h) contain future time clauses.
(i) Maybe it will rain tomorrow. **If it rains** tomorrow, I'm going to stay home.	In (i): *If it rains tomorrow* is an *if*-clause. *if* + subject and verb = an *if*-clause When the meaning is future, the simple present (not **will** or **be going to**) is used in an *if*-clause.

EXERCISE 30 ▶ Looking at grammar. (Chart 3-7)
Choose the correct verbs.

1. Before   I'm going to return / (I return)   to my country next year, I'm going to finish my graduate degree in computer science.
2. My boss will review my work after she   will return / returns   from vacation next week.
3. I'll text you as soon as my plane   will land / lands.
4. I don't especially like my current job, but I'm going to stay with this company until I   find / will find   something better.
5. I need to find someone to water my vegetable garden when I   am / will be   away next week.
6. If it   won't be / isn't   cold tomorrow, we'll go to the beach. If it   is / will be   cold tomorrow, we'll go to a movie.
7. When you   will be / are   in Australia next month, are you going to explore the Great Barrier Reef?

EXERCISE 31 ▶ Looking at grammar. (Chart 3-7)
Use the given verbs to complete the sentences. Use **be going to** for the future.

To-Do List

1. *take / reread*   I _'m going to reread_ the textbook **before** I _take_ the final exam next month.
2. *clean / finish*   Tim _____ his desk **as soon as** he _____ class.
3. *make / go*   **Before** I _____ to my job interview next week, I _____ _____ a list of questions I want to ask about the company.
4. *visit / fix*   Tom _____ the leak in his mom's roof **when** he _____ her next week.
5. *look for / find*   I _____ cell phones online **until** I _____ a good deal.*
6. *wash / stop*   **If** the rain _____, Dan _____ his car.
7. *work / get*   **If** Eva _____ home early, we _____ in our vegetable garden.

---

*Time clauses beginning with **until** usually follow the main clause.
    Usual: I'm going to look for cell phones online **until** *I find a good deal.*
    Possible but less usual: **Until** *I find a good deal,* I'm going to look for cell phones online.

EXERCISE 32 ▶ Let's talk: pairwork. (Chart 3-7)

Work with a partner. Take turns saying a sentence. Your partner will add a sentence using *if*. Pay special attention to the verb in the *if*-clause. Share some of your partner's answers.

Example: Maybe you'll go downtown tomorrow.
PARTNER A: Maybe you'll go downtown tomorrow.
PARTNER B: If I **go** downtown tomorrow, I'm going to look at laptop computers.

PARTNER A	PARTNER B
1. Maybe you'll have some free time tomorrow. 2. Maybe it'll rain tomorrow. 3. Maybe it won't rain tomorrow. 4. Maybe the teacher will be absent next week. 5. Maybe you'll win a new car tomorrow.	1. Maybe you'll be tired tonight. 2. Maybe you won't be tired tonight. 3. Maybe it'll be nice tomorrow. 4. Maybe we won't have class on Monday. 5. Maybe you'll win a lot of money next month. *Change roles.*

EXERCISE 33 ▶ Looking at grammar. (Chart 3-7)

Look at Sue's smartphone calendar. She has a busy morning. Make sentences using the words in parentheses and the given information. Use **be going to** for the future.

A Busy Day

1. (*after*)   go to the dentist \ pick up groceries
   → *After Sue goes to the dentist, she is going to pick up groceries.*
2. (*before*)   go to the dentist \ pick up groceries
3. (*before*)   have lunch with Hiro \ pick up groceries
4. (*after*)   have lunch with Hiro \ pick up groceries
5. (*before*)   have lunch with Hiro \ take her father to his doctor's appointment

Thu., Apr. 11
9:00 | dentist
10:00 | groceries
11:00 | lunch with Hiro
12:00 | Dr.'s appt. – Dad

EXERCISE 34 ▶ Looking at grammar. (Chapters 1, 2 and Chart 3-7)

Complete each sentence with a form of the words in parentheses. Pay attention to the time words. Use a form of **be going to** for the future.

1. Before Aiden (*go*) _____goes_____ to bed, he always (*brush*) _____brushes_____ his teeth.

2. Before Aiden (*go*) _____ to bed later tonight, he (*brush*) _____ his teeth.

3. Before Aiden (*go*) _____ to bed last night, he (*brush*) _____ his teeth.

4. While Aiden (*take*) _____ a shower last night, the smoke alarm (*go off*) _____.

5. As soon as the smoke alarm (*go off*) _____ last night, Aiden (*jump*) _____ out of the shower to turn it off.

6. As soon as Aiden (*get*) _____ up tomorrow morning, he (*fix*) _____ the smoke alarm.

7. Aiden always (*fix*) _____ things as soon as they (*break*) _____.

EXERCISE 35 ▶ Warm-up. (Chart 3-8)
Which sentences express future time?

1. I'm catching a train tonight.
2. I'm going to take the express train.
3. The trip will only take an hour.
4. My parents are picking me up.

3-8 Using the Present Progressive to Express Future Time

(a) Tim *is going to come*	to the party tomorrow.	The present progressive can be used to express future time. Each pair of example sentences has the same meaning.
(b) Tim *is coming*	to the party tomorrow.	
(c) We*'re going to go*	to a movie tonight.	The present progressive describes *definite plans for the future, plans that were made before the moment of speaking.*
(d) We*'re going*	to a movie tonight.	
(e) I*'m going to stay*	home this evening.	
(f) I*'m staying*	home this evening.	A future meaning for the present progressive is indicated either by future time words (e.g., *tomorrow*) or by the situation.*
(g) Ann *is going to fly*	to Miami next week.	
(h) Ann *is flying*	to Miami next week.	
(i) You*'re going to laugh* when you hear this joke.		The present progressive is NOT used for predictions about the future.
(j) INCORRECT: You're laughing when you hear this joke.		In (i): The speaker is predicting a future event.
		In (j): The present progressive is not possible; laughing is a prediction, not a planned future event.

*COMPARE: Present situation: *Look! Mary's coming. Do you see her?*
Future situation: *Are you planning to come to the party? Mary's coming. So is Alex.*

EXERCISE 36 ▶ Looking at grammar. (Chart 3-8)
Complete the conversations with the correct form of the present progressive. Discuss whether the present progressive expresses present or future time.

1. A: What (*you, do*) __*are you doing*__ tomorrow afternoon?

   B: I (*go*) __*am going*__ to the mall. How about you? What (*you, do*) _____ tomorrow afternoon?

   A: I (*go*) _____ to a movie with Dan. After the movie, we (*go*) _____ out to dinner. Would you like to meet us for dinner?

   B: No, thanks. I can't. I (*meet*) _____ my son for dinner.

2. A: What (*you, major*) _____ in?

   B: I (*major*) _____ in engineering.

   A: What courses (*you, take*) _____ next semester?

   B: I (*take*) _____ English, math, and physics.

3. A: Stop! Paula! What (*you, do*) _____ ?

   B: I (*cut*) _____ my hair, Mom.

EXERCISE 37 ▸ Listening. (Chart 3-8)
Listen to the conversation and write the words you hear.

Going on Vacation

A: I ___(1)___ on vacation tomorrow.

B: Where ___(2)___ you ___(3)___ ?

A: To San Francisco.

B: How are you getting there? ___(4)___ you ___(5)___ or ___(6)___ your car?

A: I ___(7)___ . I want to be at the airport by 7:00 tomorrow morning.

B: Do you need a ride to the airport?

A: No, thanks. I ___(8)___ a taxi. What about you? Are you planning to go somewhere over vacation?

B: No. I ___(9)___ here.

EXERCISE 38 ▸ Let's talk: pairwork. (Chart 3-8)
Work with a partner. Tell each other your plans. Use the present progressive.

Example:
PARTNER A: What are your plans for this evening?
PARTNER B: I'm staying home. How about you?
PARTNER A: I'm going to a coffee shop to work on my paper for a while. Then I'm meeting some friends for a movie.

What are your plans for …

1. the rest of today?
2. tomorrow?
3. this coming weekend?
4. next month?

EXERCISE 39 ▸ Warm-up. (Chart 3-9)
Choose <u>all</u> the possible completions.

1. Soccer season begins ____.
   a. today   b. next week   c. yesterday

2. The mall opens ____.
   a. next Monday   b. tomorrow   c. today

84   CHAPTER 3

3. There is a party _____ .
   a. last week
   b. tonight
   c. next weekend

4. The baby cries _____ .
   a. every night
   b. tomorrow night
   c. in the evenings

3-9 Using the Simple Present to Express Future Time

(a) My plane **arrives** at 7:35 *tomorrow evening*. (b) Tim's new job **starts** *next week*. (c) The semester **ends** *in two more weeks*. (d) There **is** a meeting at ten *tomorrow morning*.	The simple present can express future time when events are on a definite schedule or timetable. Only a few verbs are used in the simple present to express future time. The most common are **arrive, leave, start, begin, end, finish, open, close, be**.
(e) INCORRECT: *I wear my new suit to the wedding next week.* CORRECT: *I am wearing/am going to wear my new suit to the wedding next week.*	Most verbs CANNOT be used in the simple present to express future time. For example, in (e): The verb **wear** does not express an event on a schedule or timetable. It cannot be used in the simple present to express future time.

EXERCISE 40 ▶ Looking at grammar. (Charts 3-8 and 3-9)
Choose <u>all</u> the possible completions.

1. The concert _____ at eight tonight.
   a. begins
   b. is beginning
   c. is going to begin

2. I _____ seafood pasta for dinner tonight.
   a. make
   b. am making
   c. am going to make

3. I _____ to school tomorrow morning. I need the exercise.
   a. walk
   b. am walking
   c. am going to walk

4. The bus _____ at 8:15 tomorrow morning.
   a. leaves
   b. is leaving
   c. is going to leave

5. I _____ the championship game on TV at Jonah's house tomorrow.
   a. watch
   b. am watching
   c. am going to watch

6. The game _____ at 1:00 tomorrow afternoon.
   a. starts
   b. is starting
   c. is going to start

7. Alexa's plane _____ at 10:10 tomorrow morning.
   a. arrives
   b. is arriving
   c. is going to arrive

8. I can't pick her up tomorrow, so she _____ the airport bus into the city.
   a. takes
   b. is taking
   c. is going to take

9. Jonas _____ to several companies. He hopes to get a full-time job soon.
   a. applies
   b. is applying
   c. is going to apply

10. School _____ next Wednesday. I'm excited for vacation to begin.
    a. ends
    b. is ending
    c. is going to end

EXERCISE 41 ▶ Warm-up. (Chart 3-10)
Choose the scene that this sentence best describes: *He **is about to** fight a fire.*

Picture A

Picture B

3-10	Immediate Future: Using *Be About To*
(a) Ann is holding a suitcase, and she is wearing her coat. She ***is about to leave*** for the airport. (b) Shhh. The movie ***is about to begin***.	The idiom **be about to do something** expresses an activity that will happen *in the immediate future*, usually within minutes or seconds. In (a): Ann is going to leave sometime in the next few minutes. In (b): The movie is going to start in the next few minutes.

EXERCISE 42 ▶ Let's talk. (Chart 3-10)
Make sentences with **be about to**. Work in pairs, in small groups, or as a class.

EXERCISE 43 ▸ Warm-up. (Chart 3-11)
Choose all the possible completions for each sentence.

1. Fifteen years from now, my wife and I will retire and _____ all over the world.
   a. will travel
   b. travel
   c. traveling
   d. going to travel
   e. are traveling
   f. traveled

2. I opened the door and _____ my friend to come in.
   a. will invite
   b. invite
   c. inviting
   d. am going to invite
   e. am inviting
   f. invited

3-11 Parallel Verbs

(a) Jim **makes** his bed **and cleans** up his room every morning. (b) Anita **called** and **told** me about her new job.	Often a subject has two verbs that are connected by **and**. We say that the two verbs are parallel: V + **and** + V *makes and cleans* = parallel verbs
(c) Ann **is cooking** dinner and (is) **talking** on the phone at the same time. (d) I **will stay** home and (will) **study** tonight. (e) I **am going to stay** home and (am going to) **study** tonight. NOT PARALLEL: *I am going to stay home and will study tonight.*	It is not necessary to repeat a helping verb (an auxiliary verb) when two verbs are the same tense and form and are connected by **and**.

EXERCISE 44 ▸ Looking at grammar. (Chart 3-11)
Complete each sentence with the correct form of the verbs in parentheses. More than one answer may be possible.

Work Woes

1. When I (*get*) _____ to work yesterday, a new employee (*stream*) _____ a movie and (*text*) _____ on her phone. That is not a good way to start!

2. My favorite manager is going to leave soon. She (*move*) _____ to San Francisco and (*work*) _____ for a start-up company as soon as her son (*graduate*) _____ from high school.

3. My mom (*call*) _____ me every Monday morning at work and (*complain*) _____ about her neighbors and their noisy weekend parties.

4. Is the meeting (*start*) _____ or (*end*) _____ ? It's hard to tell. Our meetings never (*start*) _____ or (*end*) _____ on time, and there is a lot of wasted time.

Future Time 87

5. While Stephen (*sit*) _____ outside and (*drink*) _____ a cup of coffee during his lunch break yesterday, a bee (*land*) _____ on his wrist and (*sting*) _____ him. Paul (*drop*) _____ the cup and (*spill*) _____ coffee all over his pants.

6. I worked an 80-hour week! I'm beat.* After I (*get*) _____ home, I (*take*) _____ a hot bath and (*go*) _____ to bed.

EXERCISE 45 ▶ Looking at grammar. (Chapters 1 → 3 Review)
Complete each sentence with the correct form of the words in parentheses.

1. I usually (*ride*) __ride__ my bike to work in the morning, but it (*rain*) _____ when I left my house early this morning, so I (*take*) _____ the bus. After I (*get*) _____ to work, I (*find*) _____ out** that my briefcase was still on the bus.

2. A: Are you going to take the kids to the amusement park tomorrow morning?
   B: Yes. It (*open*) _____ at 10:00. If we (*leave*) _____ here at 9:30, we'll get there at 9:55. The kids can be the first ones in the park.

3. A: Ouch! I (*cut*) _____ my finger. It (*bleed*) _____!
   B: Put pressure on it. I (*get*) _____ some antibiotics and a bandage.
   A: Thanks.

4. A: Your phone (*ring*) _____.
   B: I (*know*) _____.
   A: (*you, want*) _____ me to get it?
   B: No.
   A: Why don't you want to answer your phone?
   B: I (*answer, never*) _____ during dinner.

5. A: Look! There (*be*) _____ a police car behind us. Its lights (*flash*) _____.
   B: I (*know*) _____. I (*know*) _____. I (*see*) _____ it.
   A: What (*go*) _____ on? (*you, speed*) _____?
   B: No, I'm not. I (*drive*) _____ the speed limit.
   A: Oh, look. The police car (*pass*) _____ us.
   B: Whew!

*be beat = be very, very tired; be exhausted

**find out = discover; learn

EXERCISE 46 ▶ Listening and speaking. (Chapters 1 → 3 Review)

Part I. Complete the sentences with the words you hear.

At a Chinese Restaurant

A: OK, let's all open our fortune cookies.

B: What _____ your cookie _____?

A: Mine says, "You _____ an unexpected gift."
Great! Are you planning to give me a gift soon?

B: Not that I know of. Mine says, "Your life _____ long and happy." Good.
I _____ a long life.

C: Mine says, "A smile _____ all communication problems." Well, that's good! After this, when I _____ someone, _____ just _____ at them.

D: My fortune is this: "If you _____ hard, you _____ successful."

A: Well, it _____ like all of us _____ good luck in the future!

Part II. Work in small groups. Together, write a fortune for each person in your group. Share a few of the fortunes with the class.

EXERCISE 47 ▶ Check your knowledge. (Chapters 1 → 3 Review)
Correct the verb errors.

My Cousin Pablo

1. I want to tell you about Pablo. He *is* my cousin.

2. He comes here four years ago.

3. Before he came here, he study biology in Chile.

4. He leaves Chile and move here.

5. Then he went to New York and stay there for three years.

6. He graduates from New York University.

7. Now he study for his medical degree.

8. After he finish his medical degree, he return to Chile.

EXERCISE 48 ▶ Reading, grammar, and writing. (Chapter 3)

Part I. Read the social media post. <u>Underline</u> the verbs that express the future.

TRAVEL

A Weekend in Nashville   November 3

My friend Sara and I <u>are taking</u> a trip to Nashville, Tennessee, soon. Nashville is the home of country music, and Sara loves country music. She wants to go to several shows. Nashville has more than 160 places to hear live music. Many country music singers become famous in Nashville. I don't know anything about country music, but I'm looking forward to going. We're leaving Friday evening as soon as Sara gets off work. We will be away for a week. We're going to take the train. It's a 14-hour trip, so we will sleep for part of the time. Sara has a cousin in Nashville. We are going to try to visit her, but it's possible she will be out of town. We are getting back on Sunday night because we both need to work on Monday. Sara and I are excited about our first trip to Nashville.

Part II. Imagine that you have a week's vacation. You can go anywhere you want. Think of a place you would like to visit, and write a paragraph to describe your plans. Use these questions as a guide. Remember to add variety by using different future verb forms and to use parallel verbs when appropriate.

1. Where and how are you going?
2. When are you leaving?
3. Who are you going with, or are you traveling alone?
4. Where are you staying?
5. Are you visiting anyone? Who?
6. How long are you staying there?
7. When are you getting back?

WRITING TIP

To express future time in writing, *will* is more common than other future forms. However, in informal writing, you can talk about the future in different ways to add interest. Look at how repetitive and dull the sentences from the reading become when only the verb *will* is used:

> We will leave Friday evening as soon as Sara gets off work. We will be away for two weeks. We will take the train. It's a 14-hour trip, so we will sleep part of the time.

As you now know, you can use not only *will* but also *be going to* and even the simple present or present progressive to express future time. These verbs will add more variety to your writing.

Part III. Edit your writing. Check for the following:

1. ☐ correct forms of **will** and **be going to**
2. ☐ use of some variety in the verb forms to express the future
3. ☐ use of simple present with time and **if**-clauses, where appropriate
4. ☐ correct use of parallel verbs
5. ☐ correct spelling (use a dictionary or spell-check)

▪▪▪▪▪ For digital resources, go to MyEnglishLab on the Pearson English Portal. You can also go to the Pearson Practice English app for mobile practice.

CHAPTER 4
Present Perfect and Past Perfect

PRETEST: What do I already know?
Write "C" if the **boldfaced** words are correct and "I" if they are incorrect.

1. _____ **Have** you ever **eaten** something really unusual? (Charts 4-1 and 4-2)
2. _____ I **have** just **finish** my homework. (Chart 4-3)
3. _____ My mom **has** recently **become** the bank manager. (Chart 4-3)
4. _____ Eva and Julia have started kindergarten **yet**. (Chart 4-3)
5. _____ Food prices **have increased** several times. (Chart 4-3)
6. _____ William **has worked** as an auto mechanic since he **finished** college. (Chart 4-4)
7. _____ My grandfather **has died** in 1990. (Chart 4-5)
8. _____ Max **has been playing** video games for several hours. (Chart 4-6)
9. _____ Katrina **has been texting** since she woke up. (Chart 4-6)
10. _____ We **have been staying** at that hotel three times. (Chart 4-7)
11. _____ By the time the movie **finished**, half of the audience **had gone** home. (Chart 4-8)

EXERCISE 1 ▸ Warm-up. (Chart 4-1)
Do you know the past participle form of these verbs? Complete the chart. What is the difference between the past participle forms in items 1–4 and 5–8?

SIMPLE FORM	SIMPLE PAST	PAST PARTICIPLE
1. help	helped	_helped_
2. work	worked	_worked_
3. stay	stayed	_____
4. visit	visited	_____
5. eat	ate	_eaten_
6. have	had	_had_
7. write	wrote	_____
8. begin	began	_____

Present Perfect and Past Perfect 91

4-1 Past Participle

This chapter introduces the present perfect and past perfect tenses. In order to form these verbs, you need to know *the past participle forms*. The past participle is one of the principal parts of a verb. (See Appendix A-1.)

	SIMPLE FORM	SIMPLE PAST	PAST PARTICIPLE	
REGULAR VERBS	finish look stop try use wait	finished looked stopped tried used waited	**finished** **looked** **stopped** **tried** **used** **waited**	The past participle of regular verbs is the same as the simple past form: both end in *-ed*.
IRREGULAR VERBS	be come do find go get have know make say see take tell	was/were came did found went got had knew made said saw took told	**been** **come** **done** **found** **gone** **got/gotten** **had** **known** **made** **said** **seen** **taken** **told**	Many common verbs have irregular past forms. The verbs in the list are the most common irregular verbs. See Appendix A-2 or the inside back cover for a more complete list of irregular verbs.

EXERCISE 2 ▶ Looking at grammar. (Chart 4-1)

Part I. Write the simple past and the past participle of the <u>regular</u> (*-ed*) verbs in the box.

be	die	know	read	teach
✓call	do	leave	speak	think
come	finish	move	study	walk

	SIMPLE FORM	SIMPLE PAST	PAST PARTICIPLE
1.	*call*	*called*	*called*
2.	_____	_____	_____
3.	_____	_____	_____
4.	_____	_____	_____
5.	_____	_____	_____
6.	_____	_____	_____

Part II. Write the simple past and the past participle of the <u>irregular</u> verbs in the box.

	SIMPLE FORM	SIMPLE PAST	PAST PARTICIPLE
7.	be	was, were	been
8.	_____	_____	_____
9.	_____	_____	_____
10.	_____	_____	_____
11.	_____	_____	_____
12.	_____	_____	_____
13.	_____	_____	_____
14.	_____	_____	_____
15.	_____	_____	_____

EXERCISE 3 ▸ Pairwork. (Chart 4-1)
Work with a partner. Give the past tense and past participle forms of the verb that your partner says.

PARTNER A: (book open) **PARTNER B:** (book closed)	**PARTNER B:** (book open) **PARTNER A:** (book closed)
1. give (*gave, given*)	8. say (*said, said*)
2. text (*texted, texted*)	9. begin (*began, begun*)
3. leave (*left, left*)	10. pay (*paid, paid*)
4. drive (*drove, driven*)	11. delete (*deleted, deleted*)
5. rent (*rented, rented*)	12. begin (*began, begun*)
6. forget (*forgot, forgotten*)	13. marry (*married, married*)
7. take (*took, taken*)	14. tell (*told, told*)

EXERCISE 4 ▸ Warm-up: pairwork. (Chart 4-2)
Work with a partner. Take turns asking and answering questions. Use the words in the box.

bought a boat	flown a drone	grown your own vegetables
climbed a tree	forgotten your age	ridden on a motorcycle

PARTNER A: Have you ever _____?
PARTNER B: Yes, I have. OR No, I've never _____.

Present Perfect and Past Perfect

4-2 Introduction to the Present Perfect: Unspecified Time with *Ever* and *Never*

(a) — *Have* you *ever lost* your ID*? — No, I *have never lost* my ID. (b) — *Has* it *ever snowed* in your hometown? — No, it *has never snowed* in my hometown.	The PRESENT PERFECT is frequently used to express some *unspecified or unknown time in the past*. *Ever* and *never* are examples of time words that do not give a specific time. *ever* = in your lifetime; from the time you were born to the present moment. In the (a) and (b) responses, the speaker uses *never* to say, "No, I haven't lost my ID from the time I was born to the present moment," and, "No, it hasn't snowed in my hometown from the time I was born to the present moment." QUESTION: *have/has* + subject + *ever* + past participle NEGATIVE: *have/has* + *never* + past participle
(c) Has Jon *ever* met your family? — No, *he has not met* my family. No, he's *not met* my family. No, he *has not*. No, he *hasn't*. — Yes, he *has met* my family. OR Yes, he *has*.	Note other ways to answer a question with *ever*. NEGATIVE: *have/has* + *not* + past participle NEGATIVE CONTRACTIONS: *have* + *not* = *haven't* *has* + *not* = *hasn't* AFFIRMATIVE STATEMENT: *have/has* + past participle CONTRACTED FORMS: *I've, You've, He's, She's, It's, We've, They've*

*ID = identification

EXERCISE 5 ▶ Looking at grammar. (Charts 4-1 and 4-2)
Complete the conversations. Use the present perfect form of the verbs in parentheses.

Unusual Experiences

1. A: (*you, see, ever*) __Have you ever seen__ a ghost?
    B: No, I __haven't__. I (*see, never*) __have never seen__ a ghost.

2. A: (*you, eat, ever*) _____ an insect?
    B: No, I _____. I (*eat, never*) _____ an insect.

3. A: (*you, find, ever*) _____ a gold coin?
    B: No, I _____. I (*find, never*) _____ a gold coin.

4. A: (*you, talk, ever*) _____ to a movie star?
    B: No, I _____. I (*talk, never*) _____ to a movie star.

5. A: (*you, go, ever*) _____ for a ride in a spaceship?
    B: No, I _____. I (*go, never*) _____ for a ride in a spaceship.

EXERCISE 6 ▶ Grammar and speaking. (Charts 4-1 and 4-2)

Complete the sentences with the correct form of the verbs in parentheses. Then choose a true answer for you. Share your answers with a partner. Use these forms: *I have* or *I have never.*

1. Have you ever (*see*) _____ snow?   yes   no
2. Have you ever (*fly*) _____ in a small plane?   yes   no
3. Have you ever (*run*) _____ for an hour without stopping?   yes   no
4. Have you ever (*do*) _____ volunteer work?   yes   no
5. Have you ever (*tear*) _____ a muscle?   yes   no
6. Have you ever (*have*) _____ a bad experience on a plane?   yes   no
7. Have you ever (*fall*) _____ out of a tree?   yes   no
8. Have you ever (*feel*) _____ so embarrassed that your face got hot?   yes   no
9. Have you ever (*speak*) _____ to a famous person?   yes   no
10. Have you ever (*win*) _____ a contest?   yes   no

EXERCISE 7 ▶ Let's talk: interview. (Charts 4-1 and 4-2)

Interview your classmates. Make questions using the present perfect form of the verbs. Share some of your information with the class.

1. you \ ever \ cut \ your own hair _____
2. you \ ever \ catch \ a big fish _____
3. you \ ever \ take care of \ an animal _____
4. you \ ever \ lose \ something very important _____
5. you \ ever \ sit \ on a bee _____
6. you \ ever \ break \ your arm or your leg _____
7. you \ ever \ throw \ a ball \ and \ hit \ a window _____
8. you \ ever \ swim \ in the Atlantic Ocean _____

EXERCISE 8 ▶ Warm-up. (Chart 4-3)

Choose the correct answer for each sentence.

1. Tyler has rented a small house _____.   a. last week   b. recently
2. I have seen it _____.   a. already   b. two days ago
3. His parents haven't seen it _____.   a. yesterday   b. yet
4. I have been there _____.   a. twice   b. yesterday

4-3 The Present Perfect with Unspecified Time: *Already, Yet, Just, Recently*

Erik has just eaten lunch.

Ty hasn't eaten lunch yet.

(before now / time? / now)	(a) Erik *has **just** eaten* lunch. (b) Jim *has **recently** changed* jobs.	The present perfect expresses an activity or situation that happened (or did not happen) *before now, at some unspecified or unknown time in the past.* As you learned in Chart 4-2, *ever* and *never* express an activity that occurred at an unknown time. Other common time words that express this idea are *just, recently, already,* and *yet*. In (a): Erik's lunch occurred before the present time. The exact time is not mentioned; it is unimportant or unknown.
(before now / now)	(c) Pete *has eaten* at that restaurant **many times**. (d) I *have eaten* there **twice**.	An activity may be repeated two, several, or more times *before now, at unspecified times in the past,* as in (c) and (d). Use of the present perfect can indicate that the activity may happen again.
	(e) Pele *has **already** left*. OR Pele *has left **already***. (f) Ty *hasn't eaten **yet***. (g) *Have* you ***already** left*? *Have* you *left **already***? *Have* you *left **yet***?	In (e): **Already** is used in affirmative statements. It can come after the helping verb or at the end of the sentence. Idea of ***already:*** Something happened before now, before this time. In (f): **Yet** is used in negative statements and comes at the end of the sentence. Idea of ***yet:*** Something did not happen before now (up to this time), but it may happen in the future. In (g): Both **yet** and **already** can also be used in questions. NOTE: Sometimes the speaker doesn't use a time word. It is implied. *Ty hasn't eaten.* = *Ty hasn't eaten yet.*

EXERCISE 9 ▸ Looking at grammar. (Chart 4-3)
Complete each question with the correct form of the verb in parentheses.

New Parents

1. Has Richard (*hold*) _____held_____ the baby a lot yet?
2. Has Lori (*give*) _____ the baby a bath already?
3. Has Richard (*change*) _____ a diaper yet?
4. Has Lori (*take*) _____ some pictures of the baby already?
5. Has Richard (*get*) _____ up in the middle of the night yet?
6. Has Lori (*have*) _____ problems sleeping already?
7. Has Richard (*feel*) _____ tired during the day yet?
8. Has the baby (*sleep*) _____ through the night already?

EXERCISE 10 ▸ Looking at grammar. (Chart 4-3)
Choose <u>all</u> the possible answers for each question. Work in small groups and then discuss your answers as a class.

SITUATION 1: Sara is at home. At 12:00 P.M., the phone rang. It was Sara's friend from high school. They had a long conversation, and Sara hung up the phone at 12:59. It is now 1:00. Which sentences describe the situation?

a. Sara has just hung up the phone.
b. She has hung up the phone already.
c. The phone has just rung.
d. Sara hasn't finished her conversation yet.

SITUATION 2: Mr. Peters is in bed. He became sick with the flu eight days ago. Mr. Peters isn't sick very often. The last time he had the flu was one year ago. Which sentences describe the situation?

a. Mr. Peters has been sick for a year.
b. He hasn't gotten well yet.
c. He has just gotten sick.
d. He has already had the flu.
e. He hasn't had the flu before.

SITUATION 3: Rob is at work. His boss, Rosa, needs a report. She sees Rob working on it at his desk. She's in a hurry, and she's asking Rob questions. What questions is she going to ask him?

a. Have you finished?
b. Have you finished yet?
c. Have you finished already?
d. Have you already finished?

EXERCISE 11 ▶ Looking at grammar. (Chart 4-3)
Look at Andy's smartphone calendar. Write answers to the questions. Make complete sentences with **yet** and **already.**

Wed., May 17	
9:00	dentist appointment
10:00	take car for an oil change
11:00	shop for groceries
12:00	have lunch with Michael
1:00	finish errands
2:00	pick up kids at school

It is 11:55 A.M. right now.

1. Has Andy had his dentist appointment yet? __Yes, he has had his dentist appointment already.__
   OR __Yes, he has already had his dentist appointment.__

2. Has Andy picked up his kids at school yet? _____

3. Has Andy taken his car for an oil change already? _____

4. Has Andy finished his errands yet? _____

5. Has Andy shopped for groceries already? _____

6. Has Andy had lunch with Michael yet? _____

EXERCISE 12 ▶ Listening. (Chart 4-3)
Both **is** and **has** can be contracted to **'s**. Listen to each sentence. Decide if the contracted verb is **is** or **has**. Before you begin, you may want to check your understanding of these words: *order, waiter.*

At a Restaurant

Examples: You will hear: My order's taking a long time.
You will choose: (is)   has

You will hear: My order's already taken a long time.
You will choose: is   (has)

1. is   has   4. is   has
2. is   has   5. is   has
3. is   has   6. is   has

EXERCISE 13 ▸ Warm-up. (Chart 4-4)

Choose the correct sentence (a. or b.) to describe each situation.

1. It's 10:00 A.M. Layla has been at the bus stop since 9:50.
   a. She is still there.
   b. The bus picked her up.

2. Toshi has lived in the same apartment for 30 years.
   a. After 30 years, he moved somewhere else.
   b. He still lives there.

4-4 Present Perfect with *Since* and *For*

	(a) I've **been** in class **since** ten o'clock this morning. (b) We **have known** Ben **for** ten years. We met him ten years ago. We still know him today. We are friends.	The present perfect tense is used in sentences with **since** and **for** to express situations that began in the past and continue to the present. In (a): Class started at ten. I am still in class now, at the moment of speaking. INCORRECT: *I am in class since ten o'clock this morning.*

Since

(c) I **have been** here	**since** eight o'clock. **since** Tuesday. **since** 2009. **since** yesterday. **since** last month.	**Since** is followed by the mention of a *specific point in time*: an hour, a day, a month, a year, etc. **Since** expresses the idea that something began at a specific time in the past and continues to the present.
(d) CORRECT: I **have lived** here since May.* CORRECT: I **have been** here since May. (e) INCORRECT: *I am living here since May.* (f) INCORRECT: *I live here since May.* (g) INCORRECT: *I lived here since May.* (h) INCORRECT: *I was here since May.*		Notice the incorrect sentences: In (e): The present progressive is NOT used. In (f): The simple present is NOT used. In (g) and (h): The simple past is NOT used.
MAIN CLAUSE (present perfect) (i) I **have lived** here (j) Al **has met** many people	SINCE-CLAUSE (simple past) since I **was** a child. since he **came** here.	**Since** may also introduce a time clause (i.e., a subject and verb may follow **since**). Notice in the examples: The present perfect is used in the main clause; the simple past is used in the *since*-clause.

For

(k) I **have been** here	**for** ten minutes. **for** two hours. **for** five days. **for** about three weeks. **for** almost six months. **for** many years. **for** a long time.	**For** is followed by the mention of a *length of time*: two minutes, three hours, four days, five weeks, etc.).

*Also correct: *I **have been living** here since May.* See Chart 4-6 for a discussion of the present perfect progressive.

EXERCISE 14 ▶ Looking at grammar. (Chart 4-4)
Complete the sentences with *since* or *for*.

Amy has been here ...

1. ___for___ two months.
2. ___since___ September.
3. _____ yesterday.
4. _____ the term started.
5. _____ a couple of hours.
6. _____ fifteen minutes.

The Smiths have been married ...

7. _____ two years.
8. _____ last May.
9. _____ five days.
10. _____ a long time.

Ms. Ellis has worked as a substitute teacher ...

11. _____ school began.
12. _____ last year.
13. _____ 2008.
14. _____ about a year.
15. _____ September.
16. _____ a long time.

I've known about Sonia's engagement ...

17. _____ almost four months.
18. _____ the beginning of the year.
19. _____ the first of January.
20. _____ yesterday.

EXERCISE 15 ▶ Looking at grammar. (Chart 4-4)
Complete the sentences with information about yourself.

1. I've been in this building
   - since _nine o'clock this morning_ .
   - for _27 minutes_ .

2. We've been in class
   - since _____ .
   - for _____ .

3. I've been in this city/town
   - since _____ .
   - for _____ .

4. I've had an ID card
   - since _____ .
   - for _____ .

5. I've had this book
   - since _____ .
   - for _____ .

6. I've been a student
   - since _____ .
   - for _____ .

EXERCISE 16 ▶ Looking at grammar. (Chart 4-4)
Complete each sentence with the present perfect form of the given verb.

A Talk-Show Host

Since 1995, Theresa, a talk-show host, ...

1. (*work*)   *has worked*   for a TV station in London.
2. (*interview*) _____ hundreds of guests.
3. (*meet*) _____ many famous people.
4. (*find*) _____ out about their lives.
5. (*make*) _____ friends with celebrities.
6. (*become*) _____ a celebrity herself.
7. (*sign*) _____ lots of autographs.
8. (*shake*) _____ hands with thousands of people.
9. (*write*) _____ two books about how to interview people.
10. (*think*) _____ a lot about the best ways to help people feel comfortable on her show.

EXERCISE 17 ▶ Let's talk. (Chart 4-4)
Your teacher will ask questions. One student will answer with ***since***. Another student will use that information and answer with ***for***. Only the teacher's book is open.

Example:
TO STUDENT A: How long have you been in this room?
    STUDENT A: I've been in this room **since** (10:00).
TO STUDENT B: How long has (*Student A*) been in this room?
    STUDENT B: She/He has been in this room **for** (15 minutes).

1. How long have you known me?
2. How long have you been up* today?
3. Where do you live? How long have you lived there?
4. Who has a cell phone? How long have you had your phone?
5. Who has a bike? How long have you had it?
6. How long have you been in this building today?
7. Who is wearing something new? What is it? How long have you had it/them?
8. Who is married? How long have you been married?

---

*be up = be awake and out of bed

EXERCISE 18 ▶ Looking at grammar. (Chart 4-4)

Put brackets [ ] around the *since-*clauses. Then choose the correct form of the verbs.

Car Problems

1. Otto   had / (has had)   a lot of problems with his car [ever since* he   (bought) / has bought   it.]
2. Ever since Tina   took / has taken   her car in for repairs, it   didn't run / hasn't run   properly.
3. Thomas's car   had / has had   engine problems since he   had / has had   an accident.
4. Ever since my friend   changed / has changed   the oil in my car, I   noticed / have noticed   smoke in the engine.
5. My tire   had / has had   a slow leak ever since I   drove / have driven   through a construction area. Maybe it has a nail in it.

EXERCISE 19 ▶ Let's talk: pairwork. (Charts 4-1, 4-2, and 4-4)

With a partner, take turns asking and answering questions. Begin questions with *How long have you* and the present perfect. Answer with *since*, *for*, or *never* and the present perfect.

Example: have a pet
PARTNER A: How long have you had a pet?
PARTNER B: I've had (*a cat, a dog, a bird, etc.*) for two years/since my 18th birthday. OR
    I've never had a pet.

PARTNER A	PARTNER B
1. live in (*this area*)	1. wear glasses
2. study English	2. have a roommate
3. be in this class	3. have a pet
4. be at this school	4. be married
5. have long/short/medium-length hair	5. be interested in (*a particular subject*)
6. have a beard/mustache	6. want to be (*a particular profession*) *Change roles.*

Ever since is similar to *since*, but *ever* adds emphasis to the clause.

EXERCISE 20 ▶ Reading, grammar, and writing. (Charts 4-1 → 4-4)
Part I. Read the passage about Ellie. <u>Underline</u> the present perfect verbs.

Ellie

I'd like to tell you a little about Ellie. She has lived in Vancouver, Canada, for six months. She has studied English for five years. She has been at this school since September. She likes it here.

She has medium-length hair. She has never worn glasses, except sunglasses. She likes to wear hats. Of course, she has never had a mustache!

Ellie doesn't have a roommate, but she has a pet bird. She has had her bird for one month. His name is Howie, and he likes to sing.

She is interested in biology. She has been interested in biology since she was a child. She has never been married. She wants to be a doctor. She would like to become a doctor before she has a family.

Part II. Write about the person you interviewed in Exercise 19. You can ask additional questions to get more information. Use the passage about Ellie as an example.

EXERCISE 21 ▶ Looking at grammar. (Chart 4-4)
Complete the sentences with the correct form of the words in parentheses.

Life with My Host Family

1. I (*know*) ____have known____ my host family ever since they (*visit*) ____visited____ my parents three years ago.

2. Ever since I (*get*) _____ here, I (*feel*) _____ a little homesick.

3. My host family (*move*) _____ twice since I (*begin*) _____ school.

4. My host family is nice, but I can't wait to get home for vacation. I (*see, not*) _____ _____ my family since I (*leave*) _____ home nine months ago.

5. Ever since my host brother (*meet*) _____ his girlfriend, he (*think, not*) _____ _____ about anything or anyone else. He's in love.

6. My host family helped me find a car to buy, but I (*have*) _____ a lot of problems with it ever since I (*buy*) _____ it. My host mom is afraid it's a lemon.*

7. So far** I (*enjoy*) _____ my time with my host family.

---

*a lemon = a car with a lot of problems

**So far + present perfect expresses situations that began in the past and continue to the present.

EXERCISE 22 ▸ Listening. (Charts 4-1 → 4-4)

Part I. When speakers use the present perfect in everyday speech, they often contract **have** and **has** with nouns. Listen to the sentences and notice the contractions.

Money Problems

1. Someone's taken my credit card.
2. Sorry. Your check's just bounced.
3. Both your credit cards've expired.
4. The bank's made an error again.
5. Checking fees've gone up for the third time.

Part II. Listen to the sentences. You will hear the contracted forms of the verbs. Complete the sentences with the non-contracted forms.

1. The cash machine _____ been out of service for two days.
2. I'm sorry. Your credit card _____ expired.
3. My checking account fees _____ increased a lot.
4. Someone _____ withdrawn money from your account.
5. Our new debit cards _____ gotten lost in the mail.

EXERCISE 23 ▸ Warm-up. (Chart 4-5)

Read the short conversation. Who is more likely to say the last sentence, Pam or Jen? Why?

PAM: I've traveled around the world several times.
JEN: I traveled around the world once.
_____: I'm looking forward to my next trip.

4-5	Simple Past vs. Present Perfect
SIMPLE PAST (a) I *exercised* yesterday. PRESENT PERFECT (b) I *have* already *exercised*.	In (a): I exercised at a specific time in the past (*yesterday*). In (b): I exercised at an unspecified time in the past (*sometime before now*).
SIMPLE PAST (c) I *was* in Europe *last year / three years ago / in 2010 / in 2012 and 2016 / when I was ten years old*. PRESENT PERFECT (d) I *have been* in Europe *many times / several times / a couple of times / once / (no mention of time)*.	The simple past expresses an activity that occurred at a specific time (or times) in the past, as in (a) and (c). The present perfect expresses an activity that occurred at an unspecified time (or times) in the past, as in (b) and (d). Use of the present perfect can indicate the activity may happen again. In (d), the speaker may return to Europe.
SIMPLE PAST (e) Ann *was* in Miami *for two weeks*. PRESENT PERFECT (f) Bob *has been* in Miami *for two weeks / since May 1st*.	In (e): In sentences where *for* is used in a time expression, the simple past expresses an activity that began and ended in the past. In (f): In sentences with *for* or *since*, the present perfect expresses an activity that began in the past and continues to the present.

EXERCISE 24 ▶ Looking at grammar. (Chart 4-5)
Look at the verbs in green. Are they simple past or present perfect? Check (✓) the correct time box.

	WE KNOW THE TIME	WE DON'T KNOW THE TIME
1. Ms. Parker **has been** in Tokyo many times. → *present perfect*	☐	☑
2. Ms. Parker **was** in Tokyo last week. → *simple past*	☑	☐
3. I'**ve met** Kaye's husband. He's a nice guy.	☐	☐
4. I **met** Kaye's husband at a party last week.	☐	☐
5. Mr. White **was** in the hospital last month.	☐	☐
6. Mr. White **has been** in the hospital many times.	☐	☐
7. I like to travel. I'**ve been** to more than 30 foreign countries.	☐	☐
8. I **was** in Morocco in 2008.	☐	☐

EXERCISE 25 ▶ Looking at grammar. (Chart 4-5)
Read the sentences about bikes and notice the verbs in green. Answer the questions that follow and explain your answers.

1. Ann **had** a fast bike.
   Sue **has had** a fast bike for two years.

   Who still has a fast bike? _____

2. Jill **rode** to work on her bike last week.
   Cathy **has ridden** to work on her bike since she got a new one.

   Who is still riding a bike to work? _____

3. In her lifetime, Aunt Alexa **had** several red bikes.
   In her lifetime, Grandma **has had** several red bikes.

   Who is still alive? _____ Who is dead? _____

4. Fernando **has had** several bikes in his lifetime.
   Jenny **had** a red bike when she was in elementary school.
   Keisha **had** a blue bike when she was a teenager.
   Chen **had** a gold bike when he lived and worked in Hong Kong.

   Who no longer has a bike?

   _____

EXERCISE 26 ▶ Looking at grammar. (Chart 4-5)
Complete the sentences. Use the present perfect or the simple past form of the verbs in parentheses.
NOTE: In informal spoken English, the simple past, rather than the present perfect, is sometimes used with **already**. In this exercise, however, practice using the present perfect with **already**.

1. A: Have you ever been to Singapore?
   B: Yes, I ___have___. I (be) ___have been___ to Singapore several times. In fact, I (be)
   ___was___ in Singapore last year.

2. A: Have you ever taken a tour of the city?
   B: Yes, I _____. I (take) _____ a few tours. Last year my wife and I (take)
   _____ a fun bike tour.

3. A: Are you going to book your flight this week?
   B: I (book, already) ___have already booked___ it. I (do) _____ it yesterday.

4. A: What African countries (you, visit) _____ so far?
   B: I (visit) _____ Kenya and Ethiopia. I (visit)
   _____ Kenya in 2002. I (be) _____ in Ethiopia last year.

5. A: When are you going to write about your trip in your blog?
   B: I (write, already) _____ it. I (write) _____
   it last night and (post) _____ it this morning.

6. A: (Romero, visit, ever) _____ family overseas?
   B: Yes, he _____. He (visit) _____ several times.

EXERCISE 27 ▶ Let's talk: pairwork. (Chart 4-5)
With a partner, ask and answer the questions. Use the present perfect or simple past.

Example:
PARTNER A: What countries have you been to?
PARTNER B: I've been to Norway and Finland.
PARTNER A: When were you in Norway?
PARTNER B: I was in Norway three years ago. How about you? What countries have you been to?
PARTNER A: I've never been to Norway or Finland, but I've been to … .

1. What countries have you been to? When were you in...?
2. Where are some interesting places you have lived? When did you live in...?
3. What are some interesting / unusual / scary things you have done in your lifetime? When did you...?
4. What are some helpful things (for a friend / your family / your community) you have done in your lifetime? When did you...?

EXERCISE 28 ▶ Listening. (Charts 2-3 and 4-5)
For each item, you will hear two complete sentences and then the beginning of a third sentence. Complete the third sentence with the past participle of the verb you heard in the first two sentences.

Example: You will hear: I eat vegetables every day. I ate vegetables for dinner last night. I have...

   You will write: I have __eaten__ vegetables every day for a long time.

1. Since Friday, I have _____ a lot of money.
2. All week, I have _____ big breakfasts.
3. Today, I have already _____ several emails.
4. I just finished dinner, and I have _____ a nice tip.
5. Since I was a teenager, I have _____ in late on weekends.
6. All my life, I have _____ very carefully.
7. Since I was little, I have _____ in the shower.

EXERCISE 29 ▶ Game. (Charts 4-1 → 4-5)
Work in groups:
1. On a piece of paper, write down two statements about yourself, one in the simple past tense and one in the present perfect tense.
2. Make one statement true and one statement false.
3. Say your sentences.
4. The other members of your group will try to guess which one is true.
5. Tell your group the answers after everyone has finished guessing.

The person with the most correct guesses at the end of the game is the winner.

Example:
STUDENT A: I've never cooked dinner.
            I saw a famous person last year.
STUDENT B: You've never cooked dinner. That is true.
            You saw a famous person last year. That is false.

EXERCISE 30 ▶ Warm-up. (Chart 4-6)
Complete the sentences with time information.
1. I am sitting at my desk right now. I have been sitting at my desk since _____.
2. I am looking at my book. I have been looking at my book for _____.

4-6 Present Perfect Progressive

Al and Ann are in their car right now. They are driving home. It is now four o'clock.

(a) They **have been driving** since two o'clock.

(b) They **have been driving** for two hours. They will be home soon.

(c) How long **have** they **been driving**?

The PRESENT PERFECT PROGRESSIVE talks about *how long* an activity has been in progress before now.

NOTE: Time expressions with *since*, as in (a), and *for*, as in (b), are frequently used with this tense.

STATEMENT:
have/has + **been** + **-ing**

QUESTION:
have/has + subject + **been** + **-ing**

Present Progressive vs. Present Perfect Progressive

PRESENT PROGRESSIVE

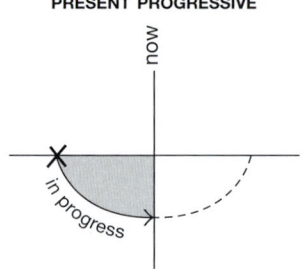

(d) Po *is sitting* in class right now.

The present progressive describes an activity that is in progress right now, as in (d). It does not discuss duration (length of time).

INCORRECT: *Po has been sitting in class right now.*

PRESENT PERFECT PROGRESSIVE

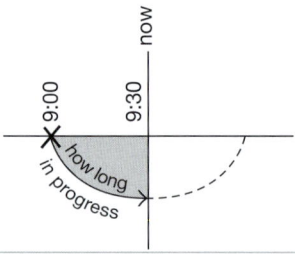

Po is sitting at his desk in class. He sat down at nine o'clock. It is now nine-thirty.

(e) Po **has been sitting** in class *since* nine o'clock.

(f) Po **has been sitting** in class *for* thirty minutes.

The present perfect progressive *emphasizes the duration* (length of time) of an activity that began in the past and is in progress right now.

INCORRECT: *Po is sitting in class since nine o'clock.*

(g) CORRECT: I **know** Yoko.
(h) INCORRECT: I am knowing Yoko.
(i) CORRECT: I **have known** Yoko **for** two years.
(j) INCORRECT: I have been knowing Yoko for two years.

NOTE: Non-action verbs (e.g., *know, like, own, belong*) are generally not used in the progressive tenses.*

In (i): With non-action verbs, the present perfect is used with *since* or *for* to express the duration of a situation that began in the past and continues to the present.

*See Chart 1-6, Verbs Not Usually Used in the Progressive, p. 18.

EXERCISE 31 ▸ Looking at grammar. (Chart 4-6)

Complete the sentences. Use the present progressive or the present perfect progressive form of the verbs in parentheses.

At School

1. I (*sit*) __am sitting__ in the cafeteria right now. I (*sit*) __have been sitting__ here since twelve o'clock.

2. Kate is standing in line at the registration counter. She (*wait*) _____ for help. She (*wait*) _____ for help for twenty minutes.

3. Scott and Rebecca (*study*) _____ together right now. They (*study*) _____ together in the library for over an hour.

4. Right now we're in class. We (*do*) _____ an exercise. We (*do*) _____ this exercise for a couple of minutes.

5. A: You look busy right now. What (*you, do*) _____?
   B: I (*work*) _____ on my physics experiment. It's a difficult experiment.
   A: How long (*you, work*) _____ on it?
   B: I started planning it last January. I (*work*) _____ on it since then.

EXERCISE 32 ▸ Let's talk. (Chart 4-6)

Answer the questions your teacher asks. Your book is closed.

Example:
TEACHER: Where are you living?
STUDENT: I'm living in an apartment on Fourth Avenue.
TEACHER: How long have you been living there?
STUDENT: I've been living there since last September.

1. Right now you are sitting in class. How long have you been sitting here?
2. When did you first begin to study English? How long have you been studying English?
3. I began to teach English in (*year*). How long have I been teaching English?
4. I began to work at this school in (*month or year*). How long have I been working here?
5. What are we doing right now? How long have we been doing it?
6. (*Student's name*), I see that you wear glasses. How long have you been wearing glasses?
7. Who drives? When did you first drive a car? How long have you been driving?
8. Who drinks coffee? How old were you when you started to drink coffee? How long have you been drinking coffee?
9. Who owns a motorcycle? How long have you owned one?
10. Who likes candy? How long have you liked candy?

EXERCISE 33 ▶ Warm-up. (Chart 4-7)

Read the sentences and answer this question: *Who is Suzanne helping right now?*

1. Roger is having trouble with math. Suzanne has been helping him with his homework tonight. She has been helping him since 6:00.

2. Suzanne likes to help students with math. She has helped Tia and Kofi this week.

4-7 Present Perfect Progressive vs. Present Perfect

Present Perfect Progressive

(a) Tarik and Gina are talking on the phone. They *have been talking* on the phone for 20 minutes.	The present perfect progressive expresses the *duration of present activities,* using action verbs, as in (a). The activity began in the past and is still in progress.

Present Perfect

(b) Tarik *has talked* to Gina on the phone many times (before now). (c) INCORRECT: *Tarik has been talking to Gina on the phone many times.* (d) Tarik *has known* Gina for two years. (e) INCORRECT: *Tarik has been knowing Gina for two years.*	The present perfect expresses (1) repeated activities that occur at *unspecified times in the past,* as in (b), OR (2) the *duration of present situations,* as in (d), using non-action verbs.

Present Perfect Progressive and Present Perfect

(f) I *have been living* here for six months. OR (g) I *have lived* here for six months. (h) Ed *has been wearing* glasses since he was ten. OR Ed *has worn* glasses since he was ten. (i) I*'ve been going* to school ever since I was five years old. OR I*'ve gone* to school ever since I was five years old.	For some (not all) verbs, duration can be expressed by either the present perfect or the present perfect progressive. Examples (f) and (g) have essentially the same meaning, and both are correct. Often either tense can be used with verbs that express the *duration of usual or habitual activities/situations* (things that happen daily or regularly). Common verbs are *live, work, study, play, teach,* and *wear glasses.*

EXERCISE 34 ▶ Looking at grammar. (Chart 4-7)

Complete the sentences with the verbs in *italics*. Use the present perfect progressive form for the activity that is still in progress.

1. *has been helping / has helped*

   a. Professor Ruiz got to his office at 7:00 A.M. He _____ a student since then.

   b. Professor Jackson is really nice. He _____ me several times with my medical school application.

2. *has been sleeping / has slept*

   a. Tony _____ this afternoon. He stayed up all night to study for a test.

   b. Gina got a new mattress for her dorm room. She _____ on it twice, but it's too hard for her.

3. *have been reading / have read*

   a. I _____ this same page in my chemistry book three times, and I still don't understand it.

   b. I _____ it for the last half hour. It's like another language!

EXERCISE 35 ▶ Looking at grammar. (Chapters 1, 2, and 4)

Look at each set of sentences. Check (✓) the sentences that are still in progress. Look at the verbs in green, and discuss the differences in meaning.

1. a. _____ Rachel **is taking** English classes.
   b. _____ Nadia **has been taking** English classes for two months.

2. a. _____ Ayako **has been living** in Jerusalem for two years. She likes it there.
   b. _____ Beatriz **has lived** in Jerusalem. She's also lived in Paris. She's lived in New York and Tokyo. She's lived in lots of cities.

3. a. _____ Jack **has visited** his aunt and uncle many times.
   b. _____ Matt **has been visiting** his aunt and uncle for the last three days.

4. a. _____ Cyril **is talking** on the phone.
   b. _____ Cyril **talks** on the phone a lot.
   c. _____ Cyril **has been talking** to his boss on the phone for half an hour.
   d. _____ Cyril **has talked** to his boss on the phone lots of times.

5. a. _____ Mr. Woods **walks** his dog in Forest Park every day.
   b. _____ Mr. Woods **has walked** his dog in Forest Park many times.
   c. _____ Mr. Woods **walked** his dog in Forest Park five times last week.
   d. _____ Mr. Woods **is walking** his dog in Forest Park right now.
   e. _____ Mr. Woods **has been walking** his dog in Forest Park since two o'clock.

EXERCISE 36 ▶ Looking at grammar. (Chapter 1 and Charts 4-1 → 4-7)
Choose the correct verb. In some sentences, more than one answer may be possible.

Frustrations

1. I _____ the windows twice, and they still don't look clean.
   a. am washing   b. have washed   c. have been washing

2. Please tell Mira to get off the phone. She _____ for over an hour.
   a. is talking   b. has talked   c. has been talking

3. Where are you? I _____ at the mall for you to pick me up.
   a. wait   b. am waiting   c. have been waiting

4. Josh _____ up all night twice this week. He has a lot of homework.
   a. stays   b. has stayed   c. has been staying

5. Where have you been? The baby _____, and I can't comfort her.
   a. cries   b. is crying   c. has been crying

EXERCISE 37 ▶ Listening. (Chart 4-7)
Listen to the weather report. Then listen again and complete the sentences with the words you hear.

Do you know these words?
- boy (as an exclamation)
- what's in store
- hail
- weather system
- high winds
- rough

TODAY'S WEATHER

The weather ___1___ certainly ___2___ today. Boy, what a day! ___3___ already ___4___ rain, wind, hail, and sun. So, what's in store for tonight? As you ___5___ probably ___6___, dark clouds ___7___. We have a weather system moving in that is going to bring colder temperatures and high winds. ___8___ all week that this system is coming, and it looks like tonight is it! ___9___ even ___10___ snow down south of us, and we could get some snow here too. So hang onto your hats! We may have a rough night ahead of us.

EXERCISE 38 ▶ Looking at grammar. (Chart 4-7)
Complete the sentences. Use the present perfect or the present perfect progressive form of the verbs in parentheses. In some sentences, either form is possible.

Enjoying the Outdoors

1. A: I'd like to take a break. We (hike) _have been hiking_ for more than an hour.
   B: OK, let's stop here. The views are beautiful.

2. A: Is the trail to Glacier Lake difficult?
   B: No, not at all. I (hike) _have hiked_ it many times with my kids.

3. A: Do you like it here?
   B: I love it! I (live) _have been living / have lived_ here since the beginning of the summer
   and (take) _____ several beautiful hikes.

4. A: I'm getting hungry. We (walk) _____ since sunrise.
   I think I'll have lunch.
   B: Good idea.

5. A: Do you like this campsite?
   B: Very much. I (stay) _____ here several times. It's my favorite place
   to camp.

6. A: It's snowing. It (snow) _____ all night.
   B: The skiing will be great!

7. A: Do you ski often?
   B: Every day! I (work) _____ as a ski instructor here for the past
   five months.
   A: (you, teach) _____ for a long time?
   B: I (teach) _____ people to ski since I was a teenager.

Present Perfect and Past Perfect 113

EXERCISE 39 ▶ Listening. (Charts 4-3 → 4-7)

Listen to each conversation and choose the sentence that best describes it.

Example: You will hear: A: This movie is silly.
B: I agree. It's really dumb.

You will choose: (a.) The couple has been watching a movie.
b. The couple finished watching a movie.

1. a. The speakers listened to the radio already.
   b. The speakers have been listening to the radio.

2. a. The man lived in Dubai a year ago.
   b. The man still lives in Dubai.

3. a. The man has called the children several times.
   b. The man called the children once.

4. a. The speakers went to a party and are still there.
   b. The speakers went to a party and have already left.

EXERCISE 40 ▶ Listening and speaking. (Chapters 1 → 4)

Part I. Listen to the phone conversation between a mother and her daughter, Lara.

A Common Illness

LARA: Hi, Mom. I was just calling to tell you that I can't come to your birthday party this weekend. I'm afraid I'm sick.

MOM: Oh, I'm sorry to hear that.

LARA: Yeah, I got sick Wednesday night, and it's just been getting worse.

MOM: Are you going to see a doctor?

LARA: I don't know. I don't want to go to a doctor if it's not serious.

MOM: Well, what symptoms have you been having?

LARA: I've had a cough, and now I have a fever.

MOM: Have you been taking any medicine?

LARA: Just over-the-counter* stuff.

MOM: If your fever doesn't go away, I think you need to call a doctor.

LARA: Yeah, I probably will.

MOM: Well, call me tomorrow, and let me know how you're doing.

LARA: OK. I'll call you in the morning.

---

*over-the-counter = medicine you can buy without a prescription from a doctor

Part II. Work with a partner. Complete the conversation and practice it. Take turns being the parent and the sick person.

Possible symptoms:				
a fever	chills	a sore throat	a runny nose	achiness
a stomachache	a cough	a headache	sneezing	nausea

A: Hi, Mom/Dad. I was just calling to tell you that I can't come to _____. I'm afraid I'm sick.

B: Oh, I'm sorry to hear that.

A: Yeah, I got sick Wednesday night, and it's just been getting worse.

B: Are you going to see a doctor?

A: I don't know. I don't want to go to a doctor if it's not serious.

B: Well, what symptoms have you been having?

A: I've had _____, and now I have _____.

B: Have you been taking any medicine?

A: Just over-the-counter stuff.

B: If your _____ doesn't go away, I think you need to call a doctor.

A: Yeah, I probably will.

B: Well, call me tomorrow and let me know how you're doing.

A: OK. I'll call you in the morning.

EXERCISE 41 ▶ Warm-up. (Charts 4-8)
Read Karen's statement. Which sentence (a. or b.) is correct?

> KAREN: Jay met me for lunch. He was so happy. He had passed his driver's test.
> a. First, Jay talked to Karen. Then he passed his test.
> b. First, Jay passed his test. Then he talked to Karen.

4-8 Past Perfect

Situation:
Jack left his office at 2:00. Mia arrived at his office at 2:15 and knocked on the door.

(a) When Mia arrived, Jack wasn't there. He *had left*.

(b) *By the time* Mia arrived, Jack *had already left*.

The PAST PERFECT is used when the speaker is talking about two different events at two different times in the past; one event ended before the second event happened.

In (a): There are two events, and both happened in the past: *Jack left his office. Mia arrived at his office.*

To show the time relationship between the two events, we use the past perfect (**had left**) to say that the first event (Jack leaving his office) was completed before the second event (Mia arriving at his office) occurred.

In (b): **By the time** is frequently used with the past perfect to indicate one event happened before another.

(c) Jack *had left* his office when Mia arrived.

(d) He*'d* left. I*'d* left. They*'d* left. Etc.

FORM: **had** + *past participle*

CONTRACTION: *I / you / she / he / it / we / they* + **'d**

(e) Jack *had left before* Mia arrived.
(f) Jack *left before* Mia arrived.
(g) Mia *arrived after* Jack had left.
(h) Mia *arrived after* Jack left.

When **before** and **after** are used in a sentence, the time relationship is already clear so the past perfect is often not necessary. The simple past may be used, as in (f) and (h).

Examples (e) and (f) have the same meaning.
Examples (g) and (h) have the same meaning.

(i) Stella was alone in a strange city. She walked down the avenue slowly, looking in shop windows. Suddenly, she turned her head and looked behind her. Someone *had called* her name.

The past perfect is more common in formal writing such as fiction, as in (i).

EXERCISE 42 ▸ Looking at grammar. (Chart 4-8)
Identify which action in the past took place first (1st) and which action took place second (2nd).

1. Before I went to bed, I **checked** the front door. My roommate **had** already **locked** it.
   a. __2nd__ I checked the door.
   b. __1st__ My roommate locked the door.

2. I **looked** for Diego, but he **had left** the building.
   a. _____ Diego left the building.
   b. _____ I looked for Diego.

3. I **laughed** when I saw my son. He **had poured** a bowl of noodles on top of his head.
   a. _____ I laughed.
   b. _____ My son poured a bowl of noodles on his head.

4. Oliver **arrived** at the theater on time, but he couldn't get in. He **had left** his ticket at home.
   a. _____ Oliver left his ticket at home.
   b. _____ Oliver arrived at the theater.

5. I **handed** Betsy the newspaper, but she didn't want it. She **had read** it during her lunch hour.
   a. _____ I handed Betsy the newspaper.
   b. _____ Betsy read the newspaper.

6. After Carl **arrived** in New York, he called his mother. He **had promised** to call her as soon as he got in.
   a. _____ Carl made a promise to his mother.
   b. _____ Carl called his mother.

7. The tennis player **jumped** in the air for joy. He **had won** the match.
   a. _____ The tennis player won the match.
   b. _____ The tennis player jumped in the air.

EXERCISE 43 ▸ Looking at grammar. (Charts 4-3, 4-4, and 4-8)
Complete the conversations with the present perfect or past perfect. Use *have*, *has*, or *had*.

1. A: There's Professor Newton. I'll introduce you.
   B: You don't need to. I _____ already met him.

2. A: Did Jack introduce you to Professor Newton?
   B: He didn't need to. I _____ already met him before I moved here.

3. A: Oh, no! We're too late. The train _____ left.
   B: That's OK. We'll catch the next one.

4. A: Tom missed the train.
   B: I know. I was with him. When we got to the station, the train _____ just left.

5. A: You sure woke up early this morning!
   B: Well, I went to bed early last night. By 6:00 A.M., I _____ already slept for eight hours.

6. A: Go back to sleep. It's only 6:00 in the morning.
   B: I can't. I _____ been awake since 5:00.

7. A: Grandpa _____ gone back into the hospital again.
   B: What happened?
   A: When Grandma got home last night, she found him on the floor. He _____ fallen and hit his head.

EXERCISE 44 ▸ Check your knowledge. (Chapter 4 Review)
Correct the errors in verb tense usage.

My Experience with English

1. I have been ~~studied~~ *studying* English for eight years, but I still have a lot to learn.

2. I start English classes at this school two months ago, and I have learned a lot of English since then.

3. I want to learn English since I am a child.

4. I have been thinking about how to improve my English skills quickly since I came here, but I hadn't found a good way.

5. Our teacher likes to give tests. We has have six tests since the beginning of the term.

6. I like learning English. When I was young, my father found an Australian girl to teach my brothers and me English, but when we move to another city, my father didn't find anyone to teach us.

7. I made many friends since school started. I meet Abdul in the cafeteria on the first day. He was friendly and kind. We are friends since that day.

8. Abdul have been study English for three months. His English is better than mine.

EXERCISE 45 ▶ Reading, grammar, and writing. (Chapters 1, 2, and 4)
Part I. Read the passage. <u>Underline</u> the words that express time. Note the verbs in green.

A Brief Introduction

My name is Tanet Sakda. I am from Thailand. <u>Right now</u> I am studying English at this school. I have been at this school since the beginning of January. I arrived here on January 2, and my classes began on January 6.

Since I came here, I have done many things, and I have met many people. Last week, I went to a party at my friend's house. I met some of the other students from Thailand at the party. Of course, we spoke Thai, so I didn't practice my English that night. There were only people from Thailand at the party.

However, since I came here, I have made friends with a lot of other people too, including people from Latin America and the Middle East. I have enjoyed meeting people from other countries, and they have become my friends. Now I know people from around the world.

Part II. Write three paragraphs about yourself. Use Part I as a model. Answer these questions:

Paragraph I:

1. What is your name? _____
2. Where are you from? _____
3. How long have you been here? _____

Paragraph II:

4. What have you done since you came here? OR What have you learned since you began studying English? _____
_____

Paragraph III:

5. Who(m) have you met in this class? OR Who(m) have you met recently?
_____
_____

6. Give a little information about these people.
_____
_____

WRITING TIP

The English verb system can seem very confusing. Small differences in verb forms can change the meaning of a sentence. A good way to check your writing is to focus on one verb form at a time. For example, choose a time word like *now*. Find all the instances of *now* and check that the verbs are in the correct tense. That is probably present progressive for this writing assignment. Note that sometimes, there is only one time word for several sentences that follow.

Then choose another time word and think about the verb tenses for that time. Check that they are correct.

Later, for a final check, go through your paragraphs sentence by sentence to check your verbs one last time.

Here are some helpful time markers and the tenses they often go with:

Time Markers	Tense(s)
now, today	present progressive
last night / week / etc. *that night / week / etc.* *yesterday* *in 2010* (specific date)	simple past
since, for	present perfect, simple past* OR present perfect progressive (for events still in progress)

*Remember: when you introduce a time clause with *since*, the main clause uses present perfect and the *since*-clause uses the simple past.

Part III. Edit your writing. Check for the following:

1. ☐ use of the simple past for finished events
2. ☐ use of the present perfect for events up to now
3. ☐ use of the present perfect for unspecified time
4. ☐ use of the present perfect progressive for events that started in the past and are still in progress
5. ☐ correct use of **have** and **has** with the present perfect and present perfect progressive
6. ☐ correct spelling (use a dictionary or spell-check)

▪▪▪▪ For digital resources, go to MyEnglishLab on the Pearson English Portal. You can also go to the Pearson Practice English app for mobile practice.

CHAPTER 5
Asking Questions

PRETEST: What do I already know?
Write "C" if the **boldfaced** words are correct and "I" if they are incorrect.

1. ____ **Has** it snowing right now? (Chart 5-1)
2. ____ **When** will you graduate from college? (Chart 5-2)
3. ____ **What** did you say that **for**? (Chart 5-3)
4. ____ Who(m) **you asked** to the wedding? (Chart 5-4)
5. ____ What **did happen** at the party last night? (Chart 5-3)
6. ____ What is your father's occupation — what **is he do**? (Chart 5-4)
7. ____ **Which websites** do you check most often? (Chart 5-5)
8. ____ **How many years** are you? (Chart 5-6)
9. ____ **How often** do you see your parents? (Chart 5-7)
10. ____ **How far is** from Tokyo to Singapore? (Chart 5-8)
11. ____ **How long it take** to fly from Berlin to Prague? (Chart 5-9)
12. ____ **How do you spell** the word *shampoo*? (Chart 5-11)
13. ____ **How about getting** takeout for dinner tonight? (Chart 5-12)
14. ____ There's enough money for the rent, **isn't it?** (Chart 5-13)

EXERCISE 1 ▶ Warm-up. (Chart 5-1)
Choose the correct completion.

A: ____ you like sweets?   B: Yes, ____.

a. Are   c. Have   a. I like   c. I have
b. Do   d. Were   b. I'm   d. I do

5-1 Yes/No Questions and Short Answers

Yes/No Question	Short Answer (+ Long Answer)	
(a) **Are** you ready? **Are** you a student?	*Yes, I **am**.* (I am ready.) *No, I **am not**.* (I'm not a student.)	A **yes/no question** is a question that can be answered by *yes* or *no*. * In (b): INCORRECT: *Yes, I like.*
(b) **Do** you **like** tea?	*Yes, I **do**.* (I like tea.) *No, I **don't**.* (I don't like tea.)	
(c) **Is** it **raining**?	*Yes, it **is**.* (It's raining.) *No, it **isn't**.* (It isn't raining.)	In an affirmative short answer (*yes*), a helping verb is NOT contracted with the subject.
(d) **Did** Liz **call**?	*Yes, she **did**.* (Liz called.) *No, she **didn't**.* (Liz didn't call.)	In (c): INCORRECT: *Yes, it's.* In (e): INCORRECT: *Yes, I've.* In (f): INCORRECT: *Yes, he'll.*
(e) **Have** you **met** Al?	*Yes, I **have**.* (I have met Al.) *No, I **haven't**.* (I haven't met Al.)	
(f) **Will** Rob **be** here?	*Yes, he **will**.* (Rob will be here.) *No, he **won't**.* (Rob won't be here.)	The spoken emphasis in a short answer is on the verb.
(g) **Is there** a restroom nearby?	*Yes, there **is**.* (There is a restroom nearby.) *No, there **isn't**.* (There isn't a restroom nearby.)	***Be*** + ***there*** asks if something exists somewhere.

*For more information on question formation with the tenses in this chart, see Charts 1-7, p. 21, 2-1, p. 31, 2-2, p. 32, 3-2, p. 66, 3-3, p. 69, and 4-2, p. 94.

EXERCISE 2 ▶ Looking at grammar. (Chart 5-1)
Choose the correct verbs.

A New Cell Phone

1. A: **Is / Does** that your new cell phone?
   B: Yes, it **is / does**.

2. A: **Are / Do** you like it?
   B: Yes, I **am / do**.

3. A: **Were / Did** you buy it online?
   B: Yes, I **was / did**.

4. A: **Was / Did** it expensive?
   B: No, it **wasn't / didn't**.

5. A: **Is / Does** it ringing right now?
   B: Yes, it **is / does**.

6. A: **Are / Do** you going to answer it?
   B: Yes, I **am / do**.

7. A: **Was / Did** the call important?
   B: Yes, it **was / did**.

8. A: **Have / Were** you turned your phone off?
   B: No, I **haven't / wasn't**.

9. A: **Will / Are** you call me later?
   B: Yes, I **will / are**.

10. A: **Do / Are** you have my new number?
    B: Yes, I **do / have**.

EXERCISE 3 ▶ Looking at grammar. (Chart 5-1)

Use the information in parentheses to make *yes/no* questions. Complete each conversation with an appropriate short answer. Do not use a negative verb in the question.

Travel Questions

1. A: _Do you take credit cards?_
   B: Yes, _we do._ (We take credit cards.)

2. A: _____
   B: No, _____ (The price doesn't include tax.)

3. A: _____
   B: Yes, _____ (You need a reservation.)

4. A: _____
   B: Yes, _____ (We are open every day.)

5. A: _____
   B: No, _____ (The tour isn't going to leave soon.)

6. A: _____
   B: Yes, _____ (The bus came.)

7. A: _____
   B: No, _____ (You haven't missed the flight.)

8. A: _____
   B: Yes, _____ (There is an express train.)

EXERCISE 4 ▶ Let's talk: interview. (Chart 5-1)

Interview seven students in your class. Make questions with the given words. Ask each student a different question.

1. you \ like \ animals?
2. you \ ever \ had \ a pet snake?
3. it \ be \ cold \ in this room?
4. it \ rain \ right now?
5. you \ sleep \ well last night?
6. you \ be \ tired right now?
7. you \ be \ here next year?

EXERCISE 5 ▶ Looking at grammar. (Chart 5-1)
Complete the questions with *Do, Does, Did, Is,* or *Are*.

Leaving for the Airport

1. We're ready to leave. _____ you have your passport?
2. _____ you almost ready?
3. _____ you already print out our boarding passes?
4. _____ you remember to pack a snack for the plane?
5. Your carry-on looks big. _____ it fit under the seat?
6. _____ you call for our ride?
7. _____ our ride coming soon?
8. _____ the driver nearby?

EXERCISE 6 ▶ Listening. (Chart 5-1)
In spoken English, it may be hard to hear the beginning of a *yes/no* question because the words are often reduced.*

Part I. Listen to these common reductions.

1. Is he absent?   →   *Ih-ze* absent? or *Ze* absent?
2. Is she absent?   →   *Ih-she* absent?
3. Does it work?   →   *Zit* work?
4. Did it break?   →   *Dih-dit* break? or *Dit* break?
5. Has he been sick?   →   *Ze* been sick? or *A-ze* been sick?
6. Is there enough?   →   *Zere* enough?
7. Is that OK?   →   *Zat* OK?

Part II. Complete the sentences with the words you hear. Write the non-reduced forms.

At the Grocery Store

1. I need to see the manager. _____ available?
2. I need to see the manager. _____ in the store today?
3. Here is one bag of apples. _____ enough?
4. I need a drink of water. _____ a drinking fountain?
5. My credit card isn't working. Hmmm. _____ expire?
6. Where's Simon? _____ left?
7. The price seems high. _____ include the tax?

a drinking fountain

---

*See also Chapter 1, Exercise 37, p. 24, and Chapter 2, Exercise 19, p. 41.

EXERCISE 7 ▶ Warm-up. (Chart 5-2)
Choose the correct answers. There may be more than one answer for each question.

1. Where did you go?
    a. To the hospital.   b. Yes, I did.   c. Outside.   d. Yesterday.

2. When is James leaving?
    a. I'm not sure.   b. Yes, he is.   c. Yes, he does.   d. Around noon.

3. Why did Mr. and Ms. Lee move?
    a. I think so.   b. They got new jobs.   c. No, they aren't.   d. Yes, they did.

5-2 Where, Why, When, What Time, How Come, What ... For

The questions in this chart ask for information. Note that most are *wh*-type questions. The answers do not begin with *yes* or *no*.*

Question	Answer	
(a) **Where** did he go?	Home.	**Where** asks about *place*.
(b) **When** did he leave?	Last night. Two days ago. Monday morning. Seven-thirty.	A question with **when** can be answered by any time expression, as in the sample answers in (b).
(c) **What time** did he leave?	Seven-thirty. Around five o'clock. A quarter past ten.	A question with **what time** asks about *time on a clock*.
(d) **Why** did he leave?	Because he didn't feel well.**	**Why** asks about *reason*.
(e) **What** did he leave **for**? (f) **How come** he left?	**Why** can also be expressed with the phrases **What ... for** and **How come**, as in (e) and (f). Note that with **How come,** usual question order is not used. The subject precedes the verb and no form of **do** is used.	

*For a comparison of *yes/no* and information questions, see Appendix A-8.
**See Chart 8-6, p. 241, for the use of *because*. *Because I didn't feel well* is an adverb clause. It is not a complete sentence. In this example, it is the short answer to a question.

EXERCISE 8 ▶ Reading and grammar. (Charts 5-1 and 5-2)
Read the information about Irina and Paul. Then make complete questions with the given words. Choose the correct short answers.

The Simple Life

Irina and Paul live a simple life. They have a one-room cabin on a mountain lake. They fish for some of their food. They also raise chickens. They pick fruit from trees and berries from bushes in the summer. They don't have electricity or TV, but they enjoy their life. They don't need a lot to be happy.

1. QUESTION: where \ Irina and Paul \ live?
    <u>Where do Irina and Paul live?</u>
    ANSWER: a. Yes, they do.   (b.) On a lake.

2. QUESTION: they \ live \ a simple life? _____
   ANSWER: a. Yes, they live.   b. Yes, they do.

3. QUESTION: when \ they \ pick \ fruit from trees? _____
   ANSWER: a. In the summer.   b. Yes, they do.

4. QUESTION: they \ have \ electricity? _____
   ANSWER: a. No, they don't.   b. No, they don't have.

5. QUESTION: they \ enjoy \ their life? _____
   ANSWER: a. Yes, they do.   b. Yes, they enjoy.

6. QUESTION: they \ be \ happy? _____
   ANSWER: a. Yes, they do.   b. Yes, they are.

EXERCISE 9 ▸ Looking at grammar. (Chart 5-2)
Restate the sentences with **How come** and **What for**.

1. Why are you going?
2. Why did they come?
3. Why does he need more money?
4. Why are they going to leave?

EXERCISE 10 ▸ Looking at grammar. (Chart 5-2)
Complete the questions using the information from Speaker A.

What was that?

1. A: I'm going downtown in a few minutes.
   B: I didn't catch that. When _are you going downtown_____? OR
   B: I didn't catch that. Where _are you going in a few minutes_____?

2. A: My kids are transferring to Lakeview Elementary School because it's a better school.
   B: What was that? Where _____? OR
   B: What was that? Why _____?

3. A: I am going to meet Taka at 10:00 at the mall.
   B: I couldn't hear you. Tell me again. What time _____? OR
   B: I couldn't hear you. Tell me again. Where _____?

4. A: Class begins at 8:15.
   B: Are you sure? When _____? OR
   B: Are you sure? What time _____?

5. A: I stayed home from work because I wanted to watch the World Cup final on TV.
   B: Huh?! Why _____? OR
   B: Huh?! What _____ for?

EXERCISE 11 ▶ Grammar and listening. (Charts 5-1 and 5-2)

Complete the conversation. Then listen to the conversation to check your answers. Use a form of **be going to** for the future verb.

Where are Roberto and Isabelle?

A: _Do you know_ ₁ Roberto and Isabelle?

B: Yes, I _____₂. They live around the corner from me.

A: _____₃ seen them recently?

B: No, I _____₄. They're out of town.

A: When _____₅ be back? I'm having a party, and I can't reach them.

B: They're going to be back Monday. They are with Roberto's parents.

A: Oh, _____₆ they there?

B: Because his dad is sick.

A: That's too bad.

B: _____₇ want Roberto's or Isabelle's cell number?

A: No, I don't, but thanks. I'll talk to them when they get back.

B: OK, sounds good.

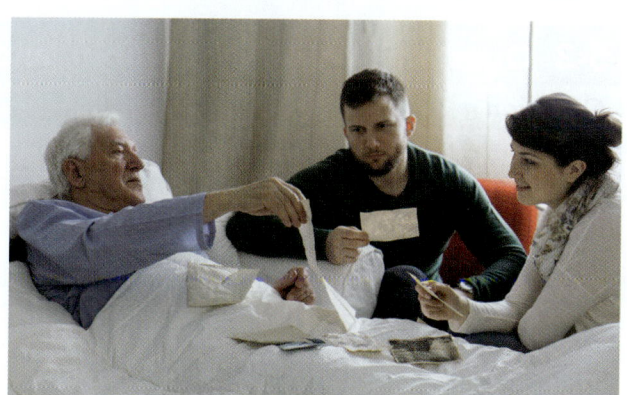

 EXERCISE 12 ▶ Listening. (Charts 5-1 and 5-2)

Listen to each question and choose the correct answer.

Example: You will hear: When are you leaving?
You will choose: a. Yes, I am.   (b.) Tomorrow.   c. In the city.

1. a. I am too.   b. Yesterday.   c. Sure.
2. a. For dinner.   b. At 6:00.   c. At the restaurant.
3. a. Outside the mall. b. After lunch.   c. Because I need a ride.
4. a. At work.   b. Because traffic was heavy.   c. A few hours ago.
5. a. The kitchen.   b. In a few minutes.   c. My parents are coming.

Asking Questions   127

EXERCISE 13 ▶ Warm-up. (Chart 5-3)

Match each question with the correct answer.

A Flight to Rome

1. Who flew to Rome? _____
2. Who did you fly to Rome? _____
3. What did you fly to Rome? _____
4. What flew to Rome? _____

a. A small plane flew to Rome.
b. I flew to Rome.
c. I flew a small plane to Rome.
d. I flew Pablo to Rome.

5-3 Questions With *Who, Whom,* and *What*

Question	Answer	
(a) **Who** came? *(S)*	**Someone** came. *(S)*	In (a): **Who** is used as the subject (S) of a question. In (b): **Who(m)** is used as the object (O) in a question.
(b) **Who(m)** did *you* see? *(O)*	I saw **someone**. *(S)(O)*	**Whom** is used in formal written and spoken English. In everyday English, **who** is usually used instead of **whom**: UNCOMMON: Whom did you see? COMMON: Who did you see?
(c) **What** happened? *(S)*	**Something** happened. *(S)*	**What** can be used as either the subject or the object in a question.
(d) **What** did *you* see? *(O)*	I saw **something**. *(S)(O)*	Note in (a) and (c): When **who** or **what** is used as the subject of a question, usual question word order is not used; no form of **do** is used: CORRECT: Who came? INCORRECT: Who did come?

EXERCISE 14 ▶ Looking at grammar. (Chart 5-3)

Make questions with **Who, Who(m)**, and **What**. Write "S" if the question word is the subject. Write "O" if the question word is the object.

What's going on?

QUESTION | ANSWER

1. _Who knows?_ (S) — **Someone** knows. (S)
2. _Who(m) did you see?_ (O) — I saw **someone**. (O)
3. _____ — **Someone** is outside.

4. _____ Talya met **someone**.

5. _____ Mike found out **something**.

6. _____ **Something** changed Gina's mind.

7. _____ Gina is talking about **someone**.*

8. _____ Gina is talking about **something**.

EXERCISE 15 ▶ Looking at grammar. (Chart 5-3)
Complete the questions with **Who** or **What**.

At the Hospital

1. A: _____ just left?
   B: That was the doctor.

2. A: _____ do you need?
   B: A glass of water.

3. A: _____ is your nurse today?
   B: I'm not sure. Maybe David or Nancy.

4. A: _____ is going on?
   B: I'm getting a new roommate.

5. A: _____ did you call?
   B: The nurse.

6. A: _____ do you need?
   B: Dr. Smith or her nurse.

EXERCISE 16 ▶ Let's talk. (Chart 5-3)
Abbreviations in text messages are very popular. Ask your classmates the meaning of these abbreviations.

Example: LOL
STUDENT A: What does *LOL* mean?
STUDENT B: *LOL* means "laughing out loud."

1. TTYL
2. BTW
3. ROTFL
4. IMO
5. IMHO
6. TYT
7. ILY
8. XOXO
9. OMW
10. GTG

---

*A preposition may come at the beginning of a question in very formal English:
  About whom (NOT **who**) is *Tina talking*?
In everyday English, a preposition usually does not come at the beginning of a question.

EXERCISE 17 ▶ Let's talk: interview. (Chart 5-3)

Walk around the room and ask your classmates questions with **Who** or **What**.

Example: _____ are you currently reading?
STUDENT A: What are you currently reading?
STUDENT B: A book about a cowboy.

1. _____ do you like to do in your free time?
2. _____ is your idea of the perfect vacation?
3. _____ is your best friend?
4. _____ was an important teacher from your childhood?
5. _____ stresses you out?
6. _____ do you need that you don't have?
7. _____ would you most like to invite to dinner? Why? (*The person can be living or dead.*)

EXERCISE 18 ▶ Listening. (Charts 5-2 and 5-3)

Listen to the conversation. Listen again and complete the sentences with the words you hear.

A Secret

A: John told me something.

B: _____ tell you?
                    1

A: It's confidential. I can't tell you.

B: _____ anyone else?
                    2

A: He told a few other people.

B: _____ tell?
                    3

A: Some friends.

B: Then it's not a secret. _____ say?
                                         4

A: I can't tell you.

B: _____ can't _____ me?
         5   6

A: Because it's about you. But don't worry. It's nothing bad.

B: Gee. Thanks a lot. That sure makes me feel better.

EXERCISE 19 ▶ Reading, grammar, and speaking. (Charts 5-2 and 5-3)

Read the passage about Nina's birthday. Make questions with the given words. Answer the questions with a partner, in small groups, or as a class.

The Birthday Present

Tom got home late last night, around midnight. His wife, Nina, was sitting on the couch waiting for him. She was quite worried because Tom is never late.

Tomorrow is Nina's birthday. Unfortunately, Tom doesn't think she will be happy with her birthday present. Yesterday, Tom bought her a bike, and he decided to ride it home from the bike shop. While he was riding down a hill, a driver came too close to him, and he landed in a ditch. Tom was OK, but the bike wasn't. Tom walked to a bus stop nearby and finally got home.

Tom told Nina the story, but Nina didn't care about the bike. She said she had a better present: her husband.

Do you know these words?
- couch
- landed
- quite
- ditch

1. When \ Tom \ get home
2. Where \ be \ his wife
3. What \ Tom \ buy
4. Why \ be \ Tom \ late
5. What present \ Nina \ get

EXERCISE 20 ▶ Warm-up. (Chart 5-4)

Answer the questions with information about yourself.

1. What do you do on weekends? I …
2. What did you do last weekend? I …
3. What are you going to do this weekend? I'm going to …
4. What will you do the following weekend? I will …

5-4 Using *What* + a Form of *Do*

Question	Answer	
(a) What **does** Bob **do** every morning?	He *goes to class.*	**What** + a form of **do** is used to ask questions about activities.
(b) What **did** you **do** yesterday?	*I went downtown.*	
(c) What **is** Anna **doing** (right now)?	*She's studying.*	Examples of forms of **do**: *am doing, will do, are going to do, did*, etc.
(d) What **are** you **going to do** tomorrow?	*I'm going to go to the beach.*	
(e) What **do** you **want to do** tonight?	*I want to go to a movie.*	In (g): *What do you do?* has a special meaning. It means *What is your occupation, your job?* Another way of asking the same question: *What do you do for a living?*
(f) What **would** you **like to do** tomorrow?	*I would like to visit Jim.*	
(g) What **do** you **do**?	*I'm a software engineer.*	

EXERCISE 21 ▶ Looking at grammar. (Chart 5-4)

Make questions beginning with ***What*** + a form of ***do***.

1. A: _____*What are you doing*_____ right now?
   B: I'm working on a monthly budget.
2. A: _____ last night?
   B: I paid my bills.

3. A: _____ tomorrow?
   B: I'm going to go run a lot of errands.

4. A: _____ tomorrow?
   B: I want to go to the beach.

5. A: _____ this evening?
   B: I would like to go to a movie.

6. A: _____ in your business classes?
   B: We do a lot of project work in small groups.

7. A: _____ for your next vacation?
   B: I'm staying home and relaxing. My wife has to work.

8. A: _____ (for a living)?
   B: My wife is a teacher. She teaches first grade.

EXERCISE 22 ▸ Let's talk: interview. (Chart 5-4)

Interview your classmates. Make questions with the given words and **What** + a form of **do**. More than one verb tense may be possible. Share a few of your classmates' answers with the class.

Example: tomorrow
STUDENT A: What are you going to do tomorrow? / What do you want to do tomorrow? / What would you like to do tomorrow? / Etc.
STUDENT B: I'm going to buy a new video game. / I want to buy a new video game. / I'd like to buy a new video game. / Etc.

1. last night
2. right now
3. next Saturday
4. this afternoon
5. tonight
6. last weekend
7. after class yesterday
8. every morning
9. since you arrived in this city
10. on weekends

EXERCISE 23 ▸ Warm-up. (Chart 5-5)

Answer the questions about ice cream. Use the flavors in the box or your own words.

| blackberry | chocolate | coffee | lemon | strawberry |
| caramel | coconut | green tea | mint | vanilla |

1. Which ice-cream flavors are popular in your country?
2. What kind of ice cream do you like?

132 CHAPTER 5

5-5 Which vs. What and What Kind Of

Which

(a) JOE: May I borrow a pen from you?
    MIA: Sure. I have two pens. This pen has black ink. That pen has red ink.
    Which pen do you want? OR
    Which one do you want? OR
    Which do you want?

In (a): Mia uses **which** (not **what**) because she wants Joe to choose.

Which is used when the speaker wants someone to make a choice, when the speaker is offering alternatives: *this one or that one; these or those.*

(b) AMY: I like these earrings, and I like those too.
    ZAC: **Which (earrings / ones)** are you going to buy?
    AMY: I think I'll get these.

Which can be used with either singular or plural nouns.

(c) LEO: Here's a photo of my daughter's class.
    TIA: Very nice. **Which one** is your daughter?

Which can be used to ask about people as well as things.

(d) JAN: My aunt gave me some money for my birthday. I'm going to take it with me to the mall.
    MAX: **What** are you going to buy with it?
    JAN: I haven't decided yet.

In (d): The question doesn't involve choosing from a particular group of items, so Max uses **what**, not **which**.

What Kind Of

QUESTION	ANSWER	
(e) **What kind of** shoes did you buy?	Boots. Sandals. Tennis shoes. Loafers. Running shoes. High heels. Clogs. Etc.	**What kind of** asks for information about a specific type (a specific kind) in a general category. In (e): general category = shoes specific kinds = boots sandals tennis shoes etc.
(f) **What kind of** fruit do you like best?	Apples. Bananas. Oranges. Grapefruit. Strawberries. Etc.	In (f): general category = fruit specific kinds = apples bananas oranges etc.

EXERCISE 24 ▶ Looking at grammar. (Chart 5-5)

Make questions beginning with **Which** or **What**.

1. A: I have two books. *Which book / Which one / Which do you want?*

   B: That one. (I want that book.)

2. A: *What did you buy when you went shopping?*

   B: A book. (I bought a book when I went shopping.)

Asking Questions 133

3. A: Could I borrow your pen for a minute?

   B: Sure. I have two. _____

   A: That one. (I would like that one.)

4. A: _____

   B: A pen. (Hassan borrowed a pen from me.)

5. A: _____

   B: Two pieces of hard candy. (I have two pieces of hard candy in my hand.) Would you like one?

   A: Yes. Thanks.

   B: _____

   A: The yellow one. (I'd like the yellow one.)

6. A: _____ the most in South America?

   B: Peru and Brazil. (I enjoyed Peru and Brazil the most.) I have family there.

EXERCISE 25 ▶ Let's talk: interview. (Chart 5-5)
Complete the questions with an appropriate word in the box. Then interview classmates. Write their answers and share some with the class.

animals	electronics	movies	podcasts	social media
desserts	ice cream	music	school subjects	TV shows

1. What kind of _____ do you like to listen to?

   STUDENT 1: _____

   STUDENT 2: _____

2. What kind of _____ do you like to watch?

   STUDENT 1: _____

   STUDENT 2: _____

3. What kind of _____ do you like to eat?

   STUDENT 1: _____

   STUDENT 2: _____

4. What kind of _____ do you use the most?

   STUDENT 1: _____

   STUDENT 2: _____

5. What kind of _____ do you know a lot about?

   STUDENT 1: _____

   STUDENT 2: _____

EXERCISE 26 ▶ Warm-up. (Chart 5-6)
Match each question with the correct answer.

1. How tall is your sister? _____
2. How old is your brother? _____
3. How did you get here? _____
4. How soon do we need to go? _____
5. How well do you know Kazu? _____

a. By bus.
b. In five minutes.
c. I don't know him at all. I only know his sister.
d. Fifteen.
e. Five feet (1.52 meters).

5-6 Using *How*

Question	Answer	
(a) ***How*** did you get here?	I drove. / By car. I took a taxi. / By taxi. I took a bus. / By bus. I flew. / By plane. I took a train. / By train. I walked. / On foot.	***How*** has many uses. One use of ***how*** is to ask about means (ways) of transportation.
(b) ***How old*** are you? (c) ***How tall*** is he? (d) ***How big*** is your apartment? (e) ***How sleepy*** are you? (f) ***How hungry*** are you? (g) ***How soon*** will you be ready? (h) ***How well*** does he speak English? (i) ***How quickly*** can you get here?	Twenty-one. About six feet (1.83 meters). It has three rooms. Very sleepy. I'm starving. In five minutes. Very well. I can get there in 30 minutes.	***How*** is often used with adjectives (e.g., *old, big*) and adverbs (e.g., *well, quickly*).

EXERCISE 27 ▶ Reading and grammar. (Chart 5-6)
Read the passage about John and then answer the questions.

Long John

John is 14 years old. He is very tall for his age. He is 6 foot, 6 inches (2 meters). His friends call him "Long John." People are surprised to find out that he is still a teenager. Both his parents are average height, so John's height seems unusual.

It causes problems for him, especially when he travels. Beds in hotels are too short, and there is never enough leg room on airplanes. He is very uncomfortable. When he can, he prefers to take a train because he can walk around and stretch his legs. But John has an advantage over his friends. He's already a great basketball player.

1. How tall is John? _____.
2. How old is John? _____.

3. How well do you think he sleeps in hotels? _____.
4. How comfortable is he on airplanes? _____.
5. How does he like to travel? _____.

EXERCISE 28 ▶ Looking at grammar. (Chart 5-6)
Make questions with ***How***.

1. A: <u>*How old is your daughter?*</u>
   B: Ten. (My daughter is ten years old.)
2. A: _____
   B: Very important. (Education is very important.)
3. A: _____
   B: By bus. (I get to school by bus.)
4. A: _____
   B: Very, very deep. (The ocean is very, very deep.)
5. A: _____
   B: By plane. (I'm going to get to Buenos Aires by plane.)
6. A: _____
   B: Not very. (The test wasn't very difficult.)
7. A: _____
   B: I ran. (I ran here.)
8. A: _____
   B: In an hour. (We are going to get there in an hour.)
9. A: _____
   B: On foot. (I'll walk to your house.)
10. A: _____
    B: It's 29,029 feet high. (Mount Everest is 29,029 feet high.)*

*29,029 feet = 8,848 meters

EXERCISE 29 ▸ Listening. (Chart 5-6)
Complete the conversations with the words you hear.

1. A: _____ are these eggs?
   B: I just bought them at the farmers' market, so they should be fine.

2. A: _____ were the tickets?
   B: They were 50% off.

3. A: _____ was the driver's test?
   B: Well, I didn't pass, so that gives you an idea.

4. A: _____ is the car?
   B: There's dirt on the floor. We need to vacuum it inside.

5. A: _____ is the frying pan?
   B: Don't touch it! You'll burn yourself.

6. A: _____ is the street you live on?
   B: There is a lot of traffic, so we keep the windows closed a lot.

7. A: _____ are you about interviewing for the job?
   B: Very. I already scheduled an interview with the company.

EXERCISE 30 ▸ Let's talk: pairwork. (Charts 5-1 → 5-6)
Work with a partner. Create a conversation between a parent and teenager. You can write any questions that make sense. Practice your conversation, and present it to the class. You can look at your book before you speak. When you speak, look at your partner.

Parent to Teen

A: _____?
B: We're not sure. Maybe we'll go to a movie.

A: _____?
B: My friends.

A: _____?
B: Not too late. Probably around 11:00.

A: _____?
B: We'll take the subway.

A: _____?
B: Because you're asking me so many questions!
A: That's my job. I'm your parent!

EXERCISE 31 ▶ Warm-up: trivia. (Chart 5-7)
Match each question with the best answer.*

1. How often does the earth go completely around the sun? _____
2. How often do the summer Olympics occur? _____
3. How often do earthquakes occur? _____
4. How many times a year can a healthy person safely donate blood? _____
5. How many times a day do the hour and minute hands on a clock overlap? _____

a. About six times a year.
b. Several hundred times a day.
c. Once a year.
d. Every four years.
e. Exactly 22 times a day.

5-7 Using How Often / How Many Times

Question	Answer	
(a) **How often** do you go shopping?	Every day. Once a week. About twice a week. Every other day or so.* Three times a month.	**How often** asks about frequency.
(b) **How many times a day** do you eat?	Three or four.	Other ways of asking **how often**:
How many times a week do you go shopping?	Two.	**how many times** { a day, a week, a month, a year
How many times a month do you go to the post office?	Once.	
How many times a year do you take a vacation?	Once or twice.	
Frequency Expressions a lot occasionally once in a while not very often hardly ever almost never never	every every other once a twice a three times a ten times a } day / week / month / year	

Every other day means "Monday yes, Tuesday no, Wednesday yes, Thursday no," etc. *Or so* means "approximately."

*See *Trivia Answers*, p. 449.

138 CHAPTER 5

EXERCISE 32 ▸ Let's talk: pairwork. (Chart 5-7)

Work with a partner. Take turns asking and answering questions with *How often* or *How many times a day/week/month/year*.

Example: eat lunch at the cafeteria
PARTNER A: How often/many times a week do you eat lunch at the cafeteria?
PARTNER B: About twice a week. How about you? How often do you eat at the cafeteria?
PARTNER A: I don't. I bring my own lunch.

1. check email
2. listen to podcasts
3. go out to eat
4. cook your own dinner
5. buy a toothbrush
6. take selfies
7. attend weddings
8. stream music from the internet

EXERCISE 33 ▸ Listening. (Charts 5-6 and 5-7)

Read the information about Ben. Then complete the questions with the words you hear.

Ben's Sleeping Problem

Ben has a problem with insomnia. He's unable to fall asleep at night very easily. He also wakes up often in the middle of the night and has trouble getting back to sleep. Right now he's talking to a nurse at a sleep disorders clinic. The nurse is asking him some general questions.

1. _____ you?
2. _____ you?
3. _____ you weigh?
4. In general, _____ you sleep at night?
5. _____ you fall asleep?
6. _____ you wake up during the night?
7. _____ you in the mornings?
8. _____ you exercise?
9. _____ you feeling right now?
10. _____ you come in for an overnight appointment?

EXERCISE 34 ▶ Warm-up. (Chart 5-8)
Look at the map and answer the questions about flying distances to these cities.

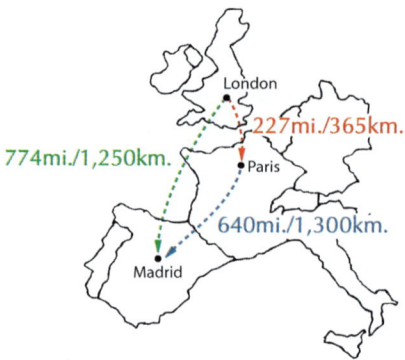

1. How far is it from London to Madrid?
2. How many miles is it from London to Paris?
3. How many kilometers is it from Paris to Madrid?

5-8 Talking About Distance

(a) *It is* 489 miles *from* Oslo *to* Helsinki by air.*	The most common way of expressing distance: *It is* + distance + *from/to* + *to/from*
(b) *It is* 3,605 miles { *from* Moscow *to* Beijing. *from* Beijing *to* Moscow. *to* Beijing *from* Moscow. *to* Moscow *from* Beijing. }	In (b): All four expressions with *from* and *to* have the same meaning.
(c) — *How far is it* from Mumbai to Delhi? — 725 miles. (d) — *How far do you* live from school? — Four blocks.	*How far* is used to ask questions about distance.
(e) *How many miles* is it from London to Paris? (f) *How many kilometers* is it to Montreal from here? (g) *How many blocks* is it to the post office?	Other ways to ask *how far*: • how many miles • how many kilometers • how many blocks

*1 mile = 1.60 kilometers; 1 kilometer = 0.621 mile

EXERCISE 35 ▶ Looking at grammar. (Chart 5-8)
Make questions with **How far** or **How many**.

1. A: <u>How far / How many miles is it from Prague to Budapest?</u>
   B: 276 miles. (It's 276 miles to Prague from Budapest.)

2. A: _____
   B: 257 kilometers. (It's 257 kilometers from Montreal to Quebec.)

3. A: _____
   B: Six blocks. (It's six blocks from here to the post office.)

4. A: _____
   B: A few miles. (It's a few miles from work to here.)

EXERCISE 36 ▶ Grammar and speaking. (Chart 5-8)
Ask about distances between major cities. Write four questions. Use this model: **How far is it from (__) to (__)?** Look up the correct distances in miles and kilometers. Ask other students your questions, and have them guess the answers.

Example: Cairo (Egypt) \ New Delhi (India) Answer: (4,438 km/2,758 miles)
STUDENT A: How far is it from Cairo to New Delhi?
STUDENT B: It's 4,000 kilometers.
STUDENT A: Almost!/Not bad!/Pretty good! It's about 4,400 kilometers.

EXERCISE 37 ▶ Warm-up. (Chart 5-9)
Complete the sentences. Then ask classmates about their weekday routine. Begin with **How long does it take you to**. Share some of their answers with the class.

1. It takes me _____ minutes to get ready for bed.
2. It takes me _____ minutes to brush my teeth.
3. It usually takes me _____ minutes/hour(s) to fall asleep.
4. It takes me _____ minutes/hour(s) to get ready in the morning.
5. It takes me _____ minutes/hour(s) to get to school.

5-9 Length of Time: *It + Take* and *How Long; How Many*

IT + TAKE + (SOMEONE) + LENGTH OF TIME + INFINITIVE					***It + take*** is often used with time words and an infinitive to express *length of time*, as in (a) and (b). An infinitive = ***to*** + *the simple form of a verb.** In (a): ***to cook*** is an infinitive.
(a)	It	takes		20 minutes	***to cook*** rice.
(b)	It	took	Al	two hours	***to drive*** to work.

(c) ***How long*** does it take to cook rice? Twenty minutes. (d) ***How long*** did it take Al to drive to work today? Two hours. (e) ***How long*** did you study last night? Four hours. (f) ***How long*** will you be in Hong Kong? Ten days.	***How long*** asks about *length of time*.
(g) ***How many days*** will you be in Hong Kong?	Other ways of asking ***how long:*** **how many** + { minutes / hours / days / weeks / months / years }

*See Chart 13-3, p. 374.

EXERCISE 38 ▶ Let's talk: pairwork. (Chart 5-9)
Work with a partner. Take turns asking and answering questions using *it + take*. Share a few of your answers with the class.

1. How long does it take you to …
   a. eat breakfast? → *It takes me ten minutes to eat breakfast.*
   b. take a shower?
   c. get to class?
   d. write a short paragraph in English?
   e. read a 300-page book?
   f. clean your room?

2. In general, how long does it take to …
   a. fly from (*a city*) to (*a city*)?
   b. get from here to your hometown?
   c. get used to living in a foreign country?
   d. get a visa?
   e. commute from (*a local place*) to (*a local place*) during rush hour?
   f. learn English well?

EXERCISE 39 ▶ Looking at grammar. (Chart 5-9)
Part I. Make questions with *How many*.

1. A: _____
   B: Five days. (It took me five days to drive to Istanbul.)
2. A: _____
   B: A week. (Mr. McNally will be in the hospital for a week.)
3. A: _____
   B: Six months. (I've been living here for six months.)

Part II. Make questions with *How long*.

4. A: _____
   B: Ten years. (I lived in Oman for six years.)
5. A: _____
   B: A long time. (It takes a long time to learn a second language.)
6. A: _____
   B: A couple of years. (I've known Mr. Pham for a couple of years.)
7. A: _____
   B: Since 2005. (He's been living in Canada since 2005.)

EXERCISE 40 ▶ Warm-up: listening. (Chart 5-10)
Listen to the questions. The question words and verbs in green are contracted. Choose the correct verb in the box for each question.

does	did	is	are	will

A Birthday

1. **When's** your birthday? _____
2. **When'll** your party be? _____
3. **Where'd** you decide to have it? _____
4. **Who're** you inviting? _____

5-10 Spoken and Written Contractions with Question Words

		Spoken	
is	(a)	"*When's* he coming?" "*Why's* she late?"	**Is, are, does, did, has, have,** and **will** are often contracted with question words in spoken English.
are	(b)	"*What're* these?" "*Who're* they talking to?"	
does	(c)	"*When's* the movie start?" "*Where's* he live?"	
did	(d)	"*Who'd* you see?" "*What'd* you do?"	
has	(e)	"*What's* she done?" "*Where's* he gone?"	
have	(f)	"*How've* you been?" "*What've* I done?"	
will	(g)	"*Where'll* you be?" "*When'll* they be here?"	
	(h)	*What do you* → *Whaddaya* think?	***What do you*** and ***What are you*** both can be reduced to ***Whaddaya*** in informal speech.
	(i)	*What are you* → *Whaddaya* thinking?	
		Written	
is	(j)	*Where's* Ed? *What's* that? *Who's* he?	Only contractions with **where, what,** or **who** + **is** are commonly used in writing — in text messages and emails, for example. They are generally not appropriate in more formal writing, such as in magazine articles or reference material.

Asking Questions 143

EXERCISE 41 ▸ Listening. (Chart 5-10)
Listen to the contractions in these questions.

1. Where is my key?
2. Where are my keys?
3. Who are those people?
4. What is in that box?
5. What are you doing?
6. Where did Bob go last night?
7. Who will be at the party?
8. Why is the teacher absent?
9. Who is that?
10. Why did you say that?
11. Who did you talk to at the party?
12. How are we going to get to work?
13. What did you say?
14. How will you do that?

EXERCISE 42 ▸ Grammar and listening. (Chart 5-10)
Write the full form of the verb in the contractions: *is*, *are*, *does*, *did*, and *will*. Then listen to the sentences and note the pronunciation of the contractions.

On an Airplane

Examples: You will hear: When's the plane taking off?
           You will write: ___is___

           You will hear: When's the plane land?
           You will write: ___does___

1. Who're you going to sit with? _____
2. How're you going to get your bag under the seat? _____
3. What'd the flight attendant just say? _____
4. Why'd we need to put our seat belts back on? _____
5. Why's the plane descending? _____
6. Why's the flight attendant look worried? _____
7. When'll the pilot tell us what's going on? _____
8. Why're we landing now? _____
9. Who'll meet you when you land? _____
10. When's our connecting flight? _____
11. How'll we get from the airport to our hotel? _____

EXERCISE 43 ▶ Listening. (Chart 5-10)
Complete the questions with the words you hear. Write the non-contracted or non-reduced forms.

A Mother Talking to Her Teenage Daughter

1. _____ going?
2. _____ going with?
3. _____ that?
4. _____ known him?
5. _____ meet him?
6. _____ go to school?
7. _____ a good student?
8. _____ be back?
9. _____ wearing that outfit?
10. _____ giving me that look?
11. _____ asking so many questions?

Because I love you!

EXERCISE 44 ▶ Listening. (Chart 5-10)
Listen to the questions and circle the correct non-reduced forms of the words you hear.

Example: You will hear: Whaddaya want?
　　　　　You will choose: What are you　(What do you)

1. What are you　　What do you　　5. What are you　　What do you
2. What are you　　What do you　　6. What are you　　What do you
3. What are you　　What do you　　7. What are you　　What do you
4. What are you　　What do you　　8. What are you　　What do you

EXERCISE 45 ▶ Warm-up. (Chart 5-11)
Part I. Both sentences in each pair are grammatically correct. Which question in each pair do you think is more common in spoken English?

1. a. How do you spell *Hawaii*?
   b. What is the spelling for *Hawaii*?

2. a. How do you pronounce G-A-R-A-G-E?
   b. What is the pronunciation for G-A-R-A-G-E?

Part II. Which two questions have the same meaning?

1. How are you doing?
2. How's it going?
3. How do you do?

5-11 More Questions with *How*

Question		Answer	
(a) *How do you spell* "coming"?		C-O-M-I-N-G.	To answer (a): Spell the word.
(b) *How do you say* "yes" in Japanese?		Hai.	To answer (b): Say the word.
(c) *How do you say / pronounce* this word?		_____	To answer (c): Pronounce the word.
(d) *How are you getting along?*	Great.		In (d), (e), and (f): How is your life? Is your life OK? Do you have any problems?
(e) *How are you doing?*	Fine.		
(f) *How's it going?*	OK.		NOTE: Example (f) is also used in greetings: *Hi, Bob. How's it going?*
	So-so.		
(g) *How do you feel?* *How are you feeling?*	Terrific! Wonderful! Great! Fine. OK. So-so. A bit under the weather. Not so good. Terrible! / Lousy. / Awful!		The questions in (g) ask about health or about general emotional state.
(h) *How do you do?*		How do you do?	In (h): *How do you do?* is used by two speakers when they meet each other for the first time in a very formal situation.*

*A: *Dr. Erickson, I'd like to introduce you to a friend of mine, Rick Brown. Rick, this is my biology professor, Dr. Erickson.*
B: **How do you do,** *Mr. Brown?*
C: **How do you do,** *Dr. Erickson? I'm pleased to meet you.*

EXERCISE 46 ▶ Game. (Chart 5-11)

Divide into teams. Take turns spelling the words your teacher gives you. The team with the most correct answers wins. Your book is closed.

Example: country
TEACHER: How do you spell *country*?
TEAM A: C-O-U-N-T-R-Y.
TEACHER: Good.
  (*If the answer is incorrect, another team tries.*)

1. together
2. people
3. daughter
4. beautiful
5. foreign
6. neighbor
7. happened
8. awful
9. beginning
10. intelligent
11. Mississippi
12. purple
13. rained
14. different
15. wonderful
16. computer

EXERCISE 47 ▶ Let's talk. (Chart 5-11)

Walk around the room and ask your classmates how to say each word or phrase in another language (Japanese, Arabic, German, French, Korean, etc.). If someone doesn't know, ask another person. Use this question: **How do you say** (___) **in** (___)?

Example:
STUDENT: A: How do you say *yes* in French?
STUDENT: B: *Yes* in French is *oui*.

1. No.
2. Thank you.
3. OK.
4. How are you?
5. Good-bye.
6. Excuse me.

EXERCISE 48 ▶ Let's talk: interview. (Chart 5-11)

Walk around the room. Interview your classmates. Practice the following questions: **How are you doing? / How's it going? / How do you feel? / How are you feeling?** Use the answers in Chart 5-11, section (g).

EXERCISE 49 ▶ Warm-up. (Chart 5-12)

In the conversation, the speakers are making suggestions. <u>Underline</u> their suggestions.

A: Let's invite the Thompsons over for dinner.

B: Good idea! How about next Sunday?

A: Let's do it sooner. What about this Saturday?

5-12 Using *How About* and *What About*

(a) A: We need one more player. B: *How about / What about Jack?* Let's ask him if he wants to play.	*How about* and *what about* have the same meaning and usage. They are used to make suggestions or offers.
(b) A: What time should we meet? B: *How about / What about three o'clock?*	*How about* and *what about* are followed by a noun (or pronoun) or the *-ing* form of a verb (gerund).
(c) A: What should we do this afternoon? B: *How about going* to the zoo?	NOTE: *How about* and *what about* are frequently used in informal spoken English, but are usually not used in writing.
(d) A: *What about asking* Sally over for dinner next Sunday? B: OK. Good idea.	
(e) A: I'm tired. *How about you?* B: Yes, I'm tired too. (f) A: Are you hungry? B: No. *What about you?* A: I'm a little hungry.	*How about you?* and *What about you?* are used to ask a question that refers to the information or question that immediately preceded it. In (e): *How about you?* = Are you tired? In (f): *What about you?* = Are you hungry?

EXERCISE 50 ▶ Grammar and listening. (Chart 5-12)
Choose the best response. Then listen to each conversation and check your answer.

Example:
SPEAKER A: What are you going to do over vacation?
SPEAKER B: I'm staying here. What about you?
SPEAKER A: a. Yes, I will. I have a vacation too.
(b.) I'm going to Jordan to visit my sister.
c. I did too.

1. A: Did you like the movie?
   B: It was OK, I guess. How about you?
   A: a. I thought it was pretty good.
   b. I'm sure.
   c. I saw it last night.

2. A: Are you going to the company party?
   B: I haven't decided yet. What about you?
   A: a. I didn't know that.
   b. Why am I going?
   c. I think I will.

3. A: Do you like living in this city?
   B: Sort of. How about you?
   A: a. I'm living in the city.
   b. I'm not sure. It's pretty noisy.
   c. Yes, I have been.

4. A: What are you going to have?
   B: Well, I'm not really hungry. I think I might just order a salad. How about you?
   A: a. I'll have one too.
   b. I'm eating at a restaurant.
   c. No, I'm not.

EXERCISE 51 ▶ Let's talk: pairwork. (Chart 5-12)
Here are some questions you can use to begin conversations. Use them to make short conversations with a partner. You can look at your book before you speak. When you speak, look at your partner.

Example:
PARTNER A: What kind of movies do you like to watch?
PARTNER B: I like comedies. I like to laugh. How about/What about you?
PARTNER A: Thrillers are my favorite. I just saw (*name of movie*). It was so exciting. Have you seen it?
PARTNER B: Yes, I really enjoyed it. My favorite part was…

1. How long have you been living in (*this city or country*)?
2. What are you going to do after class today?
3. Vacation is coming up soon. What are your plans?

Change roles.

4. How is school/are your classes going for you?
5. How often do you speak English outside of class?
6. How has your day been so far?

EXERCISE 52 ▸ Warm-up. (Chart 5-13)
What is the <u>expected</u> response? Circle *yes* or *no*.

1. You're studying English, aren't you?   Yes.   No.
2. You're not a native speaker of English, are you?   Yes.   No.

5-13 Tag Questions

(a) Jill is sick, ***isn't she?***			A tag question is a question that is added on to the end of a sentence. An auxiliary verb is used in a tag question.
(b) You didn't know, ***did you?***			
(c) There's enough time, ***isn't there?***			
(d) I'm not late, ***am I?***			Note that ***I am*** becomes ***aren't I*** in a negative tag, as in (e). (*Am I not* is also possible, but it is very formal and rare.)
(e) I'm late, ***aren't I?***			

Affirmative (+)	**Negative (−)**	**Affirmative (+) Expected Answer**	When the main verb is affirmative, the tag question is negative, and the expected answer agrees with the main verb.
(f) *You **know*** Bill,	***don't*** you?	**Yes.**	
(g) *Marie **is*** from Paris,	***isn't*** she?	**Yes.**	

Negative (−)	**Affirmative (+)**	**Negative (−) Expected Answer**	When the main verb is negative, the tag question is affirmative, and the expected answer agrees with the main verb.
(h) *You **don't know*** Tom,	***do*** you?	**No.**	
(i) *Marie **isn't*** from Athens,	***is*** she?	**No.**	

THE SPEAKER'S QUESTION	THE SPEAKER'S IDEA
(j) It will be nice tomorrow, ***won't it?*** ↗	Tag questions have two types of intonation: rising and falling. The intonation determines the meaning of the tag.
	A speaker uses rising intonation to make sure information is correct. In (j): The speaker has an idea; the speaker is checking to see if the idea is correct.
(k) It will be nice tomorrow, ***won't it?*** ↘	Falling intonation is used when the speaker is seeking agreement. In (k): The speaker thinks it will be nice tomorrow and is almost certain the listener will agree.
YES/NO QUESTIONS (l) — Will it be nice tomorrow? — **Yes, it will.** OR **No, it won't.**	In (l): The speaker has no idea. The speaker is simply looking for information. Compare (j) and (k) with (l).

EXERCISE 53 ▸ Listening and grammar. (Chart 5-13)
Listen to each pair of sentences and answer the question.

1. a. You're Mrs. Rose, aren't you?
   b. Are you Mrs. Rose?

   QUESTION: In which sentence is the speaker checking to see if her information is correct?

2. a. Do you take cream with your coffee?
   b. You take cream with your coffee, don't you?

   QUESTION: In which sentence does the speaker have no idea?

3. a. You don't want to leave, do you?
   b. Do you want to leave?

   QUESTION: In which sentence is the speaker looking for agreement?

 EXERCISE 54 ▸ Grammar and listening. (Chart 5-13)
Complete the tag questions with the correct verbs. Then listen to the questions and check your answers.

1. SIMPLE PRESENT
   a. You *like* strong coffee, _____don't_____ you?
   b. David *goes* to Ames High School, _____ he?
   c. Leila and Sara *live* on Tree Road, _____ they?
   d. Jane *has* the keys to the storeroom, _____ she?
   e. Jane*'s* in her office, _____ she?
   f. You*'re* a member of this class, _____ you?
   g. Oleg *doesn't have* a car, _____ he?
   h. Lisa *isn't* from around here, _____ she?
   i. I*'m* in trouble, _____ I?

2. SIMPLE PAST
   a. Paul *went* to Indonesia, _____ he?
   b. You *didn't talk* to the boss, _____ you?
   c. Ted's parents *weren't* at home, _____ they?
   d. That *was* Pat's idea, _____ it?

3. PRESENT PROGRESSIVE, BE GOING TO, AND PAST PROGRESSIVE
   a. You*'re studying* hard, _____ you?
   b. Greg *isn't working* at the bank, _____ he?
   c. It *isn't going to rain* today, _____ it?
   d. Michelle and Yoko *were helping*, _____ they?
   e. He *wasn't listening*, _____ he?

4. PRESENT PERFECT
   a. It *has been* warmer than usual, _____ it?
   b. You*'ve had* a lot of homework, _____ you?
   c. We *haven't spent* much time together, _____ we?

d. Fatima *has started* her new job, _____ she?

e. Bruno *hasn't finished* his sales report yet, _____ he?

f. Steve's *had to leave* early, _____ he?

EXERCISE 55 ▶ Let's talk: pairwork. (Chart 5-13)
Work with a partner. Make true statements for your partner to agree with. Remember, if your partner makes an affirmative statement before the tag, the expected answer is *yes*. If your partner makes a negative statement before the tag, the expected answer is *no*.

1. The weather is _____ today, isn't it?
2. This book costs _____, doesn't it?
3. I'm _____, aren't I?
4. The classroom isn't _____, is it?
5. Our grammar homework wasn't _____, was it?
6. Tomorrow will be _____, won't it?

EXERCISE 56 ▶ Listening. (Chart 5-13)
Listen to the tag questions and choose the <u>expected responses</u>.

Checking in at a Hotel

Example: You will hear: Our room's ready, isn't it?
You will choose: (Yes.)   No.

1. Yes.   No.   6. Yes.   No.
2. Yes.   No.   7. Yes.   No.
3. Yes.   No.   8. Yes.   No.
4. Yes.   No.   9. Yes.   No.
5. Yes.   No.   10. Yes.   No.

EXERCISE 57 ▶ Reading and speaking. (Chapter 5 Review)

Part I. Read the blog entry by co-author Stacy Hagen.

> Do you know these words?
> - casual
> - challenging
> - acceptable
> - politics
> - likely

BlackBookBlog

Small Talk

Small talk (light casual conversation for informal situations) can be challenging in any language, but it is particularly difficult for nonnative speakers. Every culture has topics that are acceptable for small talk. In English-speaking countries, it is common to talk about the weather. This is a very safe topic. An unsafe topic would be politics. People can have strong feelings about political topics and may get into arguments.

Here are some common conversation starters about the weather:
    Beautiful day, isn't it?
    Have you ever seen so much rain/snow/ice?
    Are you enjoying this beautiful day/sunny day/sunshine?
    I'm really enjoying the sun this week. How about you?

A helpful hint is to always add a detail when you answer. This will help keep the conversation going. For example:

    A: Beautiful day, isn't?
    B: Yes, I'm really enjoying the sunshine. <u>I'm not from here, and this much sun is a nice surprise</u>.

OR

    A: Have you ever seen so much snow?
    B: No, I haven't. But it's really fun. <u>I'm going to go sledding tomorrow with some friends.</u>

Note that Speaker B added the detail "I'm not from here, … " or "I'm going to go sledding tomorrow with some friends." It's very likely that Speaker A will ask in response, "Oh, where are you from?" or "Where are you going sledding?" This will take the conversation in a new direction.

It is a good idea to practice small-talk starters so you can get better at them. It will help you feel more comfortable when you want to start a conversation with someone for the first time.

Part II. Look outside at the weather. Write three conversation starters about the weather. Use at least one tag question. Then work with a partner and create a short conversation for each. Remember to add a detail in Partner B's first response. Share one of your conversations with the class.

A: _____

B: _____

A: _____

B: _____

EXERCISE 58 ▶ Listening and speaking. (Chapter 5 Review)

Part I. Listen to the conversation. A customer is ordering at a fast-food restaurant.

Ordering at a Fast-Food Restaurant

Part II. Work with a partner. Take turns being the cashier and the customer. Complete the sentences with items from the menu and practice your conversation.

burger	chicken strips	soft drinks: *cola, lemon soda, iced tea*
cheeseburger	fish burger	milkshakes: *vanilla, strawberry, chocolate*
double cheeseburger	veggie burger	(*small, medium, large*)
fries	salad	

CASHIER: So, what'll it be?
CUSTOMER: I'll have a _____.
CASHIER: Would you like fries or a salad with your burger?
CUSTOMER: I'll have (a) _____.
CASHIER: What size?
CUSTOMER: _____.
CASHIER: Anything to drink?
CUSTOMER: I'll have a _____.
CASHIER: Size?
CUSTOMER: _____.
CASHIER: OK. So that's _____
_____.
CUSTOMER: About how long'll it take?
CASHIER: We're pretty crowded right now. Probably 10 minutes or so. That'll be $6.50. Your number's on the receipt. I'll call the number when your order's ready.
CUSTOMER: Thanks.

EXERCISE 59 ▶ Check your knowledge. (Chapter 5 Review)
Correct the errors in question formation.

1. Who you saw? → *Who did you see?*

2. Where I buy subway tickets?

3. What for you are leaving?

4. What kind of tea you like best?

5. It's freezing out, and you're not wearing gloves, aren't you?

6. Who you studied with at school?

7. She is going to work this weekend, doesn't she?

8. How long take to get to the airport from here?

9. How much height your father have?

10. It's midnight. Why you so late? Why you forget to call?

EXERCISE 60 ▶ Writing (Chapter 5)
Part I. Read the text messages. Note the variety of questions in J's response.

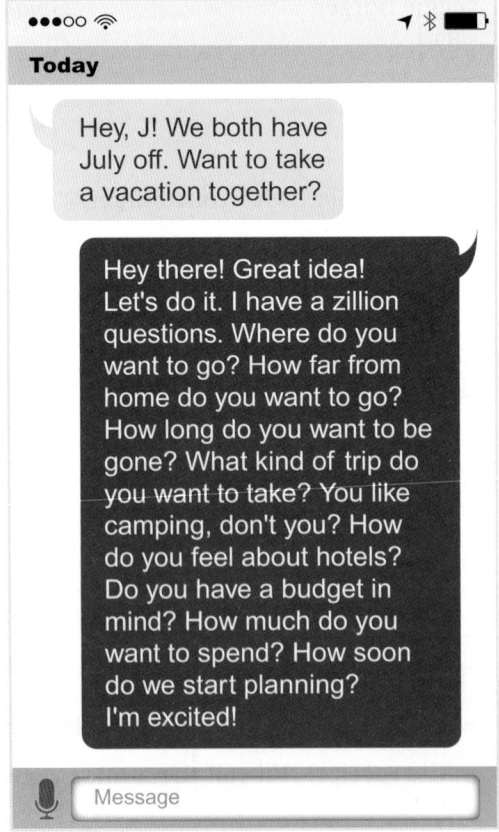

Part II. Imagine that you are going to visit a friend in another country. You decide the country — one you have never visited. What kinds of things do you need to know before you go? Respond to your friend's text message and ask a variety of questions.

> ### WRITING TIP
>
> It is easy to confuse *what* and *how* when you write or ask questions. Since you are probably more familiar with *what* questions, here are some general guidelines for *how* questions:
>
> 1. *How* is used with adjectives or adverbs:
>
>   How + far / tall / old / fast / cold / often / long / soon / late / big / much / many
>
>   How far do you want to go?
>   How soon do you want to leave?
>
> 2. *How* is used in greetings and to ask for opinions:
>
>   How are you doing?
>   How have you been?
>   How do you feel about … ?
>   How do you like … ?
>
> 3. *How* is used for weather and transportation:
>
>   How is the weather?
>   How will we get there?
>
> Watch out for these commonly confused questions with *how* and *what*:
>
> | | | | |
> |---|---|---|---|
> | CORRECT: | How do you know? | INCORRECT: | Why do you know? |
> | CORRECT: | What do you think? | INCORRECT: | How do you think? |
> | CORRECT: | What do you call this? | INCORRECT: | How do you call this? |

Part III. Edit your writing. Check for the following:

1. ☐ correct question word order
2. ☐ correct use of helping verbs in questions
3. ☐ correct use of *what* and *how* in questions
4. ☐ use of different question types
5. ☐ correct spelling (use a dictionary or spell-check)

▪▪▪▪▪ For digital resources, go to MyEnglishLab on the Pearson English Portal. You can also go to the Pearson Practice English app for mobile practice.

CHAPTER 6
Nouns and Pronouns

PRETEST: What do I already know?
Write "C" if the **boldfaced** words are correct and "I" if they are incorrect.

1. _____ There are many interesting **citys** in Asia. (Chart 6-1)
2. _____ My mom and grandma are very strong **women**. (Chart 6-1)
3. _____ **Shines the sun**. (Chart 6-3)
4. _____ I left your **phone the kitchen counter**. (Chart 6-4)
5. _____ I study English **in the night**. (Chart 6-5)
6. _____ I left **in 2015 my country**. (Chart 6-6)
7. _____ Every person in the world **needs** love. (Chart 6-7)
8. _____ Montreal and Vancouver are **places beautifuls** to visit. (Chart 6-8)
9. _____ I want to show you my **vegetables garden**. (Chart 6-9)
10. _____ This summer, my friend Mira is going to visit **my sister and me**. (Chart 6-10)
11. _____ The **two brother houses** look identical. (Chart 6-11)
12. _____ **Whose** backpack is this? (Chart 6-12)
13. _____ You have your beliefs, and I have **my**. (Chart 6-13)
14. _____ Greta's husband forgets her birthday, so she buys **herself** a present every year. (Chart 6-14)
15. _____ I brought two oranges. Do you want this one, and I'll have **other** one? (Chart 6-15)
16. _____ Green and red are not my favorite colors. Do you have this shirt in **other** colors?

EXERCISE 1 ▶ Warm-up. (Chart 6-1)
Write *one* if the noun is singular. Write *two* if the noun is plural.

In the Kitchen

1. _____ onion
2. _____ spices
3. _____ tomato
4. _____ berries
5. _____ dishes
6. _____ knives

6-1 Plural Forms of Nouns

Singular	Plural	
(a) one bird one street one rose	two *birds* two *streets* two *roses*	SINGULAR = one PLURAL = more than one To make most nouns plural, add **-s**.
(b) one dish one match one class one box	two *dishes* two *matches* two *classes* two *boxes*	Add **-es** to nouns ending in **-sh**, **-ch**, **-ss**, and **-x**.
(c) one baby one city	two *babies* two *cities*	If a noun ends in a consonant + **-y**, change the **y** to **i** and add **-es**, as in (c).
(d) one toy one key	two *toys* two *keys*	If **-y** is preceded by a vowel, add only **-s**, as in (d).
(e) one knife one shelf	two *knives* two *shelves*	If a noun ends in **-fe** or **-f**, change the ending to **-ves**. EXCEPTIONS: *beliefs, chiefs, roofs, cuffs, cliffs*.
(f) one tomato one zoo one zero	two *tomatoes* two *zoos* two *zeroes/zeros*	The plural form of nouns that end in **-o** is sometimes **-oes** and sometimes **-os**. **-oes**: *tomatoes, potatoes, heroes* **-os**: *zoos, radios, studios, pianos, solos, sopranos, photos, autos, videos* **-oes** or **-os**: *zeroes/zeros, volcanoes/volcanos, tornadoes/tornados, mosquitoes/mosquitos, echoes/echos*
(g) one child one foot one goose one man one mouse one tooth one woman ————	two *children* two *feet* two *geese* two *men* two *mice* two *teeth* two *women* two *people*	Some nouns have irregular plural forms. NOTE: The singular form of *people* can be *person, woman, man, child*. For example, one *man* and one *child* = two *people*. (Two *persons* is also possible, but not very common.)
(h) one deer one fish one sheep	two *deer* two *fish* two *sheep*	Some nouns may have the same singular and plural forms.

EXERCISE 2 ▶ Looking at grammar. (Chart 6-1)
Write the correct singular or plural form for each noun.

1. one chair   two _____chairs_____
2. a _____   a lot of windows
3. one wish   several _____
4. one _____   a lot of sheep

5. a tax   a lot of _____
6. one boy   two _____
7. a hobby   several _____
8. one leaf   two _____
9. a _____   two halves
10. a belief   many _____
11. one wolf   two _____
12. a radio   several _____
13. one _____   two feet
14. an _____   two addresses

EXERCISE 3 ▶ Game. (Chart 6-1)

Work in teams. Write the plural form of each noun under the correct heading. The number of words for each column is in parentheses. NOTE: *fish* and *thief* can go in two places.

✓butterfly	child	hero	mouse	thief
baby	city	library	✓museum	tomato
boy	fish	✓man	potato	woman
✓bean	girl	mosquito	sandwich	zoo

PEOPLE (8)	FOOD (5)	THINGS PEOPLE CATCH (5)	PLACES PEOPLE VISIT (4)
men	beans	butterflies	museums

EXERCISE 4 ▸ Looking at grammar. (Chart 6-1)

Part I. Edit the sign by giving the appropriate nouns their correct plural forms. There are eight errors.

ON SALE
(while supply last)
shirt   jean   pant   dress
Outfit and shoe for babys 50% off

Part II. Imagine you are selling some items online that you don't need any longer. Write an ad and list eight items you would like to sell. Make sure that some of your items are plural.

EXERCISE 5 ▸ Warm-up: listening. (Chart 6-2)

Listen to the nouns. Circle *yes* if you hear a plural ending. If not, circle *no*.

Examples: You will hear: books
You will choose: (yes) no

You will hear: class
You will choose: yes (no)

1. yes no
2. yes no
3. yes no
4. yes no
5. yes no
6. yes no

6-2 Pronunciation of Final -s/-es

Final **-s/-es** has three different pronunciations: /s/, /z/, and /əz/.

(a)	seats = seat/s/ maps = map/s/ lakes = lake/s/	Final **-s** is pronounced /s/ after voiceless sounds. In (a): /s/ is the sound of "s" in *bus*. Examples of voiceless* sounds: /t/, /p/, /k/.	
(b)	seeds = seed/z/ stars = star/z/ holes = hole/z/ laws = law/z/	Final **-s** is pronounced /z/ after voiced sounds. In (b): /z/ is the sound of "z" in *buzz*. Examples of voiced* sounds: /d/, /r/, /l/, /m/, /b/, and all vowel sounds.	
(c)	dishes = dish/əz/ matches = match/əz/ classes = class/əz/ sizes = size/əz/ pages = page/əz/ judges = judge/əz/	Final **-s/-es** is pronounced /əz/ after *-sh, -ch, -s, -z, -ge/-dge* sounds. In (c): /əz/ adds a syllable to a word.	

*See Appendix A-6 for more information about voiceless and voiced sounds.

EXERCISE 6 ▶ Listening. (Chart 6-2)

Listen to the words. Circle the sound you hear at the end of each word: /s/, /z/, or /əz/.

1. pan**ts** /s/ /z/ /əz/
2. ca**rs** /s/ /z/ /əz/
3. box**es** /s/ /z/ /əz/
4. pe**ns** /s/ /z/ /əz/
5. wish**es** /s/ /z/ /əz/
6. lak**es** /s/ /z/ /əz/

EXERCISE 7 ▶ Listening. (Chart 6-2)

Listen to each pair of words. Decide if the endings have the same sound or a different sound.

Examples: You will hear: maps streets
You will choose: (same) different

You will hear: knives forks
You will choose: same (different)

1. same different   5. same different
2. same different   6. same different
3. same different   7. same different
4. same different   8. same different

EXERCISE 8 ▶ Listening and pronunciation. (Chart 6-2)

Listen to the words. Write the pronunciation of each ending you hear: /s/, /z/, or /əz/. After you correct the answers, practice pronouncing the words.

1. names = name/z/
2. clocks = clock/s/
3. eyes = eye/ /
4. boats = boat/ /
5. eyelashes = eyelash/ /
6. ways = way/ /
7. lips = lip/ /
8. bridges = bridge/ /
9. cars = car/ /

EXERCISE 9 ▶ Listening. (Chart 6-2)

Listen to the sentences and circle the words you hear. Practice pronouncing them.

1. size   sizes   3. tax   taxes   5. glass glasses
2. tax   taxes   4. price prices   6. prize prizes

EXERCISE 10 ▶ Warm-up. (Chart 6-3)

Part I. Work in small groups. Make lists about the topic of friendship.

1. What qualities are important in a friendship?
2. Name things you do with friends.
3. What social media do you use to stay connected to friends?

Part II. Complete the sentences with information from Part I. Share some of your sentences with the class.

1. _____ and _____ are important qualities in a friendship.
2. I _____ and _____ with my friends.
3. I use _____ to stay connected to friends.

Part III. Answer these questions about your answers in Part II.

1. In which sentence did you write verbs?
2. In which two sentences did you write nouns?
3. In which sentence did you write subjects?
4. In which sentence did you write objects?

6-3 Subjects, Verbs, and Objects

(a) The	S **sun** (noun)	V **shines**. (verb)	An English sentence has a SUBJECT (S) and a VERB (V). The SUBJECT is a *noun*. In (a): **sun** is a noun; it is the subject of the verb **shines**. NOTE: Some nouns can also be verbs: People **plant** flowers.
(b)	S **Plants** (noun)	V **grow**. (verb)	

(c)	S
	Plants
	(noun)
		V
		need
		(verb)
			O
			water.
			(noun)
				Sometimes a VERB is followed by an OBJECT (O).
				The OBJECT of a verb is a *noun*. In (c): **water** is the object of the verb **need**. An object answers the question *What?*
				     What do plants need?
				     What is Bob reading?

(d)	S **Bob** (noun)	V **is reading** (verb)	O **a book**. (noun)	

EXERCISE 11 ▶ Looking at grammar. (Chart 6-3)
Complete each diagram with the correct subject, verb, and object.

1. Birds sing songs.

Birds	sing	songs
subject	verb	object of verb

2. Birds fly south.

Birds	fly	Ø
subject	verb	object of verb

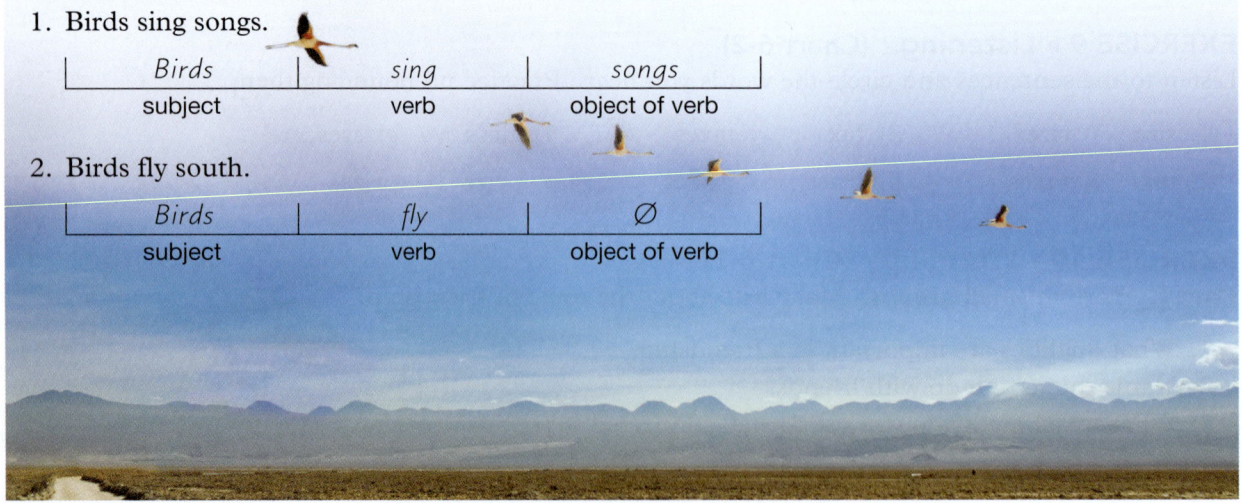

3. Birds build nests.

   | subject | verb | object of verb |

4. The sun heats the earth.

   | subject | verb | object of verb |

5. The sun sets at night.

   | subject | verb | object of verb |

6. The moon rises every evening.

   | subject | verb | object of verb |

7. Fires destroy forests.

   | subject | verb | object of verb |

8. Surprises happen every day.

   | subject | verb | object of verb |

EXERCISE 12 ▶ Looking at grammar. (Chart 6-3)
Write "N" if the word in green is a noun. Write "V" if it is a verb.

1. a. People smile when they're happy. _____
   b. Maryam has a nice smile when she's happy. _____

2. a. Please don't sign your name in pencil. _____
   b. People often name their children after relatives. _____

3. a. Airplanes land on runways at the airport. _____
   b. The land across the street from our house is vacant. _____

4. a. People usually store milk in the refrigerator. _____
   b. We went to the store to buy some milk. _____

5. a. I took the express train from New York to Boston last week. _____
   b. Lindsey trains horses as a hobby. _____

EXERCISE 13 ▶ Warm-up: pairwork. (Chart 6-4)

Work with a partner. Make true sentences about yourself using **like** or **don't like**. Share a few of your partner's answers with the class.

I like/don't like to do my homework …

1. at the library.
2. at the kitchen table.
3. in my bedroom.
4. on my bed.
5. with a friend.
6. in the evening.
7. on weekends.
8. after dinner.
9. before class.
10. during class.

6-4 Objects of Prepositions

	S	V	O	PREP		O OF PREP
(a)	Ann	put	her books	**on**	the	**desk**.
						(noun)

	S	V	PREP		O OF PREP
(b)	A leaf	fell	**to**	the	**ground**.
					(noun)

Many English sentences have prepositional phrases. In (a): **on the desk** is a prepositional phrase.

A prepositional phrase consists of a PREPOSITION (PREP) and an OBJECT OF A PREPOSITION (O of PREP). The object of a preposition is a NOUN.

Reference List of Prepositions

about	before	despite	next to	to
above	behind	down	of	toward(s)
across	below	during	off	under
after	beneath	for	on	until/till*
against	beside	from	out	up
along	besides	in	over	upon
among	between	into	since	with
around	beyond	like	through	within
at	by	near	throughout	without

*Till is a more informal way of saying *until*.

EXERCISE 14 ▶ Looking at grammar. (Chart 6-4)

Check (✓) the prepositional phrases, and underline the noun in each phrase that is the object of the preposition.

1. ✓ across the <u>street</u>
2. ____ in a minute
3. ____ daily
4. ____ down the hill
5. ____ next to the phone
6. ____ doing work
7. ____ in a few hours
8. ____ from my parents

EXERCISE 15 ▶ Looking at grammar. (Charts 6-3 and 6-4)

Check (✓) the sentences that have objects of prepositions. Identify the preposition (P) and the object of the preposition (Obj. of P).

At the Beach

1. a. _____ The wind blew loudly.
                           P   Obj. of P
   b. ✓ The wind blew loudly at the beach.
                                     P   Obj. of P
   c. ✓ The wind pushed the waves onto the beach.

2. a. _____ Emma sat on the beach.
   b. _____ She watched the waves.
   c. _____ She didn't swim in the waves.

3. a. _____ An athletic woman jumped into the water.
   b. _____ She swam in the water.
   c. _____ She swam for an hour.

4. a. _____ Annika dropped her ring.
   b. _____ Annika dropped her ring in the sand.
   c. _____ Annika dropped her ring in the sand at the beach.

EXERCISE 16 ▶ Let's talk. (Chart 6-4)

Review prepositions of place by using each phrase in a complete sentence. Demonstrate the meaning of the preposition with an action while you say the sentence. Work in pairs, in small groups, or as a class.

Example: across the room → I'm walking across the room. OR I'm looking across the room.

1. above the door
2. against the wall
3. toward(s) the door
4. between two pages of my book
5. in the classroom
6. into the classroom
7. on my desk
8. at my desk
9. below the window
10. beside my book
11. near the door
12. far from the door
13. off my desk
14. out the window
15. behind me
16. through the door

EXERCISE 17 ▶ Game: trivia. (Chart 6-4)

Work in small groups. Answer the questions without looking at a map. After you finish, look at a map to check your answers.* The team with the most correct answers wins.

1. Name a country directly under Russia.
2. Name the country directly above Germany.
3. What river flows through London?

---

*See *Trivia Answers*, p. 449.

4. What is a country near Haiti?
5. Name a country next to Vietnam.
6. Name a city far from Sydney, Australia.
7. What is the country between Austria and Switzerland?
8. Name the city within Rome, Italy.
9. Name two countries that have a river between them.
10. Name a country that is across from Saudi Arabia.

EXERCISE 18 ▶ Reading and grammar. (Chart 6-4)
Read the passage and answer the questions.

Do you know these words?
- giant   - snakes
- insects   - frogs
- vines   - gorillas
- ground

THE HABITATS OF A RAIN FOREST

Rain forests have different areas where animals live. These areas are called *habitats*. Scientists have given names to the four main habitats or layers of a rain forest.

Some animals live in the tops of giant trees. The tops of these trees are much higher than the other trees, so this layer is called the *emergent* layer.* Many birds and insects live there.

← emergent layer

← canopy

← understory

← forest floor

Under the emergent layer is the *canopy*. The canopy is the upper part of the trees. It is thick with leaves and vines, and it forms an umbrella over the rain forest. Most of the animals in the rain forest live in the canopy.

The next layer is the *understory*. The understory is above the ground and under the leaves. In the understory, it is very dark and cool. It gets only 2–5% of the sunlight that the canopy gets. The understory has the most insects of the four layers, and a lot of snakes and frogs also live there.

Finally, there is the *forest floor.* On the surface of this floor are fallen leaves, branches, and other debris.** In general, the largest animals in the rain forest live in this layer. Common animals in this habitat are tigers and gorillas.

*emergent = in botany, a plant that is taller than other plants around it, like a tall tree in a forest
**debris = loose, natural material, like dirt

1. Name two types of animals that live in the tops of giant trees.
2. What layer forms an umbrella over the rain forest?
3. Where is the understory?
4. Where do you think most mosquitoes live?
5. What are some differences between the emergent layer and the forest floor?

EXERCISE 19 ▶ Warm-up. (Chart 6-5)
Complete the sentences with information about yourself: *I was born* ...

1. in _____ (*month*).
2. on _____ (*date*).
3. on _____ (*weekday*).
4. at _____ (*time*).

6-5 Prepositions of Time

in	(a) Please be on time *in the future*. (b) I usually watch TV *in the evening*.	*in* + the past, the present, the future* *in* + the morning, the afternoon, the evening	
	(c) I was born *in October*. (d) I was born *in 1995*. (e) I was born *in the 20th century*. (f) The weather is hot *in (the) summer*.	*in* + { a month a year a century a season }	
on	(g) I was born *on October 31st, 1995*. (h) I went to a movie *on Thursday*. (i) I have class *on Thursday morning(s)*.	*on* + a date *on* + a weekday *on* + (a) weekday morning(s), afternoon(s), evening(s)	
at	(j) We sleep at night. I was asleep *at midnight*. (k) I fell asleep *at 9:30 (nine-thirty)*. (l) He's busy *at the moment*. Can I take a message?	*at* + noon, night, midnight *at* + "clock time" *at* + the moment, the present time, present	

*Possible in British English: *in future* (e.g., *Please be on time in future.*)

EXERCISE 20 ▶ Looking at grammar. (Chart 6-5)
Complete the sentences with *in*, *at*, or *on*. All the sentences contain time expressions.

Studious Stan has college classes ...

1. _____ the morning.
2. _____ the afternoon.
3. _____ the evening.
4. _____ night.
5. _____ weekdays.
6. _____ Saturdays.
7. _____ Saturday mornings.
8. _____ noon.
9. _____ midnight.

Unlucky Lisa has a birthday every four years. She was born ...

10. _____ February 29th.
11. _____ February 29th, 1976.
12. _____ February.
13. _____ 1976.
14. _____ February 1976.
15. _____ the winter.

Cool Carlos is a fashion designer. He's thinking about clothing designs ...

16. _____ the moment.
17. _____ the present time.
18. _____ the past.

EXERCISE 21 ▶ Let's talk: interview. (Chart 6-5)
Complete each question with an appropriate preposition. Interview seven classmates. Ask each person one question. Share a few of the answers with the class.

1. What do you like to do _____ the evening?
2. What do you usually do _____ night before bed?
3. What do you like to do _____ Saturday mornings?
4. What did you do _____ January 1st of this year?
5. What were you doing _____ this time last year?
6. How do you spend your free time _____ the summer?
7. What will you do with your English skills _____ the future?

EXERCISE 22 ▶ Warm-up. (Chart 6-6)
Check (✓) all the grammatically correct sentences.

1. a. ____ I left Athens in 2005.
   b. ____ I left in 2005 Athens.
   c. ____ In 2005, I left Athens.

2. a. ____ Lee sold his car yesterday.
   b. ____ Yesterday Lee sold his car.
   c. ____ Lee sold yesterday his car.

6-6 Word Order: Place and Time

	S	V	PLACE	TIME	In a typical English sentence, "place" usually comes before "time," as in (a).
(a)	Mia moved		to Paris	in 2008.	INCORRECT: Mia moved in 2008 to Paris.
	We went		to a movie	yesterday.	
	S	V	O	P	T	S-V-O-P-T = Subject-Verb-Object-Place-Time
(b)	We bought a house in Miami in 2005.					(basic English sentence structure)
	TIME	S	V	PLACE		Expressions of time can also come at the beginning of a sentence, as in (c) and (d).
(c)	In 2008,	Mia	moved	to Paris.		A time phrase at the beginning of a sentence is often followed by a comma, as in (c).
(d)	Yesterday	we	went	to a movie.		

EXERCISE 23 ▶ Looking at grammar. (Chart 6-6)
Put the phrases in the correct sentence order.

Updates

1. to Paris \ next month

   Monique's company is going to transfer her _____.

2. last week \ through Turkey

   William began a bike trip _____.

3. at his uncle's bakery \ Alexi \ on weekends \ works

   _____.

4. am taking \ tomorrow \ a flight \ I \ to Cairo

   _____.

EXERCISE 24 ▶ Warm-up. (Chart 6-7)
Add a final **-s** or **Ø**.

1. Lions roar____.
2. A lion roar____.
3. Lions, tigers, and leopards roar____.
4. A tiger in the jungle roar____.
5. Tigers in the jungle roar____.
6. Tigers in jungles roar____.

6-7 Subject-Verb Agreement

(a) SINGULAR SINGULAR The **sun** shine**s**. PLURAL PLURAL (b) Bird**s** sing.	A singular subject takes a singular verb, as in (a). A plural subject takes a plural verb, as in (b). NOTE: verb + **-s** = singular (*shines*) noun + **-s** = plural (*birds*)
(c) SINGULAR SINGULAR My *brother* lives in Jakarta. PLURAL PLURAL (d) My *brother* and *sister* live in Jakarta.	Two subjects connected by **and** take a plural verb, as in (d).
(e) The **glasses** over there under the window by the sink **are** clean. (f) The **information** in those magazines about Vietnamese culture and customs **is** very interesting.	Sometimes phrases come between a subject and a verb. These phrases do not affect the agreement of the subject and verb.
V S (g) *There **is** a **book** on the desk.* V S (h) *There **are** some **books** on the desk.*	**There** + **be** + *subject* expresses that something exists in a particular place. The verb agrees with the noun that follows **be**.
(i) **Every student is** sitting down. (j) **Everybody/Everyone hopes** for peace.	**Every** is a singular word. It is used with a singular, not plural, noun. INCORRECT: *Every students* ... Subjects with **every** take singular verbs, as in (i) and (j).
(k) **People** in my country **are** friendly.	**People** is a plural noun and takes a plural verb.

EXERCISE 25 ▶ Looking at grammar. (Chart 6-7)
Identify the subject (S) and the verb (V). Correct errors in agreement.

My Apartment Building

1. The <u>apartments</u> (S) in this building <u>is</u> (V) modern. → are
2. Five <u>students</u> (S) from my class <u>live</u> (V) in this building. → OK (no error in agreement)
3. There is a vacant apartment in my building.
4. The people on my floor is helpful.
5. The neighbors in the apartment next to mine is very friendly.
6. My aunt and uncle live next door.
7. Every person in this building have a pet.
8. All apartments have air-conditioning.

EXERCISE 26 ▶ Looking at grammar. (Chart 6-7)
Work in small groups. Complete the sentences with the correct form of the verbs in the box. Discuss the words you use to describe different animal sounds in your native language.

| bark | buzz | scream | squeak |

What sounds do these animals make?

1. A dog _____ .
2. Dogs _____ .
3. Monkeys and chimpanzees _____ .
4. A monkey in the jungle _____ .
5. Monkeys in the jungle _____ .
6. A mouse and a rat _____ .
7. Mice and rats _____ .
8. Bees in a hive _____ .
9. Every bee _____ .
10. Every bee in a hive _____ .

EXERCISE 27 ▸ **Listening.** (Charts 6-2 and 6-7)

Listen to the passage. Listen a second time and add *-s* where necessary.

> Do you know these words?
> - sweat
> - fur
> - paw
> - flap
> - mud

HOW SOME ANIMALS STAY COOL

How do animal___(1) stay cool in hot weather? Many animal___(2) don't sweat like human___(3), so they have other way___(4) to cool themselves.

Dog___(5), for example, have a lot of fur___(6) and can become very hot. They stay___(7) cool mainly by panting. If you don't know what *panting* means, this is the sound of panting.

Cat___(8) lick___(9) their paw___(10) and chest___(11). When their fur ___(12) is wet, they become cooler.

Elephant___(13) have very large ear___(14). When they are hot, they can flap their huge ear___(15). The flapping ear___(16) act___(17) like a fan, and it cool___(18) them. Elephant___(19) also like to roll in the mud___(20) to stay cool.

EXERCISE 28 ▸ **Warm-up.** (Chart 6-8)

Think about the very first teacher you had. Choose words from below to describe him/her.

| young | elderly | unfriendly | serious | impatient |
| middle-aged | friendly | fun | patient | helpful |

6-8 Using Adjectives to Describe Nouns

(a) Rob is reading a **ADJECTIVE** *good* **NOUN** *book*.	Words that describe nouns are called ADJECTIVES. In (a): *good* is an adjective; it describes the book.	
(b) The *tall* woman wore a *new* dress. (c) The *short* woman wore an *old* dress. (d) The *young* woman wore a *short* dress.	We say that adjectives "modify" nouns. *Modify* means "change a little." An adjective changes the meaning of a noun by giving more information about it.	
(e) Roses are *beautiful* flowers. INCORRECT: Roses are beautifuls flowers.	Adjectives are neither singular nor plural. They do NOT have a plural form.	
(f) He wore a *white* shirt. INCORRECT: He wore a shirt white. (g) Roses *are beautiful*. (h) His shirt *was white*.	Adjectives usually come immediately before nouns, as in (f). Adjectives can also follow the main verb *be*, as in (g) and (h).	

Nouns and Pronouns 171

EXERCISE 29 ▶ Looking at grammar. (Chart 6-8)
Check (✓) the phrases that have adjectives. <u>Underline</u> the adjectives.

1. __✓__ a <u>scary</u> story
2. _____ on Tuesday
3. _____ going to a famous place
4. _____ a small, dark, uncomfortable room
5. _____ quickly and then slowly
6. _____ long or short hair

EXERCISE 30 ▶ Looking at grammar. (Chart 6-8)
Add the given adjectives to the sentences. Only <u>two</u> of the three adjectives in each item will work.

Example: hard, heavy, strong   A man lifted the box.
→ *A strong man lifted the heavy box.*

1. beautiful, safe, red   Roses are flowers.
2. empty, wet, hot   The waiter poured coffee into my cup.
3. fresh, clear, hungry   Mrs. Fields gave the kids a snack.
4. dirty, modern, delicious   After our dinner, Frank helped me with the dishes.

EXERCISE 31 ▶ Grammar and reading. (Chart 6-8)
Part I. Add your own nouns, adjectives, and prepositions to the list. Don't look at Part II.

1. an adjective __old__
2. a person's name _____
3. a plural noun _____
4. a plural noun _____
5. a singular noun _____
6. an adjective _____
7. an adjective _____
8. a preposition of place _____
9. an adjective _____
10. a plural noun _____

Part II. Complete the sentences with the same words you added in Part I. Some of your completions might sound a little odd or funny. Read your completed passage aloud to a partner, group, or the rest of the class.

    One day a/an __old__ girl was walking in the city. Her name was _____.
              1   2
She was carrying a package for her grandmother. It had some _____, some
                                                                                3
_____, and a/an _____, among other things.
    4   5
    As she was walking down the street, a/an _____ thief stole her package. The
                                                                                                     6
_____ girl pulled out her cell phone and called the police, who caught the thief
   7
_____ a nearby building and returned her package to her. She took it immediately to
   8
her _____ grandmother, who was glad to get the package because she really needed
     9
some new _____.
          10

EXERCISE 32 ▸ Warm-up. (Chart 6-9)
Combine the word **chicken** with the words in the box.

✓fresh	hot	✓legs	recipe	soup

1. _chicken legs_
2. _fresh chicken_
3. _____
4. _____
5. _____

6-9 Using Nouns as Adjectives

(a) I have a **flower** garden.	Sometimes words that are usually used as nouns are used as adjectives.
(b) The **shoe** store also sells socks.	For example, **flower** is usually a noun, but in (a), it is used as an adjective to modify **garden**.
(c) INCORRECT: a flowers garden	When a noun is used as an adjective, it is singular in form, NOT plural.
(d) INCORRECT: the shoes store	

EXERCISE 33 ▸ Looking at grammar. (Chart 6-9)
<u>Underline</u> and identify the nouns (N). Use one of the nouns in the first sentence as an adjective in the second sentence.

1. This <u>book</u> (N) is about <u>grammar</u> (N). It's a _grammar book*_.
2. My garden has vegetables. It's a _____.
3. The soup has beans. It's _____.
4. I read a lot of articles in magazines. I read a lot of _____.
5. The factory makes toys. It's a _____.
6. The villages are in the mountains. They are _____.
7. The lesson was about art. It was an _____.
8. Flags fly from poles. Many government buildings have _____.
9. This medicine stops coughs. I recommend this _____.
10. This wall has bricks. It's a _____.

---

*When one noun modifies another noun, the spoken stress is usually on the first noun: a **grammar** book.

EXERCISE 34 ▶ Grammar and speaking. (Chart 6-9)
Add *-s* to the nouns in green if necessary. Then circle *yes* or *no* to agree or disagree with each sentence. Share your answers with a partner.

What do you think?

1. One day, **computer** programs will make it possible for computers to think.   yes   no
2. **Computer** make life more stressful.   yes   no
3. **Airplane** trips are enjoyable nowadays.   yes   no
4. **Airplane** don't have enough legroom.   yes   no
5. **Bike** are better than cars for getting around in a crowded city.   yes   no
6. It's fun to watch **bike** races like the *Tour de France* on TV.   yes   no
7. **Vegetable** soups are delicious.   yes   no
8. Fresh **vegetable** are my favorite food.   yes   no

EXERCISE 35 ▶ Listening and speaking. (Charts 6-1 → 6-9)

Part I. Listen to two friends talking about finding an apartment.

Part II. Complete your own conversation. Perform it for the class. You can use words in the box. NOTE: This conversation is slightly different from Part I.

Do you know these words?
- can't afford
- subway
- walking distance
- quiet location
- dream

air-conditioning	an elevator	near a bus stop	a studio
a balcony	an exercise room	near a freeway	a two-bedroom
close to my job	a laundry room	parking	a walk-up

A: I'm looking for a new place to live.

B: How come?

A: _____. I need _____.

B: I just helped a friend find one. I can help you. What else do you want?

A: I want _____. Also, I _____.

   I don't want _____.

B: Anything else?

A: _____ would be nice.

B: That's expensive.

A: I guess I'm dreaming.

an apartment with a balcony

EXERCISE 36 ▶ Warm-up. (Chart 6-10)

Read the conversation. Look at the personal pronouns in green. Decide if they are subject or object pronouns.

A: Did **you** hear? Ivan quit his job.
          1

B: **I** know. I don't understand **him**. Between **you** and **me**, **I** think it's a bad decision.
    2   3   4   5 6

1. you   subject   object
2. I   subject   object
3. him   subject   object
4. you   subject   object
5. me   subject   object
6. I   subject   object

6-10 Personal Pronouns: Subjects and Objects

SUBJECT PRONOUNS:	I	we	you	he, she, it	they
OBJECT PRONOUNS:	me	us	you	him, her, it	them

(a) **Kate** is married. **She** has two children. (b) **Kate** is my friend. I know **her** well.	A pronoun refers to a noun. In (a): **she** is a pronoun; it refers to **Kate**. In (b): **her** is a pronoun; it refers to **Kate**. In (a): **She** is a SUBJECT PRONOUN. In (b): **her** is an OBJECT PRONOUN.
(c) Mike has **a new blue bike**. He bought **it** yesterday.	A pronoun can refer to a single noun (e.g., **Kate**) or to a noun phrase. In (c): **it** refers to the whole noun phrase **a new blue bike**.
(d) **Eric and I** are good friends. (e) Al met **Eric and me** at the museum. (f) Al walked between **Eric and me**.	Guidelines for using pronouns following **and**: If the pronoun is used as part of the subject, use a subject pronoun, as in (d). If the pronoun is part of the object, use an object pronoun, as in (e) and (f). INCORRECT: Eric and me are good friends. INCORRECT: Al met Eric and I at the museum.

SINGULAR PRONOUNS:	I	me	you	he, she, it	him, her
PLURAL PRONOUNS:	we	us	you	they	them

(g) **Nick** isn't here. **He** is working. (h) The **students** are in class. **They** are taking a test. (i) **Kate and Tom** are married. **They** have two children.	Singular pronouns refer to singular nouns; plural pronouns refer to plural nouns, as in the examples.

EXERCISE 37 ▶ Looking at grammar. (Chart 6-10)
Write the nouns that the pronouns in green refer to.

1. The desserts looked delicious, but the kids didn't eat them. They are allergic to nuts. They cause breathing problems and itchy skin.

    a. them = _____

    b. They = _____

    c. They = _____

2. Do bees sleep at night? Or do they work in their hives all night long? You never see them after dark. What do they do after night falls?

    a. they = _____

    b. them = _____

    c. they = _____

3. Table tennis began in England in the late 1800s. Today it is an international sport. My brother and I played it a lot when we were teenagers. I beat him sometimes, but he was a better player and usually won.

    a. it = _____   c. him = _____

    b. it = _____   d. he = _____

EXERCISE 38 ▶ Looking at grammar. (Chart 6-10)
Circle the correct completions.

1. Toshi ate dinner with   I / me.
2. Toshi ate dinner with Mariko and   I / me.
3. I / me   had dinner with Toshi last night.
4. Toshi drove Mariko and   I / me   to the store after dinner. He waited for   we / us   in the car.
5. We also got tickets for the soccer game. We got   it / them   right away.   It / They   is / are selling fast.

EXERCISE 39 ▶ Looking at grammar. (Chart 6-10)
Complete the sentences with *she, he, it, her, him, they,* or *them*.

1. I have a grammar book. ____*It*____ is black.
2. Brian borrowed my books. _____ returned _____ yesterday.
3. Sonya is wearing some new earrings. _____ look good on _____.
4. Don't look directly at the sun. Don't look at _____ directly even if you are wearing sunglasses. Its light can injure your eyes.
5. Recently, I read about "micromachines." _____ are machines that are smaller than a grain of sand. One scientist called _____ "the greatest scientific invention of our time."

EXERCISE 40 ▶ Warm-up. (Chart 6-11)
Match each phrase to the picture that it describes.

Picture A

Picture B

1. _____ the teacher's office
2. _____ the teachers' office

6-11 Possessive Nouns

SINGULAR:	(a) I know the *student's* name.		An apostrophe (') and an *-s* are used with nouns to show possession.
PLURAL:	(b) I know the *students'* names.		
PLURAL:	(c) I know the *children's* names.		

SINGULAR	(d) the student → my baby → a man →	the *student's* name my *baby's* name a *man's* name	SINGULAR POSSESSIVE NOUN: noun + apostrophe (') + *-s*	
	(e) James →	*James'/James's* name	A singular noun that ends in *-s* has two possible possessive forms: *James'* or *James's*.	
PLURAL	(f) the students → my babies →	the *students'* names my *babies'* names	PLURAL POSSESSIVE NOUN: noun + *-s* + apostrophe (')	
	(g) men → the children →	*men's* names the *children's* names	IRREGULAR PLURAL POSSESSIVE NOUN: noun + apostrophe (') + *-s* (An irregular plural noun is a plural noun that does not end in *-s*: *children, men, people, women*. See Chart 6-1.)	

COMPARE: (h) *Tom's* here. (i) *Tom's* brother is here.	In (h): *Tom's* is not a possessive noun. It is a contraction of *Tom is*, used in informal writing. In (i): *Tom's* is a possessive noun.

EXERCISE 41 ▸ Looking at grammar. (Chart 6-11)
Decide if the meaning of the word in green is "one" or "more than one."

1. The teacher answered the *student's* questions.   (one)   more than one
2. The teacher answered the *students'* questions.   one   more than one
3. Our *daughters'* bedroom is next to our room.   one   more than one
4. Our *son's* room is downstairs.   one   more than one
5. *Men's* clothing is on sale at the department store.   one   more than one

EXERCISE 42 ▸ Game: trivia. (Chart 6-11)
Work in small groups. Use the correct possessive form of each noun to complete the sentences. Decide if the information is true or false. The group with the most correct answers wins.*

1. *earth*   The _____ surface is about 70% water.   T   F
2. *elephant*   An _____ skin is pink and wrinkled.   T   F
3. *man*   Pat is a _____ name.   T   F
4. *woman*   Pat is a _____ name.   T   F
5. *women*   The area for language is larger in _____ brains.   T   F
6. *person*   A _____ eyes blink more if he/she is nervous.   T   F
7. *People*   _____ voices always get lower as they age.   T   F

*See *Trivia Answers*, p. 449.

EXERCISE 43 ▸ Grammar and speaking. (Chart 6-11)

Part I. Look at the Nelson family tree. Complete the sentences using the correct possessive form.

1. _____Ned's_____ wife is Ella.
2. _____ husband is Sam.
3. Howard is _____ brother.
4. Howard is _____ husband.
5. _____ grandmother is Ella.
6. _____ parents are Sam and Lisa.
7. Ella and _____ grandson is William.
8. Howard and Monica are _____ aunt and uncle.

Part II. Work with a partner. Talk about the members of your family or another family. Use possessives. Your partner will create a family tree from your description.

EXERCISE 44 ▸ Warm-up. (Chart 6-12)
Choose the correct answers.

1. Who's holding the little girl in the striped shirt?
   a. That's Rachel.   b. That's Rachel's.

2. Whose granddaughter is that?
   a. That's Rachel.   b. That's Rachel's.

6-12 Using *Whose*

	Question	Answer	
(a)	*Whose* (***book***) is this?	It's John's (book).	***Whose*** asks about possession.
(b)	*Whose* (***books***) are those?	They're mine (OR my books).	The meaning in (a): *Who does this book belong to?*
(c)	*Whose* **car** did you borrow?	I borrowed Karen's (car).	NOTE: The person asking the question may omit the noun (***book***) if the meaning is clear to the listener.
COMPARE:			
(d)	***Who's*** that?	Mary Smith.	***Who's*** and ***whose*** have the same pronunciation.
(e)	***Whose*** is that?	Mary's.	***Who's*** is a contraction of ***who is***.
			Whose asks about possession.

EXERCISE 45 ▶ Looking at grammar. (Chart 6-12)

Using ***who's*** or ***whose*** with ***that***, make two questions for each picture. Then give the correct answer for each question.

QUESTION   ANSWER

1. *bag / Elise*

   a. ____Whose bag is that?____   ____Elise's____

   b. ____Who's that?____   ____Elise____

2. *Jason / apple*

   a. _____   _____

   b. _____   _____

3. *car / Roger*

   a. _____   _____

   b. _____   _____

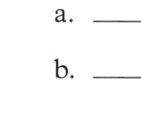

4. *Buddy / leash*

   a. _____   _____

   b. _____   _____

EXERCISE 46 ▶ Grammar and speaking. (Chart 6-12)

Part I. Complete the questions with ***Whose*** or ***Who's***.

1. _____ taking the picture?
2. _____ next to you?
3. _____ skis are those?
4. _____ standing at the end?
5. _____ the guy in the hat?

a ski vacation

180 CHAPTER 6

6. _____ house did you stay at?

Part II. Ask another student two additional questions, one with *Who's* and one with *Whose*.

EXERCISE 47 ▶ Listening. (Chart 6-12)
Listen to the each question and choose the correct word.

1. Who's   Whose
2. Who's   Whose
3. Who's   Whose
4. Who's   Whose
5. Who's   Whose
6. Who's   Whose

EXERCISE 48 ▶ Warm-up. (Chart 6-13)
Check (✓) all the grammatically correct responses.

Do you know whose camera this is?

1. _____ It's my camera.
2. _____ It's mine.
3. _____ It's my.
4. _____ It's yours.
5. _____ It's your camera.
6. _____ It's your's.
7. _____ It's theirs.
8. _____ It's their camera.
9. _____ It's theirs'.

6-13 Possessive Pronouns and Adjectives

This pen belongs to me.
(a) It's *mine*.
(b) It is *my* pen.

Examples (a) and (b) have the same meaning; they both show possession.

Mine is a *possessive pronoun*; *my* is a *possessive adjective*.

Possessive Pronouns	Possessive Adjectives
(c) I have *mine*.	I have *my* pen.
(d) You have *yours*.	You have *your* pen.
(e) She has *hers*.	She has *her* pen.
(f) He has *his*.	He has *his* pen.
(g) We have *ours*.	We have *our* pens.
(h) You have *yours*.	You have *your* pens.
(i) They have *theirs*.	They have *their* pens.
(j) ———	I have a book. *Its* cover is black.

A POSSESSIVE PRONOUN is used alone, without a noun following it.

A POSSESSIVE ADJECTIVE is used only with a noun following it.

INCORRECT: *I have mine pen.*
INCORRECT: *I have my.*

COMPARE *its* vs. *it's*:
(k) Jon gave me a book. I don't remember *its* name.
(l) Jon gave me a book. *It's* really interesting.

In (k): *its* (NO apostrophe) is a possessive adjective modifying the noun *name*.
In (l): *It's* (with an apostrophe) is a contraction of *it + is*.

COMPARE *their* vs. *there* vs. *they're*:
(m) The students have *their* books.
(n) My books are over *there*.
(o) Where are the students? *They're* in class.

Their, *there*, and *they're* have the same pronunciation, but not the same meaning.
   their = possessive adjective, as in (m)
   there = an expression of place, as in (n)
   they're = *they are*, as in (o)

EXERCISE 49 ▶ Looking at grammar. (Chart 6-13)
Circle the correct completions.

1. Alice called   (her)/ hers   friend.
2. Hasan wrote a letter to   his / he's   mother.
3. It's / Its   normal for a dog to chase   it's / its   tail.
4. The cat cleaned   its / it's   fur with   its / it's   tongue.
5. Paula drove my car to work.   Hers / Her   had a flat tire.
6. Junko fell off her bike and broke   hers / her   arm.
7. Anastasia is a good friend of   my / mine.*
8. I met a friend of   you / yours   yesterday.
9. A: Excuse me. Is this   my / mine   pen or   your / yours?
   B: This one is   my / mine.   Your / Yours   is on   your / yours   desk.
10. a. Adam and Amanda are married.   They / They're   live in an apartment building.
    b. Their / There / They're   apartment is on the fifth floor.
    c. We live in the same building.   Our / Ours   apartment has one bedroom, but   their / theirs   has two.
    d. Their / There / They're   sitting   their / there / they're   now because   their / there / they're   waiting for a visit from   their / there / they're son.

EXERCISE 50 ▶ Let's talk. (Charts 6-12 and 6-13)
Work in small groups. Take pictures of objects in the room (about 10-15 per group) with cell phones. Ask and answer questions about the objects. Use possessive pronouns, possessive adjectives, or the person's name.

Example: (picture of a backpack)
STUDENT A: Whose backpack is this?
STUDENT B: It's hers. / It's her backpack. / It's Yumi's.

EXERCISE 51 ▶ Warm-up. (Chart 6-14)
Work in small groups. Take turns saying the sentences while you or other students show the meaning with a small mirror.

1. I am looking at myself.
2. You are looking at yourself.
3. You are looking at yourselves.
4. He is looking at himself.
5. They are looking at themselves.
6. She is looking at herself.
7. We are looking at ourselves.

---

*A friend of + possessive pronoun (e.g., a *friend of mine*) is a common expression.

6-14 Reflexive Pronouns

myself	(a) I saw **myself** in the mirror.	REFLEXIVE PRONOUNS end in **-self/-selves**. They are used when the subject (e.g., *I*) and the object (e.g., *myself*) are the same person.
yourself	(b) You (one person) saw **yourself**.	
herself	(c) She saw **herself**.	
himself	(d) He saw **himself**.	INCORRECT: *I saw me in the mirror.*
itself	(e) It (e.g., the kitten) saw **itself**.	
ourselves	(f) We saw **ourselves**.	
yourselves	(g) You (plural) saw **yourselves**.	
themselves	(h) They saw **themselves**.	

(i) Greg lives **by himself**.	**By** + a reflexive pronoun = alone
(j) I sat **by myself** on the park bench.	In (i): Greg lives alone, without family or roommates.
(k) I **enjoyed myself** at the fair.	*Enjoy* and a few other verbs are commonly followed by a reflexive pronoun. See the list below.

Common Expressions with Reflexive Pronouns

believe in yourself	feel sorry for yourself	pinch yourself	tell yourself
blame yourself	give yourself (something)	be proud of yourself	work for yourself
cut yourself	help yourself	take care of yourself	wish yourself (luck)
drive yourself	hurt yourself	talk to yourself	
enjoy yourself	introduce yourself	teach yourself	

EXERCISE 52 ▶ Looking at grammar. (Chart 6-14)
Complete the sentences with reflexive pronouns.

1. Are you OK, Heidi? Did you hurt ___*yourself*___?
2. Leo taught _____ to play the piano. He never had a teacher.
3. Do you ever talk to _____? Most people talk to _____ sometimes.
4. A newborn baby can't take care of _____.
5. We need to have confidence in our own abilities. We need to believe in _____.
6. Isabel always wishes _____ good luck before a big test.
7. Kazu, there's plenty of food on the table. Please help _____.
8. I couldn't believe my luck! I had to pinch _____ to make sure I wasn't dreaming.

EXERCISE 53 ▶ Let's talk: interview. (Chart 6-14)

Interview six students. Ask each student a different question. Share some of their answers.

1. In this town, what is a good way to enjoy yourself?
2. How do people introduce themselves in your country? What do they say?
3. Have you ever wished yourself good luck? When or why?
4. Have you ever felt sorry for yourself? Or, have you ever felt proud of yourself? If so, why?
5. When athletes talk to themselves before an important event, what do you imagine they say?
6. In your country, at what age does a person usually begin living by himself or herself?

EXERCISE 54 ▶ Warm-up. (Chart 6-15)

Choose the picture that matches the description: *One flower is red. Another is yellow. The other is pink.*

Picture A

Picture B

6-15 Singular Forms of *Other*: *Another* vs. *The Other*

Another

○ ● ○ ○ ○ one　another	**another** = one more out of a group of items **Another** is a combination of *an* + *other*, written as one word.
(a) Paul is looking at baseball caps. The store has several that he likes. One is blue. **Another** is red.	

The Other

○ ● one　the other	**the other** = all that remains of a given number; the last one
(b) Paul is looking at baseball caps in the store. There are two colors. One is blue. **The other** is red.	
(c) Paul tried on one cap. Then he tried on { *another* cap. / *another* one. / *another*. }	**Another** and **the other** can be used • as adjectives in front of a noun (e.g., **another** cap). • as adjectives in front of the word **one** (e.g., **another one**). • alone as pronouns (e.g., **another**).
(d) Paul tried on one cap. Then he tried on { *the other* cap. / *the other* one. / *the other*. }	

EXERCISE 55 ▶ Looking at grammar. (Chart 6-15)
Complete the sentences with *another* or *the other*.

Picture A

Picture B

1. One appliance in Picture A is a washing machine. _____ is a dryer.

2. There are three appliances in Picture B. One is a washing machine. Another is a dryer. _____ is a stove.

a stove

a microwave

a dishwasher

a refrigerator

3. There are many, many types of appliances. One is a stove.

   a. _____ is a microwave.

   b. _____ is a dishwasher.

   c. What is the name of _____ type of appliance?

a saw

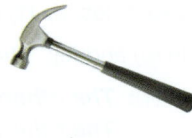
a hammer

a screwdriver

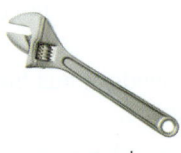
a wrench

4. Do you know the names of these tools? One is a saw. _____ is a hammer.

5. I need to borrow two tools. One is a screwdriver. _____ is a hammer.

6. Here are four tools. One is a saw. _____ is a hammer. _____ is a screwdriver. _____ is a wrench.

7. A builder needs many, many tools. One is a saw. _____ is a hammer. _____ is a screwdriver. _____ is a wrench.

EXERCISE 56 ▸ Warm-up. (Chart 6-16)
Match the sentences to the correct pictures.

Picture A

Picture B

1. _____ Some are red. The others are yellow.

2. _____ Some are red. Others are yellow.

6-16 Plural Forms of *Other*: *Other(s)* vs. *The Other(s)*

Other(s)

Jeremy has many kinds of fruit trees in his garden. Some have apples.

(a) **Other** trees have peaches.

(b) **Other** ones have peaches.

(c) **Others** have peaches.

Other(s) (without **the**) means "several more out of a group of similar items, several in addition to the one(s) already mentioned." Examples (a)–(c) have the same meaning.

In (a) and (b): **Other** is an adjective.

In (c): **Others** is a pronoun.
      Others = **Other trees**

INCORRECT: Others ones
                Others trees

The Other(s)

Lara has two kinds of fruit trees in her garden. Some have pears.

(d) **The other** trees have cherries.

(e) **The other** ones have cherries.

(f) **The others** have cherries.

The other(s) means "the last ones in a specific group, the remains from a given number of similar items." Examples (d)–(f) have the same meaning.

In (d) and (e): **The other** is an adjective.

In (f): **The others** is a pronoun.
      The others = **The other trees**

INCORRECT: The others ones
                The others trees

EXERCISE 57 ▶ Grammar and speaking. (Charts 6-15 and 6-16)
Work in pairs or small groups. Perform these actions.

1. Hold two pens. Use a form of *other* to describe the second pen.
   → *I'm holding two pens. One is mine, and the other belongs to Ahmed.*
2. Hold three pens. Use a form of *other* to describe the second and third pens.
3. Hold up your two hands. One of them is your right hand. Tell us about your left hand, using a form of *other*.
4. Hold up your right hand. One of the five fingers is your thumb. Using forms of *other*, tell us about your index finger, then your middle finger, then your ring finger, and then your little finger, the last of the five fingers on your right hand.

EXERCISE 58 ▶ Looking at grammar. (Chart 6-16)
Complete the sentences with *other*, *others*, *the other*, or *the others*.

1. There are many kinds of animals in the world. The elephant is one kind. Some ___others___ are tigers, horses, and bears.

2. There are many kinds of animals in the world. The elephant is one kind. Some _____ kinds are tigers, horses, and bears.

3. There are three colors in the Italian flag. One of the colors is red. _____ are green and white.

4. There are three colors in the Italian flag. One of the colors is red. _____ colors are green and white.

5. Many people like to get up very early in the morning. _____ like to sleep until noon.

6. There are many kinds of geometric shapes. Some are circles. _____ shapes are squares. Still _____ are rectangles.

7. There are four geometric shapes in the above drawing. One is a square. _____ shapes are a rectangle, a circle, and a triangle.

8. Of the four geometric shapes in the drawing, only the circle has curved lines. _____ have straight lines.

6-17 Summary: Forms of *Other*

	Adjective	Pronoun	
SINGULAR	another apple	another	Note that the word **others** (*other* + *final -s*) is used only as a plural pronoun.
PLURAL	other apples	other**s**	
SINGULAR	the other apple	the other	
PLURAL	the other apples	the other**s**	

EXERCISE 59 ▶ Looking at grammar. (Chart 6-17)
Look at each picture and complete the sentences with the words in the box.

| another | other | others | the other | the others |

1. There is a large bowl of apples on the table. Paul ate one apple. He is still hungry. He wants a second one.

   a. He wants to eat _____ apple.

   b. He wants to eat _____ one.

   c. He wants to eat _____.

2. There are two apples on the table. Paul is going to eat one of them.

   a. Sara is going to eat _____ apple.

   b. Sara is going to eat _____ one.

   c. Sara is going to eat _____.

3. There are many apples in Paul's kitchen. Paul is holding one apple.

   a. There are _____ apples in a bowl.

   b. There are _____ ones on a plate.

   c. There are _____ on a chair.

4. There are four apples on the table. Paul is going to take one of them, and Sara is going to take three.

   a. Sara is going to take _____ apples.

   b. Sara is going to take _____ ones.

   c. Sara is going to take _____.

EXERCISE 60 ▶ Looking at grammar. (Charts 6-15 → 6-17)
Complete the sentences with *another*, *other*, *others*, *the other*, or *the others*.

1. Juan doesn't like to wear suits. He has only one. His wife wants him to buy _____another_____ one.

2. Juan is looking at two suits. One is blue, and _____ is brown.

3. Some suits are blue. _____ are gray.

4. Some jackets have zippers. _____ jackets have buttons.

5. Some people keep dogs as pets. _____ have cats. Still _____ people have fish or birds as pets.

6. My boyfriend gave me a ring. I tried to put it on my ring finger, but it didn't fit. So I had to put it on _____ finger.

7. People have two thumbs. One is on the right hand. _____ is on the left hand.

8. Sometimes when I'm thirsty, I'll have a glass of water, but often one glass isn't enough, so I'll have _____ one.

9. There are five letters in the word *fresh*. One of the letters is a vowel. _____ are consonants.

10. Smith is a common last name in English. _____ common names are Johnson, Jones, Miller, Anderson, Moore, and Brown.

EXERCISE 61 ▶ Looking at grammar. (Charts 6-15 → 6-17)
Read each conversation and choose the correct statement (a. or b.).

1. A: Did you buy the black jacket?
   B: No. I bought the other one.

   a. Speaker B was looking at two jackets.
   b. Speaker B was looking at several jackets.

2. A: One of my favorite colors is dark blue. Another one is red.
   B: Me too.

   a. The speakers have only two favorite colors.
   b. The speakers have more than two favorite colors.

3. A: Do your friends live on campus?
   B: A few live on campus, and the others live nearby.

   a. All of Speaker B's friends live on or near campus.
   b. Some of Speaker B's friends live on or near campus.

4. A: This looks like the wrong street. Let's go back and take the other road.

   B: OK.

   a. There are several roads the speakers can take.

   b. There are two roads the speakers can take.

5. A: What's the best way to get downtown from here?

   B: It's pretty far to walk. Some people take the bus. Others prefer the subway.

   a. There are only two ways to get downtown.

   b. There are more than two ways to get downtown.

6. A: When I was a kid, I had lots of pets. One was a black dog. Another was an orange cat. Some others were a goldfish and a turtle.

   B: Pets are great for kids.

   a. Speaker A had more than four pets.

   b. Speaker A had only four pets.

7. A: I'm packing a banana for my lunch. Do you want the other?

   B: Sure, thanks.

   a. There are two bananas.

   b. There are several bananas.

EXERCISE 62 ▶ Check your knowledge. (Chapter 6 Review)
Correct the errors.

1. Jimmy had three ~~wish~~ *wishes* for his birthday.

2. I had some black beans soup for lunch.

3. The windows in our classroom is dirty.

4. People in Brazil speaks Portuguese.

5. Are around 8,600 types of birds in the world.

6. My mother and father work in Milan. Their teacher's.

7. In my family, mens and womens work as carpenter, pilot, and doctor.

8. Is a new student in our class. Have you met her?

9. There are two pool at the park. The smaller one is for childs. The another is for adults.

10. The highways in my country are excellents.

11. I don't like my apartment. Its in a bad neighborhood. Is a lot of crime. I'm going to move to other neighborhood.

EXERCISE 63 ▸ Reading and writing. (Chapter 6)

Part I. Read the passage and answer the questions.

> Do you know these words?
> - calm
> - nervous
> - anxious
> - variety
> - techniques
> - wave
> - inhale/exhale
> - heart rate

HOW TO CALM YOURSELF

Everyone feels nervous or anxious at times. Maybe it comes from an experience like going to the dentist. Or perhaps it's worrying about a big test. There are a variety of techniques that people use to calm themselves. Here are three that many people have found helpful.

One way to relax is by imagining a peaceful place, such as a tropical beach. Thinking about the warm water, cool breezes, and regular sounds of the ocean waves helps people calm themselves. Another popular method is deep breathing. A person inhales deeply and then slowly exhales as a way to slow the heart rate and relax the body. Still other people find exercise helpful. Some people benefit from a slow activity like a 20-minute walk. Others prefer activities that make them tired, like running or swimming.

After people try some of these techniques, many feel better just knowing that they can use their mind or physical exercise to help them relax.

1. What are three ways people relax when they are nervous? (Use *one* and *another* in your answer.)
2. Why do some people choose activities like running and swimming as a way to relax?
3. Imagine you are trying to relax by thinking of a peaceful place. What place would you think of?
4. How do you relax when you are nervous?

Part II. Read this paragraph by a student who tells how he relaxes when he's nervous.

How I Calm Down

Sometimes I feel nervous, especially when I have to give a speech. My body begins to shake, and I realize that I have to calm myself down. This is the technique I use: I imagine myself in a peaceful place. My favorite place in the world is the sea. I imagine myself on the water. I am floating. I feel the warm water around me. The sounds around me are very relaxing. I only hear the waves and maybe a few birds. I don't think about the past or the future. I can feel my heart rate decrease a little, and my body slowly starts to calm down. Before I give a speech, I use this technique. I find it very helpful.

Part III. Write a paragraph about how you relax when you are nervous. Follow the model in Part II. Give specific details about how you relax and what the results are.

Sometimes I feel nervous, especially when I have to _____. My _____ and I realize that I have to calm myself down. This is the technique I use: _____.

> **WRITING TIP**
>
> When you want to add interesting details to your writing, it is helpful to ask yourself these questions: *who, what, when, where, why,* and *how*. For this writing assignment, it can help you think of details to describe how you calm yourself. For example, what do you do, exactly, to calm yourself? Where are you? What do you see? How do you feel? Why do you feel better?

Part IV. Edit your writing. Check for the following:

1. ☐ use of the simple present to describe your feelings and actions
2. ☐ correct use of final *-s*/*-es*/*-ies* on singular verbs
3. ☐ correct forms of **another**/**other** if you use these words
4. ☐ use of interesting details in your paragraph
5. ☐ correct spelling (use a dictionary or spell-check)

▪▪▪▪▪ For digital resources, go to MyEnglishLab on the Pearson English Portal. You can also go to the Pearson Practice English app for mobile practice.

CHAPTER 7
Modal Auxiliaries, the Imperative, Making Suggestions, Stating Preferences

PRETEST: What do I already know?
Write "C" if the **boldfaced** words are correct and "I" if they are incorrect.

1. ____ We **have to wake** up early tomorrow. Our flight leaves at 5:00. (Chart 7-1)
2. ____ I **can read** when I was four years old. (Chart 7-2)
3. ____ The weather **might** hot this weekend. (Chart 7-3)
4. ____ Ben isn't here. He **could** still **be** asleep. (Chart 7-4)
5. ____ **May** I please **go** to a movie tonight? (Chart 7-5)
6. ____ **May** you **go** with me to the mall? (Chart 7-6)
7. ____ **Maybe** I **should** wear a warm coat. It's pretty cold outside. (Chart 7-7)
8. ____ **You better get** ready. We're going to be late. (Chart 7-8)
9. ____ I**'ve got to leave**. I need to pick up my kids at school. (Chart 7-9)
10. ____ I **must not study** this weekend. Our teacher didn't give us any homework. (Chart 7-10)
11. ____ There is only one room available at the hotel. It **must be** popular. (Chart 7-11)
12. ____ The information **could be** clearer, couldn't it? (Chart 7-12)
13. ____ Please **don't to wear** your shoes indoors. (Chart 7-13)
14. ____ It's a nice evening. Why **we don't eat** dinner outside on the patio? (Chart 7-14)
15. ____ My parents **would rather living** in a small town than a large city. (Chart 7-15)

EXERCISE 1 ▶ Warm-up. (Chart 7-1)
Check (✓) the sentences that are grammatically correct.

1. ____ I can skydive.
2. ____ He cans skydives.
3. ____ She can to skydive.
4. ____ My parents can't skydive.

7-1 Introduction to Modal Auxiliaries

The verbs in this chapter are called "modal auxiliaries." They are helping verbs that express a wide range of meanings such as ability, possibility, and necessity.*

Auxiliary + the Simple Form of a Verb

can	(a) Olga *can speak* English.	Some modal auxiliaries are immediately followed by the simple form of a verb, as in (a)–(e).
could	(b) He *couldn't come* to class.	• They are not followed by *to*.
may	(c) It *may rain* tomorrow.	INCORRECT: *Olga can to speak English.*
will	(d) I *will be* in class tomorrow.	• The main verb does not have a final *-s*.
would	(e) *Would* you please *close* the door?	INCORRECT: *Olga can speaks English.*
		• The main verb is not in a past form.
		INCORRECT: *Olga can spoke English.*
		• The main verb is not in its *-ing* form.
		INCORRECT: *Olga can speaking English.*

Auxiliary + *to* + the Simple Form of a Verb

have to	(f) I *have to study* tonight.	Some modal auxiliaries use *to* + the simple form, as in (f) and (g).
be able to	(g) Kate *is able to learn* quickly.	

*See Chart 7-16 for a summary of all the modal auxiliaries in this chapter.

EXERCISE 2 ▶ Looking at grammar. (Chart 7-1)
Make sentences with the given verbs + *come*. Add *to* where necessary. Follow the example.

Example: can → *Leo can come tonight.*

1. may
2. is able
3. has
4. will not
5. could not
6. is not able

EXERCISE 3 ▶ Listening. (Chart 7-1)
Listen to the sentences. Add *to* where necessary. If *to* isn't necessary, write Ø. Notice that *to* may sound like "ta."

Plans for Tomorrow

A: Where do you and Joe have ____₁ go tomorrow?

B: I have ____₂ go downtown. Joe has ____₃ take the kids to buy school supplies. He couldn't ____₄ do it today.

A: May I ____₅ come with you?

B: You can ____₆ if you want to get up early.

A: Would you ____₇ wake me up? Sometimes I'm not able ____₈ hear my alarm.

B: Sure. I have a great way to wake people up. You definitely won't ____₉ sleep in!

A: I can't ____₁₀ wait!

194 CHAPTER 7

💬 EXERCISE 4 ▸ Warm-up. (Chart 7-2)
Circle a completion for each sentence. Answers may vary. Discuss your answers.

1. A newborn baby   can / can't   roll over.
2. A baby of four months   can / can't   smile.
3. A newborn baby   is able to / isn't able to   see black and white shapes.
4. A baby of six months   is able to / isn't able to   see colors.
5. When I was nine months old, I   could / couldn't   crawl.
6. When I was nine months old, I   could / couldn't   walk.

7-2 Expressing Ability: *Can, Could, Be Able To*

(a) Bob **can play** the piano. (b) You **can buy** a screwdriver at a hardware store. (c) I **can meet** you at Ted's tomorrow afternoon.	***Can*** expresses *ability* in the present or future.
(d) I { **can't** / **cannot** / **can not** } understand that sentence.	The negative form of ***can*** may be written ***can't***, ***cannot***, or ***can not***.
(e) I *can gó*. (f) I *cán't go*.	In spoken English, ***can*** is usually unstressed and pronounced /kən/ = "kun." ***Can't*** is stressed and pronounced /kæn?/, with the final sound being a glottal stop.* The glottal stop replaces the /t/ in spoken English. Occasionally native speakers have trouble hearing the difference between ***can*** and ***can't*** and need to ask for clarification.
(g) Our son **could walk** when he was one year old.	The past form of ***can*** is ***could***.
(h) He **couldn't walk** when he was six months old.	The negative of ***could*** is ***couldn't*** or ***could not***.
(i) He **can read**. (j) He **is able to read**. (k) She **could read**. (l) She **was able to read**.	Ability can also be expressed with a form of ***be able to***. Examples (i) and (j) have the same meaning. Examples (k) and (l) have the same meaning.

*A glottal stop is the sound you hear in the negative "unh-uh." The air is stopped by the closing of your glottis in the back of your throat. The phonetic symbol for the glottal stop is /ʔ/.

EXERCISE 5 ▶ Looking at grammar. (Chart 7-2)
Part I. Complete the sentences with *can* or *can't*.

1. A dog _____ swim, but it _____ fly.

2. A frog _____ live both on land and in water, but a cat _____ .

3. A bilingual person _____ speak three languages, but a trilingual person _____ .

4. Many people with color blindness _____ see green and red, but people with normal color vision _____ .

Part II. Restate the sentences in Part I. Use *be able to*.

EXERCISE 6 ▶ Let's talk: interview. (Chart 7-2)
Interview your classmates. Ask each student a different question. If the answer is "yes," ask the follow-up question in parentheses. Share some of your answers with the class.

Can you …

1. speak more than two languages? (Which ones?)
2. draw well — for example, draw a picture of me? (Can you do it now?)
3. fold a piece of paper in half more than six times? (Can you show me?)
4. play chess? (How long have you played?)

Are you able to …

5. write clearly with both your right and left hands? (Can you show me?)
6. pat the top of your head with one hand and rub your stomach in a circle with the other hand at the same time? (Can you show me?)
7. hold your breath underwater for a long time? (How long?)
8. play a musical instrument? (Which one?)

EXERCISE 7 ▶ Listening. (Chart 7-2)
Listen to the conversation. You will hear reductions for *can* and *can't*. Write the words you hear.

In the Classroom

A: I _____(1)_____ this math assignment.

B: I _____(2)_____ you with that.

A: Really? _____(3)_____ this problem to me?

B: Well, we _____(4)_____ out the answer until we do this part.

A: OK. But it's so hard.

B: Yeah, but I know you _____(5)_____ it. Just go slowly.

A: I need to leave in a few minutes. _____(6)_____ me after school today to finish this?

B: Well, I _____(7)_____ you right after school, but how about at 5:00?

A: Great!

EXERCISE 8 ▶ Let's talk. (Chart 7-2)
Complete the sentences with ***could/couldn't/be able to/not be able to*** and your own words.

Example: A year ago I _____ , but now I can. → *A year ago I couldn't speak English, but now I can.*

1. When I was a child, I _____ , but now I can.
2. When I was six, I _____ , but I wasn't able to do that when I was three.
3. I _____ when I was younger, but now I can't.
4. In the past, I _____ , but now I am.

EXERCISE 9 ▶ Warm-up. (Chart 7-3)
Check (✓) the sentences in each group that have the same meaning.

GROUP A

1. _____ Maybe it will be hot tomorrow.

2. _____ It might be hot tomorrow.

3. _____ It may be hot tomorrow.

GROUP B

4. _____ You can have dessert now.

5. _____ You may have dessert now.

GROUP C

6. _____ She can't stay up late.

7. _____ She might not stay up late.

7-3 Expressing Possibility: *May, Might,* and *Maybe;* Expressing Permission: *May* and *Can*

(a) It *may rain* tomorrow. (b) It *might rain* tomorrow. (c) — Why isn't John in class? — I don't know. He { *may* / *might* } be sick today.	*May* and *might* express possibility in the present or future. They have the same meaning. There is no difference in meaning between (a) and (b).
(d) It *may not rain* tomorrow. (e) It *might not rain* tomorrow.	Negative: *may not* and *might not* (Do not contract *may* and *might* with *not*.)
(f) *Maybe* it will rain tomorrow. COMPARE: (g) *Maybe* John is sick. (adverb) (h) John *may be* sick. (verb)	In (f) and (g): *maybe* (spelled as one word) is an adverb. It means "possibly." It comes at the beginning of a sentence. INCORRECT: *It will maybe rain tomorrow.* In (h): *may be* (two words) is a verb form: the modal *may* + the main verb *be*. Examples (g) and (h) have the same meaning. INCORRECT: *John maybe sick.*
(i) Passengers with young children *may board* now. (j) Passengers with young children *can board* now.	*May* is also used to give *permission*, as in (i). *Can* is often used to give *permission*, too, as in (j). NOTE: Examples (i) and (j) have the same meaning, but *may* is more formal than *can*.
(k) You *may not have* a cookie. You *can't have* a cookie.	*May not* and *cannot* (*can't*) are used to deny permission (i.e., to say "no").

EXERCISE 10 ▶ Looking at grammar. (Chart 7-3)

Rewrite the sentences with the words in parentheses.

1. It may snow tonight.

   (*might*) _____

   (*Maybe*) _____

2. You might need to wear your boots.

   (*may*) _____

   (*Maybe*) _____
   _____

3. Maybe there will be a blizzard.

   (*may*) _____

   (*might*) _____

EXERCISE 11 ▶ **Let's talk.** (Chart 7-3)
Answer each question with *may*, *might*, and *maybe*. Include at least three possibilities in each answer. Work in pairs, in small groups, or as a class.

Example: What are you going to do tomorrow?
  → *I don't know. **I may** go downtown.* OR ***I might** go to the laundromat.*
     ***Maybe** I'll study all day. Who knows?*

1. What are you going to do tomorrow night?
2. What's the weather going to be like tomorrow?
3. What is our teacher going to do tonight?
4. (_____) isn't in class today. Where is he/she?
5. What is your occupation going to be ten years from now?

EXERCISE 12 ▶ **Looking at grammar.** (Chart 7-3)
Complete the sentences with *can*, *may*, or *might*. Identify the meaning of the modals: possibility or permission.

In a Courtroom

1. No one speaks without the judge's permission. You ___*may / can*___ not speak until the judge asks you a question. Meaning: ___*permission*___

2. The judge _____ or _____ not reduce your fine for your speeding ticket. It depends. Meaning: _____

3. You _____ not argue with the judge. If you argue, you will get a fine. Meaning: _____

4. You have a strong case, but I'm not sure if you will convince the judge. You _____ win or you _____ lose. Meaning: _____

 EXERCISE 13 ▶ **Listening.** (Charts 7-2 and 7-3)
You will hear sentences with *can*, *may*, or *might*. Decide if the speakers are expressing ability, possibility, or permission.

Example: You will hear: A: Where's Victor?
                              B: I don't know. He may be sick.

           You will choose: ability   (possibility)   permission

1. ability   possibility   permission
2. ability   possibility   permission
3. ability   possibility   permission
4. ability   possibility   permission
5. ability   possibility   permission

EXERCISE 14. Warm-up. (Chart 7-4)
In which sentence is the speaker expressing the following?

| a. past ability | b. present possibility | c. future possibility |

1. ____ The score is 80–90, but with five minutes left, our team could win.
2. ____ A player is on the ground. He could be hurt.
3. ____ Our team didn't win. We couldn't score another basket.

7-4 Using *Could* to Express Possibility

(a) — How was the movie? **Could** you **understand** the English? — Not very well. I **could** only **understand** it with the help of subtitles. (b) — Why isn't Greg in class? — I don't know. He **could be** sick. (c) Look at those dark clouds. It **could rain** any minute.	One meaning of **could** is *past ability,* as in (a).* Another meaning of **could** is *possibility*. In (b): **He could be sick** has the same meaning as *He may/might be sick,* i.e., *It is possible that he is sick.* In (b): **could** expresses a *present* possibility. In (c): **could** expresses a *future* possibility.

*See also Chart 7-2.

EXERCISE 15 ▸ Looking at grammar. (Charts 7-2 and 7-4)
Does *could* express past, present, or future time? What is the meaning: ability or possibility?

SENTENCE	PAST	PRESENT	FUTURE	ABILITY	POSSIBILITY
1. I **could be** home late tonight. Don't wait for me for dinner.			X		X
2. Thirty years ago, when he was a small child, David **could speak** Swahili fluently. Now he's forgotten a lot of it.					
3. A: Where's Alicia? B: I don't know. She **could be** at the mall.					
4. When I was a child, I **could climb** trees, but now I'm too old.					
5. Let's leave for the airport now. Yuki's plane **could arrive** early, and we want to be there when she arrives.					
6. A: What's that on the carpet? B: I don't know. It looks like a bug. Or it **could be** a piece of fuzz.					

EXERCISE 16 ▶ Let's talk. (Chart 7-4)

Suggest possible solutions for each situation. Use ***could***. Work in pairs, in small groups, or as a class.

Finding Solutions

Example: Tim has to go to work early tomorrow. His car is completely out of gas. His bike has a flat tire.
→ *He could take the bus to work.*
→ *He could get a friend to take him to a gas station to get gas.*
→ *He could try to fix his bike.*
→ *He could get up very early and walk to work.*
Etc.

1. Lisa walked to school today. Now she wants to go home. It's raining hard. She doesn't have an umbrella, and she's wearing sandals.
2. Joe and Joan want to get some exercise. They were planning to play tennis this morning, but it snowed last night, and the tennis court is full of snow.
3. Roberto just bought a new TV. He has it at home now. The remote control is complicated. It has a lot of buttons. He doesn't understand how to use all of them.
4. Albert is traveling around the world. He is 22 years old. Today he is alone in Paris. He needs to eat, and he needs to find a place to stay overnight. But while he was asleep on the train last night, someone stole his wallet. He has no money and no credit cards.

EXERCISE 17 ▶ Listening. (Charts 7-3 and 7-4)

Listen to the conversation between a husband and wife. Listen again and complete the sentences with the words you hear.

In a Home Office

A: Look at this cord. Do you know what it's for?

B: I don't know. We have so many cables and cords around here with all our electronic equipment. It _____(1)_____ for our old printer.

A: No, that isn't a printer cord.

B: It _____(2)_____ for one of the kids' toys.

A: Yeah, I _____(3)_____. But they don't have many electronic toys.

B: I have an idea. It _____(4)_____ for an old cell phone. You know — the one I had before this one.

A: I bet that's it. We _____(5)_____ probably throw this out.

B: Well, let's be sure before we do that.

EXERCISE 18 ▸ Looking at grammar. (Charts 7-2 → 7-4)

Choose the verb that has the same meaning as the phrase in **bold**. More than one answer may be correct.

1. Thomas **is able to** memorize long numbers. He   can / could   remember a lot.
2. **It's possible** the weather will be nice tomorrow. It   might / may   be sunny.
3. You **have** my **permission** to stay out late. You   can / may   stay out until 1:00 A.M.
4. **Were you able to** read the doctor's note?   Can / Could   you read her handwriting?
5. Julia isn't here. **It's possible** she's at home. She   was able to / could   still be asleep.
6. I **wasn't able to** go to the dance. I hurt my foot, and I   couldn't / may not   dance.
7. **Are you able to** find a computer virus and remove it?   May / Can   you get rid of a computer virus?

EXERCISE 19 ▸ Warm-up. (Chart 7-5)

Check (✓) all the grammatically correct sentences.

At the Airport

1. _____ May I see your ID and boarding pass?
2. _____ Can I see your ID and boarding pass?
3. _____ Could I see your ID and boarding pass?
4. _____ May you show me your ID and boarding pass?

7-5 Polite Requests with *I: May, Could, Can*

Polite Request	Possible Answers	
(a) *May I* please borrow your pen? (b) *Could I* please borrow your pen? (c) *Can I* please borrow your pen?	Yes. Yes. Of course. Yes. Certainly. Of course. Certainly. Sure. (*informal*) OK. (*informal*) Uh-huh. (*meaning "yes"*) I'm sorry, but I need to use it myself.	People use *may*, *could*, and *can* to make polite requests with *I*.* The questions ask for someone's permission or agreement. Examples (a), (b), and (c) have basically the same meaning. *Can I* is less formal than *may I* and *could I*. NOTE: *May* is not used with *you* in polite requests.
(d) *Can I* borrow your pen, please? (e) *Can I* borrow your pen?		***Please*** can come at the end of the question, as in (d). ***Please*** can be omitted from the question, as in (e).

*In a polite question, *could* is NOT the past form of *can*.

EXERCISE 20 ▶ Grammar and speaking. (Chart 7-5)

Complete the phone conversations. Use **May I**, **Could I**, or **Can I** + a verb in the box.
NOTE: The caller is always Speaker B. Practice your conversations with a partner.

| ask | help | leave | reschedule | speak/talk |

Hello?

1. A: Hello?
   B: Hello. Is Ahmed there?
   A: Yes, he is.
   B: _____ to him?
   A: Just a minute. I'll get him.

2. A: Hello? Mr. Black's office.
   B: _____ to Mr. Black?
   A: _____ who is calling?
   B: Susan Abbott.
   A: Just a moment, Ms. Abbott. I'll transfer you.

3. A: Hello?
   B: Hi. This is Bob. _____ to Pedro?
   A: Sure. Hold on.

4. A: Good afternoon. Dr. Wu's office. _____ you?
   B: Yes. I have an appointment that I need to change.
   A: Just a minute, please. I'll transfer you to our appointment desk.

5. A: Hello?
   B: Hi Emily. It's Nina. I'm still at work and can't leave. _____ our appointment.
   A: Sure. Let me get my calendar.

6. A: Hello?
   B: Hello. _____ to Maria?
   A: She's not here right now.
   B: Oh. _____ a message?
   A: Sure. Just let me get a pen.

Modal Auxiliaries, the Imperative, Making Suggestions, Stating Preferences

EXERCISE 21 ▶ Let's talk: pairwork. (Chart 7-5)

Work with a partner. Ask and answer polite questions. Begin with *May I*, *Could I*, or *Can I*. Make conversations you can perform for the class.

Polite Requests

Example: (A), you want to see (B)'s grammar book for a minute.
PARTNER A: May/Could/Can I (please) see your grammar book for a minute?
PARTNER B: Of course. / Sure. / Etc.
PARTNER A: Thank you. / Thanks. I forgot to bring mine to class today.

1. (A), you want to see (B)'s dictionary for a minute.
2. (B), you are on the phone with (A). Someone knocks on your door. You want to call (A) back.
3. (A), you are at a restaurant. (B) is your server. You have finished your meal. You want the check.
4. (B), you run into (A) on the street. (A) is carrying some heavy packages. What are you going to say to him/her?
5. (A), you are speaking to (B), who is one of your teachers. You aren't feeling well and want to leave class early today.
6. (B), you are in a store with your good friend (A). You go to pay for your groceries, but you left your wallet at home.
7. (A), you are paying for an item in a store. (B) is the cashier. You want to pay with a check, but you don't know if the store takes checks.

EXERCISE 22 ▶ Warm-up. (Chart 7-6)

Check (✓) all the correct requests.

There are a lot of dishes tonight.

1. _____ Will you help me with the dishes?
2. _____ Would you load the dishwasher?
3. _____ May you load the dishwasher?
4. _____ Can you unload the dishwasher?
5. _____ Could you unload the dishwasher?

7-6 Polite Requests with *You*: *Would, Could, Will, Can*

Polite Requests	Possible Answers	
(a) ***Would you*** please open the door? (b) ***Could you*** please open the door? (c) ***Will you*** please open the door? (d) ***Can you*** please open the door?	Yes. Yes. Of course. Certainly. I'd be happy to. Of course. I'd be glad to. Sure. (*informal*) OK. (*informal*) Uh-huh. (*meaning* "yes") I'm sorry. I'd like to help, but my hands are full.	People use ***would***, ***could***, ***will*** and ***can*** with ***you*** to make polite requests. The questions ask for someone's help or cooperation. Examples (a), (b), (c), and (d) have basically the same meaning. ***Would*** and ***could*** sound a little more formal than ***will*** and ***can***. For some speakers, ***would*** and ***could*** sound more polite, but tone of voice and the use of *please* can also determine politeness.
		NOTE: ***May*** is NOT used when ***you*** is the subject of a polite request. INCORRECT: *May you please open the door?*

EXERCISE 23 ▶ Looking at grammar. (Chart 7-6)

Make two different questions for each situation. Use *you*.

1. You're in a room and it's getting very hot.

   Formal: *Would you please open the window?*

   Informal: *Can you turn on the air conditioner?*

2. You're trying to watch TV, but your friends are talking too loud, and you can't hear it.

   Formal: _____

   Informal: _____

3. You're in a restaurant. You are about to pay and notice the bill is more than it should be. The server has made a mistake.

   Formal: _____

   Informal: _____

4. You are in an apartment building and running toward an elevator. There is a woman in it, and the door is beginning to close. You want her to hold it open for you.

   Formal: _____

   Informal: _____

EXERCISE 24 ▶ Let's talk: pairwork. (Charts 7-5 and 7-6)

Work with a partner. Make a conversation for one (or more) of the situations. Perform your conversation for the rest of the class.

Example: You're in a restaurant. You want the server to refill your coffee cup. You catch the server's eye and raise your hand slightly. He approaches your table and says: "Yes? What can I do for you?"

PARTNER A: Yes? What can I do for you?
PARTNER B: Could I please have some more coffee?
PARTNER A: Of course. Right away. Could I get you anything else?
PARTNER B: No thanks. Oh, on second thought, yes. Would you bring some cream too?
PARTNER A: Certainly.
PARTNER B: Thanks.

1. You've been waiting in a long line at a busy bakery. Finally, it's your turn. The clerk turns toward you and says: "Next!"
2. You are at work. You feel sick and you have a slight fever. You really want to go home. You see your boss, Mr. Jenkins, walking by your desk. You say: "Mr. Jenkins, could I speak with you for a minute?"
3. The person next to you on the plane has a bag on the floor that is in your space. You would like him to move it. You say: "Excuse me."

EXERCISE 25 ▶ Looking at grammar. (Charts 7-5 and 7-6)

Choose the correct verbs. In some cases, both answers may be correct.

At a Government Office

1. _____ your name please?
    a. May I have   b. May you give me

2. _____ your driver's license or passport?
    a. Can I see   b. Could you show me

3. _____ take your driver's license out of your wallet?
    a. Will you   b. Can you

4. _____ write down your address?
    a. May you   b. Could you

5. _____ please sign your name on the line?
    a. Will you   b. Would you

6. _____ also write the date?
    a. Can you   b. May you

7. _____ tell me the best way to reach you?
    a. May you   b. Would you

EXERCISE 26 ▶ Warm-up. (Chart 7-7)

Your friend Paula has a terrible headache. What advice would you give her? Check (✓) the sentences you agree with.

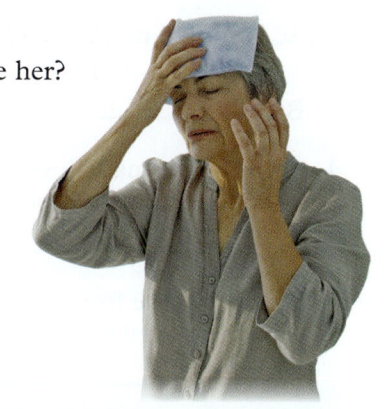

1. ____ You should lie down.
2. ____ You should take some medicine.
3. ____ You ought to call the doctor.
4. ____ You should go to the emergency room.
5. ____ You ought to put an ice-pack on your forehead.

7-7 Expressing Advice: *Should* and *Ought To*

(a) My clothes are dirty. I { *should* / *ought to* } wash them.	***Should*** and ***ought to*** have the same meaning: "This is a good idea. This is good advice." FORMS: ***should*** + *simple form of a verb* (no *to*) ***ought*** + *to* + *simple form of a verb*
(b) INCORRECT: *I should to wash them.* (c) INCORRECT: *I ought washing them.*	
(d) You need your sleep. You ***should not*** (***shouldn't***) stay up late.	NEGATIVE: ***should*** + ***not*** = ***shouldn't*** (*Ought to* is usually not used in the negative.)
(e) A: I'm going to be late for the bus. What ***should I do***? B: Run!	QUESTION: ***should*** + *subject* + *main verb* (*Ought to* is usually not used in questions.)
(f) A: I'm tired today. B: You ***should/ought to*** go home and take a nap. (g) A: I'm tired today. B: ***Maybe*** you ***should/ought to*** go home and take a nap.	The use of ***maybe*** with ***should*** and ***ought to*** "softens" advice. COMPARE: In (f): Speaker B is giving definite advice. He is stating clearly that he believes going home for a nap is a good idea and is the solution to Speaker A's problem. In (g): Speaker B is making a suggestion: going home for a nap is one possible way to solve Speaker A's problem.

EXERCISE 27 ▶ Let's talk: pairwork. (Chart 7-7)

Complete the conversations with ***should*** or ***ought to***.

Giving Advice

1. A: My computer has started to make a buzzing noise. I just bought it last month.
   B: You _____ .

2. A: For the past week, I've woken up every morning with a stiff neck. I can't figure out why. I'm not sleeping differently. My mattress and pillow are the same.
   B: You _____ .

Modal Auxiliaries, the Imperative, Making Suggestions, Stating Preferences

3. A: I worked hard and wrote a really good paper for history. My teacher doesn't think I wrote it, but I did.

   B: You _____.

4. A: My roommate doesn't clean up. The kitchen sink is full of his dirty dishes. His clothes are all over the apartment. I've talked to him many times about this.

   B: You _____.

5. A: I got home from the store and found a shirt in my bag. I didn't buy it. My four-year old son had put it there.

   B: You _____.

6. A: My daughter's friend takes really long showers when she stays with us. Sometimes she uses all the hot water.

   B: You _____.

EXERCISE 28 ▸ Let's talk: pairwork. (Chart 7-7)

Work with a partner. Partner A states the problem. Partner B gives advice using *should* or *ought to*. Include *maybe* to soften the advice if you wish. Take turns. Look at your partner before you speak.

Example: I'm sleepy.
PARTNER A: I'm sleepy.
PARTNER B: (Maybe) You should drink/ought to drink some coffee.

PARTNER A	PARTNER B
1. I can't fall asleep at night.	5. I'm starving.★
2. I have a sore throat.	6. I have the hiccups.
3. I dropped my sister's phone and cracked the screen.	7. Someone stole my lunch from the refrigerator in the staff lounge at work.
4. I sat on my friend's sunglasses. Now the frames are bent.	8. I bought some shoes that don't fit. Now my feet hurt.
	Change roles.

EXERCISE 29 ▸ Warm-up. (Chart 7-8)

Marco lost his passport. Here are some suggestions. Check (✓) the sentences you agree with. Which sentences seem more serious or urgent?

1. ____ He had better go to the embassy.

2. ____ He should wait and see if someone returns it.

3. ____ He had better report it to the police.

4. ____ He should ask a friend to help him look for it.

★*starving* (informal English) = very, very hungry

7-8 Expressing Advice: *Had Better*

(a) My clothes are dirty. I { should / ought to / had better } wash them.	**Had better** has the same basic meaning as *should* and *ought to*: "This is a good idea. This is good advice."
(b) You're driving too fast! You**'d better** slow down.	**Had better** has more of a sense of urgency than *should* or *ought to*. It often implies a warning about possible bad consequences. In (b): If you don't slow down, there could be a bad result. You could get a speeding ticket or have an accident.
(c) You**'d better not** eat that meat. It looks spoiled.	NEGATIVE: **had better not**
(d) I**'d better** send my boss an email right away.	In conversation, **had** is usually contracted: **'d**.

💬 **EXERCISE 30 ▶ Grammar and speaking.** (Chart 7-8)
Give advice using **had better**. Then mention some bad consequences if the person doesn't follow the advice. Work in pairs, in small groups, or as a class.

1. I haven't paid my electric bill.
   → *You'd better pay it by tomorrow. If you don't pay it, the electric company will turn off the power.*
2. Joe oversleeps a lot. This week he has been late to work three times. His boss is very unhappy about that.
3. I don't feel good right now. I think I'm coming down with something.*
4. I can't remember if I locked the front door when I left for work.
5. I can't find my credit card, and I've looked everywhere.
6. My ankle really hurts. I think I've sprained it.

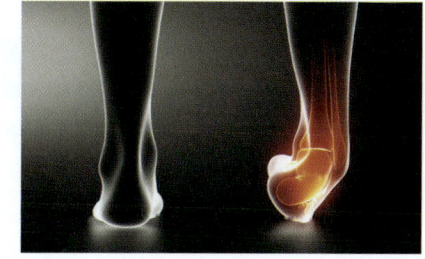

💬 **EXERCISE 31 ▶ Let's talk.** (Charts 7-7 and 7-8)
Work in small groups. Give advice using **should**, **ought to**, and **had better**. The leader states the problem, and others in the group offer suggestions. Select a different leader for each item on page 210.

Example:
LEADER: I study, but I don't understand my physics class. It's the middle of the term, and I'm failing the course. I need a science course in order to graduate. What should I do?**
STUDENT A: You**'d better** get a tutor right away.
STUDENT B: You **should** make an appointment with your teacher and see if you can get some extra help.
STUDENT C: Maybe you **ought to** drop your physics course and take a different science course next term.

---

*The idiom *come down with something* = get sick.

**Should* (NOT *ought to* or *had better*) is usually used in a question that asks for advice. The answer, however, can contain *should*, *ought to*, or *had better*. For example:
   A: *My houseplants always die. What should I do?*
   B: *You'd better get a book on plants. You should try to find out why they die. Maybe you ought to look on the internet and see if you can find some information.*

1. I forgot my dad's birthday yesterday. I feel terrible about it. What should I do?
2. I just discovered that I made dinner plans for tonight with two different people. I'm supposed to meet my parents at one restaurant at 7:00, and I'm supposed to meet my boss at a different restaurant across town at 8:00. What should I do?
3. Samira accidentally left the grocery store with an item she didn't pay for. It was under her purse in the shopping cart. What should Samira do?
4. I borrowed Karen's favorite book of poetry. It was special to her. A note on the inside cover said "To Karen." The author's signature was under it. Now I can't find the book. I think I lost it. What should I do?

EXERCISE 32 ▶ Warm-up. (Chart 7-9)

Which of these statements about writing a résumé are true in your country? Check (✓) them. Which sentence is more common in writing? Which sentences are more common in speaking?

Writing a Résumé

1. _____ You must list all your previous employers.
2. _____ You have to provide references.
3. _____ You have got to include personal information, for example, whether you are married or not.

7-9 Expressing Necessity: *Have To, Have Got To, Must*

(a) I have a very important test tomorrow. I { *have to* / *have got to* / *must* } *study* tonight.	***Have to***, ***have got to***, and ***must*** have basically the same meaning. They express the idea that something is necessary.
(b) I'd like to go with you to the movie this evening, but I can't. I ***have to go*** to a meeting. (c) Bye now! I'***ve got to go***. My wife's waiting for me. I'll call you later. (d) All passengers ***must present*** their passports at customs upon arrival. (e) Tommy, you ***must hold*** onto the railing when you go down the stairs.	***Have to*** is used much more frequently in everyday speech and writing than ***must***. ***Have got to*** is typically used in informal conversation, as in (c). ***Must*** is typically found in written instructions or rules, as in (d). Adults also use it when talking to younger children, as in (e). It sounds very strong.
(f) ***Do*** we ***have to bring*** pencils to the test? (g) Why ***did*** he ***have to leave*** so early?	QUESTIONS: ***Have to*** is usually used in questions, not ***must*** or ***have got to***. Forms of ***do*** are used with ***have to*** in questions.
(h) I ***had to study*** last night.	The PAST form of ***have to***, ***have got to***, and ***must*** (meaning necessity) is ***had to***. NOTE: ***Must*** is NOT used for the past tense.
(i) I ***have to*** ("hafta") *go* downtown today. (j) Rita ***has to*** ("hasta") *go* to the bank. (k) I've ***got to*** ("gotta") *study* tonight.	NOTE: ***Have to***, ***has to***, and ***have got to*** are commonly reduced, as in (i) through (k).

EXERCISE 33 ▶ Grammar and speaking. (Charts 7-7 and 7-9)
Choose the correct meaning for each statement. Which ones do you agree with?

Rules or Advice?

1.	Teenagers have to be respectful to their parents.	necessity	advice
2.	The elderly should live with their children.	necessity	advice
3.	Babies ought to sleep with their mothers.	necessity	advice
4.	Kids have got to obey their parents.	necessity	advice
5.	Families should have dinner together every night.	necessity	advice
6.	Parents must love their children.	necessity	advice

EXERCISE 34 ▶ Let's talk. (Charts 7-7 and 7-9)
Answer the questions. Work in pairs, in small groups, or as a class.

1. What are some things you **have to do** today? Tomorrow? Every day?
2. What is something you **had to do** yesterday?
3. What is something you**'ve got to do** soon?
4. What is something you**'ve got to do** after class today or later tonight?
5. What is something a driver **must do**, according to the law?
6. What is something a safe driver **should or shouldn't do**?
7. What are some things a person **should or shouldn't do** to stay healthy?
8. What are some things a person **must do** to stay alive?

EXERCISE 35 ▶ Grammar and speaking. (Charts 7-7 and 7-9)
Check (✓) the statement in each pair that you agree with. Discuss your answers with another student or in small groups.

At a Restaurant

1. _____ Diners must leave a tip.

   _____ Diners should leave a tip.

2. _____ Servers must wash their hands.

   _____ Servers ought to wash their hands.

3. _____ People have got to put their phones away in the restaurant.

   _____ People should put their phones away in the restaurant.

4. _____ The restaurant manager should greet customers when they enter the restaurant.

   _____ The restaurant manager has to greet customers when they enter the restaurant.

5. _____ The servers must wear uniforms.

   _____ The servers should wear their own clothes.

EXERCISE 36 ▶ Looking at grammar. (Charts 7-2 → 7-4, 7-7, and 7-9)
Part I. Choose the correct completions for the sentences. Sometimes both choices may be correct.

Many English names have two forms: a formal or legal name and an informal one. For example, you **should / may** know a person as Andy, but his legal name is Andrew. Or, for a woman, Kathy **could / may** have the formal name Katherine or Kathleen. Why is this important? Imagine you **have to / maybe** look up a phone number, either in a phone book or on the internet. People **might / can** use their formal name for registration, and this **could / may** show up on the internet or elsewhere.

Look at these names: Nick, Lilly. **Can you / Are you able to** give the formal names?

Part II. Work with a partner. Write a formal name for each of the following.

1. Bob, Bobby → _____
2. Danny → _____
3. Jon, Jonny → _____
4. Bill, Billy → _____
5. Debbie → _____
6. Sue → _____
7. Alex → _____
8. Terry → _____

EXERCISE 37 ▶ Listening. (Chart 7-9)
Complete the sentences with the words you hear.

EMPLOYMENT APPLICATION

Applications are considered for all positions without regard to race, color, religion, sex, national origin, age, marital or veteran status, or in the presence of a non-related medical condition or handicap.

Donna	N/A	Frost	May 4, 2019
First Name	Middle Initial	Last Name	Date

1443 Maple Ridge Heights		052-555-5454	
Address		Phone #	

Happyville	PA	04321	123-000-7890
City	State	Zip Code	Social Security #

Do you know these words?
- employment   - previous
- applicable   - employer
- legal   - apply
- nickname

Filling out a Job Application

1. The application _____ be complete. You shouldn't skip any parts. If a section doesn't fit your situation, you can write N/A (not applicable).

2. If you fill out the form by hand, your writing _____ be easy to read.

3. _____ use your full legal name, not your nickname.

4. _____ list the names and places of your previous employers.

5. _____ list your education, beginning with either high school or college.

6. All spelling _____ be correct.

7. A: _____ write the same thing twice, like a phone number?

   B: No, you can just write "same as above."

8. A: _____ apply in person?

   B: No, for a lot of companies, you can do it online.

EXERCISE 38 ▶ Reading and speaking. (Charts 7-7 → 7-9)
Part I. Read the passage.

A Family Problem

Mr. and Mrs. Hill don't know what to do about their 15-year-old son, Mark. He's very intelligent but has no interest in learning. His grades are getting worse, and he won't do any homework. Sometimes he skips school and spends the day at the mall.

His older sister Kathy is a good student, and she never causes any problems at home. Kathy hasn't missed a day of school all year. Mark's parents keep asking him why he can't be more like Kathy. Mark is jealous of Kathy and picks fights* with her.

All Mark likes to do is stay in his bedroom and listen to loud music or play video games. He often refuses to eat meals with his family. He argues with his parents, his room is a mess, and he won't** help around the house.

Part II. This family needs advice. Work with a partner. What should they do? What shouldn't they do? Make a list, and compare your suggestions with the advice of other classmates.

Use each of these words at least once in the advice you give.

| should | have got to/has got to | ought to | must |
| shouldn't | had better | have to/has to | |

EXERCISE 39 ▶ Warm-up. (Chart 7-10)
Which sentence (a. or b.) completes the idea of the given sentence?

We have lots of time.
   a. You must not hurry!
   b. You don't have to hurry!

---
*pick a fight = start a fight

**won't is used here to express refusal: He refuses to help around the house.

7-10 Expressing Lack of Necessity: *Do Not Have To*; Expressing Prohibition: *Must Not*

(a) I finished all of my homework this afternoon. I **don't have to study** tonight. (b) Tomorrow is a holiday. Mary **doesn't have to go** to class. (c) I **didn't have to work** last week. I had several days off.	**Don't / doesn't / didn't have to** express the idea that something is *not necessary*.
(d) Bus passengers *must not talk* to the driver. (e) Tommy, you *must not/mustn't* play* with matches! (f) **Do not/Don't** talk to the driver. (g) **Do not/Don't** play with matches.	**Must not** expresses *prohibition* (DO NOT DO THIS!). **Must not** is not common; it is generally used for rules or with children. Speakers more often express prohibition with imperatives**, as in (f) and (g).

*The first "t" is not pronounced.
**See also Chart 7-13.

EXERCISE 40 ▶ Looking at grammar. (Chart 7-10)
Complete the sentences with ***don't have to***, ***doesn't have to***, or ***must not***.

1. You ____must not____ drive when you are tired. It's dangerous.
2. I live only a few blocks from my office. I ____don't have to____ drive to work.
3. Liz finally got a car, so now she drives to work. She _____ take the bus.
4. Mr. Murphy is very wealthy. He _____ work for a living.
5. You _____ tell Daddy about the birthday party. We want it to be a surprise.
6. A: Did Professor Acosta give an assignment?
   B: Yes, she assigned Chapters 4 and 6, but we _____ read Chapter 5.
7. A: Listen carefully, Kristen. If a stranger offers you a ride, you _____ get in the car. Never get in a car with a stranger. Do you understand?
   B: Yes, Mom.

EXERCISE 41 ▶ Grammar and speaking. (Charts 7-9 and 7-10)
Work with a partner. Take turns making true sentences about your time in elementary school using **have to** and **didn't have to**.

Elementary School Experiences

1. study English grammar → *I had to / didn't have to study English grammar.*
2. wear a uniform
3. knock on the classroom door before I entered
4. help clean the school at the end of the day
5. bring my lunch to school

6. learn keyboarding skills for the computer
7. take a lot of tests
8. use online textbooks
9. sing by myself in front of other students
10. do a lot of homework every night

EXERCISE 42 ▶ Warm-up. (Chart 7-11)

Read the situation and the conclusions that follow. Which conclusion(s) seem(s) logical to you? Explain your answers, if necessary.

SITUATION: Mr. Ellis is a high school gym teacher. He usually wears gym clothes to work. Today he is wearing a suit and tie.

1. He must have an important meeting.
2. He must be rich.
3. He must need new clothes.
4. He must want to make a good impression on someone.
5. His gym clothes must not be clean.

7-11 Making Logical Conclusions: *Must*

(a) A: Nancy is yawning. B: She **must be** sleepy.	In (a): Speaker B is making a logical guess. He bases his guess on the information that Nancy is yawning. His logical conclusion, his "best guess," is that Nancy is sleepy. He uses **must** to express his logical conclusion.
(b) LOGICAL CONCLUSION: Lea doesn't eat meat. She **must be** vegetarian. (c) NECESSITY: If you want to get into the movie theater, you **must buy** a ticket.	COMPARE: **Must** can express • a logical conclusion, as in (b). • necessity, as in (c).
(d) NEGATIVE LOGICAL CONCLUSION: Eric ate everything on his plate except the pickle. He **must not like** pickles. (e) PROHIBITION: There are sharks near the hotel beach. You **must not go** swimming there.	COMPARE: **Must not** can express • a negative logical conclusion, as in (d). • prohibition, as in (e).

EXERCISE 43 ▶ Looking at grammar. (Chart 7-11)
Complete the conversations with **must** or **must not**.

My Best Guess

1. A: Did you offer our guests something to eat?

    B: Yes, but they didn't want anything. They ___must not___ be hungry yet.

2. A: You haven't eaten since breakfast? That was hours ago. You ___must___ be hungry.

    B: I am.

3. A: Gregory has already had four glasses of water, and now he's having another.

    B: He _____ be really thirsty.

4. A: I offered Holly something to drink, but she doesn't want anything.

    B: She _____ be thirsty.

5. A: The dog won't eat.

    B: He _____ feel well.

6. A: Brian has watery eyes and has been coughing and sneezing.

    B: Poor guy. He _____ have a cold.

7. A: Erica's really smart. She always gets above 95 percent on her math tests.

    B: I'm sure she's pretty bright, but she _____ also study a lot.

8. A: Listen. Someone is jumping on the floor above us.

    B: It _____ be Sam. Sometimes he does exercises in his apartment.

EXERCISE 44 ▶ Looking at grammar. (Chart 7-11)
Make a logical conclusion for each situation. Use **must**.

1. Alima is crying. → *She must be unhappy.*
2. Mrs. Chu has a big smile on her face.
3. Samantha is shivering.
4. Olga watches ten movies a week.
5. James is sweating.
6. Toshi can lift one end of a compact car by himself.

EXERCISE 45 ▶ Let's talk. (Chart 7-11)
Make logical conclusions with **must** or **must not**. Use the suggested phrases and/or your own words.

1. I am at Cyril's apartment door. I've knocked on the door and have rung the doorbell several times. Nobody has answered the door. *(be at home? be out somewhere?)*
    → *Cyril must not be at home. He must be out somewhere.*

2. Jennifer reads all the time. She sits in a quiet corner and reads even when people come to visit her. (*love books? like books better than people? like to talk to people?*)

3. Lara has a full academic schedule, plays on the volleyball team, takes piano lessons, and has a part-time job at an ice-cream store. (*be busy all the time? have a lot of spare time? be a hard worker?*)

4. Simon gets on the internet every day as soon as he gets home from work. He stays at his computer until he goes to bed. (*be a computer addict? have a happy home life? have a lot of friends?*)

EXERCISE 46 ▶ Looking at grammar. (Charts 7-9 and 7-11)
Complete the sentences with **must**, **have to**, or **had to** and the correct form of the verbs in parentheses.

At Work

A: Your eyes are red. You (*be*) _____₁_____ really tired.

B: Yeah, I (*stay*) _____₂_____ up all night working on a project.

A: Did you finish?

B: No, I (*work*) _____₃_____ on it later today, but I have a million other things to do.

A: You (*be*) _____₄_____ really busy.

B: I am!

EXERCISE 47 ▶ Looking at grammar. (Charts 7-7 → 7-11)
Choose the verb that has the same meaning as the phrase in **bold**. More than one answer may be correct.

Buying a Car

1. You really **don't have a choice**. You   have to / should   test-drive the car before you buy it.

2. **It's a good idea** to get information about cars on the internet before you go to the dealer. You   should / must   find out about things like reliability ratings and paying a fair price.

3. You **don't need to** buy a car today. You   don't have to / must not   make your decision right now. You can take some time and shop around.

4. You **need to** find out the insurance costs. You   have got to / have to   call your insurance company first. Some cars are very expensive to insure.

5. **It's a bad idea** to pay full price for a car. You   shouldn't / couldn't   pay the sticker price.

6. **That's my best guess**. The price is low. The dealer   must / had better   want to sell it quickly.

7. **That's a good idea**. You   ought to / should   find out the invoice price (the price the dealer pays for the car) before you make an offer.

EXERCISE 48 ▶ Warm-up. (Chart 7-12)
Complete the questions with the correct words in the box. Two words don't fit any questions.

| can't | couldn't | do | does | will | wouldn't |

1. You can work this weekend, _____ you?
2. He won't be late, _____ he?
3. We'd like you to stay, _____ we?
4. They don't have to leave, _____ they?

7-12 Tag Questions with Modal Auxiliaries

(a) You *can* come, ***can't you***? (b) She *won't* tell, ***will she***? (c) He *should* help, ***shouldn't he***? (d) They *couldn't* do it, ***could they***? (e) We *would like* to help, ***wouldn't we***?	Tag questions are common with these modal auxiliaries: ***can***, ***will***, ***should***, ***could***, and ***would***.*
(f) They *have to* leave, ***don't they***? (g) They *don't have to* leave, ***do they***? (h) He *has to* leave, ***doesn't he***? (i) He *doesn't have to* leave, ***does he***? (j) You *had to* leave, ***didn't you***? (k) You *didn't have to* leave, ***did you***?	Tag questions are also common with ***have to***, ***has to***, and ***had to***. Notice that forms of ***do*** are used for the tag in (f) through (k).

*See Chart 5-13, p. 149, for information on how to use tag questions.

EXERCISE 49 ▶ Looking at grammar. (Chart 7-12)
Complete the tag questions.

1. You can answer these questions, _____ you?
2. Melinda won't tell anyone our secret, _____ she?
3. Alice would like to come with us, _____ she?
4. I don't have to do more chores, _____ I?
5. Steven shouldn't come to the meeting, _____ he?
6. Flies can fly upside down, _____ they?
7. You would rather have your own apartment, _____ you?
8. Jill has to renew her driver's license, _____ she?
9. If you want to catch your bus, you should leave now, _____ you?
10. Ms. Baxter will be here tomorrow, _____ she?
11. You couldn't hear me, _____ you?
12. We had to work hard in our chemistry class, _____ we?

EXERCISE 50 ▸ Warm-up. (Chart 7-13)
Read each group of sentences. Decide who the speaker is and a possible situation for each group.

GROUP A
1. Show me your driver's license.
2. Take it out of your wallet, please.
3. Give me your registration and proof of insurance.
4. Step out of the car.

GROUP B
1. Open your mouth.
2. Stick out your tongue.
3. Say "ahhh."
4. Let me take a closer look.
5. Don't bite me!

7-13 Imperative Sentences: Giving Instructions

COMMAND:
(a) Captain: **Open** the door!
    Soldier: Yes, sir!
 	
REQUEST:
(b) Teacher: **Open** the door, please.
    Student: Sure.
 	
DIRECTIONS:
(c) Barbara: Could you tell me how to get to the post office?
    Stranger: Sure. **Walk** two blocks down this street. **Turn** left *and* **walk** three more blocks. It's on the right-hand side of the street.
	Imperative sentences are used to give commands, make polite requests, and give directions. The difference between a command and a request lies in the speaker's tone of voice and the use of **please**.
	
	Please can come at the beginning or end of a request:
	    Open the door, please.
	    Please open the door.
	
	INCORRECT: *You open the door please.*

(d) **Close** the window. (e) Please **sit** down. (f) **Be** quiet! (g) **Don't walk** on the grass. (h) Please **don't wait** for me. (i) **Don't be** late.	The simple form of a verb is used in imperative sentences. In (d): The understood subject of the sentence is *you* (meaning the person the speaker is talking to): *Close the window = You close the window.* NEGATIVE FORM: ***Don't*** + *the simple form of a verb*

EXERCISE 51 ▸ Let's talk. (Chart 7-13)
Part I. Work with a partner or in small groups. Read the steps for cooking rice. Put them in a logical order (1–8).

Cooking Rice

a. _____ Measure the rice.
b. _____ Cook for 20 minutes.
c. _____ Pour water into a pan.
d. _____ Bring the water to a boil.
e. _____ Put the rice in the pan.
f. _____ Set the timer.
g. _____ Turn off the heat.
h. _____ Take the pan off the stove.

Part II. Write instructions for cooking something simple. Share your recipe with the class.

EXERCISE 52 ▶ Listening. (Chart 7-13)
Part I. Listen to the steps in this number puzzle, and write the verbs you hear.

> Do you know these words?
> - double
> - add
> - multiply
> - subtract

Puzzle steps:

1. _____ down the number of the month you were born. For example,

   _____ the number 2 if you were born in February.

   _____ 3 if you were born in March, etc.

2. _____ the number.

3. _____ 5 to it.

4. _____ it by 50.

5. _____ your age.

6. _____ 250.

Part II. Now follow the steps in Part I to complete the puzzle. In the final number, the last two digits on the right will be your age, and the one or two digits on the left will be the month you were born.

EXERCISE 53 ▶ Warm-up. (Chart 7-14)
Check (✓) the sentences that are suggestions.

1. _____ Why do bears hibernate?
2. _____ I have a day off. Why don't we take the kids to the zoo?
3. _____ Let's go see the bears at the zoo.

7-14 Making Suggestions: *Let's* and *Why Don't*

(a) — It's hot today. **Let's** go to the beach. — OK. Good idea. (b) — It's hot today. **Why don't we** go to the beach? — OK. Good idea.	**Let's** and **Why don't we** are used to make suggestions about activities for you and another person or other people to do. Examples (a) and (b) have the same meaning. **Let's** = *let us*
(c) — I'm tired. — **Why don't you** take a nap? — That's a good idea. I think I will.	In (c): **Why don't you** is used to make a friendly suggestion or to give friendly advice.

EXERCISE 54 ▸ Looking at grammar. (Chart 7-14)
Choose the sentences that can be suggestions.

1. a. Why don't you wear something different today?
   b. Why do you wear red on Mondays?

2. a. Why did you get to work late?
   b. Why didn't you get to work on time?
   c. Why don't we get to work early?

3. a. Why do you only check email at night?
   b. Why don't you check your email now?

EXERCISE 55 ▸ Let's talk. (Chart 7-14)
Make suggestions beginning with **Let's** and **Why don't we**.

Dinner Plans
1. Where should we go for dinner tonight?
2. Who should we ask to join us for dinner tonight?
3. What time should we meet at the restaurant?
4. Where should we go afterwards?

EXERCISE 56 ▸ Let's talk. (Chart 7-14)
Work in small groups. One person states the problem, and then others in the group offer suggestions beginning with **Why don't you**.

Help!
1. I'm freezing.
2. I'm feeling dizzy.
3. I'm so bored. I want to do something fun this weekend. Any ideas?
4. I've lost my last cell phone charger. I had three, and now I have none.
5. I haven't done my assignment for Professor Lopez. It will take me a couple of hours, and class starts in an hour. What am I going to do?

6. I've lost the key to my apartment, so I can't get in. My roommate is at the library. What am I going to do?

7. My friend and I had an argument, and now we aren't talking to each other. I've had some time to think about it, and I'm sorry for what I said. I miss her friendship. What should I do?

EXERCISE 57 ▶ Warm-up. (Chart 7-15)
Check (✓) the statements that are true for you.

1. _____ I prefer vegetables to fruit.
2. _____ I like raw vegetables better than cooked.
3. _____ I would rather eat vegetables than meat.

7-15 Stating Preferences: *Prefer, Like ... Better, Would Rather*

(a) I *prefer* apples *to* oranges. (b) I *prefer* watching TV *to* studying.	***prefer*** + noun + ***to*** + noun ***prefer*** + *-ing* verb + ***to*** + *-ing* verb
(c) I *like* apples *better than* oranges. (d) I *like* watching TV *better than* studying.	***like*** + noun + ***better than*** + noun ***like*** + *-ing* verb + ***better than*** + *-ing* verb
(e) Ann *would rather have* an apple than an orange. (f) INCORRECT: *Ann would rather has an apple.* (g) I'd rather visit a big city *than live* there. (h) INCORRECT: *I'd rather visit a big city than to live there.* INCORRECT: *I'd rather visit a big city than living there.*	***Would rather*** is followed immediately by the simple form of a verb (e.g., *have, visit, live*), as in (e). Verbs following ***than*** are also in the simple form, as in (g).
(i) *I'd / You'd / She'd / He'd / We'd / They'd* rather have an apple.	Contraction of ***would*** = ***'d***
(j) *Would you rather* have an apple *or* an orange?	In (j): In a polite question, ***would rather*** can be followed by ***or*** to offer someone a choice.

EXERCISE 58 ▶ Looking at grammar. (Chart 7-15)
Complete the sentences with ***than*** or ***to***.

1. When I'm hot and thirsty, I **prefer** cold drinks ___to___ hot drinks.
2. When I'm hot and thirsty, I **like** cold drinks **better** ___than___ hot drinks.
3. When I'm hot and thirsty, I**'d rather have** a cold drink ___than___ a hot drink.
4. I **prefer** tea _____ coffee.
5. I **like** tea **better** _____ coffee.
6. I**'d rather** drink tea _____ coffee.
7. When I choose a movie to watch, I **prefer** comedies _____ drama.
8. I **like** folk music music **better** _____ rock and roll.

222 CHAPTER 7

9. My parents **would rather work** _____ retire. They enjoy their jobs.

10. Do you **like** spring **better** _____ fall?

11. I **prefer visiting** my friends in the evening _____ watching TV by myself.

12. I **would rather read** a book in the evening _____ visit with friends.

EXERCISE 59 ▸ Let's talk: pairwork. (Chart 7-15)

Work with a partner. Take turns asking and answering questions. Be sure to answer in complete sentences.

Which do you like better?

Examples: Which do you prefer: apples or oranges?*
→ *I prefer oranges to apples.*

Which do you like better: bananas or strawberries?
→ *I like bananas better than strawberries.*

Which would you rather have right now: an apple or a banana?
→ *I'd rather have a banana.*

1. Which do you like better: rice or potatoes?
2. Which do you prefer: peas or corn?
3. Which would you rather have for dinner tonight: fish or chicken?
4. Name two sports. Which do you like better?
5. Name two movies. Which one would you rather see?
6. What kind of music would you rather listen to: rock or classical?
7. Name two vegetables. Which do you prefer?
8. Name two TV programs. Which do you like better?

EXERCISE 60 ▸ Let's talk: interview. (Chart 7-15)

Interview your classmates. Use ***would rather ... than*** in your answers. Share some of your answers with the class.

Would you rather ...

1. live in an apartment or in a house?** Why?
2. be an author or an artist? Why?
3. drive a fast car or fly a small plane? Why?
4. be rich and unlucky in love or poor and lucky in love? Why?
5. surf the internet or watch TV? Why?
6. have a big family or a small family? Why?
7. be a bird or a fish? Why?
8. spend your free time with other people or by yourself? Why?

---

*Use a rising intonation on the first choice and a falling intonation on the second choice: Which do you prefer, apples or oranges?

It is possible but not necessary to repeat a preposition after **than.
CORRECT: *I'd rather live in an apartment **than in a house**.*
CORRECT: *I'd rather live in an apartment **than a house**.*

7-16 Summary: Modal Auxiliaries Taught in Chapter 7

Auxiliary + the Simple Form of a Verb		Meaning
can	(a) Olga *can speak* English. (b) You *can go* now. (c) *Can* I *leave* early?	ability permission request
could	(d) He *couldn't come* to class. (e) It *could snow* tomorrow. (f) *Could* you *help* me?	past ability possibility request
may	(g) It *may rain* tomorrow. (h) You *may leave* now. (i) *May* I *see* your passport?	possibility permission request (with *I*, not *you*)
might	(j) It *might rain* tomorrow.	possibility
should	(k) Mary *should study* harder.	advice
had better	(l) I *had better study* tonight.	advice
must	(m) You *must register* by tomorrow (n) You worked all night. You *must be* tired.	necessity logical conclusion
will	(o) I *will be* in class tomorrow. (p) *Will* you *help* me carry this box?	certainty request
would	(q) *Would* you *help* me carry this box?	request (with *you*, not *I*)
Auxiliary + *to* + the Simple Form of a Verb		
have to	(r) I *have to study* tonight. (s) I *don't have to study* tonight. (t) I *didn't have to study* last night.	necessity lack of necessity (negative)
have got to	(u) I *have got to study* tonight.	necessity
be able to	(v) Kate *is able to study* today. (w) She *wasn't able to study* yesterday.	ability
ought to	(x) Kate *ought to study* harder.	advice

EXERCISE 61 ▶ Check your knowledge. (Chapter 7 Review)

Correct the errors.

        had
1. You ˄ better call the doctor today.

2. Emma shouldn't wears shorts to work.

3. Would you please to help me clean the kitchen?

4. George was able to talking by the age of one.

5. Today might a good day to go to the zoo with the kids.

6. I ought paying my bills today.

7. You don't should stay up too late tonight.

8. Can you speak any English a few years ago?

9. May you give me your name, please?

10. We must wait a long time for the subway last night.

11. You don't has to wait for me. I'll be a little late.

12. You won't tell anyone my secret, are you?

13. Please you unlock the door for me. I can't find my key.

14. Let's to take a break.

15. I prefer cooking vegetables to eat them raw.

EXERCISE 62 ▸ Reading, speaking, and writing. (Chapter 7)
Part I. Read the blog entry by co-author Stacy Hagen. Give the meaning for each of the boldfaced words. You can use Chart 7-16 for reference. Then find at least two uses of the imperative that give advice.

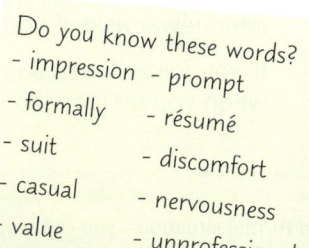

Do you know these words?
- impression
- prompt
- formally
- résumé
- suit
- discomfort
- casual
- nervousness
- value
- unprofessional

BlackBookBlog

How to Make a Good Impression in a Job Interview

As you know, it is important to make a good impression when you interview for a job. For example, the way you dress can create a positive or negative impression. When I applied for my first job, many years ago, people dressed more **formally**. At the time, women wore dresses or skirts, never pants, and men wore **suits**. Now, you can be a little more **casual**. Sometimes women wear nice pants, and men **don't have to** always wear suits. It depends on the company you want to work for. Different companies have different work cultures.

However, there are certain things you **should** and **shouldn't** do to make a good impression. For example, you shouldn't wear flip-flops or shorts. This is probably too casual unless you are applying to be a surfing instructor!

Are this man's clothes appropriate for a job interview? Why or why not?

Be sure to arrive on time or even a little early. Employers value workers who are prompt.

The interviewer will already have the résumé you sent, but you **might** want to bring extra copies. There **may** be more than one interviewer, and it's helpful if everyone has a copy of your résumé.

Greet the interviewer by name. Say, "Hello," or "Hi, Ms. Thompson*." It's common to follow with "It's nice to meet you." If you are in a culture where shaking hands is common, you can put out your hand at the same time. "Hey" is not an appropriate greeting and may create a negative impression. Save it for informal situations or for friends.

When you are answering the interviewer's questions, make eye contact. In many countries like the U.S. and Canada, this shows confidence and interest. Looking down or away may communicate discomfort or nervousness.

You probably already know this, but don't chew gum during the interview. It makes noise and looks unprofessional.

Finally, you will want to prepare for your interview. Look up common interview questions on the internet and practice answers. (There are many sites that give useful advice for different types of companies.) Also, you **ought to** research the company before you go to the interview. That way, you **can** show some knowledge of the company as you talk about the job. It can also help you think of good questions to ask. Often at the end of the interview, the interviewer asks if you have questions about the company.

If you follow these suggestions, you will have a better chance of making a good impression when you go for a job interview. Good luck!

*In formal situations, you can say, "How do you do?" instead of "Hello" or "Hi."

Part II. Work in small groups and discuss these questions.

1. What advice in the blog is the same as in your country and what advice is different?
2. What other suggestions can you think of to make a good impression at a job interview?
3. Can you think of other things a person in your country should never do at a job interview?

Part III. Choose one of the topics below. Write a three-paragraph blog entry of your own. Using Part I as a model, give general advice to people who want to …

1. improve their health.
2. get good grades.
3. improve their English.
4. find a job.
5. get a good night's sleep.
6. protect the environment by recycling.

Use this outline for writing your three paragraphs.

I. Beginning paragraph: *Do you want to … ? Here are some suggestions for you to consider.*
II. Middle paragraph: List your suggestions and add details, making use of modal verbs and the imperative.
III. Concluding paragraph: *Follow these suggestions for …*

WRITING TIP

An outline, formatted as shown below, is useful for organizing your writing.

Use roman numbers to show the topic of each paragraph. Use capital letters to show details under your topics.

    I. Introduction
   II. Suggestions
       A.
       B.
       C.
       etc.
  III. Conclusion

Part IV. Edit your writing. Check for the following:

1. ☐ use of your outline to guide your writing
2. ☐ correct use of different modal verbs or the imperative to give advice
3. ☐ use of *to* when necessary with the modal
4. ☐ no *-s* on the main verbs that come after modals
5. ☐ correct spelling (use a dictionary or spell-check)

▪▪▪▪▪ For digital resources, go to MyEnglishLab on the Pearson English Portal. You can also go to the Pearson Practice English app for mobile practice.

CHAPTER 8

Connecting Ideas: Punctuation and Meaning

PRETEST: What do I already know?
Write "C" if the punctuation, meaning, or verb form is correct. Write "I" if it is incorrect.

1. _____ My mom puts milk lemon and sugar in her tea. (Chart 8-1)
2. _____ Do you prefer coffee or tea with breakfast? (Chart 8-2)
3. _____ Martha had no vacation time, so she was very unhappy. (8-3)
4. _____ Tomorrow won't work for an appointment, but the next day will. (8-4)
5. _____ Joe went to college, but his brother didn't. (8-4)
6. _____ The supervisor doesn't leave work early, and neither don't his employees. (Chart 8-5)
7. _____ Lauren overslept because her alarm didn't ring. (Chart 8-6)
8. _____ Even though Thomas likes to cook, he often eats dinner at home. (Chart 8-7)
9. _____ Jennifer gets good grades although she studies a lot. (Chart 8-7)

EXERCISE 1 ▶ Warm-up. (Chart 8-1)
Check (✓) the sentences that have the correct punctuation.

1. _____ I ate some raspberries, and blackberries.
2. _____ I ate some raspberries and blackberries.
3. _____ I ate some raspberries, blackberries, and blueberries.
4. _____ I ate some blueberries, Julia ate some strawberries.
5. _____ I ate some blueberries, and Julia ate some strawberries.

8-1 Connecting Ideas with *And*

Connecting Items within a Sentence

(a) NO COMMA:	I saw a cat *and* a mouse.	When *and* connects only TWO WORDS (or phrases) within a sentence, NO COMMA is used, as in (a).
(b) COMMAS:	I saw a cat**,** a mouse**,** *and* a dog.	When *and* connects THREE OR MORE items within a sentence, COMMAS are used, as in (b).*

Connecting Two Sentences

(c) COMMA:	I saw a cat**,** *and* you saw a mouse.	When *and* connects TWO COMPLETE SENTENCES (also called "independent" clauses), a COMMA is usually used, as in (c).
(d) PERIOD:	I saw a cat**.** You saw a mouse.	Without *and*, two complete sentences are separated by a period, as in (d), *not* a comma.**
(e) INCORRECT:	*I saw a cat, you saw a mouse.*	A complete sentence begins with a capital letter; note that *You* is capitalized in (d).

*In a series of three or more items, the comma before *and* is optional. ALSO CORRECT: *I saw a cat, a mouse and a dog.*
**A "period" (the dot used at the end of a sentence) is called a "full stop" in British English.

EXERCISE 2 ▶ Looking at grammar. (Chart 8-1)
Underline and label the words (noun, verb, adjective) connected by *and*. Add commas as necessary.

Birthdays

1. a. The children gave <u>flowers</u> *(noun)* and <u>gift cards</u> *(noun)* to their grandma. → (*no commas needed*)
   b. The children gave <u>flowers</u>*(noun)***,** <u>gift cards</u>*(noun)***,** and <u>balloons</u>*(noun)* to their grandma. → (*commas needed*)

2. a. The cake was moist and delicious.

   b. The cake was moist sweet and delicious.

3. a. The girls at the party danced talked and laughed.

   b. The girls at the party danced and talked.

4. a. A clown made dogs cats horses and giraffes out of balloons for the children.

   b. The clown was funny friendly and kind.

EXERCISE 3 ▶ Speaking and writing. (Chart 8-1)
Interview another student in your class. Take notes and then write complete sentences using *and*. Share some of the answers with the class.

What are …

1. your three favorite sports?
2. three adjectives that describe the weather today?
3. four cities that you would like to visit?

4. two characteristics that describe this city or town?
5. five things you did this morning?
6. three things you are afraid of?
7. two or more things that make you happy?
8. the four most important qualities of a good parent?

EXERCISE 4 ▶ Looking at grammar. (Chart 8-1)
Add commas, periods, and capital letters as necessary.

Visiting Italy

1. Italy is a popular country. ~~m~~ **M**any tourists go there.
2. Italy is a popular country, and many tourists go there.*
3. High-speed trains run between major cities they are very comfortable.
4. Some interesting cities are Rome Florence Venice Milan and Naples.
5. Milan is in the north Naples is in the south.
6. I asked a question in Italian the tour guide answered in my language.
7. I asked a question in Italian and the tour guide answered in my language.
8. The west coast is beautiful many villages have spectacular views of the sea.
9. You should also visit the east coast Venice is a good place to start.

EXERCISE 5 ▶ Warm-up. (Chart 8-2)
Complete the sentences with your own ideas. Make true statements.

1. When I'm not sure of the meaning of a word in English, I _____ or _____.

2. Sometimes I don't understand native speakers of English, but I _____.

*Sometimes the comma is omitted when **and** connects two very short independent clauses: *The rain fell **and** the wind blew.* In longer sentences, the comma is helpful and usual.

8-2 Connecting Ideas with *But* and *Or*

(a) I *went* to bed *but couldn't* sleep. (b) Is a lemon *sweet or sour*?	***And***, ***but***, and ***or*** are called "coordinating conjunctions." Similar to ***and***, ***but*** and ***or*** can connect items within a sentence.
(c) Did you order *coffee, tea, or milk*? (d) Did you order *coffee, tea or milk*?	When there are three or more items in a series, a comma is used between the first items in the series. A comma before the conjunction is optional, as in (c) and (d).
I dropped the vase. = a sentence *It didn't break.* = a sentence (e) I dropped the vase**,** ***but*** it didn't break. (f) Do we have class on Monday**,** ***or*** is Monday a holiday?	A comma is usually used when ***but*** or ***or*** combines two complete (independent) sentences into one sentence, as in (e) and (f). A conjunction can also come at the beginning of a sentence, except in formal writing. ALSO CORRECT: I dropped the vase. But it didn't break. I saw a cat. And you saw a mouse.

EXERCISE 6 ▶ Looking at grammar. (Charts 8-1 and 8-2)
Complete the sentences with ***and***, ***but***, or ***or***. Add commas as necessary.

Sports

1. Golf __and__ tennis are popular sports in my country.
2. Sara is a good tennis player**,** __but__ she doesn't enjoy it.
3. Which would you prefer? Would you like to play tennis __or__ golf Saturday?
4. Who won? Did your team _____ the other team score the extra point?
5. Jason doesn't do any exercise _____ he is out of shape. He doesn't care.
6. I got a baseball a basketball _____ a soccer ball for my birthday.
7. Do you like baseball _____ basketball better?
8. I hit the baseball hard _____ it didn't go very far.
9. I play baseball _____ I don't play basketball.
10. Julia kicked the ball _____ didn't score a goal.

EXERCISE 7 ▶ Looking at grammar. (Charts 8-1 and 8-2)
Add commas, periods, and capital letters as necessary.

Electronic Devices* on Airplanes

1. Laptops are electronic devices**.** ͨcell phones are electronic devices.
2. Laptops and portable DVD players are electronic devices but flashlights aren't.

*device = a thing, often electric or electronic, that has a specific purpose

3. In the past, passengers couldn't use these electronic devices during takeoffs and landings they could use them the rest of the flight.
4. Now passengers can use DVD players electronic readers and cell phones for the entire flight but they need to be in airplane mode.
5. Passengers need to put their laptops away for takeoffs and landings they are too big for passengers to hold safely during this time.

EXERCISE 8 ▸ Warm-up. (Chart 8-3)
Choose the logical completion for each sentence.

1. I was tired, so I _____.   a. didn't sleep
2. I was tired, but I _____.   b. slept

8-3	Connecting Ideas with *So*	

(a)	The room was dark, *so* I turned on a light.	**So** can be used as a conjunction, as in (a). It is preceded by a comma. It connects the ideas in two independent clauses.
		
		So expresses *results*:
		  cause: *The room was dark.*
		  result: *I turned on a light.*

(b)	COMPARE: The room was dark, *but* I didn't turn on a light.	**But** often expresses an unexpected result, as in (b).

EXERCISE 9 ▸ Looking at grammar. (Charts 8-2 and 8-3)
Complete the sentences with *so* or *but*.

Traffic Problems

1. a. It began to rain hard, __so__ traffic slowed down.
   b. It began to rain hard, __but__ traffic didn't slow down.
   c. Traffic didn't slow down, _____ there were several accidents.
   d. Traffic didn't slow down, _____ there weren't any accidents.
2. a. The roads were icy, _____ many people drove on them.
   b. The roads were icy, _____ many people took the subway.
3. a. A train hit a car, _____ no one was hurt.
   b. A train hit a car, _____ police closed the road.
   c. Police closed the road, _____ traffic backed up.

232 CHAPTER 8

EXERCISE 10 ▶ Looking at grammar. (Charts 8-1 → 8-3)
Add commas, periods, and capital letters as necessary.

Surprising Animal Facts

1. Some tarantulas can go two and a half years without food. When they eat, they like grasshoppers beetles small spiders and sometimes small lizards.

2. A female elephant is pregnant for approximately twenty months and almost always has only one baby a young elephant stays close to its mother for the first ten years of its life.

3. Dolphins sleep with one eye open they need to be conscious or awake in order to breathe if they fall asleep when they are breathing, they will drown so they sleep with half their brain awake and one eye open.

 EXERCISE 11 ▶ Grammar and listening. (Charts 8-1 → 8-3)
Listen to the passage. Then add commas, periods, and capital letters as necessary. Listen again as you check your answers.

Do you know these words?
- blinker
- do a good deed
- motioned
- wave someone on

PAYING IT FORWARD*

(1) A few days ago, a friend and I were driving from Benton Harbor to Chicago. We didn't have any delays for the first hour but we ran into some highway construction near Chicago the traffic wasn't moving my friend and I sat and waited we talked about our jobs our families and the terrible traffic slowly it started to move

(2) we noticed a black sports car on the shoulder its blinker was on the driver obviously wanted to get back into traffic car after car passed without letting him in I decided to do a good deed so I motioned for him to get in line ahead of me he waved thanks and I waved back at him

(3) all the cars had to stop at a toll booth a short way down the road I held out my money to pay my toll but the toll-taker just smiled and waved me on she told me that the man in the black sports car had already paid my toll wasn't that a nice way of saying thank you?

*paying it forward = doing something nice for someone after someone does something nice for you. For example, imagine you are at a coffee stand waiting to buy a cup of coffee. The person in front of you is chatting with you and pays for your cup of coffee. You then buy a cup of coffee for the next person in line. You are *paying it forward*.

Paying it forward means the opposite of *paying it back* (repaying a debt or an obligation).

EXERCISE 12 ▶ Warm-up. (Chart 8-4)
Complete the sentences. Make true statements. Share a few of your sentences with the class.

1. I like ____fish____, but ____my sister____ doesn't.
2. I don't like _____, but _____ does.
3. I've seen _____, but _____ hasn't.
4. I'm not _____, but _____ is.
5. I wasn't _____ at 1:00 this morning, but _____ was.
6. I will _____, but _____ won't.

8-4 Using Auxiliary Verbs After *But*

(a) I **don't like** coffee, **but** my husband **does**.
(b) I **like** tea, **but** my husband **doesn't**.
(c) I **won't be** here tomorrow, **but** Sue **will**.
(d) I've **seen** that movie, **but** Joe **hasn't**.
(e) He **isn't** here, **but** she **is**.*
	After **but**, often only an auxiliary verb is used. It has the same tense or modal as the main verb.
	
	In (a): **does** = likes coffee
	
	Note in the examples:
	  negative + **but** + affirmative
	  affirmative + **but** + negative

*A verb is not contracted with a pronoun at the end of a sentence after **but** and **and**:
   CORRECT: … but she is.
   INCORRECT: … but she's.

EXERCISE 13 ▶ Looking at grammar. (Chart 8-4)
Part I. Complete each sentence with the correct negative auxiliary verb.

1. Alan listens to podcasts, but his brother ____doesn't____.
2. Alan listens to podcasts, but his brothers ____don't____.
3. Alan is listening to a podcast, but his brother _____.
4. Alan is listening to a podcast, but his brothers _____.
5. Alan listened to a podcast last week, but his brother(s) _____.
6. Alan has listened to some podcasts recently, but his brother _____.
7. Alan has listened to some podcasts recently, but his brothers _____.
8. Alan is going to listen to a podcast soon, but his brother _____.
9. Alan is going to listen to a podcast soon, but his brothers _____.
10. Alan will listen to a podcast soon, but his brother(s) _____.

Part II. Complete each sentence with the correct affirmative auxiliary verb.

1. Nicole doesn't use a laptop for her homework, but her sister ____does____.
2. Nicole doesn't use a laptop for her homework, but her sisters ____do____.
3. Nicole isn't using a laptop for her homework, but her sister _____.

234 CHAPTER 8

4. Nicole isn't using a laptop for her homework, but her sisters _____.

5. Nicole didn't use a laptop for her homework, but her sister(s) _____.

6. Nicole hasn't used a laptop recently, but her sister _____.

7. Nicole hasn't used a laptop recently, but her sisters _____.

8. Nicole isn't going to use a laptop tomorrow, but her sister _____.

9. Nicole isn't going to use a laptop tomorrow, but her sisters _____.

10. Nicole won't use a laptop tomorrow, but her sister(s) _____.

EXERCISE 14 ▶ Grammar and speaking. (Chart 8-4)

Complete the sentences with true statements about your classmates. You may need to check with them to get more information. Use appropriate auxiliary verbs.

1. __Kira__ has long hair, but __Yuki doesn't_____.
2. _____ isn't hungry right now, but _____.
3. _____ lives nearby, but _____.
4. _____ can speak (*a language*) _____, but _____.
5. _____ plays a musical instrument, but _____.
6. _____ wasn't here last year, but _____.
7. _____ will be at home tonight, but _____.
8. _____ doesn't wear a ring, but _____.
9. _____ didn't study here last year, but _____.
10. _____ has lived here for a long time, but _____.

EXERCISE 15 ▶ Listening. (Chart 8-4)

Complete the sentences with appropriate auxiliary verbs.

A Strong Storm

Example: You will hear: My husband saw a tree fall, but I …
          You will write: __didn't__.

1. _____. 5. _____.
2. _____. 6. _____.
3. _____. 7. _____.
4. _____. 8. _____.

EXERCISE 16 ▶ Warm-up. (Chart 8-5)
Match each sentence with the correct picture. NOTE: One picture doesn't match any of the sentences.

Picture A   Picture B   Picture C

1. _____ Alice has a motorcycle, and her husband does too.
2. _____ Alice has a motorcycle, and so does her husband.
3. _____ Alice doesn't have a motorcycle, and her husband doesn't either.
4. _____ Alice doesn't have a motorcycle, and neither does her husband.

8-5 Using And + Too, So, Either, Neither

(a)	S + AUX + TOO
	Sue works, *and Tom does too*.
		In affirmative statements, an auxiliary verb + *too* or *so* can be used after *and*.
		
		Examples (a) and (b) have the same meaning.
		
		Word order:
		  subject + auxiliary + **too**
		  so + auxiliary + subject

(b)	SO + AUX + S Sue works, *and so does Tom*.	

(c)	S + AUX + EITHER
	Ann doesn't work, *and Joe doesn't either*.
		An auxiliary verb + **either** or **neither** are used with negative statements.
		
		Examples (c) and (d) have the same meaning.
		
		Word order:
		  subject + auxiliary + **either**
		  neither + auxiliary + subject
		
		NOTE: An affirmative auxiliary is used with *neither*.

(d)	NEITHER + AUX + S Ann doesn't work, *and neither does Joe*.	
(e)	— I'm hungry. — *I am too. / So am I.*	**And** is not usually used when there are two speakers.
(f)	— I never eat meat. — *I don't either. / Neither do I.*	
(g)	— I'm hungry. — *Me too.* (informal)	**Me too**, **me either**, and **me neither** are often used in informal spoken English.
(h)	— I never eat meat. — *Me (n)either.* (informal)	

EXERCISE 17 ▶ Looking at grammar. (Chart 8-5)

Complete the sentences with the given words. Pay special attention to word order.

Omar James Marco Ivan

1. a. *too* Marco has a mustache, and ___James does too___.
   b. *so* Marco has a mustache, and _____.

2. a. *either* Omar doesn't have a mustache, and _____.
   b. *neither* Omar doesn't have a mustache, and _____.

3. a. *too* Marco is wearing a hat, and _____.
   b. *so* Marco is wearing a hat, and _____.

4. a. *either* Ivan isn't wearing a hat, and _____.
   b. *neither* Ivan isn't wearing a hat, and _____.

5. a. *so* Omar looks serious, and _____.
   b. *too* Omar looks serious, and _____.

EXERCISE 18 ▶ Looking at grammar. (Chart 8-5)

Part I. Complete each sentence with the correct affirmative auxiliary verb.

1. Andy walks to work, and his roommate ___does___ too.
2. Andy walks to work, and his roommates _____ too.
3. Andy is walking to work, and his roommate _____ too.
4. Andy is walking to work, and his roommates _____ too.
5. Andy walked to work last week, and his roommate(s) _____ too.
6. Andy has walked to work recently, and so _____ his roommate.
7. Andy has walked to work recently, and so _____ his roommates.
8. Andy is going to walk to work tomorrow, and so _____ his roommate.
9. Andy is going to walk to work tomorrow, and so _____ his roommates.
10. Andy will walk to work tomorrow, and so _____ his roommate(s).

Part II. Complete each sentence with the correct negative auxiliary verb.

1. Karen doesn't watch TV, and her sister ___doesn't___ either.
2. Karen doesn't watch TV, and her sisters _____ either.
3. Karen isn't watching TV, and her sister _____ either.
4. Karen isn't watching TV, and her sisters _____ either.
5. Karen didn't watch TV last night, and her sister(s) _____ either.
6. Karen hasn't watched TV recently, and neither _____ her sister.
7. Karen hasn't watched TV recently, and neither _____ her sisters.
8. Karen isn't going to watch TV tomorrow, and neither _____ her sister.
9. Karen isn't going to watch TV tomorrow, and neither _____ her sisters.
10. Karen won't watch TV tomorrow, and neither _____ her sister(s).

EXERCISE 19 ▶ Grammar and speaking. (Chart 8-5)

Work in small groups. Complete the sentences with **too, so, either,** or **neither**. Make true statements. Answers will vary. You can research information on the internet.

Around the World

1. Haiti is a small country, and ___Cuba is too_____.
2. Japan produces rice, and _____.
3. Turkey has had many strong earthquakes, and _____.
4. Iceland doesn't grow coffee, and _____.

238 CHAPTER 8

5. Most Canadian children will learn more than one language, and _____.

6. Norway joined the United Nations in 1945, and _____.

7. Argentina doesn't lie on the equator, and _____.

8. Somalia lies on the Indian Ocean, and _____.

9. Monaco has never* hosted the Olympic Games, and _____.

10. South Korea had a Nobel Prize winner in 2000, and _____.

EXERCISE 20 ▶ Let's talk: pairwork. (Chart 8-5)

Work with a partner. Partner A says a sentence. Partner B agrees with Speaker A's statement by using *so* or *neither*. Take turns.

Example: I'm confused.
PARTNER A (*book open*):   I'm confused.
PARTNER B (*book closed*): So am I.

PARTNER A	PARTNER B
1. I studied last night.	1. I overslept this morning.
2. I study grammar every day.	2. I don't like mushrooms.
3. I'd like a cup of coffee.	3. Swimming is an Olympic sport.
4. I'm not hungry.	4. Denmark doesn't have any volcanoes.
5. I've never seen a vampire.	5. I've never seen a ghost.
6. Running is an aerobic activity.	6. Chickens lay eggs.
7. Snakes don't have legs.	7. Elephants can swim.
8. Coffee contains caffeine.	8. I'd rather go to (*name of a place*) than (*name of a place*).

EXERCISE 21 ▶ Listening and speaking. (Chart 8-5)

Part I. There are responses you can use if you want to get more information or if you disagree with someone else's statement. Listen to the examples. Pay special attention to the sentence stress in items 4–6 when Speaker B is disagreeing.

To get more information:
1. A: I'm going to drop this class.
   B: **You are? Why? What's the matter?**

2. A: My phone doesn't have enough memory for this app.
   B: **Really? Are you sure?**

3. A: I can read Braille.
   B: **You can? How did you learn to do that?**

To disagree:
4. A: I love this weather.
   B: **I don't.**

Never makes a sentence negative: *The teacher is **never** late, and **neither** am I.* OR *I'm **not** either.*

5. A: I didn't like the movie.
   B: **I did!**

6. A: I'm excited about graduation.
   B: **I'm not.**

Part II. Work with a partner. Partner A will make a statement, and Partner B will ask for more information. Take turns saying the sentences.

1. I'm feeling tired.
2. I don't like grammar.
3. I've seen a ghost.
4. I didn't eat breakfast this morning.
5. I haven't slept well all week.
6. I'm going to leave class early.

Part III. Now take turns disagreeing with the statements.

7. I believe in ghosts.
8. I didn't study hard for the last test.
9. I'm going to exercise for an hour today.
10. I like strawberries.
11. I haven't worked very hard this week.
12. I don't enjoy birthdays.

EXERCISE 22 ▶ Grammar and speaking. (Charts 8-4 and 8-5)

Make true statements about your classmates using **and** and **but**. You may need to interview them to get more information. Use the appropriate auxiliary verbs. Share some of your sentences with the class.

1. _____Kunio_____ lives in an apartment, and _____Boris does too_____.
2. _____Ellen_____ is wearing jeans, but _____Ricardo isn't_____.
3. _____ is absent today, but _____.
4. _____ didn't teach English last year, and _____ either.
5. _____ can cook, and _____ too.
6. _____ has a baseball cap, and _____ too.
7. _____ doesn't have a motorcycle, and _____ either.
8. _____ doesn't have a pet, but _____.
9. _____ will get up early tomorrow, but _____.
10. _____ has studied English for more than a year, and _____ too.

EXERCISE 23 ▶ Warm-up. (Chart 8-6)
Choose <u>all</u> the logical completions.

Because Roger felt tired, _____ .
- a. he took a nap.
- b. he didn't take a nap.
- c. he went to bed early.
- d. he didn't go to bed early.

8-6 Connecting Ideas with *Because*

(a) He drank water **because** he was thirsty.	**Because** expresses a cause; it gives a reason. Why did he drink water? *Reason:* He was thirsty.
(b) MAIN CLAUSE: *He drank water.*	A main clause is a complete sentence: **He drank water** = a complete sentence
(c) ADVERB CLAUSE: *because he was thirsty*	An adverb clause is NOT a complete sentence: ***because he was thirsty*** = NOT a complete sentence ***Because*** introduces an adverb clause: ***because*** + *subject* + *verb* = *an adverb clause*
(d) MAIN CLAUSE | ADVERB CLAUSE He drank water **because** he was thirsty. (no comma) ADVERB CLAUSE | MAIN CLAUSE (e) **Because** he was thirsty, he drank water. (comma)	An adverb clause is connected to a main clause, as in (d) and (e). In (d): *main clause + no comma + adverb clause* In (e): *adverb clause + comma + main clause* Examples (d) and (e) have exactly the same meaning.
(f) INCORRECT IN WRITING: He drank water. *Because he was thirsty.*	Example (f) is incorrect in written English: **Because he was thirsty** cannot stand alone as a sentence that starts with a capital letter and ends with a period. It has to be connected to a main clause, as in (d) and (e).
(g) CORRECT IN SPEAKING: — Why did he drink some water? — **Because he was thirsty.**	In spoken English, an adverb clause can be used as the short answer to a question, as in (g).

EXERCISE 24 ▶ Looking at grammar. (Chart 8-6)
Combine each pair of sentences in two different orders. Use ***because***. Punctuate carefully.

Tom's car is a lemon!

1. Tom knew he bought a lemon. \ He had problems the first week.
    → *Tom knew he bought a lemon because he had problems the first week.*
    → *Because he had problems the first week, Tom knew he bought a lemon.*

2. The battery was dead. \ His car didn't start the other day.
3. The Check Engine light is on. \ The car is leaking oil.
4. The heater isn't working. \ It's freezing inside.
5. The windows are foggy. \ The defroster is broken.

EXERCISE 25 ▶ Looking at grammar. (Chart 8-6)
Add periods, commas, and capital letters as necessary.

Nighttime Fears

1. Jimmy is very young. *B*/because he is afraid of the dark, he likes to have a light on in his bedroom at night.

2. Andrew thinks a wolf lives under his bed because he is so scared his dad looks under his bed every night.

3. Kim believes a ghost lives in her bedroom closet because she thinks the ghost comes out at night she sleeps with the closet door closed.

4. Lesley is afraid of spiders in her bed because she once saw a spider web over her bed she checks under her covers every night.

EXERCISE 26 ▶ Looking at grammar. (Charts 8-3 and 8-6)
Part I. Restate the sentences, paying attention to punctuation. Use *so*.

Making Decisions

1. Alberto is meeting with his advisor because he hasn't decided on a major.
   → *Alberto hasn't decided on a major, so he is meeting with his advisor.*
2. Because Clarita has trouble making decisions, she calls her mom every day for advice.
3. Julia is a popular manager because she asks her employees for their opinions before she makes important decisions.

Part II. Restate the sentences, paying attention to punctuation. Use *because*.

4. Taylor's parents were very controlling, so she doesn't have much experience making decisions.
   → *Because Taylor's parents were very controlling, she doesn't have much experience making decisions.*
   → *Taylor doesn't have much experience making decisions because her parents were very controlling.*

5. Annika likes to think about the pros and cons of a problem, so she doesn't make decisions quickly.

6. Jonathan thinks he knows everything, so he never asks anyone for advice.

EXERCISE 27 ▸ Looking at grammar. (Charts 8-1 → 8-6)
Add commas, periods, and capital letters as necessary. Don't change any of the words or the order of the words.

Cooling Off

1. Jim was hot. He sat in the shade.
2. Jim was hot and tired so he sat in the shade.
3. Jim was hot tired and thirsty.
4. Because he was hot Jim sat in the shade.
5. Because they were hot and thirsty Jim and Susan sat in the shade and drank iced-tea.
6. Jim and Susan sat in the shade and drank iced-tea because they were hot and thirsty.
7. Jim sat in the shade drank iced-tea and fanned himself with his cap because he was hot tired and thirsty.
8. Because Jim was hot he stayed under the shade of the tree but Susan went back to work.

EXERCISE 28 ▸ Grammar and listening. (Charts 8-1 → 8-6)
Add commas, periods, and capital letters as necessary. Then listen to the passage to help you check your answers.

Do you know these words?
- allergies
- dust
- flower pollen
- sneeze
- metal
- itch
- reaction

STRANGE ALLERGIES

Allergies make people sneeze, cough, itch, or turn red. Common causes of allergies are dust flower pollen animal fur and nuts there are other things that cause allergies but they are not so well known dark chocolate can make some people sneeze the metal in cell phones can cause some people's skin to turn red and itch cold weather and leather clothing can also cause redness and itching in some people.

EXERCISE 29 ▶ Warm-up. (Chart 8-7)

In which sentences is the result (in green) the opposite of what you expect?

1. Even though Silvia took a cooking class, she often burns the food.
2. Because Silvia burned the food, no one wanted to eat it.
3. Although Silvia took a cooking class, she often burns the food.

8-7 Connecting Ideas with *Even Though/Although*

(a)	**Even though** I was hungry, I did not eat. I did not eat **even though** I was hungry.	**Even though** and **although** introduce an adverb clause.
(b)	**Although** I was hungry, I did not eat. I did not eat **although** I was hungry.	Examples (a) and (b) have the same meaning: *I was hungry, but I did not eat.*
COMPARE:		**Because** expresses an expected result, as in (c).
(c)	**Because** I was hungry, *I ate*.	**Even though/although** expresses an unexpected or opposite result, as in (d).
(d)	**Even though** I was hungry, *I did not eat*.	

EXERCISE 30 ▶ Looking at grammar. (Chart 8-7)

Complete the sentences with the words in *italics*.

1. *is / isn't*

   a. Because Dan is sick, he _____ going to work.

   b. Although Dan is sick, he _____ going to work.

   c. Even though Dan is sick, he _____ going to work.

2. *went / didn't go*

   a. Even though it was late, we _____ home.

   b. Although it was late, we _____ home.

   c. Because it was late, we _____ home.

EXERCISE 31 ▶ Looking at grammar. (Chart 8-7)

Complete the sentences with **even though** or **because**.

Special Talents

1. *Because* Po has a photographic memory, he does well on tests.
2. *Even though* Po has a photographic memory, his grades aren't good.
3. _____ Amir can do complicated math in his head, he doesn't understand geometry.
4. _____ Janette can draw a perfect circle, her teacher asks her to draw shapes on the board.

5. _____ Sabrina can do magic tricks, people ask her to entertain at parties.

6. _____ Alberto can crack an egg with one hand, he uses two.

7. _____ Philip can't read music, he can play the piano perfectly.

8. _____ Lilly can juggle several objects at one time, she is popular with children.

EXERCISE 32 ▸ Looking at grammar. (Charts 8-6 and 8-7)
Choose the best completion for each sentence.

1. Even though the test was fairly easy, most of the class _____.
   a. failed
   b. passed
   c. did pretty well

2. Jack hadn't heard or read about the bank robbery even though _____.
   a. he was the robber
   b. it was all over social media
   c. he was out of town when it occurred

3. Although _____, she finished the race in first place.
   a. Miki was full of energy and strength
   b. Miki was leading all the way
   c. Miki was far behind in the beginning

4. We can see the light from an airplane at night before we can hear the plane because _____.
   a. light travels faster than sound
   b. airplanes travel at high speeds
   c. our eyes work better than our ears at night

5. My partner and I worked all day and late into the evening. Even though _____, we stopped at our favorite restaurant before we went home.
   a. we were very hungry
   b. we had finished our report
   c. we were very tired

6. Although Jenna says she is vegetarian, she _____.
   a. eats meat
   b. doesn't eat meat
   c. eats a lot of vegetables

7. In the spring, the snow melts into mountain rivers. The water carries dirt and rocks. Mountain rivers turn brown because _____.
   a. mountains have a lot of snow
   b. the water from melting snow brings soil and rocks to the river
   c. ice is frozen water

Connecting Ideas: Punctuation and Meaning   245

EXERCISE 33 ▶ Listening. (Charts 8-6 and 8-7)
Choose the best completion for each sentence.

Example: You will hear: Because there was a sale at the mall, …
You will choose: a. it wasn't busy.
ⓑ. there were a lot of shoppers.
c. prices were very high.

1. a. they were under some mail.
   b. my roommate helped me look for them.
   c. I never found them.

2. a. the rain had stopped.
   b. a storm was coming.
   c. the weather was nice.

3. a. he was feeling sick.
   b. he wanted to.
   c. he was happy for me.

4. a. I mailed it.
   b. I decided not to mail it.
   c. I sent it to a friend.

5. a. Carlo bought a big car.
   b. Carlo doesn't take the bus.
   c. Carlo drives a small car.

6. a. the coaches celebrated afterwards.
   b. the fans cheered loudly.
   c. the players didn't seem very excited.

EXERCISE 34 ▶ Let's talk. (Charts 8-6 and 8-7)
Answer the questions in complete sentences. Use either *because* or *even though*. Work in pairs, in small groups, or as a class.

Example: Last night you were tired. Did you go to bed early?
   → *Yes, I went to bed early because I was tired.* OR
   → *Yes, because I was tired, I went to bed before nine.* OR
   → *No, I didn't go to bed early even though I was really tired.* OR
   → *No, even though I was really tired, I didn't go to bed until after midnight.*

1. Last night you were tired. Did you stay up late?
2. Vegetables are good for you. Do you eat a lot of them?
3. Space exploration is exciting. Would you like to be an astronaut?
4. What are the winters like here? Do you like living here in the winter?
5. (*A recent movie*) has had good reviews. Do you want to see it?
6. Are you a good artist? Will you draw a picture of me on the board?
7. Where does your family live? Are you going to visit them over the next holiday?

EXERCISE 35 ▸ **Reading and grammar.** (Chapter 8 Review)

Part I. Read the blog entry by co-author Stacy Hagen.

Do you know these words?
- nervous
- breathe
- score
- energy
- identify
- athletes
- pressure

BlackBookBlog

Choking Under Pressure

Do tests make you nervous? If they do, you are not alone. Many students become very nervous, and this causes problems during the test. They sometimes can't think, or they forget information that they studied. English has an idiom for this: They "choke under pressure." Usually, we use the word *choke* when we talk about eating. The food doesn't go down our throats, and we can't breathe correctly. "Choking under pressure" means that we do poorly, for example, at school or in sports.

Psychologist Sian Beilock wrote a book called *Choke*. Beilock says that thinking too much, or overthinking, is the problem. Imagine some baseball players. Their team needs to score, and they are thinking about how to do this. They want to hit, throw, or catch the ball really well, and they begin to worry. This takes energy. Our minds don't do two things well, such as playing and worrying, at the same time. When we worry, we may not do the other activity well.

Beilock says the same is true for test-taking. In one of her studies, students took ten minutes to write down their worries before they took a test. They scored higher than students who didn't. Beilock says that by writing thoughts down, students identify their worries. They may see that the situation is not so bad and that they can deal with it. This helps them worry less when they take the test.

Of course, athletes can't stop and write down their thoughts. Beilock recommends that they think about something else. For example, a baseball player can look at the stitching on the ball. That can stop him or her from worrying about throwing a really good ball or winning the game.

The next time you feel the pressure of a test or sporting event, try one of Beilock's techniques. There is a good chance you will feel more relaxed when you are able to identify the worry or think about something else.

stitching

Part II. Complete the sentences with words and phrases in the box. More than one answer may be correct. Add punctuation as necessary.

| students | want to do well | they forget information | they begin to worry |
| athletes | identify their worries | they choke | they sometimes do poorly |

1. _____ and _____ can choke under pressure.

2. Some students get very nervous before a test so _____.

3. Nervous students _____ but _____.

4. Because athletes think about doing really well _____.

5. Students can write their thoughts down and _____.

6. Even though athletes and students prepare very well _____.

7. Although people often try to do better by thinking about doing well _____.

EXERCISE 36 ▸ Check your knowledge. (Chapter 8 Review)
Correct the errors in sentence structure. Pay special attention to punctuation.

1. Even though I was sick, ~~but~~ I went to work.

2. Gold silver and copper. They are metals.

3. The children crowded around the teacher. Because he was doing a magic trick.

4. I had a cup of coffee, and so does my friend.

5. My roommate didn't go. Neither I went either.

6. Even I was exhausted, I didn't stop working until after midnight.

7. Although I like chocolate, but I can't eat it because I'm allergic to it.

8. I like to eat eggs for breakfast and everybody else in my family too.

9. A home improvement store sells tools and paint and flooring and appliances.

10. Most insects have wings, spiders do not.

EXERCISE 37 ▸ Writing. (Chapter 8)
Part I. Write about an animal that interests you. Follow these steps:

1. Choose an animal you want to know more about.

    Hint: If you are doing your research on the internet, type in "interesting facts about _____" (*name of animal*).

2. Take notes on the information you find. For example, here is some information about giraffes from an internet site.

    Sample notes:

    Giraffes …
    → have long necks (6 feet or 1.8 meters)
    → can reach the tops of trees
    → need very little sleep (20 minutes to two hours out of 24 hours)
    → eat about 140 pounds of food a day
    → can go for weeks without drinking water
    → get a lot of water from the plants they eat
    → can grab and hold onto objects with their tongues
    → don't have vocal cords
    → can communicate with one another (but humans can't hear them)

→ are now having a hard time living in the wild. (There are only 80,000 left and the population is getting smaller.)
→ need protection

3. Write sentences based on your facts. Combine some of the ideas using **and**, **but**, **or**, **so**, **because**, **although**, **even though**.

   Sample sentences:

   → Giraffes have long necks, so they can reach the tops of trees.
   → Although they eat about 140 pounds of food a day, they can go for weeks without drinking water.
   → Even though giraffes don't have vocal cords, they can communicate with one another.
   → Giraffes can communicate, but people can't hear their communication.

4. Put your sentences into a paragraph, with a topic sentence, logical order of ideas, and a concluding sentence.

   Sample paragraph:

   Interesting Facts About Giraffes

   Giraffes are interesting animals. They have long necks, so they can reach the tops of trees. They eat flowers, fruit, climbing plants, and the twigs and leaves from trees. Although they eat about 140 pounds of food a day, they can go for weeks without drinking water. But they get water from the plants they eat too. They have very long tongues, and these tongues are useful. Because they are so long, they can grab objects with them. Even though giraffes don't have vocal cords, they can communicate. The noises are very low, and people can't hear them. Giraffe populations are getting smaller. There are about 80,000 left in the world, and to survive, these amazing creatures need protection.

WRITING TIP

In addition to a topic sentence and major (big) details, paragraphs also have minor (small) details. The minor details add more information to the major detail:

Major: They have long necks, so they can reach the tops of trees.
Minor: They eat flowers, fruit, climbing plants, and the twigs and leaves from trees.

Major: They have very long tongues, and these tongues are useful.
Minor: Because they are so long, they can grab objects with them.

Your writing is stronger if you have at least one additional sentence to support each major detail.

Part II. Edit your writing. Check for the following:

1. ☐ use of connecting words: **and, but, or, so, because, even though, although**
2. ☐ correct punctuation with connecting words
3. ☐ a topic sentence and a concluding sentence
4. ☐ enough minor details to support all major details
5. ☐ correct spelling (use a dictionary or spell-check)

■■■■■ For digital resources, go to MyEnglishLab on the Pearson English Portal. You can also go to the Pearson Practice English app for mobile practice.

CHAPTER 9
Comparisons

PRETEST: What do I already know?
Write "C" if the **boldfaced** words are correct and "I" if they are incorrect.

1. _____ What is **more good** to have: high grades or good test scores? (Chart 9-1)
2. _____ Is love **more importanter than** money? (Chart 9-1)
3. _____ My hometown has **the friendliest people in** my country. (Chart 9-2)
4. _____ Lisa works **harder than** her co-workers do. (Chart 9-3)
5. _____ **One of the longest river in the world** is the Yangtze River in China. (Chart 9-3)
6. _____ Silvia is a fast driver. She **drives more fastly than** her husband. (Chart 9-4)
7. _____ **The longer** Daniel talked, **the more excited** he became. (Chart 9-5)
8. _____ My grandfather is **very healthier** than my grandmother. (Chart 9-6)
9. _____ This dessert has a lot of sugar. I've never tasted **a sweeter** dessert. (Chart 9-7)
10. _____ English is **as hard as** math for me. (Chart 9-8)
11. _____ A compact car is **not as large as** an SUV (sport utility vehicle). (Chart 9-9)
12. _____ There are **more vegetables** in the garden this year **than** last year. (Chart 9-10)
13. _____ You look **the same like** your brother. (Chart 9-11)

EXERCISE 1 ▶ Warm-up. (Chart 9-1)
Compare the people.

Raj

Daniel

Taka

1. Raj looks younger than _____.
2. Daniel looks younger than _____.
3. Taka looks older than _____.

9-1 Introduction to Comparative Forms of Adjectives

(a) "A" is *older than* "B."
(b) "A" and "B" are *older than* "C" and "D."
(c) Ed is *more generous than* his brother.

The comparative compares *this* to *that* or *these* to *those*.

Form: *-er* or *more*

NOTE: A comparative is followed by *than*.

	ADJECTIVE	COMPARATIVE	
ONE-SYLLABLE ADJECTIVES	old wise	**older** **wiser**	For most one-syllable adjectives, *-er* is added.
TWO-SYLLABLE ADJECTIVES	famous pleasant	**more famous** **more pleasant**	For most two-syllable adjectives, *more* is used.
	clever gentle friendly	**cleverer/more clever** **gentler/more gentle** **friendlier/more friendly**	Some two-syllable adjectives use either *-er* or *more*: able, angry, clever, common, cruel, friendly, gentle, handsome, narrow, pleasant, polite, quiet, simple, sour.
	busy pretty	**busier** **prettier**	*-Er* is used with two-syllable adjectives that end in *-y*. The *-y* is changed to *-i*.
ADJECTIVES WITH THREE OR MORE SYLLABLES	important fascinating	**more important** **more fascinating**	*More* is used with long adjectives. NOTE: The opposite of *more* is *less*: *less important, less fascinating*
IRREGULAR ADJECTIVES	good bad	**better** **worse**	*Good* and *bad* have irregular comparative forms.

EXERCISE 2 ▶ Looking at grammar. (Chart 9-1)

Complete the sentences with comparisons. Think about people, places, school subjects, and objects. Use *is* or *are* for the verbs. Share a few of your answers with the class.

In my opinion ...

1. _____ harder than _____.
2. _____ more beautiful than _____.
3. _____ more interesting than _____.
4. _____ more exciting than _____.
5. _____ safer than _____.
6. _____ more famous than _____.
7. _____ more important than _____.
8. _____ more useful than _____.
9. _____ simpler than _____.
10. _____ better than _____.

EXERCISE 3 ▶ Looking at grammar. (Chart 9-1)
Write the comparative forms for these adjectives.

1. healthy   _healthier than_
2. difficult   _____
3. easy   _____
4. boring   _____
5. dangerous   _____
6. cold   _____
7. pretty   _____
8. relaxing   _____
9. funny   _____
10. bad   _____
11. angry   _____
12. lazy   _____
13. quiet   _____
14. hot   _____

EXERCISE 4 ▶ Game: trivia. (Chart 9-1)
Work in teams. Complete each sentence with the correct comparative form of the adjective. Then decide if the sentences are true (T) or false (F). The team with the most correct answers wins.*

1. Canada is (*large*) _____ than France.   T F
2. The South Pole is generally (*cold*) _____ than the North Pole.   T F

---

*See *Trivia Answers*, p. 449.

3. Africa is (*big*) _____ than Asia. T F

4. In general, Libya is (*hot*) _____ than Mexico. T F

5. London is (*wet*) _____ than Madrid. T F

6. The Atlantic Ocean is (*deep*) _____ than the Pacific Ocean. T F

7. Malaysia is (*humid*) _____ than Paris. T F

8. Canada is (*crowded*) _____ than China. T F

9. The Nile River is (*long*) _____ than the Mississippi River. T F

10. The Andes Mountains are (*high*) _____ than the
    Himalaya Mountains. T F

EXERCISE 5 ▶ Looking at grammar. (Chart 9-1)
Complete the sentences with the correct comparative form (***more/-er***) of the adjectives in the box.

| clean | dangerous | funny | ✓ sweet |
| confusing | dark | pretty | wet |

1. Oranges are _____sweeter_____ than lemons.

2. I heard some polite laughter when I told my jokes, but everyone laughed loudly when Janet told hers. Her jokes are always _____ than mine.

3. Many more people die in car accidents than in plane accidents. Statistics show that driving your own car is _____ than flying in an airplane.

4. Professor Sato speaks clearly, but I have trouble understanding Professor Larson's lectures. Professor Larson's lectures are much _____ than Professor Sato's.

5. Is there a storm coming? The sky looks _____ than it did an hour ago.

6. That tablecloth has some stains on it. Take this one. It's _____.

7. We're having another beautiful sunrise. It looks like an orange fireball. The sky is even _____ than yesterday.

8. If a cat and a duck are out in the rain, the cat will get much _____ than the duck. The water will just roll off the duck's feathers, but it will soak into the cat's hair.

EXERCISE 6 ▶ Let's talk: pairwork. (Chart 9-1)

Work with a partner. Make comparisons with **more/-er** and the adjectives in the box. Share some of your answers with the class.

Opinions

beautiful	enjoyable	light	soft
cheap	expensive	relaxing	stressful
deep	fast	shallow	thick
easy	heavy	short	thin

1. traveling by air \ traveling by train
   → *Traveling by air is faster than traveling by train.*
   → *Traveling by air is more stressful than traveling by train.*
       Etc.
2. a pool \ a lake
3. a final exam \ a quiz
4. taking a trip \ staying home
5. iron furniture \ wood furniture
6. going to the doctor \ going to the dentist
7. gold jewelry \ silver jewelry
8. plastic toys \ wood toys
9. an emerald \ a diamond
10. a feather \ a blade of grass

EXERCISE 7 ▶ Listening. (Chart 9-1)

Listen to the statements. Do you agree or disagree? Circle *yes* or *no*.

Opinions

1. yes   no   5. yes   no
2. yes   no   6. yes   no
3. yes   no   7. yes   no
4. yes   no   8. yes   no

Do you know these words?
- raw
- history

EXERCISE 8 ▶ Warm-up. (Chart 9-2)

Compare the three handwriting samples.

A:
B:
C: The meeting starts at eight!

1. __C__ is neater than __A (or B)__ .
2. ____ is messier than _____ .
3. ____ is the messiest.
4. ____ is the best.
5. ____ is the worst.

9-2 Introduction to Superlative Forms of Adjectives

(a) "A," "B," "C," and "D" are sisters. "A" is **the oldest of all** four sisters.

(b) A woman in Turkey claims to be **the oldest person in the world**.

(c) Ed is **the most generous person** in his family.

The superlative compares one person or one part of a whole group to all the rest of the group.

Form: **-est** or **most**

NOTE: A superlative begins with **the**.

	ADJECTIVE	SUPERLATIVE	
ONE-SYLLABLE ADJECTIVES	old wise	**the oldest** **the wisest**	For most one-syllable adjectives, **-est** is added.
TWO-SYLLABLE ADJECTIVES	famous pleasant	**the most famous** **the most pleasant**	For most two-syllable adjectives, **most** is used.
	clever gentle friendly	**the cleverest** **the most clever** **the gentlest** **the most gentle** **the friendliest** **the most friendly**	Some two-syllable adjectives use either **-est** or **most**: able, angry, clever, common, cruel, friendly, gentle, handsome, narrow, pleasant, polite, quiet, simple, sour.
	busy pretty	**the busiest** **the prettiest**	**-Est** is used with two-syllable adjectives that end in **-y**. The **-y** is changed to **-i**.
ADJECTIVES WITH THREE OR MORE SYLLABLES	important fascinating	**the most important** **the most fascinating**	**Most** is used with long adjectives. NOTE: The opposite of **most** is **least**: the least important, the least fascinating
IRREGULAR ADJECTIVES	good bad	**the best** **the worst**	**Good** and **bad** have irregular superlative forms.

EXERCISE 9 ▶ Looking at grammar. (Charts 9-1 and 9-2)
Write the comparative and superlative forms of the following adjectives.

1. high   _higher, the highest_
2. good   _____
3. lazy   _____
4. hot★   _____
5. neat★   _____
6. late★   _____
7. sweet   _____
8. dangerous   _____
9. slow   _____
10. common   _____
11. friendly   _____
12. careful   _____
13. bad   _____
14. ugly   _____

★Spelling notes:
- When a one-syllable adjective ends in *one vowel + a consonant*, double the consonant and add **-er/-est**: **sad, sadder, saddest** (except for adjectives that end in **-e**: **wide, wider, widest**).
- When an adjective ends in *two vowels + a consonant*, do NOT double the consonant: **cool, cooler, coolest**.

EXERCISE 10 ▶ Game: trivia. (Chart 9-2)
Work in teams. Make true sentences with the given words. Use superlatives. The team with the most correct answers wins.*

In the World

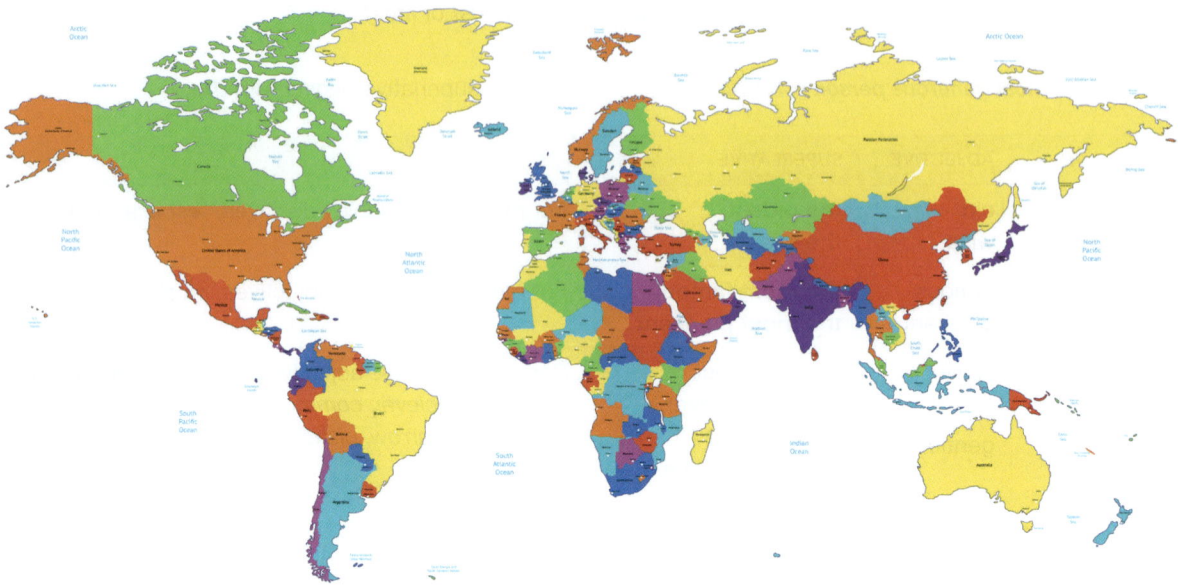

Oceans: *the Atlantic / the Pacific / the Arctic / the Indian*

1. (*deep*)   The deepest ocean is the Pacific. **OR** The Pacific is the deepest ocean.
2. (*cold*) _____
3. (*big*) _____

Continents: *Africa / Antarctica / Australia / Asia / South America*

4. (*windy*) _____
5. (*hot*) _____
6. (*populated*) _____

Countries in Asia: *India / China / Singapore / the Maldives*

7. (*large*) _____
8. (*small*) _____

Mountains: *Denali / Mount Fuji / Mount Kilimanjaro / Mount Blanc*

9. (*tall*) _____
10. (*low*) _____

Animals: *the whale / the elephant / the greyhound dog / the cheetah / the kangaroo*

11. (*heavy*) _____
12. (*fast*) _____

*See *Trivia Answers*, p. 449.

EXERCISE 11 ▸ Looking at grammar. (Chart 9-2)

Complete the sentences with your own words and the superlative form of the words in parentheses. Share a few of your answers with the class.

In My Opinion

1. (*difficult*) ___Physics___ is ___the most difficult___ subject.
2. (*easy*) _____ is _____ class.
3. (*good*) _____ is _____ time for me to fall asleep.
4. (*bad*) _____ is _____ food I have ever eaten.
5. (*happy*) _____ is _____ person in my family.
6. (*neat*) _____ is _____ person in my family.
7. (*interesting*) _____ is _____ athlete right now.
8. (*busy*) _____ is _____ person I know.

EXERCISE 12 ▸ Let's talk: interview. (Chart 9-2)

Make questions with the given words and the superlative form. Then interview your classmates, and share some of their answers with the class.

1. what \ bad movie \ you have ever seen
   → *What is the worst movie you have ever seen?*
2. what \ interesting sport to watch \ on TV
3. what \ crowded city \ you have ever visited
4. where \ good restaurant \ around here
5. what \ fun place to visit \ in this area
6. who \ kind person \ you know
7. what \ important thing \ in life
8. what \ serious problem \ in the world
9. who \ interesting person \ in the news right now

EXERCISE 13 ▸ Listening. (Charts 9-1 and 9-2)

The endings *-er* and *-est* can be hard to hear. Listen to the sentences and choose the words that you hear.

My Family

Example: You will hear: I am the shortest person in our family.
You will choose: short   shorter   (shortest)

1. short   shorter   shortest
2. tall   taller   tallest
3. happy   happier   happiest
4. happy   happier   happiest
5. old   older   oldest
6. funny   funnier   funniest
7. wise   wiser   wisest
8. wise   wiser   wisest

EXERCISE 14 ▶ Warm up. (Chart 9-3)
Complete the sentences with true information.

1. _____ is the oldest person in my family/group of friends.

2. I'm older than _____ is.

3. _____ is one of the oldest people I know.

9-3 Completing Comparatives and Superlatives

(a) I'm older *than my brother* (*is*). (b) I'm older *than he is*. (c) I'm older *than him*. (*informal*)	In formal English, a subject pronoun (e.g., *he*) follows *than*, as in (b). In informal spoken English, you may sometimes hear an object pronoun (e.g., *him*) after *than*, as in (c).
(d) *Ann's* hair is longer *than Kate's*. (e) *Jack's* apartment is smaller *than mine*.	A possessive noun (e.g., *Kate's*) or pronoun (e.g., *mine*) may follow *than*.
(f) Tokyo is one of *the largest cities in the world*. (g) David is *the most generous person I have ever known*. (h) I have three books. These two are quite good, but this one is the *best* (book) *of all*.	Typical completions when a superlative is used: In (f): *superlative* + *in* a place (*the world, this class, my family, the company*, etc.) In (g): *superlative* + *adjective clause** In (h): *superlative* + *of all*
(i) Ali is *one of* the best *students* in this class. (j) *One of* the best *students* in this class *is* Ali.	Note the pattern with *one of*: *one of* + *superlative* + *plural noun* *One of* can also begin a sentence, as in (j). NOTE: A singular verb is used with *one of*.

*See Chapter 12 for more information about adjective clauses.

EXERCISE 15 ▶ Looking at grammar. (Chart 9-3)
Complete the sentences. Use pronouns in the completions.

My Neighbors

1. Mr. Hanson is younger than his wife. He's five years younger than ___*she is*___ OR (informally) ___*her*___.

2. Mrs. Hanson works full-time. Mr. Hanson works part-time. She is busier than _____.

3. Twins Marta and Mira are shy. Their friends are more talkative than _____.

4. Isabel's school is difficult, but mine is easy. Isabel's school is more difficult than _____. My school is easier than _____.

5. The Lees' house is big. Our house is smaller than _____. Theirs is bigger than _____.

6. My dad and I like to work on cars in our free time. We are good mechanics, but Mr. Lu is a professional mechanic. He is more knowledgeable about cars than _____.

EXERCISE 16 ▸ Looking at grammar. (Chart 9-3)
Complete the sentences with superlatives of the words in *italics* and the preposition *in* or *of*, where appropriate.

My English Class

1. Ken is *lazy*. He is ____the laziest____ student ____in____ the class.

2. Phillip and Julia were *nervous*, but Erika was ____the most nervous of all____.

3. Lucy doesn't need to study. She is naturally *smart*. She is one of _____ students I have ever met.

4. Majda got a *bad* score on the test. It was one of _____ scores _____ the class.

5. There are a lot of *good* speakers in our class, but Daniel gives _____ speeches _____ all.

6. Our teacher is very *kind*. She is one of _____ teachers I have ever met.

7. Our classroom is always *hot* and *uncomfortable*. It is one of _____ and _____ classrooms _____ the building.

8. Everyone was *exhausted* after the final exam, but I was _____ all.

EXERCISE 17 ▸ Looking at grammar. (Chart 9-3)
Complete the sentences with the superlative form of the words in *italics*.

1. I have had many *good experiences*. Of those, my vacation to Honduras was one of _____ _____ I have ever had.

2. Ayako has had many *nice times*, but her birthday party was one of _____ _____ she has ever had.

3. I've taken many *difficult courses*, but statistics is one of _____ _____ I've ever taken.

4. I've made some *bad mistakes* in my life, but lending money to my cousin was one of _____ _____ I've ever made.

5. We've seen many *beautiful buildings* in the world, but the Taj Mahal is one of _____ _____ I've ever seen.

6. The *final exam* I took was pretty *easy*. In fact, it was one of _____ _____ I've ever taken.

EXERCISE 18 ▶ Let's talk: pairwork. (Chart 9-3)

Work with a partner. Take turns asking and answering questions. Use superlatives in your answers. Pay special attention to the use of plural nouns after *one of*.

Example:
PARTNER A: You have known many interesting people. Who is one of them?
PARTNER B: **One of the most interesting people** I've ever known *is* (____). OR
(____) *is* **one of the most interesting people** I've ever known.

1. There are many beautiful countries in the world. What is one of them?
2. There are many famous people in the world. Who is one of them?
3. You've probably seen many good movies. What is one of them?
4. You've probably done many interesting things in your life. What is one of them?
5. Think of some happy days in your life. What was one of them?
6. There are a lot of interesting animals in the world. What is one of them?
7. You have probably had many good experiences. What is one of them?
8. You probably know several funny people. Who is one of them?

EXERCISE 19 ▶ Game. (Charts 9-1 → 9-3)

Work in teams. Compare each list of items using the words in *italics*. Write sentences using the comparative (*-er/more*) and the superlative (*-est/most/one of the*). The group with the most correct sentences wins.

Example: streets in this city: *wide / narrow / busy / dangerous*
→ *First Avenue is **wider** than Market Street (is).*
→ *First Avenue is **narrower** than Interstate Highway 70.*
→ ***The busiest** street is Main Street.*
→ *Main Street is **busier** than Market Street.*
→ *Olive Boulevard is **one of the busiest** street**s** in the city.*
→ ***The most dangerous** street in the city is Olive Boulevard.*

1. a lemon, a grapefruit, and an orange: *sweet / sour / large / small*

2. a kitten, a cheetah, and a lion: *weak / powerful / wild / gentle / fast*

3. boxing, soccer, and golf: *dangerous / safe / exciting / boring*

4. the food at (*three places in this city where you have eaten*): *delicious / appetizing / inexpensive / good / bad*

EXERCISE 20 ▶ Looking at grammar. (Charts 9-1 → 9-3)
Complete the sentences with any appropriate form of the words in parentheses. Add any other necessary words.

Interesting Facts

1. Diamonds are very hard. They are (*hard*) __harder than__ rocks. They are one of (*hard*) __the hardest__ materials __of__ all.

2. Crocodiles and alligators are different. The snout of a crocodile is (*long*) _____ and (*narrow*) _____ than an alligator's snout. An alligator has a (*wide*) _____ upper jaw than a crocodile.

3. The Great Wall of China is (*long*) _____ structure that a country has ever built.

4. World Cup Soccer is (*big*) _____ sporting event _____ the world.

5. Young people have (*high*) _____ rate of car accidents _____ all drivers.

6. No animals can travel (*fast*) _____ than birds. Birds are (*fast*) _____ animals of all.

7. Bears are fast runners. Bears can run (*quick*) _____ than humans. Among bears, humans, and horses, bears can run short distances (*quick*) _____ of all.

8. One of (*active*) _____ volcanoes _____ the world is Mount Kilauea in Hawaii.

9. It's possible that the volcanic explosion of Krakatoa near Java in 1883 was (*loud*) _____ noise _____ recorded history. People heard it 2,760 miles/4,441 kilometers away.

EXERCISE 21 ▶ Warm-up. (Chart 9-4)
Complete the sentences with the names of people you know. Make true statements.

1. I speak English more slowly than _____.

2. I read English faster than _____.

9-4 Making Comparisons with Adverbs

(a) Ryan runs *slowly*. (b) Ryan runs *more slowly than* Tim. (c) Ryan runs *the most slowly* of all his friends. (d) Tim runs *faster than* Ryan. He runs *the fastest* of all his friends.	Adverbs modify verbs. Most adverbs end in *-ly*. Adverbs can be used in comparisons, as in (b)–(d). NOTE: The comparative and superlative forms of some adverbs like *fast* and *hard* do not end in *-ly*, as in (d).
(e) He works harder *than I do*. (f) I arrived earlier *than they did*.	Frequently an auxiliary verb follows the subject after *than*. In (e): *than I do* = *than I work* In (f): *than they did* = *than they arrived*

	ADVERB	COMPARATIVE	SUPERLATIVE	
-LY ADVERBS	carefully slowly	**more carefully** **more slowly**	the most carefully the most slowly	*More* and *most* are used with adverbs that end in *-ly*.*
ONE-SYLLABLE ADVERBS	fast hard	**faster** **harder**	the fastest the hardest	The *-er* and *-est* forms are used with one-syllable adverbs.
IRREGULAR ADVERBS	well badly far	**better** **worse** **farther/further**	the best the worst the farthest/the furthest	Both *farther* and *further* are used to compare physical distances: *I walked farther than my friend did*. OR *I walked further than my friend did*. As an adjective, *further* also means "additional": *I need further information*. Note that *farther* cannot be used when the meaning is "additional."

*Exception: *early* is both an adjective and an adverb. Forms: *earlier*, *earliest*.

EXERCISE 22 ▶ Looking at grammar. (Chart 9-4)
Complete the sentences with the correct form of the adverbs in parentheses.

My Teachers

1. Professor Gomez speaks (*quick*) ___quickly___ .
2. Professor Gomez speaks (*quick*) ___more quickly___ than Professor Thom.
3. Professor Thom writes the answers (*slow*) _____ on the board.
4. My writing teacher corrects our essays (*careful*) _____ .
5. My writing teacher correct our essays (*careful*) _____ than the other writing teachers.

6. Dr. Gupta comes to school at 6:00 A.M. He comes (*early*) _____ than the director of the school.

7. Dr. Gupta comes to school (*early*) _____ of all the teachers.

8. Ms. Lee works (*hard*) _____ every day.

9. Ms. Lee works (*hard*) _____ than any other teacher I have.

10. Ms. Lee works (*hard*) _____ of all.

EXERCISE 23 ▶ Looking at grammar. (Charts 9-1 → 9-4)

Complete each sentence with the correct form of an adjective or adverb in the box. Use each choice only once.

| careful | more careful | more carefully | the most careful | the most carefully |

1. Patrick drives _____ than his friends.

2. Patrick is a _____ driver.

3. Patrick is _____ driver of all his friends.

4. Patrick is a _____ driver than his friends.

5. Patrick drives _____ of all his friends.

| quick | quicker | more quickly | the quickest | the most quickly |

6. Andrea is a _____ runner.

7. Andrea runs _____ of all the members on her team.

8. Andrea runs _____ than the members on her team.

9. Andrea is a _____ runner than her friends.

10. Andrea is _____ runner of all her friends.

EXERCISE 24 ▶ Looking at grammar. (Chart 9-4)
Choose the correct completions for each sentence. In some cases, both answers are correct.

1. Ron and his friend went jogging. Ron ran two miles, but his friend got tired after one mile. Ron ran _____ than his friend did.
   - (a.) farther
   - (b.) further

2. If you have any _____ questions, don't hesitate to ask.
   - a. farther
   - b. further

3. I gave my old computer to my younger sister because I had no _____ use for it.
   - a. farther
   - b. further

4. Paris is _____ north than Tokyo.
   - a. farther
   - b. further

5. I like my new apartment, but it is _____ away from school than my old apartment was.
   - a. farther
   - b. further

6. Thank you for your help, but I'll be fine now. I don't want to cause you any _____ trouble.
   - a. farther
   - b. further

7. Which is _____ from here: the subway or the train station?
   - a. farther
   - b. further

EXERCISE 25 ▶ Warm-up. (Chart 9-5)
Do you agree or disagree with these statements? Choose *yes* or *no*.

1. The grammar in this book is getting harder and harder.   yes   no
2. My English is getting better and better.   yes   no
3. The longer I study English, the better I get.   yes   no

9-5 Repeating a Comparative; Using Double Comparatives

(a) Because he was afraid, he walked *faster and faster*. (b) Life in the modern world is getting *more and more complicated*.	Repeating a comparative gives the idea that something becomes progressively greater, i.e., that it increases in intensity, quality, or quantity.
(c) *The harder* you study, *the more* you will learn. (d) *The more* she studied, *the more* she learned. (e) *The warmer* the weather (is), *the better* I like it.	A double comparative has two parts; both parts begin with *the*, as in the examples. The second part of the comparison is the *result* of the first part. In (c): If you study harder, the *result* will be that you will learn more.
(f) — Do you want to ask Jenny and Jim to the party too? — Why not? *The more, the merrier*. (g) — When should we leave? — *The sooner, the better*.	*The more, the merrier* and *the sooner, the better* are two common expressions. In (f): It is good to have more people at the party. In (g): We should leave as soon as we can.

EXERCISE 26 ▶ Looking at grammar. (Chart 9-5)
Complete the sentences by repeating a comparative. Use the words in the box.

big	✓ fast	hard	long	tired
discouraged	good	hot	loud	wet

1. When I get nervous, my heart beats ___faster and faster___.

2. When you blow up a balloon, it gets _____ _____.

3. Brian's health is improving. It's getting _____ _____ every day.

4. As the ambulance came closer to us, the siren became _____ _____.

5. The line of people waiting to get into the theater got _____ _____ until it went around the building.

6. I've been looking for a job for a month and still haven't been able to find one. I'm getting _____.

7. As we traveled south toward the equator, the weather got _____ _____.

8. The rain started as soon as I left my office. As I walked to the bus stop, it rained _____, and I got _____.

9. I tried to run up the steep hill, but my legs got _____, so I walked for a while.

EXERCISE 27 ▶ Looking at grammar. (Chart 9-5)
Part I. Complete the sentences with double comparatives (***the more/-er … the more/-er***) and the words in *italics*.

1. If the fruit is *fresh*, it tastes *good*.
   ___The fresher___ the fruit (is), ___the better___ it tastes.

2. We got *close* to the fire. We felt *warm*.
   _____ we got to the fire, _____ we felt.

3. If a knife is *sharp*, it is *easy* to cut something with.
   _____ a knife (is), _____ it is to cut something.

Comparisons 265

4. The party got *noisy* next door. I got *angry*.

   _____ it got, _____ I got.

5. I exercise for a *long* time. I get *thirsty*.

   _____ I exercise, _____ I get.

Part II. Combine each pair of sentences. Use double comparatives (***the more/-er ... the more/-er***) and the words in *italics*.

6. Rosa offered to take me to the airport, and I was grateful. But we got a late start, so she began to drive faster.

   She drove *fast*. \ I became *nervous*.

   <u>The faster she drove, the more nervous I became.</u>

7. Pierre tried to concentrate on his studies, but he kept thinking about his family and home.

   He *thought* about his family. \ He became *homesick*.

   _____

8. A storm was coming. We needed to get home.

   The sky grew *dark*. \ We ran *fast*.

   _____

EXERCISE 28 ▶ Warm-up. (Chart 9-6)
Do you agree or disagree with these statements? Choose *yes* or *no*.

1. I enjoy very cold weather.   yes   no
2. It's a little cooler today than yesterday.   yes   no
3. It's much warmer today than yesterday.   yes   no

9-6 Modifying Comparatives with Adjectives and Adverbs

(a) Tom is **very** old. (b) Ann drives **very** carefully.	**Very** often modifies adjectives, as in (a), and adverbs, as in (b).
(c) INCORRECT: Tom is very older than I am. INCORRECT: Ann drives very more carefully than she used to.	**Very** is NOT used to modify comparative adjectives and adverbs.
(d) Tom is **much / a lot / far** older than I am. (e) Ann drives **much / a lot / far** more carefully than she used to.	**Much, a lot,** or **far** are used to modify comparative adjectives and adverbs, as in (d) and (e).
(f) Ben is **a little (bit)** older than I am OR (informally) me.	Another common modifier is **a little/a little bit**, as in (f).

EXERCISE 29 ▸ Looking at grammar. (Chart 9-6)
Add **very**, **much**, **a lot**, or **far** to the sentences.

1. a. It's hot today. → It's **very** hot today.
   b. It's hotter today than yesterday. → It's **much** / **a lot** / **far** hotter today than yesterday.

2. a. An airplane is fast.
   b. Taking an airplane is faster than driving.

3. a. Learning a second language is difficult for many people.
   b. Learning a second language is more difficult than learning chemistry formulas.

4. a. You can live more inexpensively in student housing than in a rented apartment.
   b. You can live inexpensively in student housing.

EXERCISE 30 ▸ Warm-up. (Chart 9-7)
Which sentence matches this meaning? *The food is very spicy.*

a. I've never tasted spicier food.
b. I've never tasted spicy food.

9-7 Negative Comparisons

(a) I've **never** taken a **harder** test. (b) I've **never** taken a **hard** test.	**Never** + comparative = superlative Example (a) means "It was the hardest test I've ever taken. I've never taken a harder test than this." Compare (a) and (b).

EXERCISE 31 ▸ Grammar and listening. (Chart 9-7)
Part I. Choose the sentence (a. or b.) that is closest in meaning to the given sentence.

1. I've never been on a bumpier plane ride.
   a. The flight was very bumpy.   b. The flight wasn't bumpy.

2. I've never tasted hot chili peppers.
   a. The peppers are hot.   b. I haven't eaten hot chili peppers.

3. The house has never looked cleaner.
   a. The house looks very clean.   b. The house doesn't look clean.

4. We've never visited a more beautiful city.
   a. The city was beautiful.   b. The city wasn't beautiful.

 Part II. Listen to the sentences. Choose the sentence (a. or b.) that is closest in meaning to the one you hear.

5. a. His jokes are funny.   b. His jokes aren't funny.
6. a. It tastes great.   b. It doesn't taste very good.
7. a. The mattress is hard.   b. I haven't slept on hard mattresses.
8. a. The movie was very scary.   b. I haven't watched scary movies.

EXERCISE 32 ▸ **Warm-up.** (Chart 9-8)
Compare the lengths of the lines.

1. Line D is as long as Line ____.
2. Line A isn't as long as Line ____.
3. Line E is almost as long as Line ____.

Line A _____
Line B _____
Line C _____
Line D _____
Line E _____

9-8 Using *As ... As* to Make Comparisons

(a) Niki is 19 years old. Emilio is also 19. Niki is **as old as** Emilio (is). (b) Mike came **as quickly as** he could.	***As ... as*** is used to say that the two parts of a comparison are equal or the same in some way. In (a): ***as*** + *adjective* + ***as*** In (b): ***as*** + *adverb* + ***as***
(c) Alex is 17. Niki is 19. Alex is **not as old as** Niki. (d) Alex is **not quite as old as** Niki. (e) Maya is 45. Alex is **not nearly as old as** Maya.	Negative form: ***not as ... as.*** *Quite* and *nearly* are often used with the negative. In (d): ***not quite as ... as*** = a small difference In (e): ***not nearly as ... as*** = a big difference
(f) Niki is **just as old as** Emilio. (g) Alex is **nearly/almost as old as** Emilio.	Common modifiers of *as ... as* are ***just*** (meaning "exactly") and ***nearly/almost***.

Niki 19   Alex 17   Emilio 19   Maya 45

*Also possible: ***not so ... as***: Alex is ***not so old as*** Niki.

EXERCISE 33 ▸ **Looking at grammar.** (Chart 9-8)
Complete the sentences with ***just as***, ***almost as***, ***not quite as***, or ***not nearly as***. Answers may vary.

Part I. Compare the fullness of the glasses.

1. Glass 4 is ___almost as / not quite as___ full as Glass 2.
2. Glass 3 is _____ full as Glass 2.
3. Glass 1 is _____ full as Glass 2.

Part II. Compare the size of the boxes.

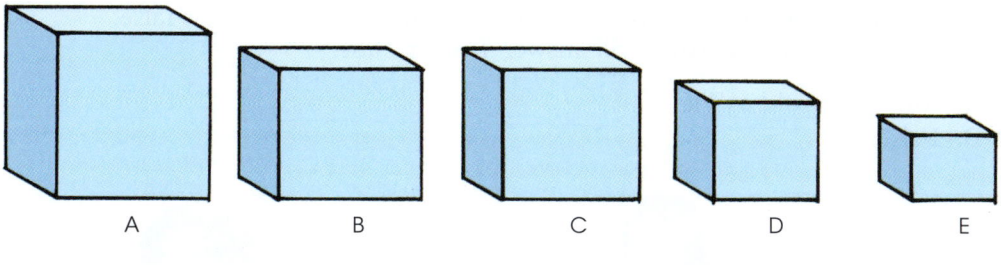

4. Box B is _____ big as Box A.
5. Box E is _____ big as Box A.
6. Box C is _____ big as Box B.
7. Box E is _____ big as Box D.

EXERCISE 34 ▸ Looking at grammar. (Chart 9-8)
Complete the sentences with *as ... as* and words in the box or your own words. Give your own opinion. Use negative verbs where appropriate.

✓ a housefly / an ant	good health / money
a lake / an ocean	honey / sugar
a lemon / a lime	monkeys / people
✓ a lion / a tiger	physics / computer science
a shower / a bath	reading a book / watching a movie
a speck of sand / a speck of dust	the sun / the moon

1. _An ant isn't as_____ big as _a housefly_____.
2. _A lion is as_____ dangerous and wild as _a tiger_____.
3. _____ large as _____.
4. _____ sweet as _____.
5. _____ important as _____.
6. _____ sour as _____.
7. _____ hot as _____.
8. _____ good at climbing trees as _____.
9. _____ relaxing as _____.
10. _____ as tiny as _____.
11. _____ as entertaining as _____.
12. _____ as difficult as _____.

EXERCISE 35 ▸ Let's talk: pairwork. (Chart 9-8)

Work with a partner. Take turns comparing the people in the photos. Use *as ... as* or *not as ... as*. You can also use *quite*, *almost*, and *nearly*. Your sentences can be true or false. Say your sentence to your partner. Your partner will answer *True* or *False*.

Example: PARTNER A: Amira is as old as Tia.
PARTNER B: False.

Tia, 30

Amira, 28

Jasmine, 10

Sachi, 50

Emily, 50

EXERCISE 36 ▸ Game. (Chart 9-8)

As ... as is used in many traditional phrases. These phrases are generally spoken rather than written. See how many of them you're familiar with by completing the sentences with the given words. Work in teams. The team with the most correct answers wins.

| ✓ a bear | a cat | a hornet | a mule | an ox |
| a bird | a feather | a kite | a rock | the hills |

1. When will dinner be ready? I'm **as** hungry **as** ___*a bear*___ .

2. Did Toshi really lift that heavy box all by himself? He must be **as** strong **as** _____ .

3. It was a lovely summer day. School was out, and there was nothing in particular that I had to do. I felt **as** free **as** _____ .

270 CHAPTER 9

an ox

a mule

a hornet

4. Marco won't change his mind. He's **as** stubborn **as** _____.

5. How can anyone expect me to sleep in this bed? It's **as** hard **as** _____.

6. Of course I've heard that joke before! It's **as** old **as** _____.

7. Why are you walking back and forth? What's the matter? You're **as** nervous **as** _____.

8. Thanks for offering to help, but I can carry the box alone. It looks heavy, but it isn't. It's **as** light **as** _____.

9. When Erica received the good news, she felt **as** high **as** _____.

10. A: Was he angry?

    B: You'd better believe it! He was **as** mad **as** _____.

EXERCISE 37 ▶ Listening. (Charts 9-1 → 9-3, 9-7, and 9-8)
Listen to each sentence and choose the statement (a. or b.) that has a similar meaning.

Example: You will hear: I need help! Please come as soon as possible.
            You will choose: (a.) Please come quickly.
                               b. Please come when you have time.

1. a. Business is better this year.
   b. Business is worse this year.

2. a. Steven is a very friendly person.
   b. Steven is an unfriendly person.

3. a. The test was difficult for Sam.
   b. The test wasn't so difficult for Sam.

4. a. We can go farther.
   b. We can't go farther.

5. a. Jon made a very good decision.
   b. Jon made a very bad decision.

6. a. I'm going to drive faster.
   b. I'm not going to drive faster.

7. a. Your work was careful.
   b. Your work was not careful.

8. a. I'm not hungry.
   b. I would like to eat.

9. a. My drive and my flight take the same amount of time.
   b. My drive takes more time.

EXERCISE 38 ▶ Warm-up. (Chart 9-9)
Complete the sentences with your own words.

1. Compare the cost of two cars:

    (A/An) _____ is more expensive than (a/an) _____.

2. Compare the cost of two kinds of fruit:

    _____ are less expensive than _____.

3. Compare the cost of two kinds of shoes (boots, sandals, tennis shoes, flip-flops, etc.):

    _____ are not as expensive as _____.

4. Compare the cost of two kinds of heat: (gas, electric, solar, wood, coal, etc.):

    _____ is not as cheap as _____.

9-9 Using Less ... Than and Not As ... As

MORE THAN ONE SYLLABLE: (a) A pen is **less** expensive **than** a book. (b) A pen is **not as** expensive **as** a book.	The opposite of **-er/more** is expressed by **less** or **not as ... as**. Examples (a) and (b) have the same meaning. **Less** and **not as ... as** are used with adjectives and adverbs of *more than one syllable*.
ONE SYLLABLE: (c) A pen is **not as** large **as** a book. INCORRECT: A pen is less large than a book.	Only **not as ... as** (NOT **less**) is used with *one-syllable adjectives or adverbs*, as in (c).

EXERCISE 39 ▶ Looking at grammar. (Chart 9-9)
Choose the correct completions for each sentence. In some cases, both answers are correct.

1. My nephew is ____ old ____ my niece.
    a. less ... than   b. not as ... as

2. My nephew is ____ hard-working ____ my niece.
    a. less ... than   b. not as ... as

3. A bee is ____ big ____ a bird.
    a. less ... than   b. not as ... as

4. My brother is ____ interested in computers ____ I am.
    a. less ... than   b. not as ... as

5. Some students are ____ serious about their schoolwork ____ others.
    a. less ... than   b. not as ... as

6. I am ____ good at repairing things ____ Diane is.
    a. less ... than   b. not as ... as

EXERCISE 40 ▶ Game. (Charts 9-1 → 9-3 and 9-7 → 9-9)
Work in teams. Compare the given words using (*not*) *as ... as*, *less*, and *more/-er*. How many comparison sentences can you think of? The team with the most correct sentences wins.

Example: trees and flowers (*big, colorful, useful, etc.*)
→ *Trees are bigger than flowers.*
→ *Flowers are usually more colorful than trees.*
→ *Flowers are less useful than trees.*
→ *Flowers aren't as tall as trees.*

1. the sun and the moon
2. teenagers and adults
3. two restaurants in this area
4. two famous people in the world

EXERCISE 41 ▶ Listening. (Charts 9-1, 9-8, and 9-9)
Listen to each sentence and the statements that follow it. Choose "T" for true or "F" for false.

Examples: France \ Brazil
You will hear: a. France isn't as large as Brazil.
You will choose: (T)   F

You will hear: b. France is bigger than Brazil.
You will choose: T   (F)

1. a sidewalk \ a road
   a. T   F
   b. T   F

2. a hill \ a mountain
   a. T   F
   b. T   F

3. hiking along a mountain path \ climbing a mountain peak
   a. T   F
   b. T   F

4. toes \ fingers
   a. T   F
   b. T   F
   c. T   F

5. basic math \ algebra
   a. T   F
   b. T   F
   c. T   F
   d. T   F

EXERCISE 42 ▶ Warm-up: trivia. (Chart 9-10)
Compare Manila, Seattle, and Singapore. Which two cities have more rain in December?*

_____ and _____ have more rain than _____ in December.

*See *Trivia Answers*, p. 449.

9-10 Using *More* with Nouns

(a)	Would you like some *more coffee*?	In (a): **Coffee** is a noun. When *more* is used with nouns, it often has the meaning of "additional." It is not necessary to use *than*.
(b)	Not everyone is here. I expect *more people* to come later.	
(c)	There are *more people* in China *than* there are in Canada.	*More* is also used with nouns to make complete comparisons by adding *than*.
(d)	Do you have enough coffee, or would you like some *more*?	When the meaning is clear, the noun may be omitted and *more* can be used by itself.

EXERCISE 43 ▶ Looking at grammar. (Charts 9-1, 9-4, and 9-10)
Use the words in the box to complete the sentences. Add *more* as necessary.

cheap	cleaner	noisier	safer
cheaper	✓ money	noisy	safely
cheaply	noise	pollution	traffic

Country Life

1. Prices are lower outside the city, and I'm saving _____*more money*_____ than I did in the city.

2. The city was expensive. I'm living _____ in the country than in the city.

3. Apartments are _____ in the country than in the city.

4. It took me only a day to find a comfortable and _____ apartment.

5. I didn't drive in the city. There were so many cars. A city has _____ than a small town.

6. I used to take the bus and subway, but now I drive a lot on two-lane highways. I have to be careful and drive _____ because I don't want to have an accident.

7. There is less crime in my town. Life is _____ for me in the country than in the city.

8. The air is very clean in my town. The city has more _____ than the country.

9. The air in the country is _____ than the air in the city.

10. The city was very loud. I heard traffic all day long. There is _____ in the city than in the country.

11. I didn't sleep well at night. Ambulances often woke me up. The city is _____ than the country.

12. I'm glad to live in a quiet area. The city was a very _____ place for me.

EXERCISE 44 ▶ Game: trivia. (Chart 9-10)
Work in teams. Write true sentences using the given information. The team with the most correct sentences wins.*

1. more kinds of mammals: South Africa \ Kenya
   → *Kenya has more kinds of mammals than South Africa.*
2. more volcanoes: Indonesia \ Japan
3. more moons: Saturn \ Venus
4. more people: Saõ Paulo, Brazil \ New York City
5. more islands: Greece \ Finland
6. more mountains: Switzerland \ Nepal
7. more sugar (per 100 grams): an apple \ a banana
8. more fat (per 100 grams): the dark meat of a chicken \ the white meat of a chicken

EXERCISE 45 ▶ Warm-up. (Chart 9-11)
Solve the math problems and then complete the sentences. Some answers may vary.

PROBLEM A: $2 + 2 =$
PROBLEM B: $\sqrt{900} + 20 =$
PROBLEM C: $3 \times 127 =$
PROBLEM D: $2 + 3 =$
PROBLEM E: $127 \times 3 =$

1. Problem _____ and Problem _____ have **the same** answers.
2. Problem _____ and Problem _____ have **similar** answers.
3. Problem _____ and Problem _____ have **different** answers.
4. The answer to Problem _____ is **the same as** the answer to Problem _____.
5. The answers to Problem _____ and Problem _____ are **similar**.
6. The answers to Problem _____ Problem _____ are **different**.
7. Problem _____ has **the same answer as** Problem _____.
8. Problem _____ is **like** Problem _____.
9. Problem _____ and Problem _____ are **alike**.

*See *Trivia Answers*, p. 449.

9-11 Using *The Same, Similar, Different, Like, Alike*

(a) Paul and Mia have **the same books**. (b) Paul and Mia have **similar books**. (c) Paul and Mia have **different books**. (d) Their books are **the same**. (e) Their books are **similar**. (f) Their books are **different**.	**The same**, **similar**, and **different** are used as adjectives. NOTE: **the** always precedes **same**.
(g) This book is **the same as** that one. (h) This book is **similar to** that one. (i) This book is **different from** that one.	NOTE: **the same** is followed by **as**; **similar** is followed by **to**; **different** is followed by **from**.*
(j) She is **the same age as** my mother. My shoes are **the same size as** yours.	A noun may come between **the same** and **as**, as in (j).

(k) My pen **is like** your pen.
(l) My pen **and** your pen **are alike**.
	Note in (k) and (l):
	   noun + **be like** + *noun*
	   noun **and** *noun* + **be alike**

(m) She **looks like** her sister. It **looks like** rain. It **sounds like** thunder. This material **feels like** silk. That **smells like** gas. This chemical **tastes like** salt. Stop **acting like** a fool. He **seems like** a nice guy.	In addition to following **be**, **like** also follows certain verbs, primarily those dealing with the senses. Note the examples in (m).
(n) The twins **look alike**. We **think alike**. Most four-year-olds **act alike**. My sister and I **talk alike**. The little boys are **dressed alike**.	**Alike** may follow a few verbs other than **be**. Note the examples in (n).

*In informal speech, native speakers might use **than** instead of **from** after **different**. **From** is considered correct in formal English, unless the comparison is completed by a clause: *I have a different attitude now than I used to have.*

EXERCISE 46 ▶ Looking at grammar. (Chart 9-11)
Complete the sentences with *as*, *to*, *from*, or *Ø*.

1. a. Geese are similar __to__ ducks. They are both large water birds.

    b. But geese are not the same _____ ducks. Geese are usually larger and have longer necks.

    c. Geese are different _____ ducks.

    d. Geese are like _____ ducks in some ways, but geese and ducks are not exactly alike _____ .

geese

a duck

an orange   a peach

2. a. An orange is not the same _____ a peach.

   b. An orange is like _____ a peach in some ways, but they are not exactly alike _____.

   c. An orange is similar _____ a peach. They are both round, sweet, and juicy.

   d. An orange is different _____ a peach.

EXERCISE 47 ▶ **Looking at grammar.** (Chart 9-11)
Compare the diagrams. Complete the sentences with *the same* (*as*), *similar* (*to*), *different* (*from*), *like*, or *alike*. Answers may vary.

1. All of the diagrams are ___similar to___ each other.
2. A is _____ B.
3. A and B are _____.
4. A and C are _____.
5. A and C are _____ D.
6. C is _____ A.
7. B isn't _____ D.

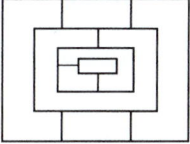
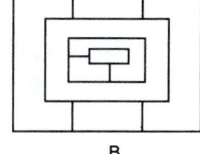

A   B

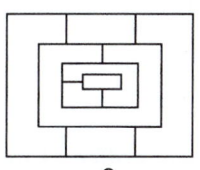
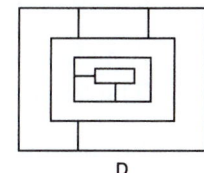

C   D

EXERCISE 48 ▶ **Grammar and listening.** (Charts 9-1 and 9-11)
Complete the sentences with the words in the box. Then listen to each passage and correct your answers.

alike	from	more	the
as	like	than	to

Gold vs. Silver

Gold is similar _____(1)_____ silver. They are both valuable metals that people use for jewelry, but they aren't _____(2)_____ same. Gold is not _____(3)_____ same color _____(4)_____ silver. Gold is also different _____(5)_____ silver in cost: gold is _____(6)_____ expensive _____(7)_____ silver.

Do you know these words?
- metals   - stripes
- valuable   - unique
- pattern

Two Zebras

Look at the two zebras in the picture. Their names are Zee and Bee. Zee looks _____(1)_____ Bee. Is Zee exactly _____(2)_____ same _____(3)_____ Bee? The pattern of the stripes on each zebra in the world is unique. No two zebras are exactly _____(4)_____. Even though Zee and Bee are similar _____(5)_____ each other, they are different _____(6)_____ each other in the exact pattern of their stripes.

EXERCISE 49 ▶ Looking at grammar. (Chart 9-11)
Complete the sentences with **the same** (*as*), **similar** (*to*), **different** (*from*), **like**, or **alike**. In some cases, more than one completion may be possible.

1. Jennifer and Jack both come from Rapid City. In other words, they come from ___the same___ town.

2. This city is ___the same as / similar to / like___ my hometown. Both are quiet and conservative.

3. You and I don't agree. Your ideas are _____ mine.

4. Sergio never wears _____ clothes two days in a row.

5. A male mosquito is not _____ size _____ a female mosquito. The female is larger.

6. I'm used to stronger coffee. I think the coffee at this cafe tastes _____ dishwater.

7. *Meet* and *meat* are homonyms; in other words, they have _____ pronunciation.

8. *Flower* has _____ pronunciation _____ *flour*.

9. My twin sisters act _____, but they don't look _____.

10. Trying to get through school without studying is _____ trying to go swimming without getting wet.

EXERCISE 50 ▶ Check your knowledge. (Chapter 9 Review)
Correct the errors in comparison structures.

1. Did you notice? My shoes and your shoes are ~~a~~ *the* same.

2. Alaska is largest state in the United States.

3. A pillow is soft, more than a rock.

4. Who is most generous person in your family?

5. The harder you work, you will be more successful.

6. One of a biggest disappointment in my life was when my soccer team lost the championship.

7. My sister is very more talkative than I am.

8. A firm mattress is so comfortable for many people than a soft mattress.

9. One of the most talkative student in the class is Frederick.

10. Professor Bennett's lectures were the confusingest I have ever heard.

EXERCISE 51 ▶ Reading. (Chapter 9 Review)
Part I. Read the passage and the statements that follow it. Underline five comparative or superlative structures.
NOTE: *He* and *she* are used interchangeably.

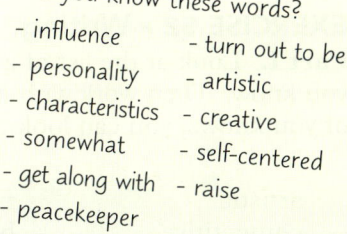

Do you know these words?
- influence
- personality
- characteristics
- somewhat
- get along with
- peacekeeper
- turn out to be
- artistic
- creative
- self-centered
- raise

BIRTH ORDER

In your family, are you the oldest, youngest, middle, or only child? Some psychologists believe your place in the family, or your birth order, has a strong influence on your personality. Let's look at some of the personality characteristics of each child.

The oldest child has all the parents' attention when she is born. As she grows up, she may want to be the center of attention. Because she is around adults, she might act more like an adult around other children and be somewhat controlling. As the oldest, she might have to take care of the younger children, so she may be more responsible. She may want to be the leader when she is in groups.

The middle child (or children) may feel a little lost. Middle children have to share their parents' attention. They may try to be different from the oldest child. If the oldest child is "good," the second child may be "bad." However, since they need to get along with both the older and younger sibling(s), they may be the peacekeepers of the family.

The youngest child is the "baby" of the family. Other family members may see him as weaker, smaller, or more helpless. If the parents know this is their last child, they may not want the child to grow up as quickly as the other children. As a way to get attention, the youngest child may be the funniest child in the family. He may also have more freedom and turn out to be more artistic and creative.

An only child (no brothers or sisters) often grows up in an adult world. Such children may use adult language and prefer adult company. Only children may be more intelligent and more serious than other children their age. They might also be more self-centered because of all the attention they get, and they might have trouble sharing with others.

Of course, these are general statements. A lot depends on how the parents raise the child, how many years are between each child, and the culture the child grows up in. How about you? Do you see any similarities to your family?

Part II. Read the statements. Circle "T" for true and "F" for false according to the information in the passage.

1. The two most similar children are the oldest and only child.   T   F
2. The middle child often wants to be like the oldest child.   T   F
3. The youngest child likes to control others.   T   F
4. Only children may want to spend more time with adults.   T   F
5. All cultures share the same birth order characteristics.   T   F

EXERCISE 52 ▸ Writing. (Chapter 9)

Part I. Look at the list of adjectives that describe personality characteristics. Check (✓) the words you know. Then work with a partner. Ask your partner about the words you don't know. If neither of you knows, you can look them up.

artistic	funny	rebellious
competitive	hard-working	relaxed
controlling	immature	secretive
cooperative	loud	sensitive
creative	mature	serious
flexible	outgoing	shy

Part II. Read the paragraph. <u>Underline</u> the comparative structures.

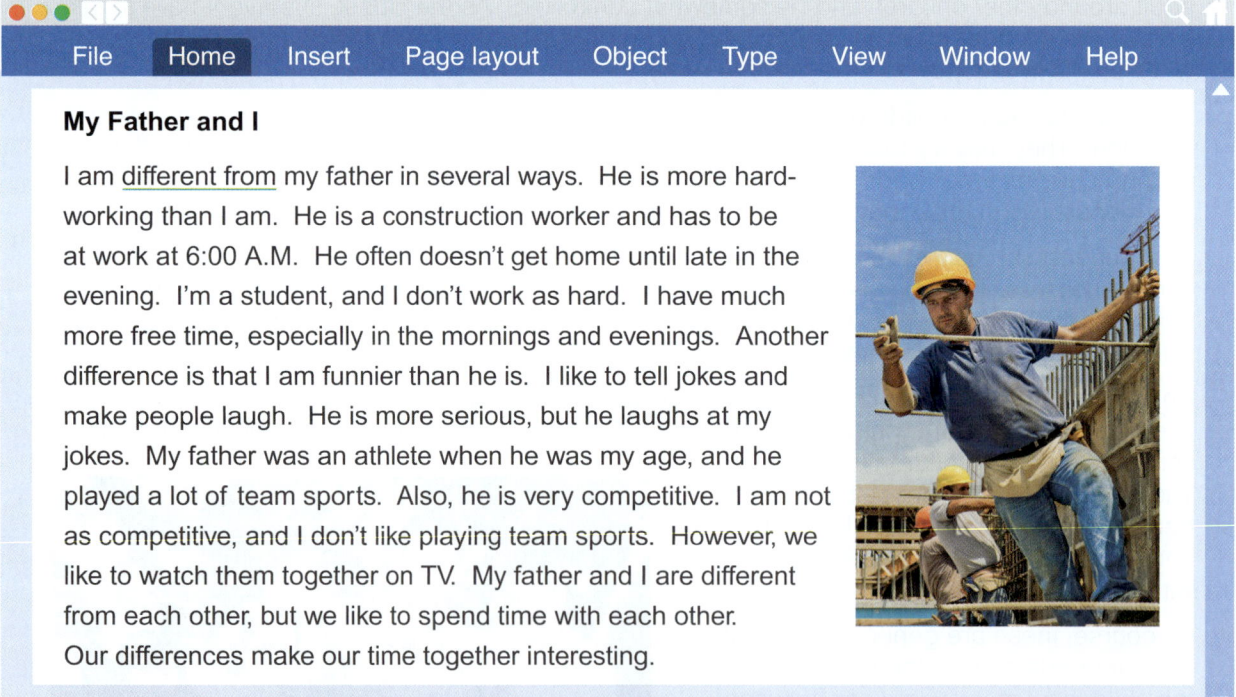

My Father and I

I am <u>different from</u> my father in several ways. He is more hard-working than I am. He is a construction worker and has to be at work at 6:00 A.M. He often doesn't get home until late in the evening. I'm a student, and I don't work as hard. I have much more free time, especially in the mornings and evenings. Another difference is that I am funnier than he is. I like to tell jokes and make people laugh. He is more serious, but he laughs at my jokes. My father was an athlete when he was my age, and he played a lot of team sports. Also, he is very competitive. I am not as competitive, and I don't like playing team sports. However, we like to watch them together on TV. My father and I are different from each other, but we like to spend time with each other. Our differences make our time together interesting.

Part III. Write a paragraph comparing your personality to that of another member of your family or a friend. Follow these steps:

1. Write an introductory sentence: *I am different from / similar to my . . . .*
2. Choose at least four characteristics from the word list. For each one, write a comparison. Use these structures:
   - *different from / (not) the same as / similar to*
   - *-er / more ... than*
   - *(not) as ... as*
3. Write a few details that explain each comparison.
4. Write a concluding sentence.

> **WRITING TIP**
>
> Transitional words like *but, however*, and *also* can help you to connect your comparative sentences better. These words make it easier for the reader to follow your ideas. *But* and *however* have the same meaning; *however* is a little more formal.
>
> - He is more serious, but he laughs at my jokes.
> - However, we like to watch them together on TV.
>
> If you want to talk about a new difference or similarity, *another* is a useful word: *Another difference is . . .* or *Another similarity is . . . .*
>
> - Another difference is that I am funnier than he is.
>
> Look at the paragraph again, and underline the words that help connect the ideas.

Part IV. Edit your writing. Check for the following:

1. ☐ correct use of comparative and superlative adjectives and adverbs (*-er/est* or ***more/the most***)
2. ☐ correct prepositions with these phrases: ***the same as/different from/similar to***
3. ☐ correct use of ***as ... as*** (no *than*)
4. ☐ use of some words to help connect your ideas, such as ***but, however, also, another***
5. ☐ correct spelling (use a dictionary or spell-check)

▪▪▪▪▪ For digital resources, go to MyEnglishLab on the Pearson English Portal. You can also go to the Pearson Practice English app for mobile practice.

CHAPTER 10
The Passive

PRETEST: What do I already know?
Write "C" if the **boldfaced** words are correct and "I" if they are incorrect.

1. _____ Books **written** by authors. (Charts 10-1 and 10-2)
2. _____ The patient **is being seen** by Dr. Vinh. (Chart 10-3)
3. _____ The bus driver **was died** in the accident. (Chart 10-4)
4. _____ What **was happened**? (Chart 10-4)
5. _____ My watch **was made** in China. (Chart 10-5)
6. _____ Your passport **must be checked** by the customs officer. (Chart 10-6)
7. _____ Michael **is married to** Helena. (Chart 10-7)
8. _____ Water **is composed oxygen** and hydrogen. (Chart 10-7)
9. _____ I have a headache. The lecture was so **bored**. (Chart 10-8)
10. _____ Rika **got** really **nervous** before her final exam. (Chart 10-9)
11. _____ We **are not accustomed to live** in a small town. (Chart 10-10)
12. _____ I **am used to sleeping** on a hard mattress. (Chart 10-11)
13. _____ You **supposed to** be home before midnight. (Chart 10-12)

EXERCISE 1 ▶ Warm-up. (Charts 10-1 and 10-2)
Choose the sentence in each pair that describes the picture above it. More than one answer may be correct.

1. a. The worm is watching the bird.
   b. The bird is watching the worm.

2. a. The bird caught the worm.
   b. The worm was caught by the bird.

3. a. The bird ate the worm.
   b. The worm was eaten.

10-1 Active and Passive Sentences

Active

(a) The mouse *ate* the cheese.

Passive

(b) The cheese *was eaten* by the mouse.

Examples (a) and (b) have the same meaning.

Active

Passive

Active

```
           s                    o
(c)      Bob      mailed     the package.
```

Passive

```
           s                   by + o
(d)   The package   was mailed   by Bob.
```

Sentence (c) is an active sentence: *Bob* is the subject and *the package* is the object.

Sentence (d) is a passive sentence. The object of the active sentence becomes the subject. The subject of the active sentence is the object of **by**.

10-2 Forming the Passive

	BE	+	PAST PARTICIPLE		
(a) Corn	is		grown	by farmers.	
(b) The fish	was		caught	by Ava.	

Form of all passive verbs: **be** + *past participle*

Be can be in any of its forms: *am, is, are, was, were, has been, have been, will be*, etc.

	Active	Passive
SIMPLE PRESENT	Farmers *grow* corn. ⟶	Corn *is grown* by farmers.
SIMPLE PAST	Farmers *grew* corn. ⟶	Corn *was grown* by farmers.
PRESENT PERFECT	Farmers *have grown* corn. ⟶	Corn *has been grown* by farmers.
FUTURE	Farmers *will grow* corn. ⟶	Corn *will be grown* by farmers.
	Farmers *are going to grow* corn. ⟶	Corn *is going to be grown* by farmers.

EXERCISE 2 ▶ Looking at grammar. (Charts 10-1 and 10-2)
Write the **be** verb and the past participle if a sentence has them.
Then write "P" if the sentence is passive.

At the Dentist

		BE	+	PAST PARTICIPLE	
1.	The dentist checks your teeth.	Ø		Ø	
2.	Your teeth are checked by the dentist.	are		checked	P
3.	The dental assistant cleaned your teeth.				
4.	Your teeth were cleaned by the dental assistant.				
5.	You have a cavity.				
6.	You are going to need a filling.				
7.	Fillings are done by the dentist.				
8.	You will need to schedule another appointment.				
9.	Another appointment will be needed.				

EXERCISE 3 ▶ Looking at grammar. (Charts 10-1 and 10-2)
Who does what? Work in pairs. Complete the sentences with the simple present form of the passive and the correct word in the box.

authors	construction workers	pharmacists	plumbers
✓auto mechanics	firefighters	pilots	vets/veterinarians

1. Cars (*repair*) ____are repaired____ by ____auto mechanics____ .
2. Toilets (*fix*) _____ by _____ .
3. Planes (*fly*) _____ by _____ .
4. Fires (*fight*) _____ by _____ .
5. Animals (*treat*) _____ by _____ .
6. Books (*write*) _____ by _____ .
7. Buildings (*build*) _____ by _____ .
8. Prescriptions (*fill*) _____ by _____ .

EXERCISE 4 ▶ Looking at grammar. (Charts 10-1 and 10-2)
Change the active verbs to passive by adding the correct subjects and forms of **be**.

1. SIMPLE PRESENT

   a. The teacher *helps* **me**.   ____I____   ____am_____ **helped** by the teacher.

   b. The teacher *helps* **Eva**. ____Eva____ ____is_____ **helped** by the teacher.

   c. The teacher *helps* **us**.   _____ _____ **helped** by the teacher.

2. **SIMPLE PAST**

   a. The teacher *helped* **him**.   _____ _____ **helped** by the teacher.

   b. The teacher *helped* **them**. _____ _____ **helped** by the teacher.

3. **PRESENT PERFECT**

   a. The teacher *has helped* **her**.   _____ _____ **helped** by the teacher.

   b. The teacher *has helped* **Joe**.   _____ _____ **helped** by the teacher.

4. **FUTURE**

   a. The teacher *will help* **me**.   _____ _____ **helped** by the teacher.

   b. The teacher *is going to help* **us**.   _____ _____ **helped** by the teacher.

EXERCISE 5 ▶ Looking at grammar. (Charts 10-1 and 10-2)

Change the verbs from active to passive. Do not change the tenses.

Tech Tasks

		BE	+	PAST PARTICIPLE	
1. Leo *scanned* the photos.	The photos	*were*		*scanned*	by Leo.
2. A team *edits* the documents.	The documents	_____		_____	by a team.
3. An assistant *has changed* the passwords.	The passwords	_____		_____	by an assistant.
4. Mari *is going to upload* a video.	The video	_____		_____	by Mari.
5. A secretary *will delete* files.	Files	_____		_____	by a secretary.
6. Tim *fixed* the printer.	The printer	_____		_____	by Tim.

EXERCISE 6 ▶ Looking at grammar. (Charts 10-1 and 10-2)

Complete the sentences with the correct passive form of the verb.

In the News

1. The town is going to offer free Wi-Fi.

   Free Wi-Fi _____ by the town.

2. The police took the suspect to jail.

   The suspect _____ to jail by the police.

3. Government officials pay their taxes late.

   Taxes _____ late by government officials.

4. The city has designed a new park.

   A new park _____ by the city.

5. Our football team will win the championship.

   The championship _____ by our football team.

EXERCISE 7 ▶ Looking at grammar. (Charts 10-1 and 10-2)
Choose the sentences that are logical (make sense).

Laws of Nature

1. a. Big fish eat little fish.
   b. Little fish are eaten by big fish.
   c. Little fish eat big fish.

2. a. Bees make honey.
   b. Honey makes bees.
   c. Honey is made by bees.

3. a. Mice hunt cats.
   b. Mice are hunted by cats.
   c. Cats are hunted by mice.
   d. Cats hunt mice.

4. a. The earth heats the sun.
   b. The earth is heated by the sun.
   c. The sun heats the earth.

5. a. Lightning hits people.
   b. People are hit by lightning.
   c. People hit lightning.
   d. Lightning is hit by people.

6. a. Humans eat animals.
   b. Animals are eaten by humans.
   c. Animals eat humans.
   d. Humans are eaten by animals.

EXERCISE 8 ▶ Looking at grammar. (Charts 10-1 and 10-2)
Change the sentences from active to passive.

A Graduation Party

	ACTIVE	PASSIVE
1. a.	The party will surprise Sam.	*Sam will be surprised by the party* .
b.	Will the party surprise Max?	*Will Max be surprised by the party* ?
2. a.	Ana planned the party.	_____ .
b.	Did Ari plan the party too?	_____ ?
3. a.	Greta will order food.	_____ .
b.	Will Pat order food too?	_____ ?
4. a.	Jill is going to sign the card.	_____ .
b.	Is Ryan going to sign it?	_____ ?
5. a.	Joni has made decorations.	_____ .
b.	Has Kazu made decorations?	_____ ?

EXERCISE 9 ▶ Looking at grammar. (Charts 10-1 and 10-2)
Which sentences express the meaning of the given sentence? More than one answer may be possible.

At School

1. A teacher interviewed the students for the scholarship.
   a. The students were interviewed.
   b. Someone interviewed the students.
   c. The teacher was interviewed.

2. Ms. Kinea was asked to teach a photography class.
   a. Ms. Kinea asked to teach photography.
   b. Someone asked Ms. Kinea to teach photography.
   c. Ms. Kinea asked someone to teach photography.

3. The students are told to clean the classrooms at the end of the day.
   a. The students told people to clean the classrooms.
   b. The classrooms are cleaned by the students.
   c. Someone told the students to clean the classrooms.

4. The staff checks student IDs.
   a. Someone checks student IDs.
   b. Student IDs are checked by someone.
   c. The staff is checked.

5. The principal will choose the graduation speakers soon.
   a. The graduation speakers will be chosen soon.
   b. The graduation speakers will choose soon.
   c. The principal will be chosen soon.

EXERCISE 10 ▶ Warm-up. (Chart 10-3)
Check (✓) the actions that are or were in progress.

1. _____ The fish are being fed by the boy.
2. _____ The fish were fed by the boy.
3. _____ The fish were being fed by the boy.
4. _____ The boy is feeding the fish.

10-3 Progressive Forms of the Passive

	Active	Passive
PRESENT PROGRESSIVE	Lyn *is copying* the files. ⟶	The files *are being copied* by Lyn.
PAST PROGRESSIVE	Lyn *was copying* the files. ⟶	The files *were being copied* by Lyn.

EXERCISE 11 ▶ Looking at grammar. (Chart 10-3)
Change the active verbs to passive by adding the correct form of **be**. Include the subject of the passive sentence.

1. PRESENT PROGRESSIVE
   a. A tutor *is helping* **us**. _____ _____ **helped** by a tutor.
   b. A tutor *is helping* **her**. _____ _____ **helped** by a tutor.
   c. A tutor *is helping* **me**. _____ _____ **helped** by a tutor.
   d. A tutor *is helping* **them**. _____ _____ **helped** by a tutor.

2. PAST PROGRESSIVE
   a. A tutor *was helping* **me**. _____ _____ **helped** by a tutor.
   b. A tutor *was helping* **him**. _____ _____ **helped** by a tutor.
   c. A tutor *was helping* **us**. _____ _____ **helped** by a tutor.
   d. A tutor *was helping* **you**. _____ _____ **helped** by a tutor.

EXERCISE 12 ▶ Looking at grammar. (Chart 10-3)
Change each sentence from passive to active.

A Company Video

1. The script was being written by professional writers.
   → *Professional writers were writing the script.*
2. Music is being chosen by a producer.
3. Subtitles are being written by a manager.
4. The film is being edited by the director.
5. Photos were being added by an assistant.

EXERCISE 13 ▶ Looking at grammar. (Charts 10-1 → 10-3)
Complete the verbs.

An Office Building at Night

1. The janitors *clean* the building at night.

   The building ___*is*___ clean*ed*___ by the janitors at night.

2. Janitors *clean* the carpets.

   The carpets _____ clean_____ by janitors.

3. The owner *is reviewing the* rents.

   Rents _____ review_____ by the owner.

4. The owner *is going to announce* rent increases.

   Rent increases _____ announce_____ by the owner.

5. An electrician *is fixing* some lights.

   Some lights _____ fix_____ by an electrician.

6. The security guard *has checked* the offices.

   The offices _____ check_____ by the security guard.

7. The security guard *discovered* an open window.

   An open window _____ discover_____ by the security guard.

8. The security guard *found* an unlocked door.

   An unlocked door _____ found by the security guard.

EXERCISE 14 ▶ Looking at grammar. (Charts 10-1 → 10-3)
Change these questions from active to passive.

Hotel Questions

1. Has the maid cleaned our room yet?
   → *Has our room been cleaned by the maid yet?*
2. Does the hotel provide hair dryers?
3. Did housekeeping bring extra towels?
4. Has room service brought our meal?
5. Is the bellhop* bringing our luggage to our room?
6. Is maintenance going to fix the air-conditioning?
7. Will the front desk upgrade** our room?

EXERCISE 15 ▶ Warm-up. (Chart 10-4)
Check (✓) the sentences that have objects. <u>Underline</u> the objects.

1. _____ A small plane crashed.
2. _____ The plane hit a tree.
3. _____ The tree fell on the wing.
4. _____ Fortunately, the pilot didn't die.
5. _____ The crash didn't kill the pilot.

---

*bellhop = a person who carries luggage for hotel guests

**upgrade = make better; in this case, provide a better room than the original one. *Upgrade* is a regular verb.

10-4 Transitive and Intransitive Verbs

Transitive

	S	V	O
(a)	Alan	*wrote*	*the song*.
(b)	Mr. Lee	*signed*	*the check*.
(c)	A cat	*killed*	*the bird*.

A TRANSITIVE verb has an object. An object is a noun or a pronoun.

Intransitive

	S	V	
(d)	Something	*happened*.	
(e)	Kate	*came*	to our house.
(f)	The bird	*died*.	

An INTRANSITIVE verb does NOT have an object.

NOTE: *to our house* is a prepositional phrase. It is not the object of the verb *came*. See Chart 6-4, p. 164.

Transitive Verbs

(g) ACTIVE: Alan *wrote* the song.
(h) PASSIVE: The song *was written* by Alan.

Only transitive verbs can be used in the passive.

Intransitive Verbs

(i) ACTIVE: Something *happened*.
(j) PASSIVE: *(not possible)*
(k) INCORRECT: Something was happened.

An intransitive verb is NOT used in the passive.

Common Intransitive Verbs*

agree	die	happen	rise	stand
appear	exist	laugh	seem	stay
arrive	fall	live	sit	talk
become	flow	occur	sleep	wait
come	go	rain	sneeze	walk

*To find out if a verb is transitive or intransitive, look in your dictionary. The usual abbreviations are v.t. (transitive) and v.i. (intransitive). Some verbs have both transitive and intransitive uses. For example:
  transitive: *Students study books.*
  intransitive: *Students study.*

EXERCISE 16 ▶ Looking at grammar. (Chart 10-4)
Check (✓) the sentences that have an object. <u>Underline</u> the objects.

1. a. _____ Jimmy sold his car.
   b. _____ Jimmy drove a truck to work.
   c. _____ Jimmy drove in a truck to work.

2. a. _____ Mr. Ortiz died at home at midnight.
   b. _____ A heart attack killed him.

3. a. _____ We arrived late to the wedding.
   b. _____ We came to the wedding in a taxi.

4. a. _____ Something strange happened at school today.
   b. _____ A car went off the road.
   c. _____ It hit a tree near a classroom.

EXERCISE 17 ▶ Looking at grammar. (Chart 10-4)
Underline the verbs and identify them as transitive (v.t.) or intransitive (v.i.). If possible, change the sentences to the passive.

1. Omar <u>walked</u> to school yesterday. *(no change)* [v.i.]
2. Alexa <u>broke</u> the window. → *The window was broken by Alexa.* [v.t.]
3. The leaves fell to the ground.
4. I slept at my friend's house last night.
5. Many people felt an earthquake yesterday.
6. Dinosaurs existed millions of years ago.
7. I usually agree with my sister.
8. Many people die during a war.
9. Scientists will discover a cure for cancer someday.
10. Did the Italians invent spaghetti?

EXERCISE 18 ▶ Game: trivia. (Charts 10-1 → 10-4)
Work in teams. Make true statements. Match the information in the left column with the information in the right column. Some sentences are active and some are passive. Add ***was/were*** as necessary. The team with the most correct answers (facts and grammar) wins.*

Examples: 1. Alexander Eiffel __h__. *(no change)*
  2. Anwar Sadat __c__. → *Anwar Sadat was shot in 1981.*

1. Alexander Eiffel __h__.
2. Anwar Sadat __c__.
3. Princess Diana ____.
4. Marie and Pierre Curie ____.
5. Oil ____.
6. Nelson Mandela ____.
7. Michael Jackson ____.
8. Leonardo da Vinci ____.
9. John F. Kennedy ____.
10. Romeo and Juliet ____.

a. killed in a car crash in 1997
b. died in 2009
✓ c. shot in 1981
d. painted the *Mona Lisa*
e. elected president of the United States in 1960
f. discovered in Saudi Arabia in 1938
g. kept apart by their parents
✓ h. designed the Eiffel Tower
i. released from prison in 1990
j. discovered radium

*See *Trivia Answers*, p. 449.

EXERCISE 19 ▶ Warm-up. (Chart 10-5)
Complete the sentences with information from one of your textbooks.

1. _____ was written by _____.
   (name of book)

2. It was published by _____.

10-5 Using the *by*-Phrase

(a) This sweater *was made* **by my aunt**.	The *by*-phrase is used in passive sentences when it is important to know who performs an action. In (a): **by my aunt** is important information.
(b) My sweater *was made* in Korea. (c) Spanish *is spoken* in Colombia. (d) That house *was built* in 1900. (e) Rice *is grown* in many countries.	Usually there is no *by*-phrase in a passive sentence. The passive is used when it is *not known or not important to know exactly who performs an action*. In (b): The exact person (or people) who made the sweater is not known and is not important to know, so there is no *by*-phrase in the passive sentence.
(f) **My aunt** is very creative. **She** made this sweater. (g) A: I like your sweaters. B: Thanks. **This sweater** *was made by* my aunt. **That sweater** *was made by* my mother.	Usually the active is used when the speaker knows who performed the action, as in (f), where the focus of attention is on **my aunt**. In (g): Speaker B uses the passive with a *by*-phrase because he wants to focus attention on the subjects of the sentences. The focus of attention is on the two sweaters. The *by*-phrases add important information.

EXERCISE 20 ▶ Looking at grammar. (Chart 10-5)
Both a. and b. sentences are grammatically correct. Choose the better sentence in each pair.

The Taj Mahal

1. Workers began construction of the Taj Mahal in 1632.
   a. Construction of the Taj Mahal was begun in 1632.
   b. Construction of the Taj Mahal was begun in 1632 by workers.

2. About 22,000 workers, artists, and craftsmen built the Taj Mahal.
   a. The Taj Mahal was built.
   b. The Taj Mahal was built by about 22,000 workers, artists, and craftsmen.

3. Builders built the Taj Mahal with materials from all over Asia.
   a. The Taj Mahal was built with materials from all over Asia.
   b. The Taj Mahal was built with materials from all over Asia by builders.

4. More than 1,000 elephants delivered the building materials to the site.
   a. The building materials were delivered to the site.
   b. The building materials were delivered to the site by more than 1,000 elephants.

5. Decorators decorated some of the walls with gemstones.
   a. Some of the walls were decorated with gemstones.
   b. Some of the walls were decorated with gemstones by decorators.

EXERCISE 21 ▶ Looking at grammar. (Chart 10-5)
Change the sentences from active to passive. Include the *by*-phrase only as necessary.

Around the World
1. People grow rice in India. ___Rice is grown in India.___
2. Do people grow rice in Africa? _____
3. People speak Portuguese in Brazil. _____
4. Canadians speak French. _____
5. Where do people speak Spanish? _____
6. Alibaba® and Amazon® sell online products. _____
7. People eat junk food in every country. _____

EXERCISE 22 ▶ Looking at grammar. (Charts 10-1 → 10-5)
Make sentences with the given words. Some sentences are active and some are passive.

At a Pizza Restaurant

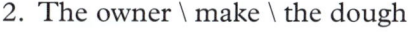

1. The dough \ make \ by the owner
   a. (*every day*) ___The dough is made by the owner every day.___
   b. (*yesterday*) _____
   c. (*tomorrow*) _____
2. The owner \ make \ the dough
   a. (*every week*) _____
   b. (*last week*) _____
3. The sauce \ prepare \ by his wife
   a. (*right now*) _____
   b. (*every day*) _____
   c. (*tomorrow*) _____
4. His wife \ prepare \ the sauce
   a. (*in the mornings*) _____
   b. (*a few minutes ago*) _____
5. The dough \ throw \ up in the air
   a. (*now*) _____
   b. (*in a few minutes*) _____
6. Pizzas \ bake \ in a pizza oven
   a. (*now*) _____
   b. (*all day long yesterday*) _____
   c. (*recently*) _____

EXERCISE 23 ▶ Looking at grammar. (Charts 10-1 → 10-5)

Make sentences with the given words, either orally or in writing. Some sentences are active and some are passive. Use the past tense. Do not change the order of the words.

A Traffic Stop

1. The police \ stop \ a speeding car
    → *The police stopped a speeding car.*
2. The driver \ ask \ to get out of the car \ by the police
3. The driver \ take out \ his license
4. The driver \ give \ his license \ to the police officer
5. The license \ check
6. The driver \ give \ a ticket
7. The driver \ tell \ to drive more carefully

 EXERCISE 24 ▶ Grammar and listening. (Charts 10-1 → 10-5)

Listen to the passage. Listen again and complete the sentences with the verbs you hear.

A Bike Accident

A: Did you hear about the accident outside the dorm entrance?

B: No. What _____1_____?

A: A guy on a bike _____2_____ by a taxi.

B: _____3_____ he _____4_____?

A: Yeah. Someone _____5_____ an ambulance.

He _____6_____ to City Hospital and _____7_____ in the emergency room for cuts and bruises.

B: What _____8_____ to the taxi driver?

A: He _____9_____ for reckless driving.

B: He's lucky that the bicyclist _____10_____.

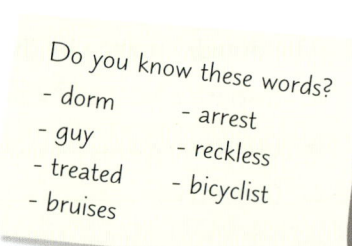

Do you know these words?
- dorm
- guy
- treated
- bruises
- arrest
- reckless
- bicyclist

EXERCISE 25 ▶ Looking at grammar. (Charts 10-1 → 10-5)

Complete the sentences with the correct form (active or passive) of the verbs in parentheses.

1. Yesterday our teacher (*arrive*) ___arrived___ five minutes late.
2. Last night class (*cancel*) _____ because of snow.
3. That's not my coat. It (*belong*) _____ to Lara.
4. Our mail (*deliver*) _____ before noon every day.

5. The "b" in *comb* (*pronounce, not*) _____. It is silent.

6. What (*happen*) _____ to John? Where is he?

7. When I (*arrive*) _____ at the airport yesterday, I (*meet*) _____ by my cousin and a couple of her friends.

8. Yesterday Lee and I (*hear*) _____ about Scott's divorce. I (*surprise, not*) _____ by the news, but Lee (*shock*) _____.

9. A new house (*build*) _____ next to ours next year.

10. Roberto (*send*) _____ that message last week. This one (*send*) _____ yesterday.

11. At the soccer game yesterday, the winning goal (*kick*) _____ by Luigi. Over 100,000 people (*attend*) _____ the soccer game.

12. A: I think American football is too violent.
    B: I (*agree*) _____ with you. I (*prefer*) _____ baseball.

13. A: When (*your bike, steal*) _____?
    B: Two days ago.

14. A: (*you, pay*) _____ your electric bill yet?
    B: No, I haven't, but I'd better pay it today. If I don't, my electricity (*shut off*) _____ by the power company.

EXERCISE 26 ▸ Warm-up. (Chart 10-6)
Read the paragraph and then the statements. Circle "T" for true and "F" for false.

Getting a Passport

Jerry is applying for a passport. He is going to fill out the application form online. He needs to take his application, proof of citizenship, and two passport photos to the passport office. He also has to pay a fee. He will receive his passport in the mail about three weeks after he applies for it.

1. All of the steps for a passport can be done online.   T   F
2. Proof of citizenship must be provided.   T   F
3. A fee has to be paid.   T   F
4. Photographs should be taken after he applies.   T   F
5. The passport will be sent by mail.   T   F

The Passive   295

10-6 Passive Modal Auxiliaries

Active Modal Auxiliaries	Passive Modal Auxiliaries (*modal* + ***be*** + *past participle*)			Modal auxiliaries are often used in the passive.
Bob *will* mail it.	It	*will be mailed*	by Bob.	**FORM:**
Bob *can* mail it.	It	*can be mailed*	by Bob.	modal + ***be*** + past participle
Bob *should* mail it.	It	*should be mailed*	by Bob.	(See Chapter 7 for information about the meanings and uses of modal auxiliaries.)
Bob *ought to* mail it.	It	*ought to be mailed*	by Bob.	
Bob *must* mail it.	It	*must be mailed*	by Bob.	
Bob *has to* mail it.	It	*has to be mailed*	by Bob.	
Bob *may* mail it.	It	*may be mailed*	by Bob.	
Bob *might* mail it.	It	*might be mailed*	by Bob.	
Bob *could* mail it.	It	*could be mailed*	by Bob.	

EXERCISE 27 ▶ Looking at grammar. (Chart 10-6)
Complete the sentences by changing the active modals to passive.

Money Matters

1. Someone must pay this bill immediately.
   This bill ___*must be paid*___ immediately.

2. The bank may request additional information.
   Additional information _____ by the bank.

3. People cannot avoid taxes.
   Taxes _____ .

4. Someone has to pay credit card interest.
   Credit card interest _____ .

5. People can reach the bank manager on his cell phone at 555-3815.
   The bank manager _____ on his cell phone at 555-3815.

6. The bank should issue* a refund.
   A refund _____ by the bank.

7. People may pay the amount now or later.
   The amount _____ now or later.

8. Be careful! If that bank app isn't secure, someone could steal your money.
   Your money _____ if that bank app isn't secure.

9. My parents say students must save money for college.
   My parents say money _____ for college.

---

*issue = give, provide

EXERCISE 28 ▶ Reading and grammar. (Charts 10-1 → 10-6)

Are you wearing jeans right now or do you have a pair at home? Who were they made by? Read the passage about jeans and choose the correct verbs.

Do you know these words?
- create
- invent
- gold miner
- rough
- tailor
- rivets

HOW JEANS WERE INVENTED

Around the world, a very popular pant for men, women, and children is jeans. Did you know that jeans **created / were created** (1) more than 100 years ago? They **invent / were invented** (2) by Levi Strauss during the California Gold Rush.

In 1853, Levi Strauss, a 24-year-old immigrant from Germany, **traveled / were travel** (3) from New York to San Francisco. His brother was the owner of a store in New York and wanted to open another one in San Francisco. When Strauss **arrived / was arrived** (4), a gold miner **asked / was asked** (5) him what he had to sell. Levi said he had strong canvas for tents and wagon covers. The miner told him he really needed strong pants because he couldn't find any that lasted very long.

So Levi Strauss took the canvas and **designed / was designed** (6) a pair of overall pants. The miners **liked / were liked** (7) them except that they were rough on the skin. Strauss **changed / was changed** (8) the canvas to a cotton cloth from France called *serge de Nimes*. Later, the fabric **called / was called** (9) "denim" and the pants **gave / were given** (10) the nickname "blue jeans."

Eventually, Levi Strauss & Company **formed / was formed** (11). Strauss and tailor David Jacobs began putting rivets in pants to make them stronger. In 1936, a red tab **added / was added** (12) to the rear pocket. This was done so "Levis" **could identify / could be identified** (13) more easily. Now the company is world famous. For many people, all jeans **know / are known** (14) as Levis.

EXERCISE 29 ▶ Warm-up: trivia. (Chart 10-7)

Complete the sentences with words in the box.* Not all words are necessary.

| China | monkeys | sand | spiders |
| Mongolia | Nepal | small spaces | whales |

1. Glass is composed mainly of _____.
2. Dolphins are related to _____.
3. The Gobi Desert is located in two countries: _____ and _____.
4. People with claustrophobia are frightened of _____.

10-7 Past Participles as Adjectives (Stative or Non-Progressive Passive)

	BE	+	ADJECTIVE	
(a)	Paul	is	young.	*Be* can be followed by an adjective, as in (a)–(c). The adjective describes or gives information about the subject of the sentence.
(b)	Paul	is	tall.	
(c)	Paul	is	hungry.	
	BE	+	PAST PARTICIPLE	
(d)	Paul	is	married.	*Be* can be followed by a past participle (the passive form), as in (d)–(f). The past participle is often like an adjective. The past participle describes or gives information about the subject of the sentence. Past participles are used as adjectives in many common, everyday expressions.
(e)	Paul	is	tired.	
(f)	Paul	is	frightened.	

(g) Paul *is married* **to** Susan.
(h) Paul *was excited* **about** the game.
(i) Paul *will be prepared* **for** the exam.

Often the past participles in these expressions are followed by particular prepositions + an object. For example:
In (g): ***married*** is followed by ***to*** (+ *an object*)
In (h): ***excited*** is followed by ***about*** (+ *an object*)
In (i): ***prepared*** is followed by ***for*** (+ *an object*)

Expressions with *Be* + Past Participle and Common Prepositions

be acquainted (*with*)	be excited (*about*)	be opposed (*to*)
be bored (*with, by*)	be exhausted (*from*)	be pleased (*with*)
be broken	be finished (*with*)	be prepared (*for*)
be closed	be frightened (*of*)	be qualified (*for*)
be composed of	be gone (*from*)	be related (*to*)
be crowded (*with*)	be hurt	be satisfied (*with*)
be devoted (*to*)	be interested (*in*)	be scared (*of*)
be disappointed (*in, with*)	be involved (*in, with*)	be shut
be divorced (*from*)	be located (*in, south of, etc.*)	be spoiled
be done (*with*)	be lost	be terrified (*of*)
be drunk (*on*)	be made of	be tired (*of, from*)*
be engaged (*to*)	be married (*to*)	be worried (*about*)

*I'm **tired of** the cold weather. = I've had enough cold weather. I want the weather to get warm.
I'm **tired from** working hard all day. = I'm tired because I worked hard all day.

*See *Trivia Answers*, p. 449.

EXERCISE 30 ▶ Looking at grammar. (Chart 10-7)

Choose all the correct completions.

1. Roger is disappointed with _____.
    a. his job   b. in the morning   c. his son's grades

2. Are you related to _____?
    a. the Browns   b. math and science   c. me

3. Finally! We are done with _____.
    a. finished   b. our chores   c. our errands

4. My boss was pleased with _____.
    a. my report   b. thank you   c. the new contract

5. The baby birds are gone from _____.
    a. away   b. their nest   c. yesterday

6. Taka and Joanne are bored with _____.
    a. their work   b. this movie   c. their marriage

7. Are you tired of _____?
    a. work   b. asleep   c. the news

EXERCISE 31 ▶ Looking at grammar. (Chart 10-7)

Part I. Complete each sentence with an appropriate preposition.

Nervous Nick is …

1. worried _____ almost everything in life.
2. frightened _____ being around people.
3. also scared _____ snakes, lizards, and dogs.
4. terrified _____ going outside and seeing a dog.
5. exhausted _____ worrying so much.
6. tired _____ his fears.

Happy Halle is …

7. excited _____ waking up every morning.
8. pleased _____ her job.
9. interested _____ having a good time.
10. involved _____ many community activities.
11. satisfied _____ just about everything in her life.
12. qualified _____ a variety of jobs.

Part II. Work in small groups. Make three statements about yourself or someone in your family. Use the adjectives in Part I.

EXERCISE 32 ▶ Looking at grammar. (Chart 10-7)
Complete the sentences with a form of **be** + the past participle of the verbs in the box.
Note the prepositions in **bold** that follow them.

| compose | interest | oppose | satisfy |
| finish | marry | prepare | ✓scare |

1. Most young children ____are scared____ **of** loud noises.
2. Jane _____ **in** ecology.
3. Don't clear the table yet. I _____ not _____ **with** my meal.
4. I _____ **with** my progress in English.
5. Tony _____ **to** Sonia. They have a happy marriage.
6. Roberta's parents _____ **to** her marriage. They don't like her fiancé.
7. The test is tomorrow. _____ you _____ **for** it?
8. A digital picture _____ **of** thousands of tiny dots called pixels.

EXERCISE 33 ▶ Looking at grammar. (Chart 10-7)
Complete each sentence with an appropriate preposition.

1. Because of the sale, the mall was crowded _____ shoppers.
2. Do you think you are qualified _____ that job?
3. Mr. Ahmad loves his family very much. He is devoted _____ them.
4. My sister is married _____ a law student.
5. I'll be finished _____ my work in another minute or two.
6. The workers are opposed _____ the new health-care plan.
7. Are you acquainted _____ this writer? I can't put her books down!*
8. Janet doesn't take good care of herself. I'm worried _____ her health.

EXERCISE 34 ▶ Let's talk. (Chart 10-7)
Interview another student in the class. You will need to add prepositions to the questions.
Share a few of the answers with the class.

1. When will you be done _____ your English studies?
2. What are you excited _____ doing next year?
3. What are you not prepared _____?
4. Have you ever been involved _____ team sports? Where? When?
5. What do kids nowadays become bored _____ quickly?
6. Are you scared or terrified _____ anything? What?

---

can't put a book down = can't stop reading a book because it's so exciting/interesting

7. What are you opposed _____ ?

8. Are you related _____ anyone famous? Who?

EXERCISE 35 ▶ Looking at grammar. (Chart 10-7)
Complete the sentences with the correct form of the expressions in the box.
Add prepositions as necessary.

be acquainted	be exhausted	be qualified
be composed	be located	be spoiled
be crowded	be made	✓ be worried
be disappointed		

1. Dennis isn't doing well in school this semester. He __is worried about__ his grades.
2. My shirt _____ cotton.
3. I live in a small apartment with six people. Our apartment _____ .
4. Vietnam _____ Southeast Asia.
5. I'm going to go straight to bed tonight. It's been a hard day. I _____ .
6. The kids _____ . I had promised to take them to the beach today, but now we can't go because it's raining.
7. Yuk! This milk tastes sour. I think it _____ .
8. Water _____ hydrogen and oxygen.
9. The job description says an applicant must have a master's degree and five years of teaching experience. I _____ not _____ that job.
10. I've never met Mrs. Novinsky. I _____ not _____ her.

EXERCISE 36 ▶ Listening. (Chart 10-7)
Complete the sentences with the words you hear.

Example: You will hear: My earrings are made of gold.

You will write: My earrings __are made of gold__ .

1. This fruit _____ . I think I'd better throw it out.
2. When we got to the post office, it _____ .
3. Oxford University _____ Oxford, England.
4. Haley doesn't like to ride in elevators. She's _____ small spaces.
5. What's the matter? _____ you _____ ?
6. Excuse me. Could you please tell me how to get to the bus station from here?
   I _____ .
7. Your name is Tom Hood? _____ you _____ Mary Hood?
8. Where's my wallet? It's _____ ! Did someone take it?

9. Oh, no! Look at my sunglasses. I sat on them, and now they _____.
10. It's starting to rain. _____ all of the windows _____?

EXERCISE 37 ▸ Warm-up. (Chart 10-8)
Match the sentences with the pictures. Two sentences do not match either picture.

Picture A

Picture B

1. The shark is terrifying. _____
2. The shark is terrified. _____
3. The swimmer is terrifying. _____
4. The swimmer is terrified. _____

10-8	Participial Adjectives: *-ed* vs. *-ing*	
	Art **interests** me. (a) I am *interested* in art. INCORRECT: *I am interesting in art.* (b) Art is *interesting*. INCORRECT: *Art is interested.* The news **surprised** Kate. (c) Kate was *surprised*. (d) The news was *surprising*.	The past participle (*-ed*)* and the present participle (*-ing*) can be used as adjectives. In (a): The past participle (*interested*) describes how a person feels. In (b): The present participle (*interesting*) describes the *cause* of the feeling. The cause of the interest is art. In (c): *surprised* describes how Kate felt. The past participle carries a passive meaning: *Kate was surprised **by the news**.* In (d): *the news* was the cause of the surprise.
	(e) Did you hear the *surprising news*? (f) Dino fixed the *broken window*.	Like other adjectives, participial adjectives may follow **be**, as in examples (a) through (d), or they may come in front of nouns, as in (e) and (f).

*The past participle of regular verbs ends in *-ed*. For verbs that have irregular forms, see Chart 2-3, p. 33, Appendix A-2, and the inside back cover.

EXERCISE 38 ▶ Looking at grammar. (Chart 10-8)

Make sentences about the pictures. Use *roller coaster, younger woman,* and *older woman*.

A Roller Coaster Ride

1. The _____ is frightened.
2. The _____ is frightening.
3. The _____ is excited.
4. The _____ is exciting.
5. The _____ is thrilling.
6. The _____ is delighted.

EXERCISE 39 ▶ Looking at grammar. (Chart 10-8)

Complete the sentences with the **-ed** or **-ing** form of the verbs in *italics*.

1. Talal's classes *interest* him.
   a. Talal's classes are ____*interesting*____ .
   b. Talal is an ____*interested*____ student.

2. Emily is going to Australia. The idea of going on this trip *excites* her.
   a. Emily is _____ about going on this trip.
   b. She thinks it is going to be an _____ trip.

3. I like to study sea life. The subject of marine biology *fascinates* me.
   a. Marine biology is a _____ subject.
   b. I'm _____ by marine biology.

4. Mike heard some bad news. The bad news *depressed* him.
   a. Mike is very sad. In fact, he is _____ .
   b. The news made Mike feel very sad. The news was _____ .

5. Robots *interest* me.
   a. I'm _____ in robots.
   b. Robots are _____ to me.

EXERCISE 40 ▸ Listening. (Chart 10-8)
Listen to the statements and choose the words you hear.

Example: You will hear: It was a frightening experience.

You will choose: frighten (frightening) frightened

1. bore   boring   bored
2. shock   shocking   shocked
3. confuse   confusing   confused
4. embarrass   embarrassing   embarrassed
5. surprise   surprising   surprised
6. scare   scary*   scared

EXERCISE 41 ▸ Looking at grammar. (Chart 10-8)
Choose the correct word in each sentence.

SITUATION: Nicki was walking on the beach with her co-worker Tyler during their lunch break. She slipped on some rocks and fell into the water.

1. Nicki felt   embarrassed / embarrassing.
2. Falling into the water was   embarrassed / embarrassing   for her.
3. It was an   embarrassed / embarrassing   experience.
4. Tyler was   surprised / surprising   when he heard the splash.
5. He had a   surprised / surprising   look on his face.
6. When Nicki went back to the office, her co-workers were   interested / interesting   in her story.
7. Nicki said her story wasn't   interesting / interested.
8. But weeks later, she could laugh about it. Now the story is   amused / amusing.
9. Nicki is   amused / amusing   when she thinks about the story.

EXERCISE 42 ▸ Warm-up. (Chart 10-9)
Are these statements true for you? Circle *yes* or *no*.

Right now …

1. I am getting tired.   yes   no
2. I am getting hungry.   yes   no
3. I am getting confused.   yes   no

---

*The adjective ending is *-y*, not *-ing*.

10-9 Get + Adjective; Get + Past Participle

GET + ADJECTIVE (a) I **am getting hungry**. Let's eat. (b) Eric **got nervous** before the job interview.	**Get** can be followed by an adjective. **Get** gives the idea of change — the idea of becoming, beginning to be, growing to be. In (a): **I'm getting hungry.** = I wasn't hungry before, but now I'm beginning to be hungry.
GET + PAST PARTICIPLE (c) **I'm getting tired**. Let's stop working. (d) Steve and Rita **got married** last month.	Sometimes **get** is followed by a past participle. The past participle after **get** is like an adjective; it describes the subject of the sentence.

Get + Adjective

get angry	get dry	get quiet
get bald	get fat	get rich
get big	get full	get serious
get busy	get hot	get sick
get close	get hungry	get sleepy
get cold	get interested	get thirsty
get dark	get late	get well
get dirty	get nervous	get wet
get dizzy	get old	

Get + Past Participle

get acquainted	get drunk	get involved
get arrested	get engaged	get killed
get bored	get excited	get lost
get confused	get finished	get married
get crowded	get frightened	get scared
get divorced	get hurt	get sunburned
get done	get interested	get tired
get dressed	get invited	get worried

EXERCISE 43 ▶ Looking at grammar. (Chart 10-9)
Complete the sentences with the words in the box.

bald	dirty	hurt	lost	rich
busy	✓full	late	nervous	serious

1. This food is delicious, but I can't eat any more. I'm getting ___*full*___.
2. Stop wasting time! We need to get _____ and finish our project!
3. I didn't understand Mariam's directions very well, so on the way to her house last night I got _____. I couldn't find her house.
4. It's hard to work on a car and stay clean. Paul's clothes always get _____ from all the grease and oil.
5. Tim doesn't like to fly. His heart beats quickly during takeoff. He gets _____.
6. We'd better go home. It's getting _____, and you have school tomorrow.
7. Simon wants to get _____, but he doesn't want to work. That's not very realistic.
8. If you plan to go to medical school, you need to get _____ about the time and money involved and start planning now.
9. Mr. Andersen is losing some of his hair. He's slowly getting _____.
10. Was the accident serious? Did anyone get _____?

EXERCISE 44 ▶ Let's talk: interview. (Chart 10-9)
Interview your classmates. Share some of their answers with the class.

1. Have you ever gotten hurt? What happened?
2. Have you ever gotten lost? What happened?
3. When was the last time you got dizzy?
4. How long does it take you to get dressed in the morning?
5. In general, do you get sleepy during the day? When?
6. Do you ever get hungry in the middle of the night? What do you do?
7. Have you ever gotten involved with a charity? Which one?

EXERCISE 45 ▶ Listening. (Chart 10-9)
Listen to the sentences and complete them with any adjectives that make sense.

Example: You will hear: This towel is soaking wet. Please hang it up so it will get _____.
You will write: ___dry___

1. _____   3. _____   5. _____
2. _____   4. _____   6. _____

EXERCISE 46 ▶ Reading. (Chart 10-9)
Read the passage and the statements that follow it. Circle "T" for true and "F" for false.

A Blended Family

   Lisa and Thomas live in a blended family. They are not related to each other, but they are brother and sister. Actually, they are stepbrother and stepsister. This is how they came to be in the same family.
   Lisa's mother got divorced when Lisa was a baby. Thomas' father was a widower. His wife had died unexpectedly. Lisa and Thomas' parents met a few years ago at a going-away party for a friend. After a year of dating, they got engaged, and a year later, they got married. Lisa is older than Thomas, but they get along well. Theirs is a happy blended family.

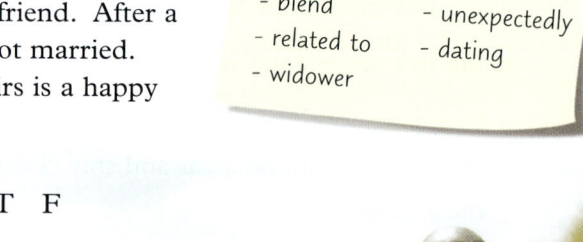

Do you know these words?
- blend
- related to
- widower
- unexpectedly
- dating

1. Lisa's mother got married. Then she got divorced. Then she got remarried.   T   F

2. Thomas' father got married, and then he got divorced. After he got divorced, he got engaged, and then he got remarried.   T   F

3. Lisa and Thomas became stepsister and stepbrother when their parents got married.   T   F

EXERCISE 47 ▶ Looking at grammar. (Chart 10-9)
Complete the sentences with appropriate forms of ***get*** and the words in the box.

angry	dark	hungry	lost	tired
cold	dressed	involve	marry	well
crowd	dry	kill	✓sunburn	worry

1. When I stayed out in the sun too long yesterday, I ___*got sunburned*___.

2. If you're sick, stay home and take care of yourself. You won't _____ if you don't take care of yourself.

3. Alima and Hasan are engaged. They are going to _____ a year from now.

4. Sarah doesn't eat breakfast, so she always _____ by ten or ten-thirty.

5. In the winter, the sun sets early. It _____ outside by six or even earlier.

6. Put these towels back in the dryer. They didn't _____ the first time.

7. Let's stop working for a while. I'm _____. I need a break.

8. Anastasia has to move out of her apartment next week, and she hasn't found a new place to live. She's _____.

9. Toshiro was in a terrible car wreck and almost _____. He's lucky to be alive.

10. The temperature is dropping. Brrr! I'm _____. Can I borrow your sweater?

11. Sorry we're late. We took a wrong turn and _____.

12. Good restaurants _____ around dinner time. It's hard to find a seat because there are so many people.

13. Calm down! Take it easy! You shouldn't _____ so _____. It's not good for your blood pressure.

14. I left when Ellen and Joe began to argue. I never _____ in other people's quarrels.

15. Sam is wearing one brown sock and one blue sock today. He _____ in a hurry this morning and didn't pay attention to the color of his socks.

EXERCISE 48 ▶ Warm-up. (Chart 10-10)
Circle the words in green that make these sentences true for you.

1. I am   used to / not used to   speaking English with native speakers.

2. I am   accustomed to / not accustomed to   speaking English without translating from my language.

3. I am   getting used to / not getting used to   English slang.

4. I am   getting accustomed to / not getting accustomed to   reading English without using a dictionary.

10-10 Using *Be Used/Accustomed To* and *Get Used/Accustomed To*

(a) I *am used to* hot weather. (b) I *am accustomed to* hot weather.	Examples (a) and (b) have the same meaning: "Living in a hot climate is usual and normal for me. I'm familiar with what it is like to live in a hot climate. Hot weather isn't strange or different to me."
(c) I *am used to living* in a hot climate. (d) I *am accustomed to living* in a hot climate.	Note in (c) and (d): *to* (a preposition) is followed by the *-ing* form of a verb (a gerund).
(e) I just moved from Florida to Alaska. I *am getting used to* (*accustomed to*) the cold weather here.	*get used to / accustomed to* = *become used to*

EXERCISE 49 ▶ Looking at grammar. (Chart 10-10)

Part I. Complete the sentences with *be used to*, affirmative or negative.

1. Juan is from Mexico. He __is used to__ hot weather. He __isn't used to__ cold weather.
2. Alice was born and raised in Miami. She _____ living in a big city.
3. My hometown is Dallas, but this year I'm moving to a small town. I _____ living in a small town. I _____ living in a big city.

Part II. Complete the sentences with *be accustomed to*, affirmative or negative.

4. Spiro recently moved to Hong Kong from Greece. He __is accustomed to__ eating Greek food. He __isn't accustomed to__ eating Chinese food.
5. I always get up around 6:00 A.M. I _____ getting up early. I _____ sleeping late.
6. Our teacher always gives us a lot of homework. We _____ having a lot of homework every day.

EXERCISE 50 ▶ Let's talk: interview. (Chart 10-10)
Ask questions with *be used to/accustomed to*. Share some answers with the class.

Example: buy \ frozen food
→ *Are you used to / accustomed to buying frozen food?*

1. get up \ early
2. sleep \ late
3. eat \ breakfast
4. skip \ lunch
5. eat \ a late dinner
6. drink \ coffee in the morning
7. have \ dessert at night
8. live \ in a big city
9. pay \ for all your expenses

EXERCISE 51 ▶ Let's talk. (Chart 10-10)
Work in small groups. Answer the questions.

1. Think of a time you traveled to another country. What did you need to get used to?
2. Think about English. What have you gotten used to or not gotten used to?
3. Think about different stages of life. What do people need to get accustomed to as they age?

EXERCISE 52 ▶ Reading and grammar. (Charts 10-1 → 10-10)

Part I. Read the blog by co-author Stacy Hagen. Underline five examples of sentences with the grammar you have studied in this chapter. Refer to the charts if necessary.

BlackBookBlog

Cultural Differences

As you know, every country has different customs, and it can take a while to get used to them. I'd like to tell you about some customs on the West Coast of the United States, where I live. Most are pretty typical for the rest of the country, too.

Although it is becoming more common to take shoes off, many people are still used to wearing them in the house. Sometimes people have a sign near the front door that says, "Please remove your shoes." Or you may be asked by your host to take them off. If you are not sure what to do, you can always ask your host. When I visit someone, I always take off my shoes and leave them near the door because I am used to doing this at my home.

When people are out walking and see someone they know, they like to smile and say, "Hi, how are you?" But this is just a quick greeting. They don't expect the other person to give a long answer. A common response is, "Pretty good, how are you?" Even when people aren't feeling so good, they often respond in a positive way. It may seem a little false, but it's just a greeting, not the start of a long conversation.

At school, teachers don't like to be interrupted in class. If a student is late, he or she enters quietly and sits at the side or the back of the room, if possible. Knocking is not necessary, and the noise bothers some teachers.

Generally, *Mr., Mrs.*, or *Ms.* is used with a teacher's last name in grades K–12. *Teacher* by itself is never used. In colleges and universities, the rules become a little more complicated. Some professors want you to use their first names. They will probably tell you this. But many are accustomed to the more formal *Professor* or *Doctor*. Sometimes your instructors will be teaching assistants who are students in graduate school. Often, first names are used, but some may ask that you use *Mr.* or *Ms. Professor* or *Doctor* is not appropriate with teaching assistants because they are not finished with their studies. If you are not sure, ask at the beginning of the term.

When people go to restaurants, it is common to leave tips for restaurant meals. Generally, the tip is left on the table or added to the credit card receipt. A tip of 15% is average. Some people tip 20–25% for excellent service. Some people will leave 10%, or even no tip, if they are not happy with the service. Money is not generally handed to the server.

It is good to research customs like these before you go to study or live in another country. Learning a language is hard, and you will feel more comfortable if you are acquainted with cultural differences.

Part II. Choose the answers for the customs in your country. Discuss them in groups and share a few of the answers with the class.

1. When I go to someone's home, shoes _____.
   a. are left outside the door
   b. are taken off after entering
   c. are kept on

2. When I am late for class, I _____.
   a. walk in and tell the teacher I am sorry
   b. walk in quietly and sit in the back of the room
   c. knock on the door and wait for the teacher to answer
   d. knock on the door one time and walk in

3. When I say my teacher's name, I use _____.
   a. the title (*Professor, Dr., Ms., Mr.*) and last name
   b. the first name only
   c. *Teacher* with no name
   d. *Sir, Madam,* or *Ma'am* with no name

4. After a meal at a restaurant, a tip _____.
   a. isn't left
   b. is left on the table
   c. is put on a credit card
   d. is handed to the server

EXERCISE 53 ▶ Warm-up. (Chart 10-11)
Complete the sentences about food preferences. Make statements that are true for you.

1. There are some foods I liked when I was younger, but now I don't eat them.

   I used to eat _____, but now I don't.

2. There are some foods I didn't like when I first tried them, but now they're OK.

   For example, the first time I ate _____, I didn't like

   it/them, but now I'm used to eating it/them.

10-11	*Used To* vs. *Be Used To*	
(a) I *used to* **live** in Chicago, but now I live in Tokyo. INCORRECT: *I used to living in Chicago.*	In (a): **Used to** expresses the habitual past (see Chart 2-9, p. 60). It is followed by the *simple form of a verb*.	
(b) I *am used to* **living** in a big city. INCORRECT: *I am used to live in a big city.*	In (b): **be used to** is followed by the *-ing* form of a verb (a gerund).*	

*NOTE: In both **used to** (habitual past) and **be used to**, the "d" is not pronounced in casual speech.

EXERCISE 54 ▸ Looking at grammar. (Chart 10-11)
Complete the sentences with an appropriate form of *be*. If no form of *be* is necessary, use **Ø**.

1. a. I have lived in Malaysia for a long time. I __am__ used to warm weather.
   b. I __Ø__ used to live in Portugal, but now I live in Spain.

2. a. I _____ used to sit in the back of the classroom, but now I prefer to sit in the front row.
   b. I _____ used to sitting at this desk. I sit here every day.

3. a. When I was a child, I _____ used to play games with my friends in a big field near my house after school every day.
   b. It's hard for my kids to stay inside on a cold, rainy day. They _____ used to playing outside in the big field near our house. They play there almost every day.

4. a. A teacher _____ used to answering questions. Students, especially good students, always have a lot of questions.
   b. I _____ used to be afraid to ask questions, but now I'm not.

5. a. People _____ used to believe the world was flat.
   b. I _____ used to believe that people on TV could see me.

EXERCISE 55 ▸ Looking at grammar. (Chart 10-11)
Complete the sentences with *used to/be used to* and the correct form of the verb in parentheses.

Habits

1. Nick stays up later now than he did when he was in high school. He (*go*) __used to go__ to bed at ten, but now he rarely gets to bed before midnight.

2. I got used to going to bed late when I was in college, but now I have a job and I need my sleep. These days I (*go*) __am used to going__ to bed around ten-thirty.

3. I am a vegetarian. I (*eat*) _____ meat, but now I eat only meatless meals.

4. Ms. Wu has had a vegetable garden all her life. She (*grow*) _____ her own vegetables.

5. Oscar has lived in Brazil for ten years. He (*eat*) _____ Brazilian food. It's his favorite.

6. Georgio moved to Germany to open his own restaurant. He (*have*) _____ a small bakery in Italy.

7. I have taken the bus to work every day for the past five years. I (*take*) _____ the bus.

8. Juanita travels by train on company business. She (*go*) _____ by plane, but now it's too expensive.

The Passive 311

EXERCISE 56 ▶ Warm-up. (Chart 10-12)
Complete the sentences about airline passengers.

1. Before getting on the plane, passengers are expected to …
2. After boarding the plane, passengers are supposed to …
3. During landing, passengers are not supposed to …

10-12 Using *Be Supposed To*

(a) Mike *is supposed to call* me tomorrow. (IDEA: I expect Mike to call me tomorrow.)	*Be supposed to* is used to talk about an activity or event that is expected to occur.
(b) We *are supposed to write* a composition. (IDEA: The teacher expects us to write a composition.)	In (a): The idea of *is supposed to* is that Mike is expected (by me) to call me. I asked him to call me. He promised to call me. I expect him to call me.
(c) Alice *was supposed to be* home at ten, but she didn't get in until midnight. (IDEA: Someone expected Alice to be home at ten.)	In the past form, *be supposed to* often expresses the idea that an expected event did not occur, as in (c).

EXERCISE 57 ▶ Looking at grammar. (Chart 10-12)
Use *be supposed to*. Make a sentence with a similar meaning.

1. The teacher expects us to be on time for class.
   → *We are supposed to be on time for class.*
2. People expect the weather to be cold tomorrow.
3. People expect the plane to arrive at 6:00.
4. My boss expects me to work late tonight.
5. I expected the mail to come an hour ago, but it didn't.

EXERCISE 58 ▶ Let's talk. (Chart 10-12)
Read the list of stereotypes. Stereotypes are beliefs that many people may have. Work with a partner. Which ones do you agree with? Which ones do you disagree with? Explain your answers.

Stereotypes

1. Little girls are supposed to play with dolls.
2. Little boys are supposed to play with toy soldiers.
3. Women are supposed to be the main caregiver for the children.
4. Women are not supposed to have careers outside the home.
5. Men are not supposed to spend much time doing housework.
6. Men are supposed to be tough.
7. Women are not supposed to fight in wars.
8. Men are supposed to act strong.
9. Women are supposed to please people.

EXERCISE 59 ▶ Check your knowledge. (Chapter 10 Review)
Correct the errors.

1. I ~~am~~ agree with him.

2. Something was happened.

3. This pen is belong to me.

4. I'm interesting in that subject.

5. He is marry with my cousin.

6. Mary's dog was died last week.

7. Were you surprise when you heard the news?

8. When I went downtown, I am get lost.

9. The bus was arrived ten minutes late.

10. We're not suppose to have pets in our apartment.

EXERCISE 60 ▶ Reading and writing. (Chapter 10)
Part I. Read the passage and underline the passive verbs.

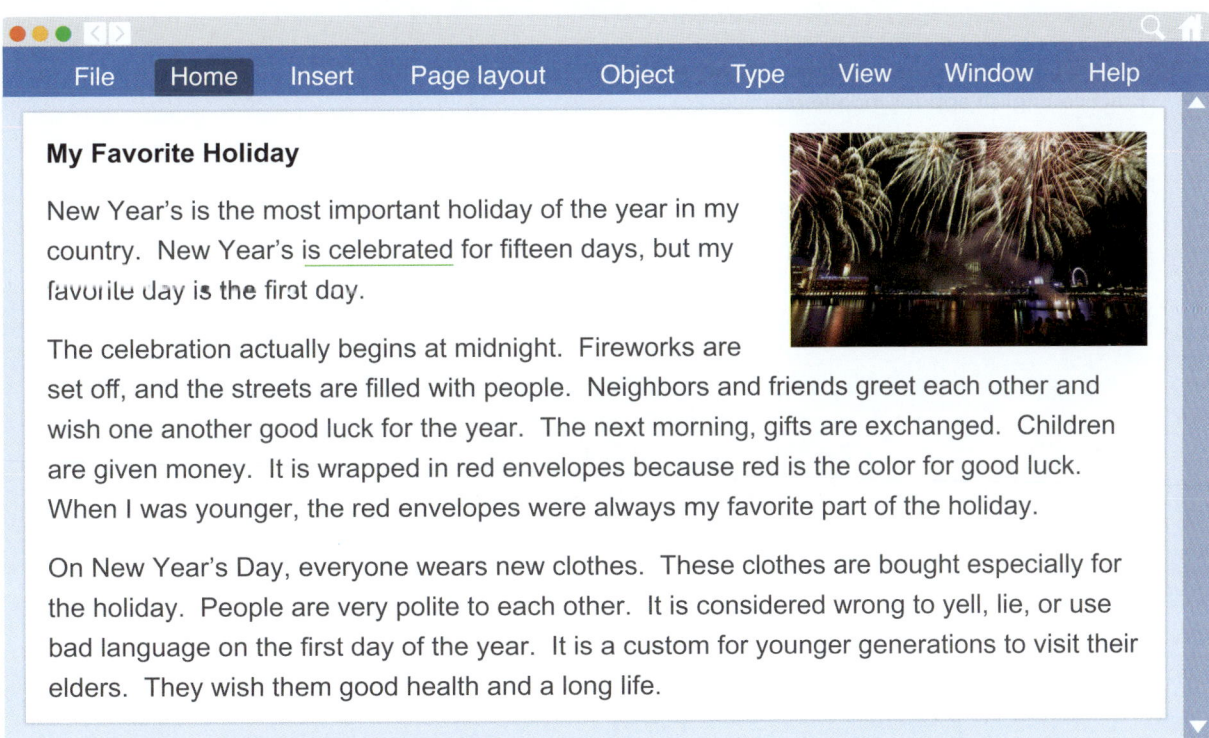

My Favorite Holiday

New Year's is the most important holiday of the year in my country. New Year's is celebrated for fifteen days, but my favorite day is the first day.

The celebration actually begins at midnight. Fireworks are set off, and the streets are filled with people. Neighbors and friends greet each other and wish one another good luck for the year. The next morning, gifts are exchanged. Children are given money. It is wrapped in red envelopes because red is the color for good luck. When I was younger, the red envelopes were always my favorite part of the holiday.

On New Year's Day, everyone wears new clothes. These clothes are bought especially for the holiday. People are very polite to each other. It is considered wrong to yell, lie, or use bad language on the first day of the year. It is a custom for younger generations to visit their elders. They wish them good health and a long life.

Part II. Choose a holiday you like. Describe the activities on this day. What do you do in the morning? Afternoon? Evening? Which activities do you enjoy the most? Make some of your sentences passive, as appropriate.

> **WRITING TIP**
>
> In most cases, it is better to use active verbs in writing. However, the passive is used when the doer of the action is not important or does not need to be mentioned. Here are some examples from the reading:
>
> Fireworks are set off. (not necessary to say: People set off fireworks.)
> Money is given to children. (not necessary to say: People give money to children.)
> These clothes are bought especially for the holiday. (not necessary to say: People buy clothes especially for the holiday.)
>
> In each of these examples, use of the passive allows the reader to focus on what is most important, the receiver of the action: the fireworks, money, and the clothes.

Part III. Edit your writing. Check for the following:

1. ☐ a form of **be** for every passive verb
2. ☐ a past participle for every passive verb
3. ☐ use of the passive when the doer of the action does not need to be mentioned
4. ☐ a description of the day's activities
5. ☐ correct spelling (use a dictionary or spell-check)

▪▪▪▪ For digital resources, go to MyEnglishLab on the Pearson English Portal. You can also go to the Pearson Practice English app for mobile practice.

CHAPTER 11

Count/Noncount Nouns and Articles

PRETEST: What do I already know?
Write "C" if the **boldfaced** words are correct and "I" if they are incorrect.

1. _____ I live in **a** old house. (Chart 11-1)
2. _____ We have **new furniture**. (Chart 11-2)
3. _____ Would you like **a** rice? (Chart 11-3)
4. _____ Many cities have **pollution**. (Chart 11-4)
5. _____ I need to buy **a** some toothpaste. I'm almost out. (Chart 11-5)
6. _____ Do you take **a little** sugar in your coffee? (Chart 11-5)
7. _____ My mom can't read small print any longer. She needs to buy **glasses**. (Chart 11-6)
8. _____ Did you pick up **carton** of eggs at the store? (Chart 11-7)
9. _____ My favorite foods are **apples** and chocolate. (Chart 11-8)
10. _____ This is **the** second time that Mr. Reyes has asked for help. (Chart 11-9)
11. _____ The tallest mountains in South America are **the** Andes. (Chart 11-10)
12. _____ Tina likes to walk in **Central Park** for exercise. (Chart 11-11)

EXERCISE 1 ▸ Warm-up. (Chart 11-1)
Check (✓) all the items you have with you right now. Do you know why some nouns have *a* before them and others have *an*?

1. _____ **a** ruler
2. _____ **an** eraser
3. _____ **a** paper clip
4. _____ **an** umbrella
5. _____ **a** used textbook
6. _____ **a** university map

11-1 A vs. An

(a)	I have **a** pencil.	***A*** and ***an*** are used in front of a singular noun (e.g., *pencil, apartment*). They mean "one."
(b)	I live in **an** apartment.	
(c)	I have **a** small apartment.	If a singular noun is modified by an adjective (e.g., *small, old*), ***a*** or ***an*** comes in front of the adjective, as in (c) and (d).
(d)	I live in **an** old building.	
		A is used in front of words that begin with a consonant (*b, c, d, f, g,* etc.): *a boy, a bad day, a cat, a cute baby.*
		An is used in front of words that begin with the vowels *a, e, i,* and *o*: *an apartment, an angry man, an elephant, an empty room,* etc.
(e)	I have **an** umbrella.	For words that begin with the letter ***u***:
(f)	I saw **an** ugly picture.	(1) ***An*** is used if the ***u*** is a vowel sound, as in *an umbrella, an uncle, an unusual day.*
(g)	I attend **a** university.	(2) ***A*** is used if the ***u*** is a consonant sound, as in *a university, a unit, a usual event.*
(h)	I had **a** unique experience.	
(i)	He will arrive in **an** hour.	For words that begin with the letter ***h***:
(j)	New Year's Day is **a** holiday.	(1) ***An*** is used if the ***h*** is silent: *an hour, an honor, an honest person.*
		(2) ***A*** is used if the ***h*** is pronounced: *a holiday, a hotel, a high grade.*

EXERCISE 2 ▸ Looking at grammar. (Chart 11-1)
Add ***a*** or ***an*** to these words.

1. _a_ mistake
2. ____ abbreviation
3. ____ dream
4. ____ interesting dream
5. ____ empty box
6. ____ box
7. ____ uniform
8. ____ email
9. ____ untrue story
10. ____ unusual message
11. ____ universal problem
12. ____ unhappy child
13. ____ hour or two
14. ____ hole in the ground
15. ____ hill
16. ____ handsome man
17. ____ honest man
18. ____ honor

EXERCISE 3 ▸ Grammar and speaking. (Chart 11-1)
Add ***a*** or ***an***. Take turns telling your partner what you did and didn't eat last week.

Example: I had an egg. I didn't have a banana. Etc.

1. ____ egg
2. ____ banana
3. ____ orange
4. ____ carrot
5. ____ tomato
6. ____ sandwich
7. ____ bowl of ice cream
8. ____ apple
9. ____ potato
10. ____ salty snack
11. ____ icy drink
12. ____ healthy meal

EXERCISE 4 ▶ Warm-up. (Chart 11-2)
Choose the correct completions. More than one answer may be correct.

1. I need one _____.
   a. chair
   b. chairs

2. There are two _____ in the room.
   a. chairs
   b. furniture

3. I found some _____ in the storage room.
   a. chair
   b. furniture

4. I found _____ in the storage room.
   a. chairs
   b. furniture

11-2 Count and Noncount Nouns

	Singular	Plural	
COUNT NOUN	*a* chair *one* chair	Ø chairs *two* chairs *some* chairs	A count noun: (1) can be counted with numbers: *one chair, two chairs, ten chairs,* etc. (2) can be preceded by *a/an* in the singular: *a chair*. (3) has a plural form ending in *-s* or *-es*: *chairs*.*

NONCOUNT NOUN	Ø furniture
	some furniture
		Ø
		Ø
			A noncount noun:
			(1) cannot be counted with numbers.
			   INCORRECT: *one furniture*
			(2) is NOT immediately preceded by *a/an*.
			   INCORRECT: *a furniture*
			(3) does NOT have a plural form (no final *-s*).
			   INCORRECT: *furnitures*

*See Chart 1-4, p. 11, Chart 6-1, p. 158, and Appendix A-6 for the spelling and pronunciation of *-s/-es*.

EXERCISE 5 ▶ Looking at grammar. (Chart 11-2)
Check (✓) the correct sentences. Correct the sentences with errors. Use *some* with the noncount nouns.

1. ✓ I bought one chair for my apartment.
2. ___ I bought ~~one~~ *some* furniture for my apartment.*
3. ___ I bought four chairs for my apartment.
4. ___ I bought four furnitures for my apartment.
5. ___ I bought a chair for my apartment.
6. ___ I bought a furniture for my apartment.
7. ___ I bought some chair for my apartment.
8. ___ I bought some furnitures for my apartment.

*CORRECT: *I bought **some furniture** for my apartment.* OR *I bought **furniture** for my apartment.* See Chart 11-5 for more information about the use of Ø and *some*.

EXERCISE 6 ▶ Warm-up. (Chart 11-3)
Write the words in the correct columns.

bills	ideas	necklaces	rings	tips
bracelets	letters	postcards	suggestions	

ADVICE **MAIL** **JEWELRY**

_____ _____ _____

_____ _____ _____

_____ _____ _____

11-3 Noncount Nouns

Individual Parts → The Whole
(Count Nouns)   (Noncount Nouns)

(a) 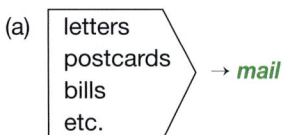 → *mail*

(b) 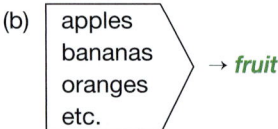 → *fruit*

(c) 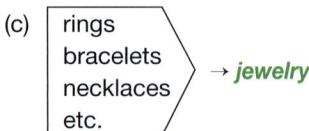 → *jewelry*

Noncount nouns usually refer to a whole group of things that is made up of many individual parts, a whole category made of different varieties.

For example, *furniture* is a noncount noun; it describes a whole category of things: *chairs, tables, beds*, etc.

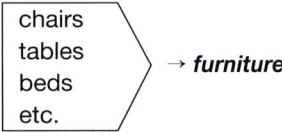 → *furniture*

Mail, fruit, and *jewelry* are other examples of noncount nouns that refer to a whole category made up of individual parts.

Some Common Noncount Nouns: Whole Groups Made up of Individual Parts

A. baggage	B. homework	E. grammar	G. chalk
clothing	housework	slang	corn
equipment	work	vocabulary	dirt
food			flour
furniture	C. advice	F. Arabic	hair
luggage	information	Chinese	pepper
money		English	rice
scenery	D. history	German	salt
stuff	literature	Indonesian	sand
traffic	music	Spanish	sugar
	poetry		

EXERCISE 7 ▶ Looking at grammar. (Charts 11-2 and 11-3)
Complete the sentences with *a/an* or *some*. Decide if the nouns in green are count or noncount.

1. I often have ___some___ fruit for dessert.	count	**(noncount)**
2. I had ___a___ peach for dessert.	**(count)**	noncount
3. I got _____ letter today.	count	noncount
4. I got _____ mail today.	count	noncount
5. Anna wears _____ ring on her left hand.	count	noncount
6. Maria is wearing _____ jewelry today.	count	noncount
7. I have _____ homework to finish.	count	noncount
8. I have _____ assignment to finish.	count	noncount
9. I needed _____ information.	count	noncount
10. I asked _____ question.	count	noncount

EXERCISE 8 ▶ Grammar and speaking. (Charts 11-2 and 11-3)
Add final *-s/-es* if possible. Otherwise, write **Ø**. Then decide if you agree or disagree with the statement. Discuss your answers.

Opinions

1. I'm learning a lot of **grammar** ___Ø___ this term.   yes   no
2. Count and noncount **noun** ___s___ are easy.   yes   no
3. A good way to control **traffic** _____ is to charge people money to drive in the city.   yes   no
4. Electric **car** _____ will replace gas **car** _____ .   yes   no
5. **Information** _____ from the internet is usually reliable.   yes   no
6. **Fact** _____ are always true.   yes   no
7. Many **word** _____ in English are similar to those in my language.   yes   no
8. The best way to learn new **vocabulary** _____ is to memorize it.   yes   no
9. I enjoy singing karaoke **song** _____ .   yes   no
10. I enjoy listening to classical **music** _____ .   yes   no
11. I like to read good **literature** _____ .   yes   no
12. I like to read mystery **novel** _____ .   yes   no
13. **Beach** _____ are relaxing places to visit.   yes   no
14. Walking on **sand** _____ is good exercise for your legs.   yes   no
15. Parents usually have helpful **suggestion** _____ for their kids.   yes   no
16. Sometimes kids have helpful **advice** _____ for their parents.   yes   no

EXERCISE 9 ▶ Warm-up. (Chart 11-4)
Complete the sentences with words in the box. Make sentences that are true for you.

beauty	health	milk	pollution	traffic
coffee	honesty	money	smog	violence
happiness	juice	noise	tea	water

1. During the day, I drink _____ or _____.
2. Two things I don't like about big cities are _____ and _____.
3. _____ is more important than _____.

11-4 More Noncount Nouns

(a) **Liquids**		**Solids and Semi-Solids**				**Gases**
coffee	soup	bread	meat	glass	paper	air
milk	tea	butter	beef	silver	soap	pollution
oil	water	cheese	chicken	gold	toothpaste	smog
		ice	fish	iron	wood	smoke
(b) **Things That Occur in Nature**						
weather	darkness	sunshine				
rain	light	thunder				
snow	sunlight	lightning				
(c) **Abstractions***						
beauty	fun	health	ignorance	love	peace	time
courage	generosity	help	kindness	luck	progress	violence
experience	happiness	honesty	knowledge	patience	selfishness	

*An abstraction is an idea. It has no physical form. A person cannot touch it.

EXERCISE 10 ▶ Looking at grammar. (Charts 11-2 → 11-4)
Add final -s/-es if possible. Otherwise, write Ø. Choose the correct verb as necessary.

1. I made some **mistake**_s_ on my algebra test.
2. In the winter in Siberia, there (**is**) / **are** **snow**_Ø_ on the ground.
3. Siberia has very cold **weather**____.
4. Be sure to give the new couple my best **wish**____.
5. I want to wish them good **luck**____.
6. **Silver**____ **is** / **are** expensive. **Diamond**____ **is** / **are** expensive too.
7. I admire Professor Yoo for her extensive **knowledge**____ of organic farming methods.
8. Professor Yoo has a lot of good **idea**____ and strong **opinion**____.

9. Teaching children to read requires **patience**____.
10. Doctors take care of **patient**____.
11. Mr. Fernandez's English is improving. He's making **progress**____.
12. Wood stoves are a source of **pollution** ____ in many cities.

EXERCISE 11 ▶ Listening. (Charts 11-2 → 11-4)
Listen to the sentences. Add **-s** if the given nouns have plural endings. Otherwise, write **Ø**.

Example: You will hear: Watch out! The steps are icy.
You will write: step *s*____

1. chalk____
2. soap____
3. suggestion____
4. suggestion____
5. gold____
6. storm____
7. storm____
8. toothpaste____
9. stuff____
10. equipment____

EXERCISE 12 ▶ Let's talk. (Chart 11-4)
Work in small groups. Can you figure out the meaning of each saying? Choose one to explain to the class.

Common Sayings

Example: Ignorance is bliss.
→ **Ignorance** means you don't know about something. **Bliss** means "happiness." This saying means that you are happier if you don't know about a problem.

1. Honesty is the best policy.
2. Time is money.
3. Laughter is the best medicine.
4. Knowledge is power.
5. Experience is the best teacher.

EXERCISE 13 ▶ Let's talk. (Chart 11-4)
Complete the sentences. Give two to four answers for each item. Share your answers with a partner. See how many of your answers are the same. REMINDER: Abstract nouns are usually noncount. To find out if a noun is count or noncount, check your dictionary or ask your teacher.

In my opinion …

1. some nice qualities in a person are …
2. some bad qualities people can have are …
3. some of the most important things in life are …
4. certain bad conditions exist in the world. Some of them are …
5. some things in nature that cause problems are …

EXERCISE 14 ▸ Game. (Charts 11-1 → 11-4)
Work in small teams. Imagine your team is at one of the places in the box. Make a list of the things you see. Share your team's list with the class. The team with the most complete and grammatically correct list wins.

a restaurant	an island	an airport
a museum	a hotel	a popular department store

Example: a teacher's office
→ *two windows*
→ *a lot of grammar books*
→ *office equipment — a computer, a printer*
→ *office supplies — a stapler, paper clips, pens, pencils, a ruler*
→ *some pictures*
→ *some furniture*
→ *three chairs*
→ *a backpack*
→ *two bookshelves*
   etc.

EXERCISE 15 ▸ Warm-up. (Chart 11-5)
Complete the sentences with *apples* or *fruit*.

1. I bought several _____ yesterday.
2. Do you eat a lot of _____?
3. Do you eat many _____?
4. Do you eat much _____?
5. I eat a few _____ every week.
6. I eat a little _____ for breakfast.

11-5 Using *A Lot Of, Some, Several, Many/Much,* and *A Few/A Little*

	Count	Noncount	
(a)	*a lot of* chairs	*a lot of* furniture	**A lot of** and **some** are used with both count and noncount nouns.
(b)	*some* chairs	*some* furniture	
(c)	*several* chairs	Ø	**Several** is used only with count nouns.
(d)	*many* chairs	*much* furniture	**Many** is used with count nouns. **Much** is used with noncount nouns.
(e)	*a few* chairs	*a little* furniture	**A few** is used with count nouns. **A little** is used with noncount nouns.

EXERCISE 16 ▶ Looking at grammar. (Charts 11-2 and 11-5)
Check (✓) the correct sentences. Correct the sentences that have errors. One sentence has a spelling error.

1. ____ Jakob learned ~~several~~ *some/Ø* new vocabulary.

2. ✓ He learned several new words.

3. ____ Takashi learned a lot of new words.

4. ____ Sonia learned a lot of new vocabulary too.

5. ____ Lydia doesn't like learning too much new vocabulary in one day.

6. ____ She can't remember too much new words.

7. ____ Mr. Lee assigned a few vocabulary to his class.

8. ____ He assigned a few new words.

9. ____ He explained several new vocabulary.

10. ____ There is alot of new word at this level.

11. ____ There are a lot of new vocabulary at this level.

EXERCISE 17 ▶ Looking at grammar: pairwork. (Charts 11-2 → 11-5)
Work with a partner. Take turns completing the questions with ***How many*** or ***How much*** and each of the given nouns.* Make the nouns plural as necessary.

1. How ____ does Mr. Miller have?
   - a. son → *many sons*
   - b. child → *many children*
   - c. work → *much work*
   - d. car
   - e. stuff
   - f. experience

2. How ____ did you buy?
   - a. fruit
   - b. vegetable
   - c. banana
   - d. tomato
   - e. orange
   - f. food

3. How ____ did you have?
   - a. fun
   - b. help
   - c. time
   - d. information
   - e. fact
   - f. money

*****Much*** and ***many*** are more commonly used in questions than in affirmative statements.

EXERCISE 18 ▶ Let's talk: interview. (Chart 11-5)

Interview your classmates. Begin your questions with **How much** or **How many**. Share some of your answers with the class.

How much/How many ...

1. pages does this book have?
2. coffee do you drink every day?
3. cups of tea do you drink every day?
4. homework do you have to do tonight?
5. assignments have you had this week?
6. many times during the week do you make your own lunch?
7. many hours do you usually sleep at night?
8. snow does this area get in the winter?

EXERCISE 19 ▶ Looking at grammar. (Charts 11-2 → 11-5)

Complete the sentences with **a few** or **a little** and the given noun. Use the plural form of the noun as necessary.

1. *music*   I feel like listening to ____a little music____ tonight.
2. *song*   We sang ____a few songs____ at the party.
3. *help*   Do you need _____ with that?
4. *pepper*   The soup just needs _____.
5. *thing*   I need to pick up _____ at the store on my way home from work tonight.
6. *apple*   I bought _____ at the store.*
7. *fruit*   I bought _____ at the store.
8. *advice*   I need _____.
9. *money*   If I accept that job, I'll make _____ more _____.
10. *friend*   _____ came by last night to visit us.
11. *rain*   It looks like we might get _____ today. I think I'll take my umbrella with me.
12. *French*   I can speak _____, but I don't know any Italian at all.
13. *hour*   Ron's plane will arrive in _____ more _____.

---

*I bought a few apples. = I bought a small number of apples.
I bought a little apple. = I bought one apple, and it was small, not large.

EXERCISE 20 ▸ Warm-up. (Chart 11-6)
Match the sentences to the pictures.

Picture A

Picture B

Picture C

1. Do you need one glass or two? _____
2. Your glasses fit nicely. _____
3. A: What happened?
   B: Some kids threw a ball and hit the glass. _____

11-6 Nouns That Can Be Count or Noncount

Quite a few nouns can be used as either count or noncount nouns. Examples of both count and noncount usages for some common nouns follow.

Noun	Used as a Noncount Noun	Used as a Count Noun
glass	(a) Windows are made of *glass*.	(b) I drank *a glass* of water. (c) Janet wears *glasses* when she reads.
hair	(d) Rita has brown *hair*.	(e) There's *a hair* on my jacket.
iron	(f) *Iron* is a metal.	(g) I pressed my shirt with *an iron*.
light	(h) I opened the curtain to let in *some light*.	(i) Please turn off *the lights* (lamps).
paper	(j) I need *some paper* to write a note.	(k) I wrote *a paper* for Professor Lee. (l) I bought *a paper* (a newspaper).
time	(m) How *much time* do you need to finish your work?	(n) How *many times* have you been to Mexico?
work	(o) I have *some work* to do tonight.	(p) That painting is *a work* of art.
coffee	(q) I had *some coffee* after dinner.	(r) *Two coffees*, please.
chicken/fish	(s) I ate *some chicken/some fish*.	(t) She drew a picture of *a chicken/a fish*.
experience	(u) I haven't had *much experience* with this software. (I don't have much knowledge or skill with this software.)	(v) I had *many* interesting *experiences* on my trip. (Many interesting events happened to me on my trip.)

Count/Noncount Nouns and Articles 325

EXERCISE 21 ▶ Looking at grammar. (Chart 11-6)
Match the correct picture to each sentence. Discuss the differences in meaning.

Picture A

Picture B

Picture C

Picture D

Picture E

Picture F

1. That was a great meal. I ate a lot of chicken. Now I'm stuffed.* _____
2. Are you hungry? How about a little chicken for lunch? _____
3. When I was a child, we raised several chickens. _____
4. I bought a couple of chickens so I can have fresh eggs. _____
5. There's a little chicken in your yard. _____
6. That's a big chicken over there. Who does it belong to? _____

EXERCISE 22 ▶ Looking at grammar. (Chart 11-6)
Complete the sentences with the given words. Make words plural as necessary. Choose words in green as necessary. Discuss the differences in meaning.

1. *time*
   a. It took a lot of __*time*__ to write my composition.
   b. I really like that movie. I saw it three __*times*__.
2. *paper*
   a. Students in Professor Young's literature class have to write a lot of _____.
   b. Students who take careful lecture notes can use a lot of _____.
   c. The *New York Times* is   a / some   famous _____.

---

*stuffed = very full

3. *work*
   a. Van Gogh's painting *Irises* is a beautiful _____ of art.
   b. I have a lot of _____ to do tomorrow at my office.
4. *hair*
   a. Erin has straight _____, and Mariam has curly _____.
   b. Brian has a white cat. When I stood up from Brian's sofa, my black slacks were covered with short white _____.
5. *glass*
   a. I wear _____ for reading.
   b. In some countries, people use _____ for their tea; in other countries, they use cups.
   c. Many famous paintings are covered with _____ to protect them.
6. *iron*
   a. _____ **is / are** necessary to animal and plant life.
   b. _____ **is / are** used to make clothes look neat.
7. *experience*
   a. My grandfather had a lot of interesting _____ in his long career as a diplomat.
   b. You should apply for the job at the electronics company because you have a lot of _____ in that field.
8. *chicken*
   a. Joe, would you like **a / some** more _____?
   b. My grandmother raises _____ in her yard.
9. *light*
   a. There **is / are** a lot of _____ on the ceilings of the school building.
   b. A: If you want to take a picture outside now, you'll need a flash. The _____ **isn't / aren't** good here.
      B: Or, we could wait an hour. **It / They** will be brighter then.

EXERCISE 23 ▶ Warm-up. (Chart 11-7)
Which of the following do you have in your cupboard? Check (✓) the items.

1. _____ a can* of tuna
2. _____ a bag of flour
3. _____ a jar of jam
4. _____ a bottle of soda pop
5. _____ a box of pasta
6. _____ a bowl of sugar

___

a can in American English = *a tin* in British English

11-7 Using Units of Measure with Noncount Nouns

(a) I had some tea. (b) I had **two cups of** tea.	To mention a specific quantity of a noncount noun, speakers use units of measure such as *two cups of* or *one piece of*.
(c) I ate some toast. (d) I ate **one piece of** toast.	A unit of measure usually describes **the container** (*a cup of, a bowl of*), **the amount** (*a pound of, a quart of*),* or **the shape** (*a bar of soap, a sheet of paper*).

*Weight measure: *one pound* = 0.45 kilograms/kilos.
 Liquid measure: *one quart* = 0.95 litres/liters; four quarts = one gallon = 3.8 litres/liters.

EXERCISE 24 ▶ Let's talk. (Chart 11-7)
Work with a partner. Complete the conversation about lunchtime by combining the words in the box. Perform the conversation several times with different food choices. Take turns being Partner A and Partner B. You can look at your book before you speak. When you speak, look at your partner.

	bread	orange juice
a glass of	cake	pasta
a cup of	candy	pizza
a bowl of	cereal	popcorn
a slice of	cheese	rice
a piece of	chicken	soda
a dish of	ice cream	soup
a plate of	mineral water	strawberries
	noodles	watermelon

Example:
PARTNER A: What are you having for lunch?
PARTNER B: I don't have much time. Maybe I'll just have _____.
PARTNER A: How about you?
PARTNER B: I'm really hungry. I think I'll have _____ and _____.

EXERCISE 25 ▶ Looking at grammar. (Chart 11-7)
What units of measure are <u>usually</u> used with the given nouns? More than one unit of measure can be used with some of the nouns.

At the Store

bag	bottle	box	can	carton	jar

1. a ___can/jar___ of olives
2. a ___box/bag___ of crackers
3. a _____ of mineral water
4. a _____ of jam or jelly

5. a _____ of tuna
6. a _____ of soup
7. a _____ of sugar
8. a _____ of milk

9. a _____ of soda
10. a _____ of flour
11. a _____ of pet food
12. a _____ of breakfast cereal

EXERCISE 26 ▶ Let's talk. (Chart 11-7)

You and your partner are planning a party for the class. You still need to buy a few things at the store. Decide what you'd like to get using the sentences below as your guide. You can be serious or silly. Perform your conversation for the class. Then your classmates will tell you if they want to come to your party or not. NOTE: You can look at your conversation before you speak. When you speak, look at your partner.

Shopping List

A: So what else do we need from the store?

B: Let's see. We need a few jars of _____. We should also get a box of _____. Oh, and a couple of bags of _____.

A: Is that it? Anything else?

B: I guess a few cans of _____ would be good. I almost forgot. What should we do about drinks?

A: How about some bottles (or cans) of _____?

B: Good idea.

A: By the way, I thought we could serve slices of _____.

B: Sure.

EXERCISE 27 ▶ Warm-up. (Chart 11-8)

Which sentence best describes each picture?

Picture A

Picture B

1. I see a dog. _____
2. Do you know the dog in the yard? _____
3. I love dogs. _____

11-8 Articles with Count and Noncount Nouns: *A/an*, *The*, Ø

Singular Count Nouns: *A/An* or *The*

(a) Joe bought *a house*.	*a/an* = one In (a): The speaker is not talking about a specific house. The speaker is talking about one house (of many). A singular count noun must have an article. INCORRECT: *Joe bought house.*
(b) *The house* next door is for sale.	In (b): *the* = a specific house INCORRECT: *House next door is for sale.*

Plural Count Nouns: Ø or *The*

(c) Ø *Houses* are expensive.	In (c): *Houses* is non-specific, and no article is used. The speaker is talking about houses in general, not a specific group of houses. ***A*** is never used with plural count nouns. INCORRECT: *A houses.* See Chart 11-5 for other expressions that can be used such as *some, several, a few, a lot of*.
(d) *The houses* in my neighborhood are very nice.	In (d): *the* = a specific group of houses, the houses in my neighborhood

Noncount Nouns: Ø or *The*

(e) I like Ø *ice cream*.	In (e): *Ice cream* is noncount. The speaker is talking about any ice cream, all ice cream, ice cream in general.
(f) *The ice cream* in the dish is for you.	In (f): *The* is used because the speaker is talking about specific ice cream, the ice cream in the dish. INCORRECT: *Ice cream in the dish is for you.*

EXERCISE 28 ▶ Looking at grammar. (Chart 11-8)
Decide if the words in green have a specific or non-specific meaning.

1. The **keys** on the counter are Jason's.   specific   non-specific
2. I saw a **snake** in the grass.   specific   non-specific

3. Do you like chocolate?   specific   non-specific
4. The chocolate in the box is a gift.   specific   non-specific
5. I need information. Can you help me?   specific   non-specific
6. The information you gave me was helpful.   specific   non-specific

EXERCISE 29 ▶ Looking at grammar. (Chart 11-8)
Write *a*, *the*, or *Ø*.

1. SPECIFIC: I need to repair _____ car.
   NON-SPECIFIC: I need to repair _____ car.
2. SPECIFIC: Do you have _____ homework?
   NON-SPECIFIC: Do you have _____ homework?
3. NON-SPECIFIC: _____ phone is ringing.
   SPECIFIC: _____ phone is ringing.
4. NON-SPECIFIC: A bag of flour is on _____ shelf.
   SPECIFIC: A bag of flour is on _____ shelf.
5. SPECIFIC: I love _____ tea.
   NON-SPECIFIC: I love _____ tea.
6. NON-SPECIFIC: I have _____ vegetables from our neighbor's garden.
   SPECIFIC: I have _____ vegetables from our neighbor's garden.

EXERCISE 30 ▶ Looking at grammar. (Chart 11-8)
Read the conversations and decide whether the speakers would probably use ***the*** or ***a***.

1. A: What did you do last night?
   B: I went to ___*a*___ party.
   A: Oh? Where was it?
2. A: Did you have a good time at ___*the*___ party last night?
   B: Yes.
   A: So did I. I'm glad that you decided to go with me.
3. A: Do you have _____ car?
   B: No. But I have _____ motorcycle.
4. A: Is Mr. Jones _____ graduate student?
   B: No. He's _____ professor.
5. A: I liked your presentation at _____ meeting yesterday.
   B: Thanks. I worked really hard on it.
6. A: Does San Diego have _____ zoo?
   B: Yes. It's world famous.
7. A: Did you like _____ apartment you saw yesterday?
   B: Yes. It has _____ big kitchen.

EXERCISE 31 ▶ Listening. (Chart 11-8)

Articles are hard to hear. Listen to the conversation. Decide if you hear *a*, *an*, *the*, or *Ø* (no article).

Example: You will hear: I have an idea.
You will choose: a (an) the Ø

1. a	an	the	Ø		6. a	an	the	Ø
2. a	an	the	Ø		7. a	an	the	Ø
3. a	an	the	Ø		8. a	an	the	Ø
4. a	an	the	Ø		9. a	an	the	Ø
5. a	an	the	Ø		10. a	an	the	Ø

EXERCISE 32 ▶ Warm-up. (Chart 11-9)

Look at the articles in green. Why do the speakers use *the*? Discuss your answers.

1. A: Did you find **the** keys?
   B: Not yet. I'm still looking for **the** light switch!
2. A: Where is **the** moon?
   B: It's behind **the** clouds.
3. A: Did you see Mika's pets?
   B: Yes, **the** dog is friendlier than **the** cat.

11-9 More About Articles

(a) Did you feed **the** dog? (b) Please turn off **the** lights. (c) **The** moon is very bright tonight. (d) Where is **the** library?	Use **the** when the speaker and listener are thinking about the same specific person or thing. In (a): The speaker and the listener are thinking about the same dog, for example, the dog in their house. In (b): The speaker and listener are thinking about the same lights, for example, the lights in the room. In (c): There is only one moon for the speaker and listener to think of. In (d): Both the speaker and listener know the library, for example, at their school, or in their town.
(e) I had **a** banana and **an** apple. I gave **the** banana to Joe. (f) That was **a great meal**. **The food** was excellent.	Use **the** for the second mention of a noun, as in (e). The speaker and listener know whom or what is being talked about. The noun in the second mention doesn't need to be the exact same word as in the first mention. In (f), **food** refers to **meal**.

(g) I spoke with **Ø my** advisor.
(h) You need to take **Ø this** bus.
(i) Mari is **Ø** helpful.
	Do not use articles before possessive adjectives (e.g., **my**), demonstrative adjectives (e.g., **this**), and adjectives by themselves.
	INCORRECT: *a my advisor*
	                a this bus
	                a helpful

(j) What is **the first** step? (k) **The last** time we met was in high school. (l) This is **the second** time I've called. (m) Tony and I have **the same** class schedule. (n) What is **the best** solution?	In (j)–(l): Nouns with **first**, **last**, and ordinal numbers generally take **the**. In (m) and (n): **Same** and **best** always takes **the**.
(o) Lyn is *in bed*. (p) Andrew is *at school*.	Expressions that refer to activities do not use **the**. In (o): Lyn is lying down, probably sleeping. In (p): Andrew is studying.
Common Expressions Without *The* in jail/prison (staying as a prisoner) in class (studying) in college (attending school—college or university) at work (working) at church (praying) at home (doing a variety of activities)	

EXERCISE 33 ▶ Looking at grammar. (Chart 11-9)
Complete the conversation with the correct articles.

Last-Minute Check

A: Did you lock _____ door?
       1

B: Yes.

A: Did you check _____ stove?
         2

B: Yes.

A: Did you close all _____ windows downstairs?
              3

B: Yes.

A: Did you set _____ alarm?
       4

B: Yes.

A: Then let's turn out _____ lights.
               5

B: Goodnight, dear.

A: Oh, don't forget your appointment with _____ doctor tomorrow.
                                6

B: Yes, dear. Goodnight.

EXERCISE 34 ▶ Looking at grammar. (Chart 11-9)
Choose the sentence that describes the given sentence.

1. We found the cat in the tree.
   a. We know the cat.
   b. We don't know the cat.

2. We found a cat in the tree.
   a. We know the cat.
   b. We don't know the cat.

3. Do you need help?
   a. Do you need specific help?
   b. Do you need help in general?

4. I left my car keys in the library.
   a. You know the library I am talking about.
   b. You don't know the library I am talking about.

5. Who fixed the TVs?
   a. I'm asking about TVs in general.
   b. I'm asking about specific TVs.

6. Mmmm. The coffee smells fresh.
   a. I'm talking about specific coffee.
   b. I'm talking about coffee in general.

EXERCISE 35 ▶ Looking at grammar. (Chart 11-9)
Complete the sentences with *a/an* or *the*.

1. I had ___*a*___ banana and ___*an*___ apple. I gave ___*the*___ banana to Mary. I ate ___*the*___ apple.

2. I had _____ bananas and _____ apples. I gave _____ bananas to Mary. I ate _____ apples.

3. I forgot to bring my things with me to class yesterday, so I borrowed _____ pencil and _____ calculator from Joe. I returned _____ calculator, but I used _____ pencil for my homework.

4. A: What did you do last weekend?
   B: I went on _____ picnic Saturday and saw _____ movie Sunday.
   A: Did you have fun?
   B: _____ picnic was fun, but _____ movie was boring.

EXERCISE 36 ▸ Looking at grammar. (Chart 11-9)
Complete the sentences with *a, the*, or Ø.

An Unlucky Purchase

I bought _____(1)_____ butter, eggs, and _____(2)_____ bag of flour to make _____(3)_____ cookies. _____(4)_____ butter and eggs were OK, but I had to return _____(5)_____ flour. When I opened it, I found _____(6)_____ little bugs in it. I took it back to the people at the store and showed them _____(7)_____ little bugs. They gave me _____(8)_____ new bag of flour. _____(9)_____ second bag didn't have any bugs in it.

EXERCISE 37 ▸ Looking at grammar. (Charts 11-8 and 11-9)
Complete the sentences with *a/an, the*, or Ø.

Online Security

1. I got _____ email. _____ message asked me to call a number because they needed _____ my bank information. I didn't respond to _____ message.
2. Did you choose _____ password yet? _____ password you have is too short.
3. The email was _____ fake message because it had too many misspellings.
4. Do not put _____ personal information in a password.
5. _____ unknown hacker stole my personal information from _____ online company.
6. Hacking is _____ crime. _____ Hackers can end up in _____ jail.

EXERCISE 38 ▸ Looking at grammar. (Charts 11-8 and 11-9)
Complete the sentences with *a/an, the*, or Ø.

1. I have __*a*__ window above my bed. I keep __*the*__ window open at night.
2. Kathy likes to listen to _____ music when she studies.
3. Would you please turn _____ radio down? _____ music is too loud.
4. Last week I read _____ book about _____ life of Indira Gandhi, India's only female prime minister, who was assassinated in 1984.
5. Let's go swimming in _____ lake today. My cousins will be there.
6. When I was in Memorial Hospital, _____ nurses were wonderful.
7. I'm studying _____ grammar. I'm also studying _____ vocabulary.
8. This room is so hot, and I feel dizzy. I'm going outside. I need _____ air.
9. _____ air is humid today.

Count/Noncount Nouns and Articles

10. Ted, pass _____ salt, please. And _____ pepper. Thanks.
11. It was too cold to walk, so I took _____ taxi.
12. What a great dinner! _____ food was excellent — especially _____ fish. And _____ service was wonderful. Let's leave _____ server a good tip.
13. I can't get in _____ car. _____ doors are locked.
14. Liam isn't at _____ work. He stopped at _____ university to see his son.

EXERCISE 39 ▶ Listening. (Charts 11-8 and 11-9)
Listen to the passage. Then listen again and write *a/an*, *the*, or *Ø*.

Do you know these words?
- roof (of your mouth)
- nerves
- blood vessels
- swell up
- avoid

ICE-CREAM HEADACHES

Have you ever eaten something really cold like ice cream and suddenly gotten ___(1)___ headache? This is known as ___(2)___ "ice-cream headache." About 30 percent of the population gets this type of headache. Here is one theory about why ice-cream headaches occur. ___(3)___ roof of your mouth has a lot of nerves. When something cold touches ___(4)___ these nerves, they want to warm up ___(5)___ your brain. Your blood vessels swell up, and this causes pain. ___(6)___ ice-cream headaches generally go away after about 30–60 seconds. ___(7)___ best way to avoid these headaches is to keep ___(8)___ cold food off ___(9)___ roof of your mouth.

EXERCISE 40 ▶ Warm-up. (Chart 11-10)
Complete the questions with *the* or *Ø*.

Would you like to see …

1. _the_ Andes Mountains?
2. _Ø_ Korea?
3. _____ Mexico City?
4. _____ Indian Ocean?
5. _____ Amazon River?
6. _____ Australia?
7. _____ Red Sea?
8. _____ Lake Michigan?
9. _____ Mount Fuji?

11-10 Using *The* or Ø with People and Places

(a) We met Ø *Mr. Wang*. I know Ø *Doctor Smith*. Ø *President Rice* has been in the news.	***The*** is NOT used with titled names. INCORRECT: We met the Mr. Wang.
(b) He lives in Ø *Europe*. Ø *Asia* is the largest continent. Have you ever been to Ø *Africa*?	***The*** is NOT used with the names of continents. INCORRECT: He lives in the Europe.
(c) He lives in Ø *France*. Ø *Brazil* is a large country. Have you ever been to Ø *Thailand*?	***The*** is NOT used with the names of most countries. INCORRECT: He lives in the France.
(d) He lives in ***the*** *United States*. ***The*** *Netherlands* is in Europe. Have you ever been to ***the*** *Philippines*?	***The*** is used in the names of only a few countries, as in (d). Others: *the Czech Republic, the United Arab Emirates, the Dominican Republic*.
(e) He lives in Ø *Paris*. Ø *New York* is the largest city in the United States. Have you ever been to Ø *Istanbul*?	***The*** is NOT used with the names of cities. INCORRECT: He lives in the Paris.
(f) ***The*** *Nile River* is long. They crossed ***the*** *Pacific Ocean*. ***The*** *Yellow Sea* is in Asia. (g) Chicago is on Ø *Lake Michigan*. Ø *Lake Titicaca* lies on the border between Peru and Bolivia.	***The*** is used with the names of rivers, oceans, and seas. ***The*** is NOT used with the names of lakes.
(h) We hiked in ***the*** *Alps*. ***The*** *Andes* are in South America. (i) He climbed Ø *Mount Everest*. Ø *Mount Fuji* is in Japan.	***The*** is used with the names of mountain ranges. ***The*** is NOT used with the names of individual mountains.

💬 EXERCISE 41 ▸ Game. (Chart 11-10)

Work in groups. Choose a place in the world. It can be a continent, country, city, sea, river, mountain, etc. Your classmates will try to guess where it is by asking *yes/no* questions. Try to limit the number of questions to ten for each place.

Example:
STUDENT A: (*thinking of the Mediterranean Sea*)
STUDENT B: Is it a continent?
STUDENT A: No.
STUDENT C: Is it hot?
STUDENT A: No.
STUDENT D: Is it big?
STUDENT A: Yes.
Etc.

EXERCISE 42 ▶ Game: trivia. (Chart 11-10)
Work in teams. Complete the sentences with **the** or **Ø**. Then decide if the statements are true or false. Circle "T" for true and "F" for false. The team with the most correct answers wins.*

1. _____ Moscow is the biggest city in _____ Russia.   T   F
2. _____ Rhine River flows through _____ Germany.   T   F
3. _____ Vienna is in _____ Australia.   T   F
4. _____ Yangtze is the longest river in _____ Asia.   T   F
5. _____ Atlantic Ocean is bigger than _____ Pacific.   T   F
6. _____ Rocky Mountains are located in _____ Canada and _____ United States.   T   F
7. _____ Dr. Sigmund Freud is famous for his studies of astronomy.   T   F
8. _____ Lake Victoria is located in _____ Tanzania.   T   F
9. Another name for _____ Holland is _____ Netherlands.   T   F
10. _____ Swiss Alps are the tallest mountains in the world.   T   F

EXERCISE 43 ▶ Game. (Chart 11-10)
Work in groups of 8-10 students. Each student says two sentences about two different places. One is true and one is false. Your classmates will guess which one is true and which one is false. Each correct answer is worth one point. If you use an article in your sentence incorrectly, you lose one point from your total. The student with the most points wins.

Example: I have hiked in the Alps. (*Students guess true or false.*)
I grew up in Kuala Lumpur. (*Students guess true or false.*)

EXERCISE 44 ▶ Warm-up. (Chart 11-11)
Complete the sentences with information about yourself.

1. I was born in _____.
   (country)
2. I have lived most of my life in _____.
   (continent)
3. This term I am studying _____.
4. Two of my favorite movies are _____ and _____.

---

*See *Trivia Answers*, p. 449.

11-11 Capitalization

Capitalize

1. The first word of a sentence	We saw a movie last night. It was very good.	*Capitalize* = use a big letter, not a small letter
2. The names of people	I met George Adams yesterday.	
3. Titles used with the names of people	I saw Doctor (Dr.) Smith. There's Professor (Prof.) Lee.	I saw a doctor. BUT I saw Doctor Wilson.
4. Months, days, holidays	I was born in April. Bob arrived last Monday. It snowed on New Year's Day.	NOTE: Seasons are not capitalized: *spring, summer, fall/autumn, winter*.

5. The names of places:
   city
   state/province
   country
   continent
 	
   ocean
   lake
   river
   desert
   mountain
 	
   school
   business
 	
   street
   building
   park, zoo
	He lives in Chicago.
	She was born in California.
	They are from Mexico.
	Tibet is in Asia.
	
	They crossed the Atlantic Ocean.
	Chicago is on Lake Michigan.
	The Nile River flows north.
	The Sahara Desert is in Africa.
	We visited the Rocky Mountains.
	
	I go to the University of Florida.
	I work for the Boeing Company.
	
	He lives on Grand Avenue.
	We have class in Ritter Hall.
	I went jogging in Forest Park.
		She lives in a city. BUT
		She lives in New York City.
		
		They crossed a river. BUT
		They crossed the Yellow River.
		
		I go to a university. BUT
		I go to the University of Texas.
		
		We went to a park. BUT
		We went to Central Park.

6. The names of courses	I'm taking Chemistry 101.	Here's your history book. BUT I'm taking History 101.
7. The titles of books, articles, movies	*Gone with the Wind* *The Sound of the Mountain*	Capitalize the first word of a title. Capitalize all other words except articles (*the, a/an*), coordinating conjunctions (*and, but, or*), and short prepositions (*with, in, at, etc.*).
8. The names of languages and nationalities	She speaks Spanish. We discussed Japanese customs.	Words that refer to the names of languages and nationalities are always capitalized.
9. The names of religions	Buddhism, Christianity, Hinduism, Islam, and Judaism are major religions in the world. Talal is a Muslim.	Words that refer to the names of religions are always capitalized.

EXERCISE 45 ▶ Looking at grammar. (Chart 11-11)
Capitalize the words in the sentences as necessary.

1. a. Do you know richard smith? He is a professor at this university.
   b. I know that professor smith teaches at the university of arizona.

2. a. I'm taking a history course this semester.
   b. I'm taking modern european history 101 this semester.

3. a. The amazon is a river in south america.
   b. The mississippi river flows south.

4. a. Canada is in north america.*
   b. Canada is north of the united states.

5. a. I find english grammar a little confusing.
   b. English grammar 099 is a difficult class.
   c. The title of this book is *fundamentals of english grammar*.

EXERCISE 46 ▶ Looking at grammar. (Chart 11-11)
Write "C" for correct and "I" for incorrect sentences. Add capital letters where necessary.

1. __I__ We're going to have a test next Tuesday.
2. _____ Where was your mother born?
3. _____ John is a catholic. ali is a Muslim.
4. _____ Anita speaks French. She studied in France for two years.
5. _____ Venezuela is a spanish-speaking country.
6. _____ The sun rises in the east.
7. _____ We went to a zoo. My grandfather took me.
8. _____ On valentine's day (february 14th), sweethearts give each other presents.
9. _____ I read a book called *the cat and the mouse in my aunt's house*.
10. _____ We went to Vancouver, British Columbia, for our vacation last summer.

EXERCISE 47 ▶ Check your knowledge. (Chapter 11 Review)
Correct the errors.

1. Our teacher gave us a lot of new vocabularies to study.

2. Would you like to have little chicken and rice for lunch?

3. The school advisor had many suggestion for the student.

---

*When **north**, **south**, **east**, and **west** refer to the direction on a compass, they are not capitalized: *Japan is **east** of China*.
When they are part of a geographical name, they are capitalized: *Japan is in the Far **East***.

4. There is a urgent message for you to call the doctor.

5. My algebra 101 course is a fairly easy.

6. There were many interesting idea and strong opinion at the meeting.

7. My Father and I share the same Birthday.

8. What time did you feed a cats?

9. We're not going to order lunch. We just want coffee. Could we have two coffee, please?

10. Many students have trouble with a slang when they learn the English.

EXERCISE 48 ▶ Reading and grammar. (Chapter 11)
Read the passage. Add capital letters as necessary.

Do you know these words?
- recognize
- apes
- penny
- guidance
- trust
- observations

JANE GOODALL

(1) Do you recognize the name jane goodall? Perhaps you know her for her studies of chimpanzees. She became very famous from her work in tanzania.

(2) Jane goodall was born in england, and as a child, was fascinated by animals. Her favorite books were *the jungle book*, by rudyard kipling, and books about tarzan, a fictional character who was raised by apes.

(3) Her childhood dream was to go to africa. After high school, she worked as a secretary and a waitress to earn enough money to go there. During that time, she took evening courses in journalism and english literature. She saved every penny until she had enough money for a trip to africa.

(4) In the spring of 1957, she sailed through the red sea and southward down the african coast to mombasa in kenya. Her uncle had arranged a job for her in nairobi with a british company. When she was there, she met dr. louis leakey, a famous anthropologist. Under his guidance, she began her lifelong study of chimpanzees on the eastern shore of lake tanganyika.

(5) Jane goodall lived alone in a tent near the lake. Through months and years of patience, she won the trust of the chimps and was able to watch them closely. Her observations changed forever how we view chimpanzees — and many other animals we share the world with.

EXERCISE 49 ▶ Reading, grammar, and writing. (Chapter 11)

Part I. Read the paragraph.

Do you know these words?
- roots
- shoots
- observe
- organization
- global
- deforestation
- service projects
- environment

ROOTS AND SHOOTS

Jane Goodall went to Africa to study animals. She spent 40 years observing and studying chimpanzees in Tanzania. As a result of Dr. Goodall's work, an organization called Roots and Shoots was formed. This organization focuses on work that children and teenagers can do to help the local and global community. The idea began in 1991. A group of 16 teenagers met with Dr. Goodall at her home in Dar Es Salaam, Tanzania. They wanted to discuss how to help with a variety of problems, such as pollution, deforestation, and helping animals survive. Dr. Goodall was involved in the meetings, but the teenagers chose the service projects and did the work themselves. The first Roots and Shoots community project was a local one. The group educated villagers about better treatment of chickens at home and in the marketplace. Today, there are tens of thousands of members in almost 100 countries. They work to make the environment and the world better through community-service projects.

Part II. Choose the best description for each noun in green.

1. *chimpanzees*
    a. a specific group of chimpanzees in Tanzania
    b. not a specific group of chimpanzees in Tanzania

2. *the idea*
    a. a specific idea (work to help the local and global community)
    b. a non-specific idea (one idea among many)

3. *pollution*
    a. not specific (pollution around the world)
    b. specific (pollution in one place)

4. *the meetings*
    a. non-specific meetings
    b. specific meetings about a variety of problems

5. *the teenagers*
    a. a specific group of teenagers (16)
    b. teenagers in general

6. *the work*
    a. work in general
    b. specific work (service project work)

7. *the environment*
   a. one environment among many
   b. the environment we know, in our world

8. *the world*
   a. we know the world (the world we live in)
   b. one world of many

Part III. Write your own paragraph about an organization that is doing something to help people or animals. Focus on correct article usage and capitalization. Follow these steps:

1. Choose an organization you are interested in.
2. Research the organization. Find the organization's website if possible. Take notes on the information you find. Include details about its history, why it was formed, its goals and benefits, and the person or people who formed it. You can use the outline below as a model (add more capital letters if you have more than two details).

   I. History of the organization
      A.
      B.
   II. Purpose/goals of the organization
      A.
      B.
   III. Key people in the organization (if not already mentioned)
      A.
      B.
   IV. Results/Benefits of the organization
      A.
      B.

> **WRITING TIP**
>
> When you are taking notes from websites, books, or other media, write down the information in your own words. Don't copy directly from a source and present it as your own words. This is called *plagiarism*. Plagiarism is not acceptable in high schools, colleges, and universities.
>
> Putting information in your own words also forces you to think about the meaning of the reading. This will help you understand and present the information more clearly.
>
> Use the grammar you know. This will probably be simpler than how you write in your own language. If you try to write at a higher level before you are ready, you will probably translate a lot from your language into English. This can result in writing that has many errors.

Part IV. Edit your writing. Check for the following:

1. ☐ use of *the* for nouns with a specific meaning
2. ☐ use of *a/an* or Ø for nouns with a non-specific meaning
3. ☐ correct article usage for people and places
4. ☐ correct capitalization (review Chart 11-11)
5. ☐ the information is in your own words, not copied
6. ☐ correct spelling (use a dictionary or spell-check)

▪▪▪▪▪ For digital resources, go to MyEnglishLab on the Pearson English Portal. You can also go to the Pearson Practice English app for mobile practice.

CHAPTER 12
Adjective Clauses

PRETEST: What do I already know?
Write "C" if the sentences are correct and "I" if they are incorrect.

1. _____ A teacher who is patient with students. (Chart 12-1)
2. _____ The neighbor started her own online business has been very successful. (Chart 12-1)
3. _____ I have a friend that recently got a part in a Hollywood movie. (Chart 12-2)
4. _____ A friend whom I've known since childhood recently recommended me for a job. (Chart 12-3)
5. _____ The movies that I enjoy the most have happy endings. (Chart 12-4)
6. _____ Have you met the woman who are in your class? (Chart 12-5)
7. _____ The hotel at which we are staying is offering the third night free. (Chart 12-6)
8. _____ The host family Erik is living is very nice. (Chart 12-6)
9. _____ The couple whose car died on their way to their wedding missed their flight for their honeymoon. (Chart 12-7)

EXERCISE 1 ▶ Warm-up. (Chart 12-1)
Check (✓) the completions that are true for you.

I have a friend who …

1. _____ likes to do exciting things.
2. _____ is interested in space.
3. _____ is studying to be an astronaut.

12-1 Adjective Clauses: Introduction

Adjectives	Adjective Clauses
An ADJECTIVE modifies a noun. *Modify* means to change a little. An adjective describes or gives information about a noun. (See Chart 6-8, p. 171.)	An ADJECTIVE CLAUSE modifies a noun. It describes or gives information about a noun.
An adjective usually comes in front of a noun.	An adjective clause follows a noun.
(a) I met a **kind** man. [ADJECTIVE + NOUN] (b) I met a **famous** man. [ADJECTIVE + NOUN]	(c) I met a man **who is kind to everybody**. [NOUN + ADJECTIVE CLAUSE] (d) I met a man **who is a famous writer**. [NOUN + ADJECTIVE CLAUSE] (e) I met a man **who lives in Oslo**. [NOUN + ADJECTIVE CLAUSE]

Grammar Terminology

(1) *I met a man* = an independent clause; it is a complete sentence.

(2) *He lives in Oslo* = an independent clause; it is a complete sentence.

(3) *who lives in Oslo* = a dependent clause; it is NOT a complete sentence.

(4) *I met a man who lives in Oslo* = an independent clause + a dependent clause; a complete sentence.

A *clause* is a structure that has a subject and a verb.

There are two kinds of clauses: *independent* and *dependent*.

- An *independent clause* is a main clause and can stand alone as a sentence, as in (1) and (2).
- A *dependent clause*, as in (3), is not a complete sentence. It must be connected to an independent clause, as in (4).

EXERCISE 2 ▶ Looking at grammar. (Chart 12-1)
Check (✓) the complete sentences.

1. _____ I know a teenager. She flies airplanes.
2. _____ I know a teenager who flies airplanes.
3. _____ A teenager who flies airplanes.
4. _____ Who flies airplanes.
5. _____ Who flies airplanes?
6. _____ I know a teenager flies airplanes.
7. _____ I know a teenager who is a pilot.
8. _____ I know a teenager is a pilot.

EXERCISE 3 ▶ Warm-up. (Chart 12-2)
Complete the sentences with the correct words in the box. <u>Underline</u> the word that follows **doctor** in each sentence.

| A dermatologist | An orthopedist | A pediatrician | A surgeon |

1. _____ is a doctor who performs operations.
2. _____ is a doctor that treats skin problems.
3. _____ is a doctor who treats bone injuries.
4. _____ is a doctor that treats children.

12-2 Using *Who* and *That* in Adjective Clauses to Describe People

(a) The man is friendly.	S V **He** lives next to me. ↓ **who** ↓ S V **who** lives next to me.	In adjective clauses, **who** and **that** are used as subject pronouns to describe people. In (a): **He** is a subject pronoun. **He** refers to "the man." To make an adjective clause, change **he** to **who**. **Who** is a subject pronoun. **Who** refers to "the man."
(b) The man **who** *lives next to me* is friendly.		
(c) The woman is talkative.	S V **She** lives next to me. ↓ **that** ↓ S V **that** lives next to me.	**That** is also a subject pronoun and can replace **who**, as in (d). The subject pronouns **who** and **that** cannot be omitted from an adjective clause. INCORRECT: *The woman lives next to me is talkative.* As subject pronouns, both **who** and **that** are common in conversation, but **who** is more common in writing.
(d) The woman **that** *lives next to me* is talkative.		In (b) and (d): The adjective clause immediately follows the noun it modifies. INCORRECT: *The woman is talkative that lives next to me.*

EXERCISE 4 ▶ Looking at grammar. (Chart 12-2)

Underline the adjective clause in the given sentence. Then change the given sentence to two shorter sentences with the same meaning.

Rescuers

1. The policewoman **who rescued the boy** was on her way home from work.
   a. _The policewoman rescued the boy_.
   b. _The policewoman was on her way home from work_.

2. The firefighter who answered the call broke a car window and rescued the injured person.
   a. _____.
   b. _____.

3. The EMT* restarted the heart of the man who collapsed at work.
   a. _____.
   b. _____.

4. The lifeguard who rescued the two swimmers had only been a lifeguard for one day.
   a. _____.
   b. _____.

5. The dog found the child who disappeared on a walk in the mountains.
   a. _____.
   b. _____.

EXERCISE 5 ▶ Looking at grammar. (Chart 12-2)

Choose the sentences that express the ideas in the given sentence.

The Vet

1. The veterinarian that took care of my daughter's pony is very gentle.
   a. The veterinarian is gentle.
   b. The veterinarian took care of a pony.
   c. The pony is gentle.
   d. The veterinarian took care of my daughter.

2. The veterinarian that treated our dog and cat recently passed away.
   a. The cat passed away.
   b. The veterinarian treated our dog.
   c. The veterinarian passed away.
   d. The veterinarian treated our cat.

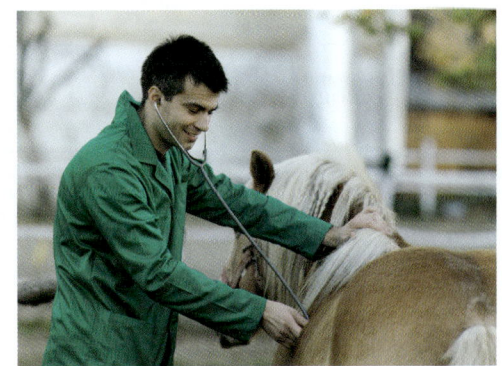

*EMT = emergency medical technician

EXERCISE 6 ▶ Looking at grammar. (Charts 12-1 and 12-2)
<u>Underline</u> each adjective clause. Draw an arrow to the noun it modifies.

The People I Work With

1. The assistant <u>who manages the schedules</u> speaks several languages.
2. The manager that hired me has less experience than I do.
3. I like the supervisor that works in the office next to mine.
4. My boss is a person who wakes up every morning with a positive attitude.
5. It's nice to work with people who have a positive attitude.

EXERCISE 7 ▶ Looking at grammar. (Charts 12-1 and 12-2)
Combine each pair of sentences with **who** or **that**. The b. sentences will form adjective clauses.

At a Restaurant

1. a. Do you know the people?　　　　b. They are sitting next to the window.
    Do you know the people who/that are sitting next to the window?

2. a. The manager was very friendly.　　b. He took us to our table.
   _____

3. a. The server didn't write anything down.　b. She took our order.
   _____

4. a. The chef has won awards.　　　　b. He makes the pasta.
   _____

5. a. My friends want to open another.　b. They run the restaurant.
   _____

6. a. I recognized a woman.　　　　　b. She was in my high school class.
   _____

EXERCISE 8 ▶ Let's talk. (Charts 12-1 and 12-2)
Work in pairs or small groups. Complete the sentences. Make true statements. Share some of your sentences with the class.

1. I know a man/woman who …
2. I have a friend who …
3. I like athletes who …
4. Workers who … are brave.
5. People who … make me laugh.
6. Doctors who … are admirable.

EXERCISE 9 ▶ Looking at grammar. (Charts 12-1 and 12-2)
Add *who* or *that*.

At a Swim Competition

1. I talked to the people <u>who OR that</u> were in line with me to get tickets for the swim meet.

2. The swimmer had the fastest time was my cousin.

3. The man coached the visiting team was my teacher in high school.

4. The parents yelled at the swimmers were asked to leave.

5. I like to sit next to fans cheer the swimmers.

EXERCISE 10 ▶ Warm-up. (Chart 12-3)
Complete the sentences with your own words.

1. The teacher that I had for first grade was _____.

2. The first English teacher I had was _____.

3. The first English teacher who I had wasn't _____.

12-3 Using Object Pronouns in Adjective Clauses to Describe People

(a) The man was friendly.	s v o I met *him*. ↓ *that*	In adjective clauses, pronouns are used as the object of a verb to describe people. In (a): *him* is an object pronoun. *Him* refers to "the man." One way to make an adjective clause is to change *him* to *that*. *That* is the object pronoun. *That* refers to "the man."
(b) The man *that* I met was friendly. (c) The man Ø I met was friendly.	o s v	*That* comes at the beginning of an adjective clause. An object pronoun can be omitted from an adjective clause, as in (c).
(d) The man was friendly.	s v o I met *him*. ↓ *who* *whom*	*Him* can also be changed to *who* or *whom*, as in (e) and (f). As an object pronoun, *that* is more common than *who* in speaking. Ø is the most common choice for both speaking and writing. *Whom* is generally used only in very formal English.
(e) The man *who* I met was friendly. (f) The man *whom* I met was friendly.	o s v	

EXERCISE 11 ▶ Looking at grammar. (Charts 12-2 and 12-3)
Part I. Check (✓) the sentences that have object pronouns.

A Tech Repair

1. _____ The technician that the company sent wasn't able to fix my Wi-Fi.
2. _____ The technician that came had just finished his training.
3. _____ The technician whom I spoke with asked his supervisor for help.
4. _____ The supervisor who arrived figured out the problem.
5. _____ The supervisor who the technician called was helpful.
6. _____ The supervisor who figured out the problem was very experienced.

Part II. Choose the correct word(s) for each sentence.

1. The tech   (who) / (whom)   I called wasn't able to help me.
2. The tech   who / whom   the company hired just graduated from high school.
3. The tech   who / whom   looked at my computer understood the problem immediately.
4. The tech   who / whom   reconnected my Wi-Fi worked very quickly.
5. The manager   who / whom   supervised the tech also came to my house.
6. The manager   who / whom   I contacted first had several suggestions.

EXERCISE 12 ▶ Looking at grammar. (Charts 12-2 and 12-3)
Choose <u>all</u> the correct completions.

Last Night's Party

1. The man _____ teaches at a well-known cooking school.
   a. that prepared the food
   b. prepared the food
   c. who prepared the food
   d. whom prepared the food

2. A woman _____ has climbed Mount Everest.
   a. that I met last night
   b. I met last night
   c. who I met last night
   d. whom I met last night

3. The people _____ just moved into the neighborhood last month.
   a. that had the party
   b. had the party
   c. who had the party
   d. whom had the party

4. The friend _____ knew several people there.
   a. that I invited
   b. I invited
   c. who I invited
   d. whom I invited

EXERCISE 13 ▶ Looking at grammar. (Chart 12-3)
<u>Underline</u> the object pronouns in the b. sentences and change the sentences to adjective clauses. Use *that* or *whom*.

My Flight to New York

1. a. A woman snored the entire flight.   b. I sat in front of <u>her</u> on the plane.
   A woman that/whom I sat in front of on the plane snored the entire flight.

2. a. A man asked me for my phone number.   b. I hadn't met him before.
   _____

3. a. A woman had twin babies.   b. The flight attendant helped her.
   _____

4. a. A man tried to board early.   b. Security stopped him.
   _____

5. a. A man gave me his window seat.   b. I didn't know him.
   _____

EXERCISE 14 ▶ Let's talk: pairwork. (Charts 12-2 and 12-3)
Work with a partner. Take turns making adjective clauses by combining the given sentences with the main sentence. Use *who*, *that*, or *whom*.

Main sentence: The man was helpful.
Example: He answered my question. → *The man who/that answered my question was helpful.*

1. He was working at the information desk.
2. I walked up to him.
3. I called him.
4. You recommended him.
5. He is the owner.
6. You invited him to the party.
7. He gave us a tour of the city.
8. I talked to him at the train station.
9. He sold us our museum tickets.
10. He gave me directions.

EXERCISE 15 ▸ Looking at grammar. (Charts 12-2 and 12-3)
Complete the sentences with *that*, *Ø*, *who*, or *whom*. Write all the possible completions.

Family Connections

1. a. The man _____ married my mother is my best friend's uncle.

    b. The man _____ my mother married is my best friend's uncle.

2. a. The baby _____ my brother and his wife adopted was born to our cousin.

    b. The baby _____ was born to our cousin was adopted by my brother and his wife.

3. a. I don't know the cousin _____ is talking to Aunt Elsa.

    b. I don't know the cousin _____ Aunt Elsa is talking to.

EXERCISE 16 ▸ Warm-up. (Chart 12-4)
Read the paragraph about James and then check (✓) the sentences that you agree with. What do you notice about the adjective clauses in green?

Wanted: A Pet

   James is looking for a pet. He is single and a little lonely. He isn't sure what kind of pet would be best for him. He lives on a large piece of property in the country. He is gone during the day from 8:00 A.M. to 5:00 P.M. but is home on weekends. He travels about two months a year but has neighbors that can take care of a pet, as long as it isn't too big. What kind of pet should he get?

1. _____ He should get a pet **that likes to run and play**, like a dog.

2. _____ He needs to get a pet **which is easy to take care of**, like a fish or turtle.

3. _____ He should get an animal **that he can leave alone for a few days**, like a cat.

4. _____ He needs to get an animal **his neighbors will like**.

5. _____ A pet **that will talk to him**, like a bird, is a good choice.

12-4 Using Pronouns in Adjective Clauses to Describe Things

(a) The river is polluted. **It** [→ **that** / **which**] flows through the town.	**Who** and **whom** refer to people. **Which** refers to things. **That** can refer to either people or things. In (a): To make an adjective clause, change **it** to **that** or **which**. **It**, **that**, and **which** all refer to a thing (the river).
(b) The river **that** flows through the town is polluted. (c) The river **which** flows through the town is polluted.	(b) and (c) have the same meaning, but (b) is more common than (c) in speaking and writing.
	When **that** and **which** are used as the subject of an adjective clause, they CANNOT be omitted. INCORRECT: *The river flows through the town is polluted.*
(d) The books were expensive. I bought **them.** [→ **that** / **which**]	**That** or **which** can be used as an object in an adjective clause, as in (e) and (g). As you have learned, an object pronoun can be omitted from an adjective clause, as in (f).
(e) The books **that** I bought were expensive. (f) The books **Ø** I bought were expensive. (g) The books **which** I bought were expensive.	(e), (f), and (g) have the same meaning. In speaking, **that** and **Ø** are common. In writing, **Ø** is rare. The use of **which**, as in (g), is more common in British English than contemporary American English.* INCORRECT: *The books that I bought them were expensive.*

*Another use of *which* is in nonrestrictive clauses. This usage is taught in *Understanding and Using English Grammar*, the next level textbook in this series.

EXERCISE 17 ▶ Looking at grammar. (Chart 12-4)
Underline each adjective clause. Draw an arrow from the adjective clause to the noun it modifies.

Lost and Found

1. The lost-and-found office <u>that we went to</u> was at the far end of the train station.

2. I left the scarf that I borrowed from my roommate on the train.

3. I turned in a cell phone that I found on my seat.

4. Some people post photos on social media of things that they find.

5. Lost items which are not claimed after 30 days are given to charity.

EXERCISE 18 ▶ Looking at grammar. (Chart 12-4)
Combine each pair of sentences into one sentence. Give all possible forms.

Complaints

1. a. The pill made me too dizzy.
   b. I took it.

   The pill that / Ø / which I took made me dizzy.

2. a. I bought a computer.
   b. It doesn't connect to the internet.

   _____

3. a. The clothes never came.
   b. I ordered them online.

   _____

4. a. The bus is usually late.
   b. It goes downtown.

   _____

5. a. I have a class.
   b. It has hours and hours of homework.

   _____

6. a. The soup was too salty.
   b. I bought it for lunch.

   _____

EXERCISE 19 ▶ Looking at grammar. (Charts 12-2 → 12-4)
Complete the sentences with *who* or *that*. In some cases, both answers are possible.

What makes you "like" a video?

1. I "like" videos _____ make me feel hopeful.

2. I watch stories _____ are emotional.

3. People _____ make videos of their pets' funny behavior get a lot of "likes."

4. It's important to have clips _____ don't go on for a long time.

5. I have friends _____ think their lives are really interesting and film everyday activities. I don't "like" these videos.

EXERCISE 20 ▶ **Looking at grammar.** (Charts 12-3 and 12-4)
Cross out the incorrect pronouns in the adjective clauses.

On Campus

1. The library I like to study in ~~it~~ is brand new.
2. The books I bought ~~them~~ at the bookstore were expensive.
3. I like the lunch special the cafeteria served ~~it~~ yesterday.
4. Professor Gomez is a teacher I would like to have ~~him~~.
5. My roommate and I are really enjoying the TV that we bought ~~it~~ for our room.
6. The basketball player you see ~~her~~ on your way to class is an Olympic athlete.
7. The student center has a café that ~~it~~ serves wonderful coffee.
8. The coffee that the café serves ~~it~~ is organic.

EXERCISE 21 ▶ **Let's talk.** (Charts 12-2 → 12-4)
Work with a partner. Take turns making true sentences by using a word or phrase from each column. Use **who** or **that**.

I know I would like to meet I have I like	a person people students parents grandparents cousins a pet a co-worker books music a hobby movies	works/work really hard relaxes/relax me makes/make me happy is/are interesting teaches/teach me a lot like/likes to have fun is/are surprising has an interesting life have interesting lives is/are funny

EXERCISE 22 ▶ **Looking at grammar.** (Charts 12-2 → 12-4)
Cross out the words **who** or **that** where possible.

Help Desk

1. Tom called the help desk to talk with someone who could help with a password problem. (*no change*)
2. The manager ~~that~~ Tom called didn't know the answer.
3. The manager who helped Tom found the answer quickly.
4. The question that you asked is a common one.
5. The people who work in the office next door can help you.
6. The agent who my brother contacted put him on hold for twenty minutes.
7. I can find the information that you need.
8. The receptionist who I spoke with didn't understand my accent.

EXERCISE 23 ▶ Listening. (Charts 12-2 → 12-4)
Listen to the sentences. They all have adjective clauses. Choose the words you hear. If there is no subject or object pronoun, choose Ø. NOTE: In spoken English, *that* often sounds like "thut."

My Mother's Hospital Stay

Example: You will hear: The doctor who treated my mother was very knowledgeable.
You will choose: (who)   that   which   whom   Ø

1. who	that	which	whom	Ø
2. who	that	which	whom	Ø
3. who	that	which	whom	Ø
4. who	that	which	whom	Ø
5. who	that	which	whom	Ø
6. who	that	which	whom	Ø
7. who	that	which	whom	Ø
8. who	that	which	whom	Ø

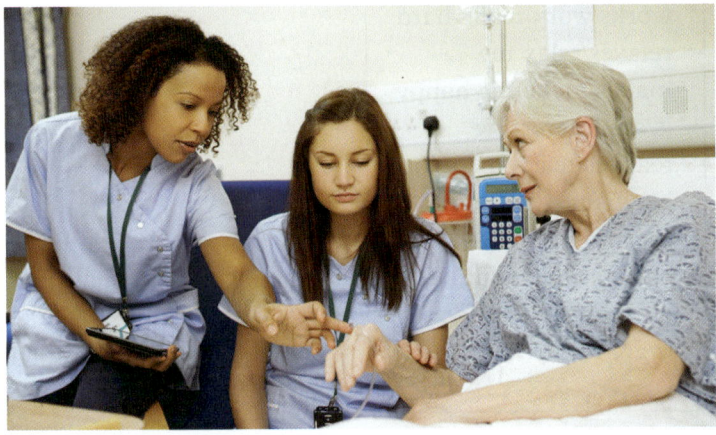

 EXERCISE 24 ▶ Let's talk. (Charts 12-1 → 12-4)
Answer the questions in complete sentences. Use any appropriate pattern for the adjective clause. Use *the* with the noun that is modified by the adjective clause.

1. • One phone wasn't ringing.
   • The other phone was ringing.
   QUESTIONS: Which phone did Hasan answer? Which phone didn't he answer?
   → Hasan answered **the** phone that was ringing.
   → He didn't answer **the** phone that wasn't ringing.

2. • One student raised her hand in class.
   • Another student sat quietly in his seat.
   QUESTIONS: Which student asked the teacher a question? Which one didn't?

3. • One girl won the bike race.
   • The other girl lost the bike race.
   QUESTIONS: Which girl is happy? Which girl isn't happy?

4. • We ate some food from our garden.
   • We ate some food at a restaurant.
   QUESTIONS: Which food was expensive? Which food was inexpensive?

5. • One man was sleeping.
   • Another man was listening to the radio.
   QUESTIONS: Which man heard the special report about the earthquake in China? Which one didn't?

6. • One person bought a small car.
   • Another person bought a large car.
   QUESTION: Which person probably spent more money than the other?

EXERCISE 25 ▶ Game. (Charts 12-2 and 12-4)
Work in teams. Connect each phrase in the left column with the correct phrase in the right column. Use *that* or *who*. Check your dictionary if necessary. The team that finishes first and has the most grammatically correct sentences wins.

Definitions

Example: 1. A hammer is a tool.
g. It is used to pound nails.
→ *A hammer is a tool that is used to pound nails.*

1. A hammer is a tool. __g__
2. A comedian is someone. ____
3. An obstetrician is a doctor. ____
4. Plastic is a chemical material. ____
5. An architect is someone. ____
6. A puzzle is a problem. ____
7. A carnivore is an animal. ____
8. Steam is a gas. ____
9. A turtle is an animal. ____
10. A hermit is a person. ____
11. A pyramid is a structure. ____

a. She/He leaves society and lives completely alone.
b. He/She tells jokes.
c. It forms when water boils.
d. It is square at the bottom and has four sides that come together in a point at the top.
e. She/He designs buildings.
f. He/She delivers babies.
✓ g. It is used to pound nails.
h. It can be shaped and hardened to form many useful things.
i. It can be difficult to solve.
j. It eats meat.
k. It has a hard shell and can live in water or on land.

EXERCISE 26 ▶ Warm-up. (Chart 12-5)
Read the sentences. What do you notice about the verbs in green and the nouns that precede them?

1. I have a friend who *is* vegetarian. He doesn't eat any meat.
2. I have friends who *are* vegetarian. They don't eat any meat.

12-5	Singular and Plural Verbs in Adjective Clauses	
(a) I know the **man** who **is** sitting over there.	In (a): The verb in the adjective clause (**is**) is singular because **who** refers to a singular noun, **man**.
(b) I know the **people** who **are** sitting over there.	In (b): The verb in the adjective clause (**are**) is plural because **who** refers to a plural noun, **people**.

EXERCISE 27 ▶ Looking at grammar. (Chart 12-5)
Choose the correct word for each sentence. Underline the noun that determines whether the verb should be singular or plural.

1. a. A saw is a <u>tool</u> that   (cuts) / cut   wood.

   b. Shovels are tools that   is / are   used to dig holes.

2. a. I am tutoring a student that   wants / want   to move to Montreal.

   b. Most people that   live / lives   in Montreal speak French as their first language.

3. a. I have a cousin who   climbs / climb   cell phone towers to repair them.

   b. People who   repairs / repair   cell phone towers can't be afraid of heights.

4. a. A professional athlete who   plays / play   tennis is called a tennis pro.

   b. Professional athletes who   plays / play   tennis for a living can make a lot of money.

5. a. Biographies are books which   tells / tell   the stories of people's lives.

   b. A book that   tells / tell   the story of a person's life is called a biography.

6. a. I sat next to some teens who   was / were   texting during a movie.

   b. A woman that   was / were   sitting near me complained to the manager.

EXERCISE 28 ▶ Warm-up. (Chart 12-6)
Complete the sentences with your own words.

1. A person that I recently spoke to was _____.
2. A person whom I recently spoke to wasn't _____.
3. The room which we are sitting in is _____.
4. The room we are sitting in has _____.
5. The room in which we are sitting doesn't have _____.

12-6 Using Prepositions in Adjective Clauses

		PREP	OBJ	
(a) The man was nice.	I talked	**to**	**him**.	

		OBJ		PREP	
(b) The man		**that**	I talked	**to**	was nice.
(c) The man		**Ø**	I talked	**to**	was nice.
(d) The man		**whom**	I talked	**to**	was nice.
		PREP	OBJ		
(e) The man		**to**	**whom**	I talked	was nice.

That, ***whom***, and ***which*** can be used as the object (OBJ) of a preposition (PREP) in an adjective clause.

REMINDER: An object pronoun can be omitted from an adjective clause, as in (c) and (h).

In very formal English, a preposition comes at the beginning of an adjective clause, followed by either ***whom*** or ***which***, as in (e) and (j). This is not common in spoken English.

NOTE: In (e) and (j), ***that*** or ***who*** cannot be used, and the pronoun CANNOT be omitted.

(b), (c), (d), and (e) have the same meaning.

(g), (h), (i), and (j) have the same meaning.

		PREP	OBJ	
(f) The chair is hard.	I am sitting	**in**	**it**.	

	OBJ		PREP	
(g) The chair	**that**	I am sitting	**in**	is hard.
(h) The chair	**Ø**	I am sitting	**in**	is hard.
(i) The chair	**which**	I am sitting	**in**	is hard.
	PREP	OBJ		
(j) The chair	**in**	**which**	I am sitting	is hard.

EXERCISE 29 ▶ Looking at grammar. (Chart 12-6)

Combine each pair of sentences. The b. sentence will form an adjective clause. Give <u>all</u> the possible forms of these clauses and <u>underline</u> them.

1. a. The movie was funny.   b. We went **to** it.

   → The movie <u>that we went **to**</u> was funny.
   → The movie <u>**Ø** we went **to**</u> was funny.
   → The movie <u>which we went **to**</u> was funny.
   → The movie <u>**to** which we went</u> was funny.

2. a. The man is over there.   b. I told you **about** him.

3. a. The woman pays me a fair salary.   b. I work **for** her.

4. a. Alicia likes the family.   b. She is living **with** them.

5. a. The job has 30 applicants.   b. You are applying **for** it.

6. a. I enjoyed the music.   b. We listened **to** it in the car.

7. a. The class is closed.   b. The students want to sign up **for** it.

EXERCISE 30 ▶ Looking at grammar. (Chart 12-6)
Complete the sentences with appropriate prepositions.* Draw brackets around the adjective clauses.

1. I spoke ___to___ a person. The person [I spoke ___to___] was friendly.
2. We went _____ a movie. The movie we went _____ was very good.
3. We stayed _____ a motel. The motel we stayed _____ was clean and comfortable.
4. We listened _____ a podcast. I enjoyed the podcast we listened _____.
5. Sally was waiting _____ a friend. The friend Sally was waiting _____ never came.
6. I talked _____ a clerk. The clerk _____ whom I talked was helpful.
7. I never found the book that I was looking _____.
8. The interviewer wanted to know the name of the college I had graduated _____.
9. My father is someone I've always been able to depend _____ when I need advice or help.
10. The person you waved _____ is waving back at you.

EXERCISE 31 ▶ Looking at grammar. (Chart 12-6)
Complete each sentence with the information in the given sentence.

1. Oscar likes the Canadian family. He is staying with them this semester.
   a. Oscar likes the Canadian family with _whom he is staying_ this semester.
   b. Oscar likes the Canadian family that _he is staying with_ this semester.

2. This man is the manager. You should complain to him.
   a. This man is the manager who _____.
   b. This man is the manager to _____.

3. My sister is the person. I usually agree with.
   a. My sister is the person with _____.
   b. My sister is the person that _____.

4. The contract hasn't come. The lawyer is waiting for it.
   a. The contract that _____ hasn't come.
   b. The contract for _____ hasn't come.

5. Who is that person? You introduced me to him at the party.
   a. Who is that person that _____?
   b. Who is that person to _____?

---

*See Appendix Chart C-2 for a list of preposition combinations.

EXERCISE 32 ▸ Listening. (Charts 12-1 → 12-6)

Listen to the sentences and choose all the true statements.

Example: You will hear: The university I want to attend is in New York.
You will choose: (a.) I want to go to a university.
b. I live in New York.
(c.) The university is in New York.

1. a. The plane is leaving Denver.
   b. I'm taking a plane.
   c. The plane leaves at 7:00 A.M.

2. a. Stores are expensive.
   b. Good vegetables are always expensive.
   c. The best vegetables are at an expensive store.

3. a. My husband made eggs.
   b. I made breakfast.
   c. The eggs were cold.

4. a. I sent an email.
   b. Someone wanted my bank account number.
   c. An email had my bank account number.

5. a. The hotel clerk called my wife.
   b. The speaker spoke with the hotel clerk.
   c. The hotel room is going to have a view.

EXERCISE 33 ▸ Reading and grammar. (Charts 12-1 → 12-6)

Part I. Work in small groups. Answer the questions.

1. Have you visited or lived in another country?
2. What differences did you notice?
3. What customs did you like? What customs seemed strange to you?

Part II. Read the passage. Write the nouns that the pronouns refer to in the list on page 362.

Do you know these words?
- political views
- sense of humor
- appreciate
- have in common

An Exchange Student in Ecuador

Hiroki is from Japan. When he was sixteen, he spent four months in South America. He stayed with a family **who** lived near Quito, Ecuador. Their
                                                        1
way of life was very different from his. At first, many things **that** they did and
                                                               2
said seemed strange to Hiroki: their eating customs, political views, ways of showing feelings, work habits, sense of humor, and more. He felt homesick for people **who** were more similar to him in their customs and habits.
              3

As time went on, Hiroki began to appreciate the way **that** his host family lived. Many activities
                                                       4
which he did with them began to feel natural, and he developed a friendship with each person in
  5
the family. At the beginning of his stay in Ecuador, he had noticed only the customs and habits
that were different between his host family and himself. At the end, he appreciated the many things
  6
which they also had in common.
  7

1. who _____   5. which _____
2. that _____   6. that _____
3. who _____   7. which _____
4. that _____

Part III. Complete the sentences with information from the passage.

1. One thing that Hiroki found strange _____ .
2. At first, he wanted to be with people _____ .
3. After a while, he began to better understand _____ .
4. At the end of his stay, he saw many things _____ .

EXERCISE 34 ▶ Warm-up. (Chart 12-7)
Check (✓) all the sentences that are true about the given statement.

I spoke with a woman whose six children have won college scholarships.

1. _____ The woman has six children.
2. _____ I told a woman about my children.
3. _____ The woman told me about her children.
4. _____ Six children won scholarships.
5. _____ The woman received scholarships.

12-7 Using *Whose* in Adjective Clauses

(a) The man called the police. **His car** → **whose car** was stolen. (b) The man **whose car** *was stolen* called the police.		***Whose*** shows possession. In (a): **His car** can be changed to **whose car** to make an adjective clause. In (b): *whose car was stolen* = an adjective clause
(c) I know a girl. **Her brother** → **whose brother** is a movie star. (d) I know a girl **whose brother** *is a movie star*.		In (c): **Her brother** can be changed to **whose brother** to make an adjective clause.
(e) The people were friendly. We bought **their house** → **whose house**. (f) The people **whose house** *we bought* were friendly.		In (e): **Their house** can be changed to **whose house** to make an adjective clause.

*****Whose** and ***who's*** have the same pronunciation but NOT the same meaning.
Who's = **who is**: **Who's** (*Who is*) *your teacher?*

EXERCISE 35 ▸ Looking at grammar. (Chart 12-7)
Combine each pair of sentences. Follow these steps:
   (1) Underline the possessive adjective in sentence b.
   (2) Draw an arrow to the noun it refers to in sentence a.
   (3) Replace the possessive adjective with **whose**.
   (4) Place **whose** + the noun that follows after the noun you drew an arrow to (in step 2).
   (5) Make one sentence by completing the **whose** phrase with the rest of the words from sentence b.

At Work

Example: a. The woman is taking some time off from work. b. Her baby is sick.
   → The woman whose baby is sick is taking some time off from work.

   a. The man isn't worried.   b. You deleted his report.
   → The man whose report you deleted isn't worried.

1. a. The C.E.O.* is resigning.   b. His company lost money.
2. a. You should talk to the woman.   b. Her firm is hiring right now.
3. a. I spoke with some engineers.   b. Their department designs robots.
4. a. The manager is happy.   b. You edited his report.
5. a. A customer is on the phone.   b. We lost his order.

EXERCISE 36 ▸ Grammar and speaking. (Chart 12-7)
Work with a partner. Take turns changing the b. sentences to adjective clauses by combining each pair of sentences with **whose**.

SITUATION: You and your friend are at a party. You are telling your friend about the people at the party.

1. a. There is the man.   b. His videos go viral.
   → There is the man whose videos go viral.
2. a. There is the woman.   b. Her husband writes movie scripts.
3. a. Over there is the man.   b. His daughter is in my English class.
4. a. Over there is the woman.   b. You met her sister yesterday.
5. a. There is the professor.   b. I'm taking her course.
6. a. That is the man.   b. His daughter is a newscaster.
7. a. That is the girl.   b. I taught her brother.
8. a. There is the boy.   b. His mother is a famous musician.

*C.E.O. = chief executive officer or head of a company

EXERCISE 37 ▶ Listening. (Chart 12-7)

Listen to the sentences and choose the words you hear: *who's* or *whose*.

Example: You will hear: The neighbor who's selling her house is moving overseas.
You will choose: (who's)   whose

1. who's   whose
2. who's   whose
3. who's   whose
4. who's   whose
5. who's   whose
6. who's   whose

EXERCISE 38 ▶ Grammar and speaking. (Chapter 12 Review)

Work in small groups. Change a. through f. to adjective clauses. Take turns completing each sentence.

1. The man _____ is an undercover police officer.
    a. His car was stolen.
       → *The man whose car was stolen is an undercover police officer.*
    b. He invited us to his party.
    c. His son broke our car window.
    d. His dog barks all night.
    e. He is standing out in the rain.
    f. His wife is an actress.

2. The nurse _____ is leaving for a trip across the Sahara Desert.
    a. Her picture was in the paper.
    b. Her father climbed Mount Everest.
    c. She helped me when I cut myself.
    d. She works for Dr. Lang.
    e. I found her purse.
    f. I worked with her father.

3. The book _____ is very valuable.
    a. Its pages are torn.
    b. It's on the table.
    c. Sam lost it.
    d. Its cover is missing.
    e. I gave it to you.
    f. I found.

EXERCISE 39 ▶ Looking at grammar. (Chapter 12 Review)

Complete the sentences with all the possible choices: *who, that, Ø, which, whose,* or *whom*.

1. The family __who / that__ moved into the house next door is from Kenya.
2. The mattress __that / Ø / which__ I bought for my bed is comfortable but expensive.
3. Everyone _____ acted in the play enjoyed the experience.
4. Ms. Rice is the teacher _____ class I enjoy most.
5. The teen _____ I helped with his schoolwork got 100% on his exam.
6. I like the people with _____ I work.

7. I have a friend _____ father is a famous artist.

8. I recycled the cell phone _____ I replaced.

9. Students _____ have part-time jobs have to budget their time very carefully.

10. The man _____ car I dented was a little upset.

11. The person to _____ you should send your application is the Director of Admissions.

12. Some people believe almost anything _____ they see on the internet.

EXERCISE 40 ▶ Listening. (Chapter 12 Review)
Listen to the conversation. Complete the sentences with *that, which, whose,* or *Ø*.

Friendly Advice

A: A magazine _____(1)_____ I saw at the doctor's office had an article _____(2)_____ you ought to read. It's about the importance of exercise in dealing with stress.

B: Why do you think I should read an article _____(3)_____ deals with exercise and stress?

A: If you stop and think for a minute, you can answer that question yourself. You're under a lot of stress, and you don't get any exercise.

B: The stress _____(4)_____ I have at work doesn't bother me. It's just a normal part of my job. And I don't have time to exercise.

A: Well, you should make time. Anyone _____(5)_____ job is as stressful as yours should make physical exercise part of their* daily routine.

---

*The use of *their* with *anyone* can be heard in informal English. In formal English, the speaker would say *his* or *her*.

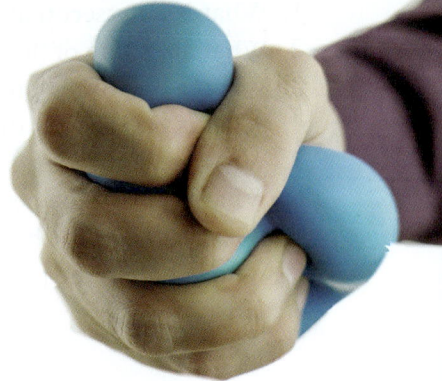

EXERCISE 41 ▶ Looking at grammar. (Chapter 12 Review)
Complete the sentences by making adjective clauses from the statements in the box.

> it erupted in Indonesia in 1883
> its mouth was big enough to swallow a whole cow in one gulp
> their license plates have names instead of numbers
> ✓ it is chosen by most people for their car
> they can't jump
> they drink coffee six hours before their bedtime
> their specialty is brain surgery

Interesting Information

1. The color _that/which is chosen by most people for their car_ is silver.

2. People _____
   may reduce their sleep time by one hour.

3. Cars _____
   get noticed more.

4. Krakatoa, a volcano _____,
   caused temperatures to drop around the world.

5. Doctors _____ generally train for six to seven
   years after medical school.

6. Elephants are the only animals _____.

7. In prehistoric times, there was a dinosaur _____
   _____.

EXERCISE 42 ▶ Let's talk: interview. (Chapter 12 Review)
Ask two classmates each question. Share their responses with the class and see which answers are the most popular.

1. What is a dessert that you like? → *A dessert that I like is ice cream.*
2. What are some of the cities in the world you would like to visit?
3. What is one of the programs which you like to watch on TV?
4. What is one subject that you would like to know more about?
5. What are some sports you enjoy playing? Watching on TV?
6. What is one of the best movies that you've ever seen?
7. What is one of the hardest classes you've ever taken?
8. Who is one of the people that you admire most in the world?

EXERCISE 43 ▶ Game. (Chapter 12 Review)

Work in teams. Answer each question with sentences that have adjective clauses. The team that has the most grammatically correct answers wins.

Example: What are the qualities of a good friend?
→ *A good friend is someone who you can depend on in times of trouble.*
→ *A good friend is a person who accepts you as you are.*
→ *A good friend is someone you can trust with secrets.*
→ *Etc.*

1. What is your idea of the ideal roommate?
2. What are the qualities of a good neighbor?
3. What kind of people make good parents?
4. What are the qualities of a good boss and a bad boss?

EXERCISE 44 ▶ Check your knowledge. (Chapter 12 Review)

Correct the errors in adjective clauses.

1. The car that I bought it used to belong to my best friend.

2. The woman was nice that I met yesterday.

3. I met a woman who her husband is a famous lawyer.

4. Do you know the people who lives in that house?

5. The professor teaches Chemistry 101 is very good.

6. The people who I painted their house want me to do other work for them.

7. The people who I met them at the party last night were interesting.

8. I enjoyed the music that we listened to it.

9. The apple tree is producing fruit that we planted it last year.

10. Before I came here, I didn't have the opportunity to speak to people who their native language is English.

11. One thing I need to get a new hair dryer.

12. The people who was waiting to buy tickets for the game they were happy because their team had made it to the championship.

EXERCISE 45 ▶ Reading and writing. (Chapter 12)

Part I. Read the passage and underline the adjective clauses. Read the passage again, but this time without the adjective clauses. Note the interesting information the adjective clauses add.

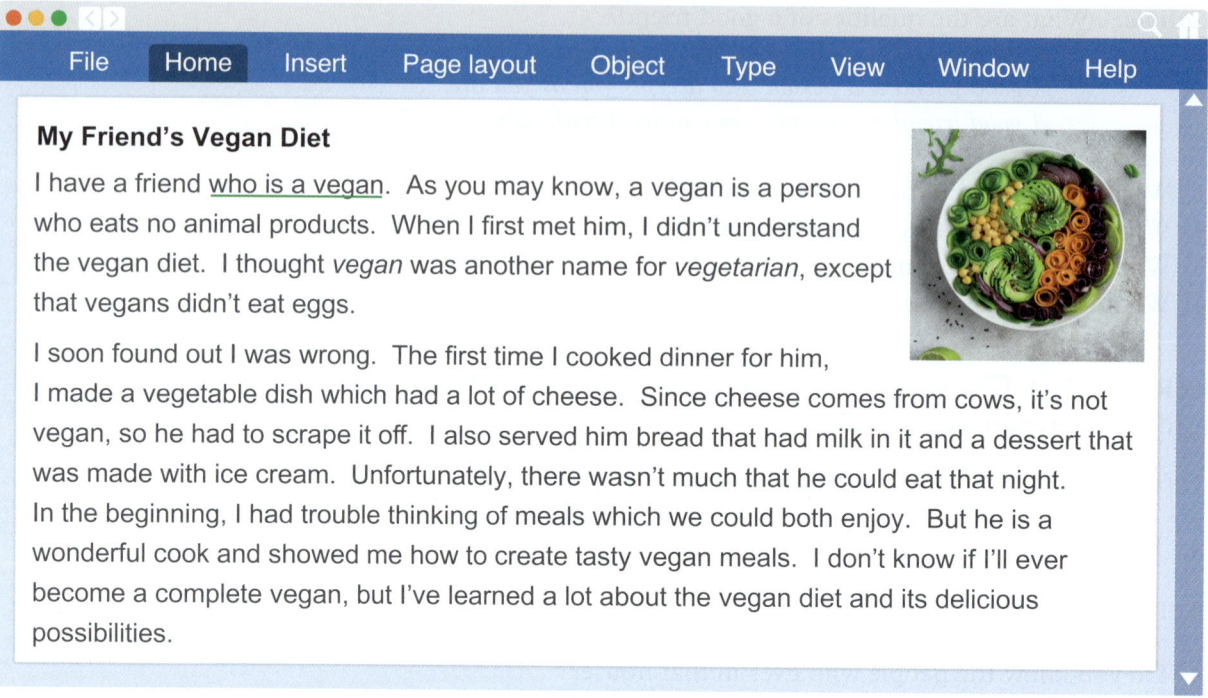

My Friend's Vegan Diet

I have a friend who is a vegan. As you may know, a vegan is a person who eats no animal products. When I first met him, I didn't understand the vegan diet. I thought *vegan* was another name for *vegetarian*, except that vegans didn't eat eggs.

I soon found out I was wrong. The first time I cooked dinner for him, I made a vegetable dish which had a lot of cheese. Since cheese comes from cows, it's not vegan, so he had to scrape it off. I also served him bread that had milk in it and a dessert that was made with ice cream. Unfortunately, there wasn't much that he could eat that night. In the beginning, I had trouble thinking of meals which we could both enjoy. But he is a wonderful cook and showed me how to create tasty vegan meals. I don't know if I'll ever become a complete vegan, but I've learned a lot about the vegan diet and its delicious possibilities.

Part II. Write a paragraph about someone interesting or unusual you know or know about. Use a few adjective clauses to add some interesting details.

Sample beginnings:

I have a friend who …
I know a person who …

WRITING TIP

When you want to describe a person and include interesting or special information, first make a list of details to mention. Then put these details into a logical order. Next, decide how you can use adjectives and adjective clauses to add interesting and special information. Finally, write your description. Don't forget to have a topic and a summary sentence.

Part III. Edit your writing. Check for the following:

1. ☐ use of some adjective clauses
2. ☐ correct forms for the adjective clauses (*who, whom, which, that, whose, Ø*)
3. ☐ correct subject-agreement with adjective clauses
4. ☐ a topic sentence, details, and a summary sentence
5. ☐ correct spelling (use a dictionary or spell-check)

▪▪▪▪ For digital resources, go to MyEnglishLab on the Pearson English Portal. You can also go to the Pearson Practice English app for mobile practice.

CHAPTER 13
Gerunds and Infinitives

PRETEST: What do I already know?
Choose **all** the correct answers.

1. Have you discussed _____ jobs with anyone yet? (Chart 13-1)
   a. to change   b. changing   c. about changing

2. We'll have a few hours before the train leaves. Do you want to _____? (Chart 13-2)
   a. sightseeing   b. go to sightseeing   c. go sightseeing

3. A new car is too expensive for Tom. He can't afford _____ one. (Chart 13-3)
   a. buy   b. to buy   c. buying

4. When the test was over, a few students continued _____. (Chart 13-4)
   a. to write   b. writing   c. to writing

5. Instead _____, let's walk to the mall. (Chart 13-5)
   a. of driving   b. driving   c. drive

6. Many people go _____ to the airport. (13-6)
   a. with the train b. by a train   c. by train

7. It is hard _____ 100% on the driver's license test. (Chart 13-7)
   a. to get   b. get   c. getting

8. In many places, _____ drivers to text while driving. (Chart 13-8)
   a. it is illegal   b. is illegal for c. it is illegal for

9. I ordered the clothes online _____ time. (Chart 13-9)
   a. to save   b. in order to save   c. saving

10. Are you _____ to sleep right now? (Chart 13-10)
    a. enough tired   b. tired enough   c. tired

EXERCISE 1 ▶ Warm-up. (Chart 13-1)
Check (✓) all the completions that are true for you.

I enjoy …

1. _____ traveling.
2. _____ going to museums.
3. _____ visiting tourist sites.
4. _____ learning about ancient history.

Gerunds and Infinitives   369

13-1 Verb + Gerund

VERB GERUND (a) I *enjoy walking* in the park.	A gerund is the *-ing* form of a verb. It is used as a noun. In (a): *walking* is a gerund. It is used as the object of the verb *enjoy*.

Common Verbs Followed by Gerunds
enjoy   (b) I *enjoy working* in my garden.
finish   (c) Ann *finished studying* at midnight.
quit   (d) David *quit smoking*.
mind   (e) Would you *mind opening* the window?
postpone (f) I *postponed doing* my homework.
put off   (g) I *put off doing* my homework.
keep (on) (h) *Keep (on) working*. Don't stop.
consider   (i) I'm *considering going* to Hawaii.
think about (j) I'm *thinking about going* to Hawaii.
discuss   (k) They *discussed getting* a new car.
talk about (l) They *talked about getting* a new car.
	The verbs in the list are followed by gerunds. The list also contains phrasal verbs (e.g., *put off*) that are followed by gerunds.
	
	The verbs in the list are NOT followed by *to* + the simple form of a verb (an infinitive).
	  INCORRECT: *I enjoy to walk in the park.*
	  INCORRECT: *Bob finished to study.*
	  INCORRECT: *I'm thinking to go to Hawaii.*
	
	See Chart 2-5, p. 43, for the spelling of *-ing* verb forms.

(m) I *considered not going* to class.	Negative form: ***not*** + *gerund*

EXERCISE 2 ▸ Looking at grammar. (Chart 13-1)

Complete each sentence with the correct form of a verb in the box.

clean	eat	hire	sleep	work
close	hand in	pay	smoke	

1. The Boyds own a bakery. They work seven days a week and they are very tired. They are thinking about ...

   a. _____ fewer hours a day.

   b. _____ their shop for a few weeks and going on vacation.

   c. _____ more workers for their shop.

2. Joseph wants to live a healthier life. He made several New Year's resolutions. For example, he will quit ...

   a. _____ cigars.

   b. _____ high-fat foods.

   c. _____ until noon on weekends.

3. Martina is a procrastinator.* She puts off ...

   a. _____ her bills.

   b. _____ her assignments to her teacher.

   c. _____ her apartment.

---

*procrastinator = someone who postpones or delays doing things

EXERCISE 3 ▸ Let's talk: pairwork. (Chart 13-1)
Work with a partner. Complete each sentence with a gerund.

Looking Ahead

Example:
PARTNER A: It sounds like your aunt is becoming forgetful. Is she going to quit (*drive*) **driving**?
PARTNER B: Yes, she is going to quit **driving**.

PARTNER A	PARTNER B
1. Have you thought about (*take*) _____ some vacation time soon?	Yes, I've …
2. It sounds like your apartment has a lot of problems. Have you considered (*move*) _____?	Yes, I've …
3. Where's Martha? Has she finished (*study*) _____ yet?	No, she hasn't …
4. Beth doesn't like her job. Is she talking about (*find*) _____ a different one?	Yes, she is …
PARTNER B	**PARTNER A**
5. Jon and Cara fight a lot. Are they going to postpone (*get*) _____ married?	No, I don't think they are going to …
6. Do you want to take a break, or do you want to keep on (*work*) _____ for another hour or so?	I think I want to keep on …
7. I have a favor to ask. Would you mind (*drive*) _____ me to the doctor tomorrow? My car won't start.	No problem. I don't mind …
8. You look tired. Are you going to put off (*study*) _____ for a few hours?	No, I can't put off … *Change roles.*

EXERCISE 4 ▸ Listening. (Chart 13-1)
Complete each short conversation with the words you hear. NOTE: There is a gerund in each completion.

Example: You will hear: A: I enjoy watching sports on TV, especially soccer.
B: Me too.

You will write: I __*enjoy watching*__ sports on TV, especially soccer.

1. A: Do you have any plans for this weekend?
   B: Henry and I _____ the dinosaur exhibit at the museum.

2. A: When you _____ your homework, could you help me in the kitchen?

   B: Sure.

3. A: I didn't understand the answer. _____ it?

   B: I'd be happy to.

4. A: I'm _____ the meeting tomorrow.

   B: Really? Why? I hope you go. We need your input.

5. A: I've been working on this math problem for an hour, and I still don't understand it.

   B: Well, don't give up. _____ .

EXERCISE 5 ▸ Warm-up. (Chart 13-2)
Answer the questions.

1. Have you ever gone ziplining?   yes   no
2. Would you like to go ziplining?   yes   no

13-2 Go + -ing

(a) **Did** you **go shopping** yesterday? (b) I **went swimming** last week. (c) Bob **hasn't gone fishing** in years.	**Go** is followed by a gerund in certain idiomatic expressions about activities. NOTE: There is no **to** between **go** and the gerund. INCORRECT: *Did you go to shopping?*

Common Expressions with go + -ing

go boating	go dancing	go jogging/running	go sightseeing	go skydiving
go bowling	go fishing	go sailing	go (ice) skating	go swimming
go camping	go hiking	go (window) shopping	go (water) skiing	go ziplining

EXERCISE 6 ▸ Let's talk: interview. (Chart 13-2)
Make questions to ask your classmates about the activities. Use any appropriate verb tense. Share some of your answers with the class.

Example: go waterskiing in the summer
   → *Do you go waterskiing in the summer?*
   → *Do you know someone who goes waterskiing in the summer?*
   → *Have you ever gone waterskiing in the summer?*

1. go skydiving
2. go bowling with friends
3. go dancing on weekends
4. go jogging for exercise
5. go fishing in the winter
6. go snow skiing
7. go camping in the snow

EXERCISE 7 ▶ Let's talk: pairwork. (Charts 13-1 and 13-2)

Work with a partner. Complete the conversation with each picture and the given information. Use expressions with **go + -ing** from Chart 13-2. Follow the model below. You can look at your book before you speak. When you speak, look at your partner.

A: Is/Are _____ here?

B: No, _____ isn't/aren't. _____ gone _____ .

A: Oh, _____ often?

B: Yes, _____ .

Example:
A: Is Sigrid here?
B: No, she isn't. She's gone skiing.
A: Oh, does she go skiing often?
B: Yes, she really enjoys skiing.

1. Maria
2. your roommates
3. Kristin and Paul
4. Allison
5. Alexis and Brian
6. Jack and his grandson
7. Andre
8. Taka and his kids
9. Kyra and Jada

Gerunds and Infinitives 373

EXERCISE 8 ▶ Warm-up. (Chart 13-3)
Check (✓) the sentences that are true for you.

1. _____ I hope to move to another town soon.
2. _____ I would like to get married in a few years.
3. _____ I intend to visit another country next year.
4. _____ I'm planning to become an English teacher.

13-3 Verb + Infinitive

(a) Tom **offered to lend** me some money. (b) I've **decided to buy** a new car.	Some verbs are followed by an infinitive. Infinitive = **to** + the simple form of a verb
(c) I've **decided not to keep** my old car.	Negative form: **not** + infinitive

Common Verbs Followed by Infinitives

want	hope	decide	seem	learn (how)	can/can't afford
need	expect	promise	appear	try	can/can't wait
would like	plan	offer	pretend	be supposed	
would love	intend	agree			
	mean	refuse			

EXERCISE 9 ▶ Looking at grammar. (Chart 13-3)
Complete each sentence with the correct form of a word in the box.

be	✓ fly to	hear	lend	visit
buy	get to	hurt	see	want
eat	✓ go to	leave	tell	watch

1. I'm planning __to fly to / to go to__ Barcelona next week.
2. Hasan promised not _____ late for the wedding.
3. My husband and I would love _____ Fiji.
4. What time do you expect _____ our house?
5. You seem _____ that dress. Are you going to buy it?
6. Nadia appeared _____ asleep, but she wasn't. She was only pretending.
7. Nadia pretended _____ asleep. She pretended not _____ me when I spoke to her.
8. The Millers can't afford _____ a house.
9. My friend offered _____ me some money.
10. Tommy doesn't like vegetables. He refuses _____ them.

11. I try _____ class on time every day.

12. My wife and I wanted to do different things this weekend. Finally, I agreed _____ a movie with her Saturday, and she agreed _____ the football game with me on Sunday.

13. I can't wait _____ my family again! It's been a long time.

14. I'm sorry. I didn't mean _____ you.

15. I learned how _____ time when I was six.

EXERCISE 10 ▸ Let's talk: pairwork. (Chart 13-3)

Work with a partner. Take turns making sentences with a form of the given phrases. Use any appropriate verb tense.

Example: never learn how to use
PARTNER A: I will never learn how to use chopsticks.
PARTNER B: My grandmother has never learned how to drive.

1. promise to help
2. can't wait to see
3. hope to go
4. decide to try
5. plan to buy
6. can't afford to buy
7. need to finish
8. be supposed to write
9. mean to come
10. expect to get

EXERCISE 11 ▸ Warm-up. (Chart 13-4)

Check (✓) the grammatically correct completions.

Many children love …

1. _____ to drink milkshakes.
2. _____ drinking milkshakes.
3. _____ drink milkshakes.

13-4 Verb + Gerund or Infinitive

(a) It began *raining*. (b) It began *to rain*.	Some verbs take either a gerund, as in (a), or an infinitive, as in (b). Usually there is no difference in meaning. Examples (a) and (b) have the same meaning.

Common Verbs That Take Either a Gerund or an Infinitive

begin	like*	hate
start	love*	can't stand
continue		

*COMPARE: *Like* and *love* can be followed by either a gerund or an infinitive:
    I like **going** / **to go** to movies. I love **playing** / **to play** chess.

Would like and *would love* are followed by infinitives:
    I would like **to go** to a movie tonight. I'd love **to play** a game of chess right now.

EXERCISE 12 ▶ Looking at grammar. (Chart 13-4)
Choose the correct verbs.

Snow

1. It started _____ around noon.
   a. snow
   (b.) snowing
   (c.) to snow

2. I continued _____ in the city.
   a. drive
   b. driving
   c. to drive

3. I don't like _____ out in the snow.
   a. be
   b. being
   c. to be

4. I would like _____ new snow tires for my car.
   a. get
   b. getting
   c. to get

5. My kids love _____ in the snow.
   a. play
   b. playing
   c. to play

6. They would love _____ near a big hill for sledding.
   a. live
   b. living
   c. to live

7. My parents hate _____ with icy sidewalks and roads.
   a. deal
   b. dealing
   c. to deal

8. They can't stand _____ the snow from their driveway and sidewalk.
   a. shovel
   b. shoveling
   c. to shovel

EXERCISE 13 ▶ Let's talk: pairwork. (Charts 13-1, 13-3, and 13-4)
Work with a partner. Take turns combining the words in the box with the given phrases to make sentences about what you like and don't like to do.

| I like | I enjoy | I hate | I don't mind |
| I love | I don't like | I can't stand | |

Example: cook → *I like to cook. / I like cooking. / I hate to cook. / I hate cooking. / I don't mind cooking. / I don't enjoy cooking. / Etc.*

Partner A	Partner B
1. live in this city	1. speak in front of a large group
2. wash dishes	2. travel by plane
3. wait in airports	3. wake up early
4. go to parties where I don't know anyone	4. listen to music while I'm falling asleep
5. eat food slowly	5. eat vegetables
6. get in between two friends who are having an argument	6. travel to unusual places *Change roles.*

EXERCISE 14 ▶ Grammar and speaking. (Charts 13-1, 13-3, and 13-4)
Complete each sentence with the infinitive or gerund form of the verb in parentheses. Then agree or disagree with the statement. Discuss your answers.

What do you do when you can't understand a native English speaker?

1. I pretend (*understand*) _____.   yes   no
2. I keep on (*listen*) _____ politely.   yes   no
3. I think, "I can't wait (*get*) _____ out of here!" or   yes   no
   "I can't wait for this person (*stop*) _____ talking."   yes   no
4. I say, "Would you mind (*repeat*) _____ that?"   yes   no
5. I begin (*nod*) _____ my head so I look like I understand.   yes   no
6. I start (*look*) _____ at my watch, so it appears I'm in a hurry.   yes   no
7. As soon as the person finishes (*speak*) _____, I say I have to leave.   yes   no

EXERCISE 15 ▶ Looking at grammar. (Charts 13-1, 13-3, and 13-4)
Complete the sentences with the infinitive or gerund form of the verbs in parentheses.

Roommates

1. I don't mind (*have*) _____ two roommates.
2. We like each other. We laugh a lot. The situation appears (*be*) _____ working.
3. We sometimes try (*eat*) _____ together, but we often don't finish (*cook*) _____ until around eight.
4. We are considering (*get*) _____ a TV.
5. One of my roommates has offered (*pay*) _____ for a satellite dish.
6. All of us hate (*wake up*) _____ early for morning classes.
7. The roommate in the room next to me is noisy in the mornings. I've quit (*set*) _____ my alarm because she wakes me up.
8. A former roommate refused (*clean*) _____, so we asked her to move.
9. She also couldn't stand (*share*) _____ a bathroom.
10. We meant (*find*) _____ another roommate, but then we decided not to.
11. Our landlord seems (*want*) _____ (*raise*) _____ the rent. He keeps (*mention*) _____ it, but he hasn't done anything yet.

EXERCISE 16 ▶ Let's talk: pairwork. (Charts 13-1 → 13-4)
Work with a partner. Take turns completing the sentences with **to go**/**going** + *a place*.

Example: I would like … .
PARTNER A: **I would like to go** to the Beach Café for dinner tonight.
PARTNER B: **I would like to go** to the movies later today.

1. I like … .
2. I love … .
3. I'd love … .
4. I refuse … .
5. I expect … .
6. I promised … .
7. I can't stand … .
8. I waited … .
9. I am thinking about … .
10. Are you considering … ?
11. I can't afford … .
12. Would you mind … ?
13. My friend and I agreed … .
14. I hate … .
15. I don't enjoy … .
16. My friend and I discussed … .
17. I've decided … .
18. I don't mind … .
19. Sometimes I put off … .
20. I can't wait … .

EXERCISE 17 ▶ Looking at grammar. (Charts 13-1, 13-3, and 13-4)
Complete the sentences with the infinitive or gerund form of the verbs in parentheses.
NOTE: When infinitives are connected by **and**, it is not necessary to use **to** with the second verb.

This Weekend

1. I want (*relax*) _____ this weekend.

2. I want (*stay*) _____ home and (*relax*) _____ this weekend.

3. I want (*stay*) _____ home, (*relax*) _____, and (*binge-watch**) _____ movies this weekend.

4. Ella is thinking about (*get*) _____ up early in the morning and (*watch*) _____ the sunrise.

5. Ella is thinking about (*get*) _____ up early in the morning, (*watch*) _____ the sunrise, and (*sit*) _____ outside on her deck.

6. Mr. and Mrs. Bashir are discussing (*trade in*) _____ their old car and (*buy*) _____ a new one.

7. Kathy plans (*move*) _____ to New York City, (*find*) _____ a job, and (*start*) _____ a new life.

---

*binge-watch = watch several episodes of a show or movie, one after another

8. Would you like (*go*) _____ out to eat and (*let*) _____ someone else do the cooking?

9. Kevin is thinking about (*quit*) _____ smoking and (*begin*) _____ an exercise program.

10. I'm planning to come to the office after you this weekend. Would you mind (*leave*) _____ the heat on but (*turn off*) _____ the lights and (*lock*) _____ the door?

EXERCISE 18 ▶ Game. (Charts 13-1 → 13-4)

Work in teams. Your teacher will call out an item number. Make a sentence using the given words and any verb tense. Begin with **I**. The first team to come up with a grammatically correct sentence wins a point. The team with the most points wins the game.

Example: want \ go
→ *I want to go to Dallas next week.*

1. plan \ go
2. consider \ go
3. offer \ help
4. like \ visit
5. enjoy \ read
6. intend \ get
7. can't afford \ buy
8. seem \ be
9. put off \ write
10. would like \ go \ swim
11. postpone \ go
12. finish \ study
13. would mind \ help
14. begin \ study
15. think about \ go
16. quit \ try
17. continue \ walk
18. learn \ speak
19. talk about \ go
20. keep \ try

EXERCISE 19 ▶ Warm-up. (Chart 13-5)

Agree or disagree with the statements. Notice the use of the prepositions and gerunds in green that follow the verbs.

I know someone who …

1. never **apologizes for** being late.   yes   no
2. is **interested in** coming to this country.   yes   no
3. is **worried about** losing his/her job.   yes   no
4. is **excited about** becoming a parent.   yes   no
5. **worries about** his or her grades.   yes   no
6. is **looking forward** to an exciting vacation.   yes   no

13-5 Preposition + Gerund

(a) Kate *insisted on coming* with us. (b) We're *excited about going* to Tahiti. (c) I *apologized for being* late.	A preposition is followed by a gerund, not an infinitive. In (a): The preposition (*on*) is followed by a gerund (*coming*).

Common Expressions with Prepositions Followed by Gerunds

be afraid *of* (doing something)	apologize *for*	look forward *to*
be excited *about*	believe *in*	plan *on*
be good *at*	dream *about* / *of*	stop (someone) *from*
be interested *in*	feel *like*	thank (someone) *for*
be nervous *about*	forgive (someone) *for*	worry *about* / be worried *about*
be responsible *for*	insist *on*	
be tired *of*	instead *of*	

EXERCISE 20 ▶ Looking at grammar. (Chart 13-5)
Complete the sentences with the correct preposition.

1. Lyn … moving.

    a. feels _____
    b. dreams _____
    c. is afraid _____
    d. is nervous _____
    e. is tired _____
    f. insisted _____
    g. plans _____

2. Sai is … taking care of the kids.

    a. excited _____
    b. good _____
    c. interested _____
    d. looking forward _____
    e. planning _____
    f. responsible _____
    g. worried _____

EXERCISE 21 ▶ Looking at grammar. (Chart 13-5)

Complete the sentences with a *preposition* + *gerund* and the given words.

1. I'm looking forward   + go away for the weekend
   → I'm looking forward **to** *going away for the weekend.*

2. Thank you   + hold the door open
3. I'm worried   + be late for my appointment
4. Are you interested   + go to the beach with us
5. I apologized   + be late
6. Are you afraid   + fly in small planes
7. Are you nervous   + take your driver's test
8. We're excited   + see the soccer game
9. Tariq insisted   + pay the restaurant bill
10. Eva dreams   + become a veterinarian someday
11. I don't feel   + eat right now
12. Please forgive me   + not get in touch sooner
13. I'm tired   + live with five roommates
14. I believe   + be honest at all times
15. Let's plan   + meet at the restaurant at six
16. Who's responsible   + clean the classroom
17. The police stopped us   + enter the building
18. Jake's not very good   + cut his own hair

EXERCISE 22 ▶ Let's talk: pairwork. (Chart 13-5)

Work with a partner. Take turns asking and answering questions using the following pattern:
What + *the given words* + *preposition* + **doing**.

Examples: be looking forward
PARTNER A: What are you looking forward to **doing**?
PARTNER B: I'm looking forward **to going to a movie tonight**.

       dream
PARTNER A: What do you dream **about doing**?
PARTNER B: I dream **about becoming a professional athlete**.

PARTNER A	PARTNER B
1. be interested	1. be nervous
2. be worried	2. be excited
3. feel	3. plan
4. be good	4. be responsible
5. be afraid	5. be tired
	Change roles.

EXERCISE 23 ▶ Listening. (Charts 13-1 → 13-5)
Listen to the conversation. Then listen again and complete the sentences with the words you hear.

A Staycation

A: Have you made any vacation plans?

B: Kind of. We're going to take a staycation.

A: You mean you're going to stay home and vacation?

B: Yeah. To be honest, I _____(1)_____ so much. I _____(2)_____. It's so uncomfortable nowadays.

A: But your wife _____(3)_____, doesn't she?

B: Right. But we don't see our kids so much because they're in college. So we _____(4)_____ time here so we can see them, and we can be tourists in our own town.

A: So, what are you _____(5)_____?

B: Well, we haven't seen the new Museum of Space yet. There's also a new art exhibit downtown. And my wife _____(6)_____ in the harbor. Actually, when we _____(7)_____ about it, we discovered there were lots of things to do.

A: Sounds like a great solution!

B: Yeah, we're both really _____(8)_____ our kids and more of our own town.

EXERCISE 24 ▶ Looking at grammar. (Chart 13-5)
Complete each sentence with the correct preposition and the gerund form of the verb in parentheses.

1. Carlos is nervous __about__ (meet) __meeting__ his girlfriend's parents.

2. I believe _____ (tell) _____ the truth no matter what.

3. I don't swim in deep water. I'm afraid _____ (drown) _____.

4. I'm looking forward _____ (take) _____ a trip with my family.

5. Do you feel _____ (tell) _____ me why you're so sad?

6. My father-in-law insists _____ (pay) _____ when we go out for dinner.

7. I'm not very good _____ (remember) _____ people's names.

8. How do you stop someone _____ (do) _____ something dangerous?

9. The kids are responsible _____ (take) _____ out the garbage.

10. Monique lost her job. That's why she is afraid _____ (have, not) _____ _____ enough money to pay her rent.

11. Jo is pregnant and is looking forward _____ (have) _____ twins.

12. I sometimes (dream) _____ (quit) _____ my job, but instead _____ (leave) _____, I'll probably ask for a transfer.

EXERCISE 25 ▶ Warm-up. (Chart 13-6)
Choose the completions that are true for you.

1. I sometimes pay for things ____.   a. by credit card   b. by check   c. in cash
2. I usually come to school ____.   a. by bus   b. by car   c. on foot
3. My favorite way to travel is ____.   a. by plane   b. by boat   c. by train
4. I communicate with my family ____.   a. by email   b. by text message c. in person

13-6 Using *By* and *With* to Express How Something Is Done

(a) Pat turned off the TV **by pushing** the "off" button.	**By** + *a gerund* is used to express how something is done.
(b) Mary goes to work **by bus**. (c) Andrea stirred her coffee **with a spoon**.	**By** or **with** followed by a noun is also used to express how something is done.

By Is Used for Means of Transportation and Communication

by (air)plane	by subway*	by mail/email	by air
by boat	by taxi	by (tele)phone	by land
by bus	by train	by fax	by sea
by car	by foot (*or:* on foot)	(*but:* in person)	

Other Uses of *By*

by chance	by mistake	by check (*but:* in cash)
by choice	by hand**	by credit card

With Is Used for Instruments or Parts of the Body
I cut down the tree **with** an ax (by using an ax).
I swept the floor **with** a broom.
She pointed to a spot on the map **with** her finger.

*by subway = American English; *by underground, by tube* = British English.

The expression **by hand is usually used to mean that something was made by a person, not by a machine: *This rug was made **by hand**.* (A person, not a machine, made this rug.)
COMPARE: *I touched his shoulder **with my hand**.*

EXERCISE 26 ▸ Looking at grammar. (Chart 13-6)
Choose all the correct completions.

1. Oliver received the news by ____.
   a. mail
   b. email
   c. by an email
   d. mistake
   e. chance
   f. person

2. Christina ate her snack with ____.
   a. knife
   b. chopsticks
   c. a spoon
   d. a fork
   e. hand

3. Kevin cleaned the bedroom with ____.
   a. a broom
   b. hand
   c. a mop
   d. soap and water

4. Philippe went to the city center ____.
   a. by foot
   b. by train
   c. on foot
   d. by a car
   e. by taxi
   f. by bus
   g. by chance

EXERCISE 27 ▸ Looking at grammar. (Chart 13-6)
Complete the sentences by using **by** + *a gerund*. Use the words in the box or your own words.

eat	✓memorize	take	watch
drink	smile	wag	wave
guess	stay	wash	

1. Many students practice vocabulary ____by memorizing____ words.
2. We clean our clothes _____ them in soap and water.
3. Khalid improved his English _____ a lot of TV.
4. We show other people we are happy _____.
5. We satisfy our hunger _____ something.
6. We quench our thirst _____ something.
7. I figured out what *quench* means _____.
8. Alex caught my attention _____ his arms in the air.
9. My dog shows me she is happy _____ her tail.
10. Carmen recovered from her cold _____ in bed and _____ care of herself.

EXERCISE 28 ▸ Vocabulary and speaking. (Chart 13-6)

Part I. Write the correct vocabulary word for each picture.

| a broom | a needle and thread | a saw | a spoon |
| a hammer | a pair of scissors | a shovel | a thermometer |

  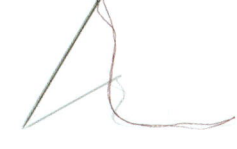

1. _____ 2. _____ 3. _____

4. _____ 5. _____

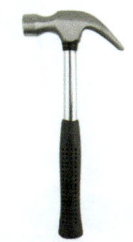  

6. _____ 7. _____ 8. _____

Part II. Take turns asking and answering questions.

Example: clean the carpet
PARTNER A: How do you clean the carpet?
PARTNER B: I clean the carpet with a vacuum.

PARTNER A	PARTNER B
How do you … 1. sweep the floor? 2. sew on a button? 3. cut wood in half? 4. take your temperature?	*How do you …* 1. eat soup? 2. dig a hole in the garden? 3. nail two pieces of wood together? 4. cut a piece of paper?

EXERCISE 29 ▶ Looking at grammar. (Chart 13-6)
Complete the sentences with **by** or **with**.

1. I opened the door ___with___ a key.
2. I went downtown ___by___ bus.
3. I dried the dishes _____ a dishtowel.
4. I went from Frankfurt to Vienna _____ train.
5. Ted drew a straight line _____ a ruler.
6. Rebecca tightened the screw in the corner of her eyeglasses _____ her fingernail.
7. I called Bill "Paul" _____ mistake.
8. I sent a copy of the contract _____ fax.
9. Talya protected her eyes from the sun _____ her hand.
10. My grandmother makes tablecloths _____ hand.

EXERCISE 30 ▶ Warm-up. (Chart 13-7)
Read the passage and then agree or disagree with the statements.

A White Lie

Rob gave his friend Paul a book for his birthday. When Paul opened it, he tried to look excited, but his wife had already given him the same book. Paul had just finished reading it, but he thanked Rob and said he was looking forward to reading it.

Paul told a "white lie." White lies are minor or unimportant lies that a person often tells to avoid hurting someone else's feelings.

1. Telling white lies is common.   yes   no
2. It is sometimes acceptable to tell a white lie. yes   no
3. I sometimes tell white lies.   yes   no

13-7 Using Gerunds as Subjects; Using *It* + Infinitive

(a) **Riding** horses is fun. (b) **It** is fun **to ride** horses. (c) **Coming** to class on time is important. (d) **It** is important **to come** to class on time.	Examples (a) and (b) have the same meaning. In (a): A gerund (**riding**) is the subject of the sentence. NOTE: The verb (*is*) is singular because a gerund is singular.* In (b): **It** is used as the subject of the sentence. **It** has the same meaning as the infinitive phrase at the end of the sentence: *it* means **to ride horses.**

*It is also correct (but less common) to use an infinitive as the subject of a sentence: *To ride horses is fun.*

EXERCISE 31 ▸ Grammar and speaking. (Chart 13-7)
Make sentences with the same meaning as the given sentences, and then decide if you agree with them. Circle *yes* or *no*. Compare your answers with a partner.

Living in This Town

Part I. Use a gerund as the subject.

1. It's hard to meet people here.
    → *Meeting people here is hard.*   yes   no
2. It takes time to make friends here.   yes   no
3. It is easy to get around the town.   yes   no
4. Is it expensive to live here?   yes   no

Part II. Use *it* + *an infinitive*.

5. Finding things to do on weekends is hard.
    → *It's hard to find things to do on weekends.*   yes   no
6. Walking alone at night is dangerous.   yes   no
7. Exploring this town is fun.   yes   no
8. Is finding affordable housing difficult?   yes   no

EXERCISE 32 ▸ Let's talk: interview. (Chart 13-7)
Interview your classmates. Ask a question and then agree or disagree with your classmate's answer. Practice using both gerunds and infinitives in your answers.

Example:
STUDENT A (*book open*):   Which is easier: to make money or to spend money?
STUDENT B (*book closed*): It's easier to spend money than (it is) to make money.
STUDENT A (*book open*):   I agree. Spending money is easier than making money. OR
                            I don't agree. I think that making money is easier than spending money.

1. Which is more fun: to visit a big city or to spend time in the countryside?
2. Which is more difficult: to write English or to read English?
3. Which is easier: to understand spoken English or to speak English?
4. Which is more expensive: to go to a movie or to go to a concert?
5. Which is more comfortable: to wear shoes or to go barefoot?

6. Which is more satisfying: to give gifts or to receive them?
7. Which is more dangerous: to ride in a car or to ride in an airplane?
8. Which is more important: to come to class on time or to get an extra hour of sleep in the morning?

EXERCISE 33 ▸ Warm-up. (Chart 13-8)
Agree or disagree with these statements.

In my culture ...

1. it is common for people to shake hands when they meet. yes no
2. it is important for people to look one another in the eye when they are introduced. yes no
3. it is strange for people to kiss one another on the cheek when they meet. yes no

13-8 It + Infinitive: Using For (Someone)

(a) *You* should study hard. (b) It is important **for you** to study hard. (c) *Mary* should study hard. (d) It is important **for Mary** to study hard. (e) *We* don't have to go to the meeting. (f) It isn't necessary **for us** to go to the meeting. (g) *A dog* can't talk. (h) It is impossible **for a dog** to talk.	Examples (a) and (b) have a similar meaning. Note the pattern in (b): ***It is*** + *adjective* + ***for*** (someone) + *infinitive phrase*

EXERCISE 34 ▸ Looking at grammar. (Chart 13-8)
Complete the sentences with the given information. Use ***for*** (***someone***) and an infinitive phrase in each completion.

1. Students should do their homework.

   It's really important _for students to do their homework_____.

2. Teachers should speak clearly.

   It's very important _____.

3. We don't have to hurry. There's plenty of time.

   It isn't necessary _____.

4. With final exams next week, I can't visit my sister this weekend.

   It's impossible _____.

5. Working parents have to budget their time carefully.

   It's necessary _____.

6. A young child usually can't sit still for a long time.

   It's difficult _____.

7. My family spends birthdays together.

   It's traditional _____.

8. My brother would love to travel to Mars someday.

   Will it be possible _____ to Mars someday?

9. I usually can't understand Mr. Alvarez. He talks too fast. How about you?

   Is it easy _____?

EXERCISE 35 ▶ Reading and grammar. (Charts 13-7 and 13-8)
Part I. Read the passage.

Do you know these words?
- *handshake*
- *impolite*
- *rude*
- *varies*
- *arm's length*
- *universal*
- *cross-cultural*
- *gesture*

BODY LANGUAGE

Different cultures use different body language. In some countries, when people meet one another, they offer a strong handshake and look the other person straight in the eye. In other countries, however, it is impolite to shake hands firmly, and it is equally rude to look a person in the eye.

The distance that people stand when they talk to one another varies from country to country. In the United States and Canada, people prefer standing just a little less than an arm's length from someone. But many people in the Middle East and Latin America like moving in closer during a conversation.

Smiling at another person is a universal, cross-cultural gesture. Although people may smile more frequently in some countries than in others, people around the world understand the meaning of a smile.

Part II. Complete the sentences with information about body language.

1. In some countries, it is important _____.
2. In some countries, _____ is impolite.
3. In my country, _____ is important.
4. In my country, it is impolite _____.

EXERCISE 36 ▶ Let's talk. (Charts 13-7 and 13-8)
In small groups, make sentences by combining the words in the box with the given phrases. Use gerunds as subjects or *it* + *an infinitive*. Share some sentences for other groups to agree or disagree with.

boring	embarrassing	hard	impossible	scary
dangerous	exciting	illegal	interesting	a waste of time
educational	fun	important	relaxing	

Example: ride a bike
→ *Riding a bike is fun.* OR *It's fun to ride a bike.*

1. ride a roller coaster
2. read newspapers
3. study economics
4. drive ten miles over the speed limit
5. walk in a cemetery at night
6. know the meaning of every word in a dictionary
7. never tell a lie
8. visit museums
9. play video games all day

EXERCISE 37 ▶ Reading and grammar. (Charts 13-1 and 13-3 → 13-8)
Part I. Read the blog entry by co-author Stacy Hagen. Note the gerunds and infinitives in green. With a partner, explain why a gerund or infinitive is used.

Do you know these words?
- casual
- challenging
- acceptable
- politics
- likely

BlackBookBlog

Service with a Smile

When you are a customer in a store or restaurant, how do you feel when an employee smiles at you? For example, let's say you are ordering a meal, and the server is very friendly and smiles a lot. Does it feel normal or strange to see such behavior?

In some cultures, as in the United States, customers expect it. It's called "service with a smile." It is important for employees to smile when they deal with the public.

Part of this expectation is also eye contact. Employees are supposed to look directly at the customer when they speak with them. Looking away is considered rude.

Imagine you are a cashier at a store right now, and you are taking a customer's money. How comfortable are you with the idea of smiling? What about looking directly at the customer?

If you are going to choose a job where you are expected to provide service with a smile, it is good to practice both eye contact and smiling until they come naturally to you. Your customer will expect you to do it, and your manager will be happier.

Part II. Agree or disagree with the statements. Discuss your answers with the class.

In my country, ...

1. it is natural to smile a lot at people.	yes	no
2. smiling a lot is too friendly.	yes	no
3. looking directly at someone is rude.	yes	no
4. customer service includes smiling at customers.	yes	no
5. customer service includes looking directly at customers.	yes	no

EXERCISE 38 ▶ Warm-up. (Chart 13-9)
Check (✓) all the sentences that are grammatically correct.

1. _____ I went to the pharmacy because I wanted to pick up a prescription.
2. _____ I went to the pharmacy in order to pick up a prescription.
3. _____ I went to the pharmacy to pick up a prescription.
4. _____ I went to the pharmacy for a prescription.
5. _____ I went to the pharmacy for to pick up a prescription.

13-9 Expressing Purpose with *In Order To* and *For*

— Why did you go to the post office? (a) I went to the post office *because I wanted to mail a letter*. (b) I went to the post office *in order to* mail a letter. (c) I went to the post office *to mail* a letter.	***In order to*** expresses purpose. It answers the question "Why?"
	In (c): ***in order*** is frequently omitted. Examples (a), (b), and (c) have the same meaning.

(d) I went to the post office *for* some stamps.
(e) I went to the post office *to buy* some stamps.
   INCORRECT: *I went to the post office for to buy some stamps.*
   INCORRECT: *I went to the post office for buying some stamps.*
	For is also used to express purpose, but it is a preposition and is followed by a noun phrase, as in (d).

EXERCISE 39 ▶ Looking at grammar. (Chart 13-9)

Make sentences by combining the phrases in the left column with those in the right column. Connect the ideas with (*in order*) *to*. Take turns saying the sentences with a partner.

Example: I called the hotel desk _____.
→ *I called the hotel desk (in order) to ask for an extra pillow.*

1. I called the hotel desk __e__.
2. I turned on the radio _____.
3. Nick went to Nepal _____.
4. People wear boots _____.
5. I looked on the internet _____.
6. Ms. Lane stood on her tiptoes _____.
7. The dentist moved the light closer to my face _____.
8. I clapped my hands and yelled _____.
9. Maria took a walk in the park _____.
10. I offered my cousin some money _____.

a. keep their feet warm and dry
b. reach the top shelf
c. listen to a baseball game
d. find the population of Malaysia
✓e. ask for an extra pillow
f. chase a mean dog away
g. help her pay the rent
h. get some fresh air and exercise
i. climb Mount Everest
j. look into my mouth

EXERCISE 40 ▶ Looking at grammar. (Chart 13-9)

Add *in order* to the sentences where possible.

1. I went to the bank to cash a check.
    → *I went to the bank in order to cash a check.*
2. I'd like to see that movie.
    → (*No change.*)
3. Sam went to the hospital to visit a friend.
4. I need to go to the bank today.
5. I need to go to the bank today to deposit my paycheck.
6. On my way home, I stopped at the store to buy some shampoo.
7. Masako went to the cafeteria to eat lunch.
8. Jack and Katya have decided to get married.
9. Pedro watches TV to improve his English.
10. I didn't forget to pay my rent.
11. Donna expects to graduate next spring.
12. Jerry needs to go to the bookstore to buy school supplies.
13. Mira hopes to complete college with a double major in physics and biology.
14. Hector asked to leave early for a doctor's appointment.

EXERCISE 41 ▶ Looking at grammar. (Chart 13-9)
Complete the sentences with *to* or *for*.

Moving to Chicago

1. I moved to Chicago ___*for*___ my education.
2. I wanted to live in the city ___*to*___ attend graduate school.
3. I needed to leave my family _____ graduate school.
4. I decided to attend graduate school _____ get a good job.
5. I like to take long walks along the lakeshore _____ relax.
6. I take long walks along the lakeshore _____ relaxation.
7. In the winter, I wear a heavy coat _____ protect myself from the wind and cold.
8. I take the train to school _____ have more time to study.
9. I go to the Art Institute of Chicago _____ fun.
10. I like to go out _____ eat Chicago-style pizza.

EXERCISE 42 ▶ Reading and grammar. (Charts 13-1 and 13-3 → 13-9)
Part I. Read the passage.

CAR SHARING

Do you know these words?
- fee
- rate
- available
- maintenance costs
- members
- effective alternative
- parking lot

In hundreds of cities around the world, people can use a car without actually owning one. It's known as car sharing.

Car sharing works like this: people pay a fee to join a car-sharing organization. These organizations have cars available in different parts of a city 24 hours a day. Members make reservations for a car and then go to one of several parking lots in the city to pick up the car. They pay an hourly or daily rate for driving it. They may also pay a charge for every mile/kilometer they drive. When they are finished, they return the car to a parking area for someone else to use.

Car sharing works well for several reasons. Some people only need to drive occasionally. Oftentimes, people only need a car for special occasions like moving items or taking long trips. Many people don't want the costs or responsibilities of owning a car. The car-sharing organization pays for gas, insurance, cleaning, and maintenance costs. Members also don't have to wait in line or fill out forms in order to get a car. They know a variety of cars will be available when they need one.

Car sharing also benefits the environment. People drive only when they need to, and fewer cars on the road means less traffic and pollution. As more cities become interested in reducing traffic, car-sharing programs are becoming an effective alternative to owning a car.

Gerunds and Infinitives 393

Part II. Complete the sentences with information from Part I. Use gerunds or infinitives.

1. _____ is helpful to people who don't own a car.
2. People pay a fee in order _____ a car-sharing organization.
3. Car-sharing members pay an hourly or daily rate for _____ a car.
4. Sometimes people need a car to _____ furniture or to _____ a trip.
5. Many people don't want the costs of _____ a car.
6. Cities are interested in _____ traffic.

EXERCISE 43 ▶ Warm-up: pairwork. (Charts 13-10)
Work with a partner. Read the conversation aloud and complete the sentences with the correct words in the box.

| strong | heavy | strength |

PARTNER A: Can you pick up a piano?

PARTNER B: No. It's too _____₁_____ for me to pick up.

How about you? Can you pick up a piano?

PARTNER A: No, I'm not _____₂_____ enough to pick

one up. What about the class? Can we pick up a piano together?

PARTNER B: Maybe. We might have enough _____₃_____ to do that as a class.

13-10 Using Infinitives with *Too* and *Enough*

	TOO + ADJECTIVE + (FOR SOMEONE) + INFINITIVE			Infinitives often follow expressions with *too*. *Too* comes in front of an adjective. In the speaker's mind, the use of *too* implies a negative result.
(a) That box is	**too** heavy		**to** lift.	
(b) A piano is	**too** heavy	**for** me	**to** lift.	
(c) That box is	**too** heavy	**for** Bob	**to** lift.	
	ENOUGH + NOUN + INFINITIVE			COMPARE: The box is too heavy. I can't lift it. The box is very heavy, but I can lift it.
(d) I don't have	**enough** money		**to** buy that car.	
(e) Did you have	**enough** time		**to** finish the test?	
	ADJECTIVE + ENOUGH + INFINITIVE			Infinitives often follow expressions with *enough*. **Enough** comes in front of a noun.* **Enough** follows an adjective.
(f) Jimmy isn't	old **enough**		**to** go to school.	
(g) Are you	hungry **enough**		**to** eat three sandwiches?	

*****Enough** can also follow a noun: *I don't have **money enough** to buy that car.* In everyday English, however, **enough** usually comes in front of a noun.

EXERCISE 44 ▶ Looking at grammar. (Chart 13-10)
Look at each picture and complete the sentences. Use *too* or *enough* + *an infinitive*.

Picture 1

1. a. *heavy / carry*   The backpack is ___too heavy___ for the boy ___to carry___.
   b. *strong / carry* The boy is not ___strong enough to carry___ the backpack.
   c. *big / carry*   The backpack is not _____ all his things.
   d. *small / carry*   The boy is _____ the backpack.
   e. *full / carry*   The backpack is _____ more things.
   f. *old / carry*   Is the boy _____ such a heavy backpack?
   g. *young / carry*   Is the boy _____ such a heavy backpack?

Picture 2

2. a. *complicated / understand* The problem is _____.
   b. *smart / figure out*   The student doesn't feel _____ the problem.
   c. *hard / figure out*   Is the problem _____ for the student _____?
   d. *clear / understand*   The explanation isn't _____.

EXERCISE 45 ▸ Looking at grammar. (Chart 13-10)
Part I. Combine each pair of sentences with ***too***.

1. We can't go swimming today. It's very cold.
   → It's ***too*** cold (*for us*) ***to go*** swimming today.
2. I couldn't finish my homework last night. I was very sleepy.
3. Mike couldn't go to his aunt's housewarming party. He was very busy.
4. This jacket is very small. I can't wear it.
5. I live far from school. I can't walk there.

Part II. Combine each pair of sentences with ***enough***.

6. I can't reach the top shelf. I'm not that tall.
   → *I'm not tall **enough to reach** the top shelf.*
7. I can't move this furniture. I'm not very strong.
8. It's not warm today. You can't go outside without a coat.
9. I didn't stay home and miss work. I wasn't really sick, but I didn't feel good all day.

EXERCISE 46 ▸ Let's talk: pairwork. (Chart 13-10)
Work with a partner. Take turns completing the sentences with infinitives.

Partner A	Partner B
1. I'm too short … .	6. A sports car is too expensive … .
2. I'm not tall enough … .	7. I don't have enough money … .
3. I'm not strong enough … .	8. Yesterday I didn't have enough time … .
4. Last night I was too tired … .	9. A teenager is old enough … but too young … .
5. Yesterday I was too busy … .	10. I know enough English … but not enough … . *Change roles.*

EXERCISE 47 ▸ Looking at grammar. (Chapter 13 Review)
Complete each sentence with the gerund or infinitive form of the word in parentheses.

1. It's difficult for me (*remember*) __to remember__ phone numbers.
2. My cat is good at (*catch*) __catching__ mice.
3. I called my friend (*invite*) _____ her for dinner.
4. Fatima talked about (*go*) _____ to graduate school.
5. Sarosh found out what was happening by (*listen*) _____ carefully to everything that was said.

6. Michelle works 16 hours a day in order (*earn*) _____ enough money (*take*) _____ care of her elderly parents and her three children.

7. No matter how wonderful a trip is, it's always good (*get*) _____ back home and (*sleep*) _____ in your own bed.

8. I keep (*forget*) _____ to call my friend Jae. I'd better write myself a note.

9. Exercise is good for you. Why don't you walk up the stairs instead of (*use*) _____ the elevator?

EXERCISE 48 ▶ Check your knowledge. (Chapter 13 Review)
Correct the errors in the use of infinitives, gerunds, prepositions, and word order.

1. It is important ~~getting~~ *to get* an education.

2. I went to the bank for cashing a check.

3. Did you go to shopping yesterday?

4. I cut the rope by a knife.

5. I thanked my friend for drive me to the airport.

6. Is difficult to learn another language.

7. Timmy isn't enough old to get married.

8. Is easy this exercise to do.

9. Last night too tired no do my homework.

10. I've never gone to sailing, but I would like to.

11. Reading it is one of my hobbies.

12. The teenagers began to built a campfire to keep themselves warm.

13. Instead of settle down in one place, I'd like to travel around the world.

14. I enjoy to travel because you learn so much about other countries and cultures.

15. My grandmother likes to fishing.

16. Martina would like to has a big family.

EXERCISE 49 ▶ Reading and grammar. (Chapter 13)

Part I. Read the passage.

Do you know these words?
- *embarrassing*
- *manufacture*
- *shipping company*
- *take a deep breath*
- *ground floor*
- *helplessly*
- *grab*
- *incident*

An Embarrassing Experience

Have you ever had an embarrassing experience? My Uncle Ernesto did while he was on a business trip in Norway.

Uncle Ernesto is a businessman from Buenos Aires, Argentina. He manufactures equipment for ships and needs to travel around the world to sell his products. Last year, he went to Norway to meet with a shipping company. While he was there, he found himself in an uncomfortable situation.

Uncle Ernesto was staying at a small hotel in Oslo. One morning, as he was getting ready to take a shower, he heard a knock at the door. He opened it, but no one was there. He stepped into the hallway. He still didn't see anyone, so he turned to go back to his room. Unfortunately, the door was locked. This was a big problem because he didn't have his key, and he was wearing only a towel.

Instead of standing in the hallway like this, he decided to get help at the front desk and started walking toward the elevator. He hoped to find an empty elevator, but the one that stopped had people in it. He took a deep breath and got in. The people in the elevator were surprised when they saw a man with a towel around him.

Uncle Ernesto thought about trying to explain his problem, but unfortunately he didn't know Norwegian. He knew a little English, so he said, "Door. Locked. No key." A businessman in the elevator nodded, but he wasn't smiling. Another man looked at Uncle Ernesto with a friendly smile.

The elevator seemed to move very slowly for Uncle Ernesto, but it finally reached the ground floor. He walked straight to the front desk and looked at the hotel manager helplessly. The hotel manager didn't have to understand any language to figure out the problem. He grabbed a key and led my uncle to the nearest elevator.

My uncle is still embarrassed about this incident. But he laughs a lot when he tells the story.

Part II. Check (✓) all the sentences that are grammatically correct.

1. a. _____ Uncle Ernesto went to Norway for a business meeting.
   b. _____ Uncle Ernesto went to Norway to have a business meeting.
   c. _____ Uncle Ernesto went to Norway for having a business meeting.

2. a. _____ Is necessary for him to travel in order to sell his products.
   b. _____ To sell his products, he needs to travel.
   c. _____ In order to sell his products, he needs to travel.

3. a. _____ Instead staying in the hall, he decided to get help.
   b. _____ Instead of staying in the hall, he decided to get help.
   c. _____ Instead to stay in the hall, he decided to get help.

4. a. _____ Uncle Ernesto thought about trying to explain his problem.
   b. _____ Uncle Ernesto considered about trying to explain his problem.
   c. _____ Uncle Ernesto decided not to explain his problem.

5. a. _____ It wasn't difficult for the hotel manager figuring out the problem.
   b. _____ It wasn't difficult for the hotel manager figure out the problem.
   c. _____ It wasn't difficult for the hotel manager to figure out the problem.

EXERCISE 50 ▶ Reading and writing. (Chapter 13)

Part I. Read the passage.

My Most Embarrassing Experience

My most embarrassing experience happened at work. One morning, I was in a hurry to get to my office, so I quickly said good-bye to my wife. She knew I was planning to give an important presentation at my firm, so she wished me good luck and kissed me on the cheek. Because traffic was heavy, I got to work a few minutes after the meeting had begun. I quietly walked in and sat down. A few people looked at me strangely, but I thought it was because I was late. During my presentation, I got more stares. I began to think my presentation wasn't very good, but I continued speaking. As soon as my talk was over, I went to the restroom. When I looked in the mirror, it wasn't hard to see the problem. There was a smudge of red lipstick on my cheek. I felt pretty embarrassed, but later in the day I started laughing about it and tried not to take myself so seriously.

Part II. Write a narrative paragraph about one of the most embarrassing experiences you have had in your life. Include some gerunds and infinitives in your writing.

WRITING TIP

A narrative paragraph tells a story or describes an event. It has a strong beginning, middle, and end. Follow these steps:

1. Set the scene with your topic sentence.
2. Tell what happened step by step. Time words/expressions help the reader follow your story. Note these examples in the above paragraph: *One morning, During my presentation, As soon as, When, later in the day.*
3. Finish with a strong concluding sentence.

Part III. Edit your writing. Check for the following:

1. ☐ use of some gerunds and infinitives
2. ☐ correct gerund forms
3. ☐ correct infinitive forms
4. ☐ use of some time words and expressions to help the reader follow the events
5. ☐ topic and concluding sentences
6. ☐ correct spelling (use a dictionary or spell-check)

▰▰▰▰▰ For digital resources, go to MyEnglishLab on the Pearson English Portal. You can also go to the Pearson Practice English app for mobile practice.

CHAPTER 14

Noun Clauses

PRETEST: What do I already know?
Write "C" if the sentences are correct and "I" if they are incorrect.

1. _____ I don't know how much this phone costs. (Chart 14-1)
2. _____ Do you know whose is this seat? (Chart 14-2)
3. _____ Dr. Mackey is wondering her patient will get better. (Chart 14-3)
4. _____ Tommy dreamed a two-headed monster was chasing him. (Chart 14-4)
5. _____ Is true that are you getting married? (Chart 14-5)
6. _____ A: Is Dorothy going to be 100 years old next week? (Chart 14-6)
    B: I think so.
7. _____ Professor Rico said, "Learning another language is hard work." "It takes a long time." (Chart 14-7)
8. _____ Thomas said that he needed a ride to work. (Chart 14-8)
9. _____ Emma said that she had studied Japanese in Tokyo. (Chart 14-9)
10. _____ Jan told to us that she needed to go home early. (Chart 14-10)

EXERCISE 1 ▸ Warm-up. (Chart 14-1)
Check (✓) all the grammatically correct sentences.

1. _____ How much does a smart watch cost?
2. _____ I don't know how much a smart watch costs.
3. _____ How much a smart watch costs?
4. _____ I don't know how much does a smart watch costs.

14-1 Noun Clauses: Introduction

(a) I know **his address**. 　　　S　V　　　O 　　　　(noun phrase)	Verbs are often followed by objects. The object is usually a noun phrase.* In (a): **his address** is a noun phrase; 　　　　**his address** is the object of the verb *know*.
(b) I know **where he lives**. 　　　S　V　　　O 　　　　(noun clause)	Some verbs can be followed by noun clauses.* In (b): **where he lives** is a noun clause; 　　　　**where he lives** is the object of the verb *know*.
(c) I know **where he lives**. 　　S　V　　S　V 　　　　　　O	A noun clause has its own subject and verb. In (c): **he** is the subject of the noun clause; 　　　　**lives** is the verb of the noun clause.
(d) I know **where my book is**. 　　　　(noun clause)	A noun clause can begin with a question word. (See Chart 14-2.)
(e) I don't know **if Ed is married**. 　　　　(noun clause)	A noun clause can begin with *if* or *whether*. (See Chart 14-3.)
(f) I know **that the world is round**. 　　　　(noun clause)	A noun clause can begin with *that*. (See Chart 14-4.)

*A *phrase* is a group of related words. It does NOT contain a subject and a verb.
A *clause* is a group of related words. It contains a subject and a verb.

EXERCISE 2 ▶ Looking at grammar. (Chart 14-1)
Underline the noun clauses. One sentence has no noun clause.

Former Neighbors

1. Where are the Smiths living?
2. I don't know where the Smiths are living.
3. We don't know what city they moved to.
4. We know that they moved a month ago.
5. Are they coming back?
6. I don't know if they are coming back.

EXERCISE 3 ▶ Warm-up: pairwork. (Chart 14-2)
Work with a partner. Ask and answer the questions. Make true statements.

1. PARTNER A: Where do I live?
   PARTNER B: I know / don't know where you live.

2. PARTNER B: Where does our teacher live?
   PARTNER A: I know / don't know where our teacher lives.

3. PARTNER B: In your last sentence, why is *does* missing?
   PARTNER A: I know / don't know why *does* is missing.

4. PARTNER A: In the same sentence, why does *lives* have an "s"?
   PARTNER B: I know / don't know why *lives* has an "s."

14-2 Noun Clauses That Begin with a Question Word

These question words can be used to introduce a noun clause: *when, where, why, how, who, (whom), what, which, whose*.

Information Question	Noun Clause	
Where *does he live*?	(a) I don't know *where he lives*.	Note in examples (a)–(f): Usual question word order is NOT used in a noun clause. INCORRECT: *I know where does he live.* CORRECT: *I know where he lives.* Note the question mark in (b), which includes a noun clause as part of the question.
When *did they leave*?	(b) Do you know *when they left*?	
What *did she say*?	(c) Please tell me *what she said*.	
Why *is Tom* absent?	(d) I wonder *why Tom is* absent.	
Who *is that boy*?	(e) Tell me *who that boy is*.	A noun or pronoun that follows main verb *be* in a question comes in front of *be* in a noun clause, as in (e) and (f).
Whose pen *is this*?	(f) Do you know *whose pen this is*?	
Who is in the office?	(g) I don't know *who is* in the office.	A prepositional phrase (e.g., *in the office*) does not come in front of *be* in a noun clause, as in (g) and (h).
Whose keys are on the counter?	(h) I wonder *whose keys are* on the counter.	
Who came to class?	(i) I don't know *who came* to class.	In (i) and (j): Question word order and noun clause word order are the same when the question word is used as a subject.
What happened?	(j) Tell me *what happened*.	

EXERCISE 4 ▸ Looking at grammar. (Charts 5-2 and 14-2)

Part I. If the sentence contains a noun clause, <u>underline</u> it and circle *noun clause*. If the question word introduces a question, circle *question*. Add final punctuation.

Campus Questions

1. Where is the library   noun clause   question
2. I'm not sure where the library is   noun clause   question
3. What time does the bookstore open   noun clause   question
4. Do you know what time the bookstore opens   noun clause   question
5. I wonder how we get tickets to the basketball game   noun clause   question
6. Do you know how we get tickets to the basketball game   noun clause   question

Part II. Compete the sentences with the given words. You may need to change the verb form. Add final punctuation.

1. *the bus / come*
    a. When __does the bus come?__
    b. I don't know when __the bus comes.__

2. *the bookstore / is*
    a. How far _____
    b. I don't know how far _____

3. *students / park their cars*
    a. Where _____
    b. Tell me where _____

4. *the gym / close early yesterday*
    a. Why did _____
    b. I'd like to know why _____

EXERCISE 5 ▸ Looking at grammar. (Chart 14-2)
Choose the correct completions.

Questions Children Ask

1. Why ____ hot?
    a. is fire   b. fire is

2. I don't know why ____ hot.
    a. is fire   b. fire is

3. Do you know what ____ made of?
    a. the moon is   b. is the moon

4. Can you tell me why ____ blue?
    a. the sky is   b. is the sky

5. Can you explain where ____ from?
    a. does wind come b. wind comes

6. Why ____ a tail?
    a. does a dog have b. a dog has

7. I don't know why ____ a tail.
    a. does a dog have b. a dog has

8. Do you know why ____?
    a. people die   b. do people die

9. How many bones _____?
   a. do I have   b. I have

10. Can you explain why _____ salt water?
    a. an ocean has   b. does an ocean have

EXERCISE 6 ▸ Let's talk: pairwork. (Chart 14-2)
Work with a partner. Take turns asking questions. Begin with **Can you tell me**.

Questions to a Teacher

1. How do I pronounce this word? → *Can you tell me how I pronounce this word?*
2. What does this mean?
3. When will I get my grades?
4. What is our next assignment?
5. How soon is the next assignment due?
6. Why is this incorrect?
7. When is a good time to meet?
8. What day does the term end?
9. Why did I fail?
10. Who will teach this class next term?

EXERCISE 7 ▸ Looking at grammar. (Chart 14-2)
Complete the responses with noun clauses.

A Subway Ride

1. A: What is the next stop?
   B: I don't know _what the next stop is_ .

2. A: How often does the train come?
   B: I don't know _how often the train comes_ .

3. A: Where do you want to sit?
   B: I don't know _____ .

4. A: Where do we get off?
   B: I'll ask _____ .

5. A: Who's going to meet us?
   B: I'm not sure _____.

6. A: Whose phone is on the floor?
   B: I don't know _____.

7. A: What's that noise?
   B: I don't know _____.

8. A: Why are we stopping now?
   B: I have no idea _____.

9. A: Why is the alarm going off?
   B: I don't know _____.

10. A: What time is the last train?
    B: I'm not sure _____.

EXERCISE 8 ▶ Let's talk: pairwork. (Chart 14-2)
Work with a partner. Take turns asking questions. Begin with **Do you know**.

Questions at Home

1. Where is the phone?
2. Why is the front door open?
3. Who just called?
4. Whose socks are on the floor?
5. Why are all the lights on?
6. There's water all over the floor. What happened?
7. What did the plumber say about the broken pipe?
8. What is the repair going to cost?

EXERCISE 9 ▶ Looking at grammar. (Charts 5-2 and 14-2)
Complete the sentences with the correct form of the words in parentheses. There may be more than one answer for some.

Parents to Teens

1. A: Where (*you, go*) ___*did you go*___ last night?
   B: I thought Dad told you where (*we, go*) ___*we went*___ last night.

2. A: It looks like you're getting ready to leave. Where (*you, go*) _____?
   B: I'm sorry. I didn't catch that.
   A: Oh, I was wondering where (*you, go*) _____.

3. A: Who (*you, text*) _____ right now?
   B: Why are you asking who (*I, text*) _____?

4. A: What time (*you, get*) _____ home last night?
   B: Who?
   A: You! I want to know what time (*you, get*) _____ home.
   B: Uh, kind of late.

5. A: Who (*you, meeting*) _____
   _____ after school tomorrow?
   B: I thought I told you who (*I, meet*) _____
   _____ after school.

6. A: When (*you, have*) _____ time to do your homework tomorrow?
   B: Pardon?
   A: I was wondering when (*you, have*) _____ time to do your homework.

7. A: What day (*your final exam, be*) _____
   _____ ?
   B: I'm not yet sure what day (*my final exam / be*) _____
   _____ .

8. A: It looks like you were up all night. How much (*you, sleep*) _____ ?
   B: You want to know how much (*I, sleep*) _____ ?
   A: Yes, you look really tired.

EXERCISE 10 ▶ Warm-up. (Chart 14-3)
Check (✓) all the grammatically correct sentences.

Is Sam at work?

1. _____ I don't know if Sam is at work.
2. _____ I don't know Sam is at work.
3. _____ I don't know if Sam is at work or not.
4. _____ I don't know whether Sam is at work.

14-3 Noun Clauses That Begin with *If* or *Whether*

Yes/No Question	Noun Clause	
Is Eric at home? Does the bus stop here? Did Ava go to Bangkok?	(a) I don't know *if Eric is at home*. (b) Do you know *if the bus stops here*? (c) I wonder *if Ava went to Bangkok*.	When a *yes/no* question is changed to a noun clause, *if* is usually used to introduce the clause.*
(d) I don't know *if Eric is at home or not*.		When *if* introduces a noun clause, the expression *or not* sometimes comes at the end of the clause, as in (d).
(e) I don't know *whether Eric is at home (or not)*.		In (e): *whether* has the same meaning as *if*.

*See Chart 14-10 for the use of *if* with *ask* in reported speech.

EXERCISE 11 ▶ Looking at grammar. (Chart 14-3)

Change the *yes/no* questions to noun clauses. Add final punctuation.

Buying a Car

1. YES/NO QUESTION: Is the price negotiable?
   NOUN CLAUSE: Can you tell me _if/whether the price is negotiable?_

2. YES/NO QUESTION: Are online prices going to be better?
   NOUN CLAUSE: I'd like to know _____

3. YES/NO QUESTION: Is there a warranty?
   NOUN CLAUSE: Could you tell me _____

4. YES/NO QUESTION: Are other colors available?
   NOUN CLAUSE: Could you check _____

5. YES/NO QUESTION: Is the car I want here?
   NOUN CLAUSE: Do you know _____

6. YES/NO QUESTION: Has the car been in an accident?
   NOUN CLAUSE: Can you check _____

7. YES/NO QUESTION: Do you take trade-ins?
   NOUN CLAUSE: I'd like to know _____

8. YES/NO QUESTION: Does this car have a backup camera?
   NOUN CLAUSE: Can you tell me _____

EXERCISE 12 ▶ Looking at grammar. (Chart 14-3)
Complete the noun clause in each conversation. Use *if* to introduce the noun clause.

What was that?

1. A: Are you leaving?

   B: Sorry, I didn't catch that.

   A: I wanted to know ___*if you are leaving*___.

2. A: Are you going to pick up the groceries?

   B: Pardon?

   A: I need to know _____ pick up the groceries.

3. A: Did you take my phone by accident?

   B: You had an accident?

   A: No! I want to know _____ my phone by accident.

4. A: Would you like to go to a movie tonight?

   B: Sorry – it's noisy in here. What was that?

   A: I'm wondering _____ to a movie tonight.

5. A: Are my car keys in the kitchen?

   B: Why are you asking me that? I have no idea _____ in the kitchen.

   A: Someone woke up on the wrong side of the bed*!

6. A: Is there gas in the car?

   B: What was that?

   A: I'm asking _____.

EXERCISE 13 ▶ Let's talk: interview. (Charts 14-2 and 14-3)
Interview your classmates. Begin your questions with ***Do you know***. Answer with ***I know*** or ***I don't know***.

1. What does it cost to fly from London to Paris?
2. When was this building built?
3. How far is it from Vancouver, Canada, to Riyadh, Saudi Arabia?
4. Is Australia the smallest continent?
5. How many eyes does a bat have?
6. What is one of the longest words in English?
7. Does a chimpanzee have a good memory?

---

*wake up on the wrong side of the bed = wake up in a bad mood

8. How old is the Great Wall of China?
9. Do all birds fly?
10. Did birds come from dinosaurs?

EXERCISE 14 ▶ Let's talk. (Charts 14-2 and 14-3)
Work in small groups. Choose a famous movie star or celebrity. Make complete statements using noun clauses and the given words. Share some of your sentences with the class. See if anyone knows the information.

1. What do you wonder about him/her?
   a. where → *I wonder where she lives.*
   b. what
   c. if
   d. who
   e. how
   f. why

2. What do you want to ask him/her?
   a. who → *I want to ask him who his friends are.*
   b. when
   c. what
   d. whether
   e. why
   f. where

EXERCISE 15 ▶ Let's talk: pairwork. (Charts 14-2 and 14-3)
Work with a partner. Partner A asks the question. Partner B restates it with *I'd like to know*.

At a Bank

PARTNER A	PARTNER B
1. What is the exchange rate?	1. Can I apply for a credit card?
2. Is there a fee for the ATM?	2. What ID do you need?
3. Are checks free?	3. What is the late fee for a credit card payment?
4. When will my debit card come?	4. What is the minimum amount to open an account?
5. What is the interest rate for a savings account?	5. Is the account free?
	Change roles.

EXERCISE 16 ▶ Warm-up. (Chart 14-4)
Check (✓) all the grammatically correct sentences. Which checked sentences do you agree with?

1. ____ I think that noun clauses are hard.
2. ____ I think that this exercise is easy.
3. ____ I suppose that this chapter is useful.
4. ____ Is interesting this chapter I think.

14-4 Noun Clauses That Begin with *That*

(a) I think *that Mr. Jones is a good teacher*. S V O (b) I hope *that you can come to the game*. (c) Mary realizes *that she should study harder*. (d) I dreamed *that I was on the top of a mountain*.	A noun clause can be introduced by the word ***that***. In (a): *that Mr. Jones is a good teacher* is a noun clause. It is the object of the verb ***think***. *That*-clauses are frequently used as the objects of verbs that express mental activity.
(e) I think *that* Mr. Jones is a good teacher. (f) I think Ø Mr. Jones is a good teacher.	The word ***that*** is often omitted, especially in speaking. Examples (e) and (f) have the same meaning.

Common Verbs Followed by *That*-clauses

agree that	dream that	know that	realize that
assume that	feel that	learn that	remember that
believe that	forget that	notice that	say that
decide that	guess that	predict that	suppose that
discover that	hear that	prove that	think that
doubt that	hope that	read that	understand that

💬 **EXERCISE 17 ▶ Grammar and speaking.** (Chart 14-4)

Add the word ***that*** to mark the beginning of a noun clause. Choose *yes* if you agree or *no* if you disagree. Then tell your partner your opinions by making true statements.

Social Media

1. I feel ^*that* people spend too much time on social media.   yes   no

2. I think social media is a good way for teens to communicate.   yes   no

3. I don't believe young children need to use social media.   yes   no

4. I think social media posts generally have correct information.   yes   no

5. Do you agree schools should teach kids how to use social media wisely?   yes   no

6. Do you think parents need to read their children's social media posts?   yes   no

EXERCISE 18 ▶ Let's talk: pairwork. (Chart 14-4)
Work with a partner. Take turns asking and answering questions. Use *that*-clauses. Share some of your partner's answers with the class.

1. What have you noticed about English grammar?
2. What have you heard in the news recently?
3. What did you dream recently?
4. What do you believe about people?
5. What can scientists prove?
6. What can't scientists prove?

EXERCISE 19 ▶ Warm-up. (Chart 14-5)
Check (✓) the sentences that you agree with.

1. ____ I'm sure that vitamins give people more energy.
2. ____ It's true that vitamins help people live longer.
3. ____ It's a fact that vitamins help people look younger.

14-5 Other Uses of *That*-Clauses

(a) **I'm sure that** the bus stops here. (b) **I'm glad that** you're feeling better today. (c) **I'm sorry that** I missed class yesterday. (d) **I was disappointed that** you couldn't come.	*That*-clauses can follow certain expressions with **be** + *adjective* or **be** + *past participle*. The word **that** can be omitted with no change in meaning: I'm sure Ø the bus stops here.

(e) **It is true that** the world is round.
 (f) **It is a fact that** the world is round.
	Note two common expressions followed by *that*-clauses:
	    It is true (that) ...
	    It is a fact (that) ...

Common Expressions Followed by *That*-clauses

be afraid that	be disappointed that	be sad that	be upset that
be angry that	be glad that	be shocked that	be worried that
be aware that	be happy that	be sorry that	
be certain that	be lucky that	be sure that	It is a fact that
be convinced that	be pleased that	be surprised that	It is true that

EXERCISE 20 ▶ Looking at grammar. (Chart 14-5)
Add *that* where possible.

At a Party

1. A: Welcome. We're glad ^*that* you could come.

   B: Thank you. I'm happy I was able to make it.

2. A: Thank you so much for your gift.

   B: I'm pleased you like it.

3. A: Are you surprised Paulo came but not Andrea?

   B: Yes! I'm certain she was invited.

4. A: Are you aware we are running out of food?

   B: No, we're not! I'm sure there's more in the kitchen.

EXERCISE 21 ▶ Let's talk. (Charts 14-4 and 14-5)
Part I. Work in small groups. Look at the health treatments below. Which ones do you know about? You may need to check your dictionary.

| acupuncture | massage | naturopathy |
| hypnosis | meditation | yoga |

Part II. Complete the sentences with words in the box. Use noun clauses. Discuss your sentences with other students.

1. I believe/think _____ is useful for _____.
2. I am certain _____.
3. I am not convinced _____.

EXERCISE 22 ▶ Listening and grammar. (Charts 14-4 and 14-5)
Listen to each conversation and then complete the sentences. Answers may vary.

Example: You will hear: MAN: I heard Jack is in jail. I can't believe it!
                          WOMAN: Neither can I! The police said he robbed a house. They must have the wrong person.

You will say: a. The man is shocked that <u>Jack is in jail</u>.
               b. The woman is sure that <u>the police have the wrong person</u>.

1. a. The woman thinks that …
   b. The man is glad that …

2. a. The mother is worried that …
   b. Her son is sure that …

3. a. The man is surprised that …
   b. The woman is disappointed that …

4. a. The man is happy that …
   b. The woman is pleased that …

5. a. The woman is afraid* that …
   b. The man is sure that …

---

*Sometimes **be afraid** expresses fear:
   I don't want to go near that dog. I'm afraid that it will bite me.
Sometimes **be afraid** expresses polite regret:
   I'm afraid you have the wrong number. = *I'm sorry, but I think you have the wrong number.*
   I'm afraid I can't come to your party. = *I'm sorry, but I can't come to your party.*

EXERCISE 23 ▶ Reading and speaking. (Charts 14-1 and 14-3 → 14-5)

Part I. Read the blog entry by co-author Stacy Hagen. Look at the sentences in green. Which ones have noun clauses? <u>Underline</u> the noun clauses.

BlackBookBlog

Do you know these words?
- step back
- step forward
- rude
- back away
- signal
- distance
- acceptable
- imagine
- scene
- misunderstandings

Personal Space

Sometimes a student stands really close to me during a conversation. I take a step back and the student steps forward. I take another step back, but the student moves forward again. What is happening? Is it rude when I step back? Do you think that I am being unfriendly?

My behavior is actually about personal space. When two people are talking, and one person backs away, this is a signal. The person is uncomfortable with the distance between the two of them.

The acceptable distance can be different in different cultures. Imagine the following scene. You get into an elevator. There are two people already there, one in each corner. Think about where you will stand. If you are in the U.S. or Canada and stand close to one of them, that person will probably move away from you. Americans and Canadians feel uncomfortable when others get too close to them. They like to have some space around them.

Let's say you are on a subway. The car is empty except for you and a woman. A man enters and sits down next to the woman. How do you think the woman will feel? Is she going to be comfortable? The answer is most likely "no." This is generally very strange behavior. It's possible that the woman will even feel that she is in danger.

It is important that you understand personal space. You don't want misunderstandings to occur because of how close you stand or sit next to someone.

Part II. Work with a partner. Answer the following questions.

1. Were you aware of the information in this blog? What specifically? Did anything surprise you?

2. What feels normal for personal space in your culture? Show it by standing and talking to one another. If you are living in another country, practice standing acceptable distances from one another.

3. Look at the picture in the blog. Imagine a woman is coming into the waiting area. She understands personal space customs. Where will she sit? Or, where won't she sit?

4. When you meet a person for the first time, how do you greet him or her? What about a friend? Is there any kind of touching, e.g., shaking hands? How much distance is there?

5. What do you do if someone is standing or sitting too close to you?

EXERCISE 24 ▸ Warm-up. (Chart 14-6)
Choose all the statements that are true for each conversation.

1. A: Did Jonathan remember to get food for dinner tonight?
   B: I think so.
   a. Speaker B thinks Jonathan got food for dinner.
   b. Speaker B is sure that Jonathan got food for dinner.
   c. Speaker B doesn't know for sure if Jonathan got food for dinner.

2. A: Is Jonathan going to cook dinner?
   B: I hope not.
   a. Speaker B says Jonathan is not going to cook dinner.
   b. Speaker B doesn't know if Jonathan is going to cook dinner.
   c. Speaker B doesn't want Jonathan to cook dinner.

14-6 Substituting *So* for a *That*-Clause in Conversational Responses

(a) A: Is Ana from Peru? B: **I think so.** (so = that Ana is from Peru) (b) A: Does Olivia live in Montreal? B: **I believe so.** (so = that Olivia lives in Montreal) (c) A: Did you pass the test? B: **I hope so.** (so = that I passed the test)	**Think**, **believe**, and **hope** are frequently followed by **so** in conversational English in response to a *yes/no* question. **So** replaces a *that*-clause. INCORRECT: *I think so that Ana is from Peru.*
(d) A: Is Jack married? B: **I don't think so. / I don't believe so.**	Negative usage of **think so** and **believe so**: *do not think so / do not believe so*
(e) A: Did you fail the test? B: **I hope not.**	Negative usage of **hope** in conversational responses: *hope not*. In (e): **I hope not** = *I hope I didn't fail the test*. INCORRECT: *I don't hope so.*

(f) A: Do you want to come with us?
B: Oh, I don't know. **I guess so.**
	Other common conversational responses:
	   I guess so. *I guess not.*
	   I suppose so. *I suppose not.*
	NOTE: In spoken English, **suppose** often sounds like "spoze."

EXERCISE 25 ▶ Looking at grammar. (Chart 14-6)

Restate Speaker B's answers by using a *that*-clause.

Weather Questions

1. A: Is the sun going to come out?

   B: I hope so.

   → *I hope that the sun is going to come out.*

2. A: Will it rain tonight?

   B: I hope not.

3. A: Is a storm coming?

   B: I don't think so.

4. A: Do I hear hail on the roof?

   B: I think so.

5. A: Will the roads be icy tomorrow?

   B: I don't believe so.

EXERCISE 26 ▶ Let's talk: pairwork. (Chart 14-6)

Work with a partner. Take turns asking the questions. If you know the answer, use **Yes** or **No**. If you are not sure, use **I think so** or **I don't think so**.

Example:
SPEAKER A (*book open*):   Does this book have more than 500 pages?
SPEAKER B (*book closed*): Yes, it does. / I don't think so. / etc.

PARTNER A	PARTNER B
1. Do you know how to spell my first name?	1. Do you know how to spell my last name?
2. Is your index finger bigger than your ring finger?	2. Is your left foot bigger than your right foot?
3. Is there a noun clause in this sentence?	3. Do any English words begin with the letter "x"?
4. Does the word *patient* have more than one meaning?	4. Does the word *dozen* have more than one meaning?
5. Do spiders have eyes?	5. Do spiders have noses?
6. Is there a fire extinguisher in this room?	6. Is there a smoke alarm in this room?
7. Is our teacher right-handed?	7. Am I left-handed?
8. Is this the last grammar exercise today?	8. Does our teacher plan to give us homework today?

EXERCISE 27 ▶ Warm-up. (Chart 14-7)
Circle the quotation marks and <u>underline</u> the punctuation inside each quotation. What are the differences in punctuation?

1. "Oh, no!" Vicki cried.

2. "Have you seen my wallet?" she asked.

3. "Maybe it's on the park bench that we were sitting on," I said.

14-7 Quoted Speech

Sometimes we want to quote a speaker's words — to write a speaker's exact words. Exact quotations are used in many kinds of writing, such as newspaper articles, stories, novels, and academic papers. When we quote a speaker's words, we use quotation marks.

(a)	**SPEAKERS' EXACT WORDS** Jane: Cats are fun to watch. Mike: Yes, I agree. They're graceful and playful. Do you have a cat?	(b)	**QUOTING THE SPEAKERS' WORDS** Jane said, "Cats are fun to watch." Mike said, "Yes, I agree. They're graceful and playful. Do you have a cat?"

(c) **HOW TO WRITE QUOTATIONS**

1. Add a comma after *said*.* ─────────────────▶ Jane said**,**
2. Add quotation marks.** ─────────────────────▶ Jane said**,** **"**
3. Capitalize the first word of the quotation. ────────▶ Jane said, **"C**ats
4. Write the quotation. Add a final period. ──────────▶ Jane said, "Cats are fun to watch**.**
5. Add quotation marks **after** the period. ──────────▶ Jane said**,** **"C**ats are fun to watch**."**

(d)	Mike said, "Yes, I agree. They're graceful and playful. Do you have a cat?"	When there are two (or more) sentences in a quotation, put the quotation marks at the beginning and end of the whole quote, as in (d).
(e)	INCORRECT: Mike said, "Yes, I agree." "They're graceful and playful." "Do you have a cat?"	Do NOT put quotation marks around each sentence. As with a period, put the quotation marks after a question mark at the end of a quote.
(f)	"Cats are fun to watch," Jane said.	In (f): Note that a comma (not a period) is used at the end of the QUOTED SENTENCE because ***Jane said*** comes after the quote.
(g)	"Do you have a cat?" Mike asked.	In (g): Note that a question mark (not a comma) is used at the end of the QUOTED QUESTION.

*Other common verbs besides *say* that introduce quotations: *admit, announce, answer, ask, complain, explain, inquire, report, reply, shout, state, write.*

**Quotation marks are called "inverted commas" in British English.

EXERCISE 28 ▸ Looking at grammar. (Chart 14-7)
Make sentences in which you quote the speaker's exact words. Use *said* or *asked*. Punctuate carefully.

Problems

1. JULIANNA: I forgot to pay my credit card bill.
   Julianna said, "I forgot to pay my credit card bill." OR
   "I forgot to pay my credit card bill," Julianna said.

2. RYAN: I'm starving, and there's nothing in the fridge.
   _____
   _____

3. MEGAN: I left my purse at home. I have no bus fare.
   _____
   _____

4. JON: Did you miss the registration deadline too?
   _____
   _____

5. HAILEY: We can't leave. I can't find the car keys.
   _____
   _____

EXERCISE 29 ▸ Looking at grammar. (Chart 14-7)
A teacher recently had a conversation with Roberto. Punctuate their quoted speech.

(TEACHER) You know sign language, don't you I asked Roberto.

(ROBERTO) Yes, I do he replied both my grandparents are deaf.

(TEACHER) I'm looking for someone who knows sign language. A deaf student is going to visit our class next Monday I said. Could you interpret for her I asked.

(ROBERTO) I'd be happy to he answered. Is she going to be a new student?

(TEACHER) Possibly I said. She's interested in seeing what we do in our English classes.

EXERCISE 30 ▶ Warm-up. (Chart 14-8)
Circle the correct words.

Noah and Jenna said that   we / they   were going to share a burger.

They wanted   our / their   sodas first.

14-8 Quoted Speech vs. Reported Speech

QUOTED SPEECH	QUOTED SPEECH = giving a speaker's exact words. Quotation marks are used.*
(a) Ann said, "**I'm** hungry."	
(b) Tom said, "**I need my** pen."	
REPORTED SPEECH	REPORTED SPEECH = giving the idea of a speaker's words. Not all of the exact words are used; pronouns and verb forms may change. Quotation marks are NOT used.*
(c) Ann said (that) **she was** hungry.	
(d) Tom said (that) **he needed his** pen.	**That** is optional; it is more common in writing than in speaking.

*Quoted speech is also called *direct speech*. Reported speech is also called *indirect speech*.

EXERCISE 31 ▶ Looking at grammar. (Chart 14-8)
Change the pronouns from quoted speech to reported speech.

Voicemail

1. Maria said, "I will need help with my project."
   → Maria said that ___she___ would need help with ___her___ project.

2. Ivan said, "I spoke with my client."

   → Ivan said that _____ spoke with _____ client.

3. Ellen said, "I am going to work from my home office the rest of the day."

   → Ellen said that _____ was going to work from _____ home office the rest of the day.

4. Rick said, "I'll meet you and Nora at your house after I finish my work at my house."

   → Rick said that _____ would meet _____ at _____ house after _____ finished _____ work at _____ house.

EXERCISE 32 ▸ Warm-up. (Chart 14-9)

Read the conversation and look at the sentences that describe it. All are correct. What differences do you notice?

JENNY: What are you doing tomorrow?
ELLA: I'm going to take my parents out to dinner.

   a. Ella said she was going to take her parents out to dinner.
   b. Ella just said she is going to take her parents out to dinner.
   c. Last week Ella said she was going to take her parents out to dinner.
   d. Ella says she is going to take her parents out to dinner.

14-9 Verb Forms in Reported Speech

(a) QUOTED: Joe said, "I *feel* good." (b) REPORTED: Joe said (that) he *felt* good. (c) QUOTED: Ken said, "I *am* happy." (d) REPORTED: Ken said (that) he *was* happy.	In formal English, if the reporting verb (e.g., *said*) is in the past, the verb in the noun clause is often also in a past form, as in (b) and (d).
— Ann said, "I am hungry." (e) — What did Ann just say? I didn't hear her. — She said (that) she *is* hungry. (f) — What did Ann say when she got home last night? — She said (that) she *was* hungry.	In informal English, often the verb in the noun clause is not changed to a past form, especially when words are reported *soon after* they are said, as in (e). In *later reporting*, however, or in formal English, a past verb is commonly used, as in (f).
(g) Ann *says* (that) she *is* hungry.	If the reporting verb is present tense (e.g., *says*), no change is made in the noun-clause verb.

QUOTED SPEECH	REPORTED SPEECH (formal or later reporting)	REPORTED SPEECH (informal or immediate reporting)
He said, "I *work* hard."	He said he *worked* hard.	He said he *works* hard.
He said, "I *am working* hard."	He said he *was working* hard.	He said he *is working* hard.
He said, "I *worked* hard."	He said he *had worked* hard.	He said he *worked* hard.
He said, "I *have worked* hard."	He said he *had worked* hard.	He said he *has worked* hard.
He said, "I *am going to work* hard."	He said he *was going to work* hard.	He said he *is going to work* hard.
He said, "I *will work* hard."	He said he *would work* hard.	He said he *will work* hard.
He said, "I *can work* hard."	He said he *could work* hard.	He said he *can work* hard.

EXERCISE 33 ▶ Looking at grammar. (Chart 14-9)
Complete the reported speech sentences. Use formal verb forms.

Updates

1. My advisor said, "I have updated your file."
   → My advisor said (that) she ____had updated____ my file.

2. Kazu said, "I will finish soon."
   → Kazu said (that) he _____ soon.

3. I said, "Leo is meeting us for lunch instead of dinner."
   → I said (that) Leo _____ us for lunch instead of dinner.

4. Ben said, "I paid the overdue electric bill."
   → Ben said (that) he _____ the overdue electric bill.

5. Cyndi said, "I am going be out of town for two weeks."
   → Cyndi said (that) she _____ out of town for two weeks.

6. Ari said, "I can help my cousin move this weekend."
   → Ari said (that) he _____ his cousin move this weekend.

7. Tarik said to me, "I will take you to your appointment tomorrow."
   → Tarik said (that) he _____ me to my appointment tomorrow.

8. Kody said, "I don't feel like going out. I'm dealing with a broken heart."
   → Kody said (that) he _____ like going out. He _____ with a broken heart.

EXERCISE 34 ▶ Looking at grammar. (Charts 14-8 and 14-9)
Change the quoted speech to reported speech. Change the verb in quoted speech to a past form in reported speech if possible.

Did I mention this?

1. Jim said, "I'm getting a pet."
   → *Jim said (that) he was getting a pet.*
2. Kristina said, "I'm allergic to chocolate, nuts, and dairy."
3. Carla said, "I just came back from a trip with my family."
4. Ahmed said, "I have already picked up food for the party."
5. Kate said, "I called my doctor."
6. Mr. Rice said, "I'm going to go to Iceland for vacation."
7. Pedro said, "I will be at your house by noon."
8. Emma said, "I can't afford to buy a new car."
9. Olivia says, "I can't afford to buy a new car."
10. My dad said, "I want to print out some of my photos from my trip on your printer."

EXERCISE 35 ▶ Warm-up. (Chart 14-10)

Choose <u>all</u> the grammatically correct sentences.

1. a. David asked Elena if she would marry him.
   b. David asked Elena would she marry him.
   c. David wanted to know if Elena would marry him.

2. a. Elena said she wasn't ready yet.
   b. Elena told she wasn't ready yet.
   c. Elena told David she wasn't ready yet.

14-10 Common Reporting Verbs: *Tell, Ask, Answer/Reply*

(a) Kay *said* that* she was hungry. (b) Kay *told me* that she was hungry. (c) Kay *told Tom* that she was hungry. INCORRECT: *Kay told that she was hungry.* INCORRECT: *Kay told to me that she was hungry.* INCORRECT: *Kay said me that she was hungry.*	A main verb that introduces reported speech is called a "reporting verb." *Say* is the most common reporting verb** and is usually followed immediately by a noun clause, as in (a). *Tell* is also commonly used. Note that *told* is followed by *me* in (b) and by *Tom* in (c). *Tell* needs to be followed immediately by a (pro)noun object and then by a noun clause.
(d) QUOTED: Ken asked me, "Are you tired?" REPORTED: Ken *asked* (*me*) *if* I was tired.	*Asked* is used to report questions.
(e) Ken *wanted to know if* I was tired. Ken *wondered if* I was tired. Ken *inquired whether or not* I was tired.	Questions are also reported by using *want to know*, *wonder*, and *inquire*.
(f) QUOTED: I said (to Kay), "I am not tired." REPORTED: I *answered / replied* that I wasn't tired.	The verbs *answer* and *reply* are often used to report replies.

*That is optional. See Chart 14-8.

Other common reporting verbs: *Kay **announced / **commented** / **complained** / **explained** / **remarked** / **stated*** that she was hungry.

EXERCISE 36 ▶ Looking at grammar. (Chart 14-10)

Complete the sentences with *said, told,* or *asked*.

By the way,

1. Karen ___told___ me that she would be here at one o'clock.

2. Jamal ___said___ that he was going to get here around two.

3. Sophia ___asked___ me what time we would arrive.

4. William _____ that you had a message.

5. William _____ me that someone had called you around ten-thirty.

6. I _____ William if he knew the caller's name.

7. Alice called. I _____ her that I would help her move into her new apartment next week. She _____ that she would welcome the help. She _____ me if I had a truck or knew anyone who had a truck. I _____ her Dan had a truck. She _____ she would call him.

8. My uncle in Toronto called and _____ that he was organizing a surprise party for my aunt's 60th birthday. He _____ me if we could come to Toronto for the party. I _____ him that we would be happy to come. I _____ when it was. He _____ it was the last weekend in August.

EXERCISE 37 ▸ Let's talk: pairwork. (Charts 14-2, 14-3, and 14-10)

Work with a partner. Write down five questions to ask your partner about his/her life or opinions. Note your partner's answers. Share some of the information with the class. Include both the question and the response. Use either formal or informal verb forms.*

Examples:
PARTNER A's question: Where were you born?
PARTNER B's response: In Nepal.
PARTNER A's report: I asked him where he was born. He told me he was born in Nepal.

PARTNER B's question: Who do you admire most in the world?
PARTNER A's response: I admire my parents.
PARTNER B's report: I asked him who he admires most in the world. He said he admires his parents the most.

EXERCISE 38 ▸ Looking at grammar. (Charts 14-8 → 14-10)

Complete the paragraph based on what the people in the picture are saying. Use the formal sequence of tenses.

---

*In everyday spoken English, native speakers sometimes change formal/later noun-clause verbs to past forms, and sometimes they don't. In an informal reporting situation, either informal/immediate reporting or reporting tenses are appropriate.

One day Katya and Pavel were at a restaurant. Katya picked up her menu and looked at it. Pavel left his menu on the table. Katya asked Pavel _what he was going to have_ . He said
_____ anything because he
                    2
_____ . He _____ already. Katya was
         3   4
surprised. She asked him why _____ . He told her
                                          5
_____ about a problem _____
              6   7
at work.

EXERCISE 39 ▶ Looking at grammar. (Charts 14-8 → 14-10)
Change the reported speech to quoted speech. Begin a new paragraph each time the speaker changes. Pay special attention to pronouns, verb forms, and word order. Answers may vary.

Example:
REPORTED SPEECH: This morning my mother asked me if I had gotten enough sleep last night. I told her that I was fine. I explained that I didn't need a lot of sleep. She told me that I needed to take better care of myself.

QUOTED SPEECH: _This morning my mother asked, "Did you get enough sleep last night?"_
"I'm fine," I replied. "I don't need a lot of sleep."
She said, "You need to take better care of yourself."

1. In the middle of class yesterday, my friend tapped me on the shoulder and asked me what I was doing after class. I told her that I would tell her later.

2. When I was putting on my coat, Robert asked me where I was going. I told him that I had a date with Anna. He wanted to know what we were going to do. I told him that we were going to a movie.

3. This afternoon, a friend called and asked me if I had time to talk. She was thinking about taking a new job in another city. I said that I was at work, and I wasn't free to take a personal call. I asked if she could talk this evening, after dinner.

Noun Clauses   423

EXERCISE 40 ▶ Listening. (Charts 14-8 → 14-10)

Listen to Roger's report of his phone conversation with Angela. Then listen again and write the missing words.

Angela called and _____(1)_____ me where Bill _____(2)_____.
I _____(3)_____ her he _____(4)_____ in the lunchroom. She _____(5)_____ when he _____(6)_____ back. I _____(7)_____ he _____(8)_____ back around 2:00. I _____(9)_____ her if I _____(10)_____ something for her.

She _____(11)_____ that Bill had the information she _____(12)_____, and only he _____(13)_____ her. I _____(14)_____ her that I _____(15)_____ him a message. She thanked me and hung up.

EXERCISE 41 ▶ Reading and speaking. (Chapter 14 Review)

Part I. Read the passage.

THE LAST LECTURE

In 2007, a 47-year-old computer science professor from Carnegie Mellon University was invited to give a lecture at his university. His name was Randy Pausch, and the lecture series was called "The Last Lecture." Pausch was asked to think about what wisdom he would give to people if he knew it was his last opportunity to do so. In Pausch's case, it really was his last lecture because he had cancer and wasn't expected to survive. Pausch gave an uplifting lecture called "Really Achieving Your Childhood Dreams." The lecture was recorded and put on the internet. A reporter for the *Wall Street Journal* was also there and wrote about it. Soon millions of people around the world heard about Pausch's inspiring talk.

Here are some quotes from Randy Pausch:

To the general public:

"Proper apologies have three parts: (1) What I did was wrong. (2) I'm sorry that I hurt you. (3) How do I make it better? It's the third part that people tend to forget."

"If I could only give three words of advice, they would be 'tell the truth.' If I got three more words, I'd add 'all the time.'"

"The key question to keep asking is, 'Are you spending your time on the right things?' Because time is all you have."

"We cannot change the cards we are dealt, just how we play the hand."

> Do you know these words?
> - lecture series
> - wisdom
> - opportunity
> - cancer
> - uplifting
> - achieving
> - inspiring
> - apology
> - tend to
> - key question

> *To his students:* "Whether you think you can or can't, you're right."
>
> *To his children:* "Don't try to figure out what I wanted you to become. I want you to become what you want to become."
>
> Sadly, in 2008, Randy Pausch died. Before his death he was able to put down his thoughts in a book, appropriately called *The Last Lecture*.

💬 **Part II.** Work in small groups. Explain the meaning of each quotation in Part I. Then, individually, choose one of the quotes to agree or disagree with. Use some of the phrases in the box and support your statement with reasons.

> I agree / disagree that
> I believe / don't believe that
> I think / don't think that
> It's true that

EXERCISE 42 ▶ Check your knowledge. (Chapter 14 Review)
Correct the errors.

1. My friend knows where ~~do~~ I live.

2. I don't know what is your email address?

3. I think so that Mr. Lee is out of town.

4. Can you tell me that where Victor is living now?

5. I asked my uncle what kind of movies does he like.

6. I think, that my English has improved a lot.

7. Is true that people are basically the same everywhere in the world.

8. A man came to my door last week. I didn't know who is he.

9. I want to know does Pedro have a laptop computer.

10. Sam and I talked about his classes. He told that he don't like his algebra class.

11. A woman came into the room and ask me Where is your brother?

12. I felt very relieved when the doctor said, you will be fine. It's nothing serious.

13. My mother asked me that: "When you will be home?

EXERCISE 43 ▶ Reading, grammar, and writing. (Chapter 14)

Part I. Read the story. Add quotation marks and other necessary punctuation to the sentences in green. You may need to capitalize some letters.

Do you know these words?
- nest
- the rest
- hatch
- feathers
- clumsy
- slender
- wander
- bed of reeds
- plenty of
- reflection

The Ugly Duckling

Once upon a time, there was a mother duck. She lived on a farm and spent her days sitting on her nest of eggs. One morning, the eggs began to move, and out came six little ducklings. But there was one egg that was bigger than the rest, and it didn't hatch. The mother didn't remember this egg. I thought I had only six, but maybe I counted incorrectly she said.

a mother duck and her ducklings

A short time later, the seventh egg hatched. But this duckling had gray feathers, not brown like his brothers, and was quite ugly. His mother thought, maybe this duck isn't one of mine. He grew faster than his brothers and ate more food. He was very clumsy, and none of the other animals wanted to play with him. Much of the time he was alone.

He felt unloved by everyone, and he decided to run away from the farm. He asked other animals on the way, do you know of any ducklings that look like me? But they just laughed and said you are the ugliest duck we have ever seen. One day, the duckling looked up and saw a group of beautiful birds overhead. They were white, with long, slender necks and large wings. I want to look just like them, the duckling thought.

He wandered alone most of the winter and finally found a comfortable bed of reeds in a pond. He thought to himself, no one wants me. I'll just hide here for the rest of my life. There was plenty of food there, and although he was lonely, he felt a little happier.

By springtime, the duck was quite large. One morning, he saw his reflection in the water. He didn't even recognize himself. A group of swans that was coming back from the south saw him and flew down to the pond. Where have you been? they cried. You're a swan like us. As they began to swim across the pond, a child saw them and exclaimed, look at the youngest swan. He's the most beautiful of all. The swan was filled with happiness, and he lived happily ever after.

a swan

Part II. Work in small groups and answer this question: What lessons does this story teach? Share your answers with the class.

Part III. Write a story that includes quoted speech. Tell the actions or events of your story using verbs in a past tense.

1. Write a fable from your country in which animals speak. (A fable is a traditional story that teaches a lesson about life.) OR Write a story that you learned when you were young.
2. Take five minutes to tell a student your story. Then tell it to another student in four minutes. Finally, take three minutes to tell your story to a third student. The last time you speak should feel more comfortable and easier than the first time.

> **WRITING TIP**
>
> The use of quoted speech can make a story feel more real or immediate to the reader. When you use quotes, it is a good idea to vary the style. *Say* is a common verb for introducing quoted speech, but, as you can see from this story, there are other verbs you can use. You can also vary the position of the verbs used with quoted speech: they can go at the beginning, in the middle, or at the end of a quotation.
>
> Note the different verbs the writer used to introduce quotations in "The Ugly Duckling" and where they are placed. In general, the verb tense used in quoted speech is either in the present or present perfect. Of course, there are exceptions, such as the first quote in the story, which uses the simple past.

Part IV. Edit your writing. Check for the following:

1. ☐ use of some quoted speech
2. ☐ correct punctuation with quotation marks
3. ☐ correct capitalization with quotation marks
4. ☐ in general, use of the present or present perfect tense in quoted speech
5. ☐ in general, use of a past tense to tell the story
6. ☐ correct spelling (use a dictionary or spell-check)

▪▪▪▪▪ For digital resources, go to MyEnglishLab on the Pearson English Portal. You can also go to the Pearson Practice English app for mobile practice.

Appendix

Supplementary Grammar Charts

UNIT A

A-1 The Principal Parts of a Verb

Regular Verbs

SIMPLE FORM	SIMPLE PAST	PAST PARTICIPLE	PRESENT PARTICIPLE
call	called	called	calling
clean	cleaned	cleaned	cleaning
plan	planned	planned	planning
play	played	played	playing
try	tried	tried	trying

Irregular Verbs

eat	ate	eaten	eating
break	broke	broken	breaking
come	came	come	coming
sing	sang	sung	singing
put	put	put	putting

Principal Parts of a Verb

(1)	THE SIMPLE FORM	English verbs have four principal forms, or "parts." *The simple form* is the form that is found in a dictionary. It is the base form with no endings on it (no final *-s*, *-ed*, or *-ing*).
(2)	THE SIMPLE PAST	*The simple past* ends in *-ed* for regular verbs. Most verbs are regular, but many common verbs have irregular past forms.
(3)	THE PAST PARTICIPLE	*The past participle* also ends in *-ed* for regular verbs. Other verbs have irregular past participles. Past participles are used with the perfect tenses (Chapter 4) and the passive (Chapter 10).
(4)	THE PRESENT PARTICIPLE	*The present participle* ends in *-ing* (for both regular and irregular verbs). It is used in progressive tenses (e.g., the present progressive and the past progressive).

The woman *is calling* for help again. Her car *broke* down in the snow. She *called* for a tow truck an hour ago, but no one *has come* yet.

A-2 Common Irregular Verbs: A Reference List

SIMPLE FORM	SIMPLE PAST	PAST PARTICIPLE	SIMPLE FORM	SIMPLE PAST	PAST PARTICIPLE
be	was, were	been	lend	lent	lent
beat	beat	beaten	let	let	let
become	became	become	lie	lay	lain
begin	began	begun	light	lit/lighted	lit/lighted
bend	bent	bent	lose	lost	lost
bite	bit	bitten	make	made	made
blow	blew	blown	mean	meant	meant
break	broke	broken	meet	met	met
bring	brought	brought	pay	paid	paid
build	built	built	put	put	put
burn	burned/burnt	burned/burnt	quit	quit	quit
buy	bought	bought	read	read	read
catch	caught	caught	ride	rode	ridden
choose	chose	chosen	ring	rang	rung
come	came	come	rise	rose	risen
cost	cost	cost	run	ran	run
cut	cut	cut	say	said	said
dig	dug	dug	see	saw	seen
do	did	done	sell	sold	sold
draw	drew	drawn	send	sent	sent
dream	dreamed/dreamt	dreamed/dreamt	set	set	set
drink	drank	drunk	shake	shook	shaken
drive	drove	driven	shoot	shot	shot
eat	ate	eaten	shut	shut	shut
fall	fell	fallen	sing	sang	sung
feed	fed	fed	sink	sank	sunk
feel	felt	felt	sit	sat	sat
fight	fought	fought	sleep	slept	slept
find	found	found	slide	slid	slid
fit	fit	fit	speak	spoke	spoken
fly	flew	flown	spend	spent	spent
forget	forgot	forgotten	spread	spread	spread
forgive	forgave	forgiven	stand	stood	stood
freeze	froze	frozen	steal	stole	stolen
get	got	got/gotten	stick	stuck	stuck
give	gave	given	swim	swam	swum
go	went	gone	take	took	taken
grow	grew	grown	teach	taught	taught
hang	hung	hung	tear	tore	torn
have	had	had	tell	told	told
hear	heard	heard	think	thought	thought
hide	hid	hidden	throw	threw	thrown
hit	hit	hit	understand	understood	understood
hold	held	held	upset	upset	upset
hurt	hurt	hurt	wake	woke/waked	woken/waked
keep	kept	kept	wear	wore	worn
know	knew	known	win	won	won
leave	left	left	write	wrote	written

A-3 The Present Perfect vs. The Past Perfect

PRESENT PERFECT	(a) I am not hungry now. I *have* already *eaten*.	The PRESENT PERFECT expresses an activity that *occurred before now*, at *an unspecified time in the past*, as in (a).
PAST PERFECT	(b) I was not hungry at 1:00 P.M. I *had* already *eaten*.	The PAST PERFECT expresses an activity that *occurred before **another** time in the past*. In (b): I ate at noon. I was not hungry at 1:00 P.M. because I had already eaten before 1:00 P.M.

A-4 The Past Progressive vs. The Past Perfect

PAST PROGRESSIVE	(a) I *was eating* when Bob came.	The PAST PROGRESSIVE expresses an activity that was *in progress at a particular time in the past*. In (a): I began to eat at noon. Bob came at 12:10. My meal was in progress when Bob came.
PAST PERFECT	(b) I *had eaten* when Bob came.	The PAST PERFECT expresses an activity that was *completed before a particular time in the past*. In (b): I finished eating at noon. Bob came at 1:00 P.M. My meal was completed before Bob came.

A-5 Regular Verbs: Pronunciation of -ed Endings

(a)	talked = talk/t/ stopped = stop/t/ missed = miss/t/ watched = watch/t/ washed = wash/t/	Final **-ed** is pronounced /t/ after voiceless sounds. You make a voiceless sound by pushing air through your mouth. No sound comes from your throat. Examples of voiceless sounds: /k/, /p/, /s/, /ch/, /sh/.	
(b)	called = call/d/ rained = rain/d/ lived = live/d/ robbed = rob/d/ stayed = stay/d/	Final **-ed** is pronounced /d/ after voiced sounds. You make a voiced sound from your throat. Your voice box vibrates. Examples of voiced sounds: /l/, /n/, /v/, /b/, and all vowel sounds.	
(c)	waited = wait/əd/ needed = need/əd/	Final **-ed** is pronounced /əd/* after "t" and "d" sounds. In (c): /əd/ adds a syllable to a word.	

*/əd/ is pronounced "ud."

A-6 Pronunciation of Final -s/-es for Verbs and Nouns

Final **-s/-es** on verbs and nouns has three different pronunciations: /s/, /z/, and /əz/.

(a)	meets = meet/s/ helps = help/s/ books = book/s/	Final **-s** is pronounced /s/ after voiceless sounds. In (a): /s/ is the sound of "s" in *bus*. Examples of voiceless sounds: /t/, /p/, /k/.
(b)	needs = need/z/ wear = wear/z/ calls = call/z/ views = view/z/	Final **-s** is pronounced /z/ after voiced sounds. In (b): /z/ is the sound of "z" in *buzz*. Examples of voiced sounds: /d/, /r/, /l/, /m/, /b/, and all vowel sounds.
(c)	wishes = wish/əz/ watches = watch/əz/ passes = pass/əz/ sizes = size/əz/ pages = page/əz/ judges = judge/əz/	Final **-s/-es** is pronounced /əz/* after *-sh, -ch, -s, -z, -ge/-dge* sounds. In (c): /əz/ adds a syllable to a word.

*/əz/ is pronounced "uz."

A-7 Review: Subject and Object Pronouns, Possessive Pronouns, and Possessive Adjectives

SUBJECT PRONOUNS	OBJECT PRONOUNS	POSSESSIVE PRONOUNS	POSSESSIVE ADJECTIVES
I	me	mine	**my** name(s)
you	you	yours	**your** name(s)
she	her	hers	**her** name(s)
he	him	his	**his** name(s)
it	it	its	**its** name(s)
we	us	ours	**our** name(s)
you	you	yours	**your** name(s)
they	them	theirs	**their** name(s)

(a) *We* saw an accident. (b) Sonya saw *it* too. (c) I have my pen. Ella has *hers*. (d) *Her* pen is blue.	Personal pronouns are used as: • subjects, as in (a); • objects, as in (b); OR • to show possession, as in (c) Possessive adjectives also show possession, as in (d).
(e) I have a *book*. *It* is on my desk. (f) I have some *books*. *They* are on my desk.	Use a singular pronoun to refer to a singular noun. In (e): *book* and *it* are both singular. Use a plural pronoun to refer to a plural noun. In (f): *books* and *they* are both plural.
(g) *It's* sunny today. (h) I'm studying about India. I'm interested in *its* history. INCORRECT: *I'm interested in it's history.*	COMPARE: In (g): ***it's*** = *it is* In (h): ***its*** is a possessive adjective: *its history* = *India's history* A possessive adjective has NO apostrophe.

A-8 Comparison of *Yes/No* and Information Question Forms

(Question Word)	Helping Verb	Subject	Main Verb	(Rest of Sentence)	
(a)	*Does*	Leo	*live*	in Montreal?	
(b) Where	*does*	Leo	*live*?		
(c)	*Is*	Sara	*studying*	at the library?	
(d) Where	*is*	Sara	*studying*?		
(e)	*Will*	you	*help*	me?	
(f) When	*will*	you	*help*	me?	
(g)	*Did*	they	*see*	Mario?	
(h) Who(m)	*did*	they	*see*?		
(i)	*Is*	Olaf		at home?	
(j) Where	*is*	Olaf?			
(k)		Who	*came*?		When the question word (e.g., *who* or *what*) is the subject of the sentence, *do* or *does* is never used.
(l)		What	*happened*?		

Supplementary Grammar Charts

UNIT B: Phrasal Verbs

NOTE: See the *Fundamentals of English Grammar Workbook* appendix for practice exercises for phrasal verbs.

B-1 Phrasal Verbs

(a) We **put off** our trip. We'll go next month instead of this month. (*put off = postpone*) (b) Jimmy, **put on** your coat before you go outdoors. (*put on = place clothes on one's body*) (c) Someone left the scissors on the table. They didn't belong there. I **put** them **away**. (*put away = put something in its usual or proper place*) (d) After I used the dictionary, I **put** it **back** on the shelf. (*put back = return something to its original place*)	In (a): **put off** = a phrasal verb A PHRASAL VERB = a verb and a particle that together have a special meaning. For example, *put off* means "postpone." A PARTICLE = a "small word" (e.g., *off, on, away, back*) that is used in a phrasal verb. Note that the phrasal verbs with **put** in (a), (b), (c), and (d) all have different meanings.
Separable (e) We *put off our trip*. = (VERB + **particle** + NOUN) (f) We *put our trip off*. = (VERB + NOUN + **particle**) (g) We *put it off*. = (VERB + PRONOUN + **particle**)	Some phrasal verbs are **separable**: A NOUN OBJECT can either (1) follow the particle, as in (e), OR (2) come between (separate) the verb and the particle, as in (f). If a phrasal verb is separable, a PRONOUN OBJECT comes between the verb and the particle, as in (g). INCORRECT: *We put off it.*
Nonseparable (h) I *ran into Bob*. = (VERB + **particle** + NOUN) (i) I *ran into him*. = (VERB + **particle** + PRONOUN)	If a phrasal verb is **nonseparable**, a NOUN or PRONOUN always follows (never precedes) the particle, as in (h) and (i). INCORRECT: *I ran Bob into.* INCORRECT: *I ran him into.*
Phrasal Verbs: Intransitive (j) The machine *broke down*. (k) Please *come in*. (l) Mr. Lim *passed away*.	Some phrasal verbs are intransitive; i.e., they are not followed by an object.
Three-Word Phrasal Verbs (m) Last night some friends *dropped in*.	Some two-word verbs (e.g., *drop in*) can become three-word verbs (e.g., *drop in on*).
	In (m): **drop in** is not followed by an object. It is an intransitive phrasal verb (i.e., it is not followed by an object).
(n) Let's *drop in on* Alice this afternoon.	In (n): **drop in on** is a three-word phrasal verb. Three-word phrasal verbs are transitive (they are followed by objects).
(o) We *dropped in on her* last week.	In (o): Three-word phrasal verbs are nonseparable (the noun or pronoun follows the phrasal verb).

B-2 Phrasal Verbs: A Reference List

A ask out = ask (someone) to go on a date

B blow out = extinguish (a match, a candle)
break down = stop functioning properly
break out = happen suddenly
break up = separate, end a relationship
bring back = return
bring up = (1) raise (children)
(2) mention, start to talk about

C call back = return a telephone call
call off = cancel
call on = ask (someone) to speak in class
call up = make a telephone call
cheer up = make happier
clean up = make neat and clean
come along (with) = accompany
come from = originate
come in = enter a room or building
come over (to) = visit the speaker's place
cross out = draw a line through
cut out (of) = remove with scissors or knife

D dress up = put on nice clothes
drop in (on) = visit without calling first or without an invitation
drop out (of) = stop attending (school)

E eat out = eat at a restaurant

F fall down = fall to the ground
figure out = find the solution to a problem
fill in = complete by writing in a blank space
fill out = write information on a form
fill up = fill completely with gas, water, coffee, etc.
find out (about) = discover information
fool around (with) = have fun while wasting time

G get on = enter a bus/an airplane/a train/a subway
get out of = leave a car, a taxi

get over = recover from an illness or a shock
get together (with) = join, meet
get through (with) = finish
get up = get out of bed in the morning
give away = donate, get rid of by giving
give back = return (something) to (someone)
give up = quit doing (something) or quit trying
go on = continue
go back (to) = return to a place
go out = not stay home
go over (to) = (1) approach
(2) visit another's home
grow up (in) = become an adult

H hand in = give homework, test papers, etc., to a teacher
hand out = give (something) to this person, then to that person, then to another person, etc.
hang around/out (with) = spend time relaxing
hang up = (1) hang on a hanger or a hook
(2) end a telephone conversation
have on = wear
help out = assist (someone)

K keep away (from) = not give to
keep on = continue

L lay off = stop employment
leave on = (1) not turn off (a light, a machine)
(2) not take off (clothing)
look into = investigate
look over = examine carefully
look out (for) = be careful
look up = look for information in a dictionary, a telephone directory, an encyclopedia, etc.

P pay back = return borrowed money to (someone)
pick up = lift
point out = call attention to

(*continued*)

B-2 Phrasal Verbs: A Reference List *(continued)*

    print out = create a paper copy from a computer
    put away = put (something) in its usual or proper place
    put back = return (something) to its original place
    put down = stop holding or carrying
    put off = postpone
    put on = put clothes on one's body
    put out = extinguish (stop) a fire, a cigarette

R **run into** = meet by chance
    run out (of) = finish the supply of (something)

S **set out (for)** = begin a trip
    shut off = stop a machine or a light, turn off
    sign up (for) = put one's name on a list
    show up = come, appear
    sit around (with) = sit and do nothing
    sit back = put one's back against a chair back
    sit down = go from standing to sitting
    speak up = speak louder
    stand up = go from sitting to standing
    start over = begin again
    stay up = not go to bed

T **take back** = return
    take off = (1) remove clothes from one's body (2) ascend in an airplane
    take out = invite out and pay
    talk over = discuss
    tear down = destroy a building
    tear out (of) = remove (paper) by tearing
    tear up = tear into small pieces
    think over = consider
    throw away/out = put in the trash, discard
    try on = put on clothing to see if it fits
    turn around } change to the opposite direction
    turn back
    turn down = decrease the volume
    turn off = stop a machine or a light
    turn on = start a machine or a light
    turn over = turn the top side to the bottom
    turn up = increase the volume

W **wake up** = stop sleeping
    watch out (for) = be careful
    work out = solve
    write down = write a note on a piece of paper

UNIT C: Prepositions

NOTE: See the *Fundamentals of English Grammar Workbook* appendix for practice exercises for preposition combinations.

C-1 Preposition Combinations: Introduction

ADJ + PREP (a) Ali is **absent from** class today. V + PREP (b) This book **belongs to** me.	*At, from, of, on,* and *to* are examples of prepositions. Prepositions are often combined with adjectives, as in (a), and verbs, as in (b).

C-2 Preposition Combinations: A Reference List

A
be absent from
be accustomed to
   add (*this*) to (*that*)
be acquainted with
   admire (*someone*) for (*something*)
be afraid of
   agree with (*someone*) about (*something*)
be angry at / with (*someone*) about / over (*something*)
   apologize to (*someone*) for (*something*)
   apply for (*something*)
   approve of
   argue with (*someone*) about / over (*something*)
   arrive at (*a building / a room*)
   arrive in (*a city / a country*)
   ask (*someone*) about (*something*)
   ask (*someone*) for (*something*)
be aware of

B
be bad for
   believe in
   belong to
be bored with / by
   borrow (*something*) from (*someone*)

C
be clear to
   combine with
   compare (*this*) to / with (*that*)
   complain to (*someone*) about (*something*)
be composed of
   concentrate on
   consist of
be crazy about
be crowded with
be curious about

D
   depend on (*someone*) for (*something*)
be dependent on (*someone*) for (*something*)

be devoted to
   die of / from
be different from
   disagree with (*someone*) about (*something*)
be disappointed in
   discuss (*something*) with (*someone*)
   divide (*this*) into (*that*)
be divorced from
be done with
   dream about / of
   dream of

E
be engaged to
be equal to
   escape from (*a place*)
be excited about
   excuse (*someone*) for (*something*)
   excuse from
be exhausted from

F
be familiar with
be famous for
   feel about
   feel like
   fill (*something*) with
be finished with
   forgive (*someone*) for (*something*)
be friendly to / with
be frightened of / by
be full of

G
   get rid of
be gone from
be good for
   graduate from

(*continued*)

C-2 Preposition Combinations: A Reference List *(continued)*

H
happen to
be happy about *(something)*
be happy for *(someone)*
hear about / of *(something)* from *(someone)*
help *(someone)* with *(something)*
hide *(something)* from *(someone)*
hope for
be hungry for

I
insist on
be interested in
introduce *(someone)* to *(someone)*
invite *(someone)* to *(something)*
be involved in

K
be kind to
know about

L
laugh at
leave for (a *place*)
listen to
look at
look for
look forward to
look like

M
be made of
be married to
matter to
be the matter with
multiply *(this)* by *(that)*

N
be nervous about
be nice to

O
be opposed to

P
pay for
be patient with
be pleased with / about
play with
point at
be polite to
prefer *(this)* to *(that)*

be prepared for
protect *(this)* from *(that)*
be proud of
provide *(someone)* with

Q
be qualified for

R
read about
be ready for
be related to
rely on
be responsible for

S
be sad about
be satisfied with
be scared of / by
search for
separate *(this)* from *(that)*
be similar to
speak to / with *(someone)* about *(something)*
stare at
subtract *(this)* from *(that)*
be sure of / about

T
take care of
talk about *(something)*
talk to / with *(someone)* about *(something)*
tell *(someone)* about *(something)*
be terrified of / by
thank *(someone)* for *(something)*
think about / of
be thirsty for
be tired from
be tired of
translate from *(one language)* to *(another)*

U
be used to

W
wait for
wait on
warn about / of
wave at
wonder about
be worried about

Listening Script

Getting Started

EXERCISE 1 ▶ p. xiii.
Part I

It's Nice to Meet You

DANIEL: Hi. My name is Daniel.
SOFIA: Hi. I'm Sofia. It's nice to meet you.
DANIEL: Nice to meet you too. Where are you from?
SOFIA: I'm from Montreal. How about you?
DANIEL: I'm from Miami.
SOFIA: Are you a new student?
DANIEL: Yes, and no. This is my third year of college, but I'm new here.
SOFIA: This is my second year here. I'm in the business school. I really like it.
DANIEL: Oh, my major is economics! Maybe we'll have a class together. So, tell me a little more about yourself. What do you like to do in your free time?
SOFIA: I love the outdoors. I spend a lot of time in the mountains. I hike on weekends. I write about it on social media.
DANIEL: I spend a lot of time outdoors too. I like the beach. In the summer, I swim every day.
SOFIA: This town has a great beach.
DANIEL: Yeah, I want to go there! Now, when I introduce you to the group, I have to write your full name on the board. What's your last name, and how do you spell it?
SOFIA: It's Sanchez. S-A-N-C-H-E-Z.
DANIEL: My last name is Willson — with two "l"s: W-I-L-L-S-O-N.
SOFIA: Oh, it looks like our time is up. I enjoyed our conversation.
DANIEL: Thanks. I enjoyed it too.

Chapter 1: Present Time

EXERCISE 9 ▶ p. 7.
1. Irene designs video games.
2. She is working on a new project.
3. She is sitting in front of her computer.
4. She spends her weekends at the office.
5. She's finishing plans for a new game.

EXERCISE 10 ▶ p. 8.
A Problem with the Printer

1. Does it need more paper?
2. Does it have enough ink?
3. Are you fixing it yourself?
4. Do you know how to fix it?
5. Do we have another printer in the office?
6. Hmmm. Is it my imagination, or is it making a strange noise?

EXERCISE 14 ▶ p. 10.
Natural Disasters: A Flood

1. The weather causes some natural disasters.
2. Heavy rains sometimes create floods.
3. A big flood causes a lot of damage.
4. In towns, floods can damage buildings, homes, and roads.
5. After a flood, a town needs a lot of financial help for repairs.

EXERCISE 18 ▶ p. 12.
1. talks
2. fishes
3. hopes
4. teaches
5. moves
6. kisses
7. pushes
8. waits
9. mixes
10. watches
11. studies
12. buys
13. enjoys
14. tries
15. carries

EXERCISE 37 ▶ p. 24.
Part II

1. Do you have pain anywhere?
2. Does it hurt anywhere else?
3. Does she have a cough or sore throat?
4. Does he have a fever?
5. Does she need lab tests?
6. Am I very sick?
7. Is it serious?
8. Does he need to make another appointment?
9. Do they want to wait in the waiting room?
10. Do we pay now or later?

EXERCISE 39 ▶ p. 25.

Getting Ready to Leave

1. We have a few minutes before we need to leave. Do you want a cup of coffee?
2. I'm ready. Do you need help?
3. Look outside. Is it raining hard?
4. Do we need to take an umbrella?
5. Mr. Smith has his coat on. Is he leaving now?
6. I'm looking for the elevators. Are they near here?

EXERCISE 41 ▶ p. 28.

Part III

Many people do aerobic exercise. It is a special type of exercise. Aerobic exercise makes the heart beat fast. Running, fast walking, and dancing are some examples of this exercise.

Right now some people are exercising in an exercise class. They are listening to music, and they are dancing. Their hearts are beating fast. Many parts of their body are getting exercise.

How about you? Do you exercise every day? Do you do aerobic exercise?

Chapter 2: Past Time

EXERCISE 17 ▶ p. 40.

1. watch, watched
2. called, called
3. works, worked
4. decided, decided

EXERCISE 18 ▶ p. 41.

In the Classroom

1. The teacher explains the homework …
2. The teacher explained the homework …
3. We review new vocabulary …
4. Our teacher surprised us …
5. My friend practices pronunciation …
6. We watched an interesting video …
7. We started a project …
8. We finish a chapter …

EXERCISE 19 ▶ p. 41.

Part II

1. Alex hurt his finger. Did he cut it with a knife?
2. Ms. Jones doesn't have any money in her wallet. Did she spend it all yesterday?
3. Karen's parents visited. Did you meet them yesterday?
4. The Browns don't have a car anymore. Did they sell it?
5. I dropped the glass. Did I break it?
6. Ann didn't throw away her old clothes. Did she keep them?
7. John gave a book to his son. Did he read it to him?
8. You don't have your glasses. Did you lose them?
9. Mr. Jones looked for his passport in his desk drawer. Did he find it?
10. The baby is crying. Did I upset her?

EXERCISE 20 ▶ p. 42.

Part II

At a Wedding

1. The bride wasn't nervous before the ceremony.
2. The groom was nervous before the ceremony.
3. His parents weren't nervous about the wedding.
4. The bride and groom were excited about their wedding.
5. The ceremony was in the evening.
6. The wedding reception wasn't after the wedding.
7. It was the next day.
8. It was at a popular hotel.
9. A lot of guests were there.
10. Some relatives from out of town weren't there.

EXERCISE 25 ▶ p. 45.

Part I

A: Did you have a good weekend?
B: Yeah, I went to a waterslide park.
A: Really? That sounds like fun!
B: It was great! I loved the fast slides. How about you? How was your weekend?
A: I visited my aunt.
B: Did you have a good time?
A: Not really. She didn't like my clothes or my haircut.

EXERCISE 40 ▶ p. 55.

Jennifer's Problem

Jennifer works for an insurance company. When people need help with their car insurance, they call her. Right now it is 9:05 a.m., and Jennifer is working at her desk.

She came to work on time this morning. Yesterday Jennifer was late to work because she had a car accident. While she was driving to work, her cell phone rang. She reached for it. While she was reaching for her phone, Jennifer lost control of the car. It hit a telephone pole.

Jennifer is OK now, but her car isn't. She feels very embarrassed. She made a bad decision, especially since it is illegal to talk on a cell phone and drive at the same time in her city.

EXERCISE 41 ▶ p. 56.

At a Checkout Stand in a Grocery Store

1. CASHIER: Hi. Did you find what you needed?
   CUSTOMER: Almost everything. I was looking for sticky rice, but I didn't see it.
   CASHIER: It's on aisle 10, in the Asian food section.
2. CASHIER: This is the express lane. Ten items only. It looks like you have more than ten. Did you count them?
   CUSTOMER: I thought I had ten. Oh, I guess I have more. Sorry.
   CASHIER: The checkout stand next to me is open.

3. CASHIER: Do you have any coupons you wanted to use?
   CUSTOMER: I had a couple in my purse, but I can't find them now.
   CASHIER: What were they for? I might have some extras here.
   CUSTOMER: One was for eggs, and the other was for ice cream.
   CASHIER: I think I have those.

Chapter 3: Future Time

EXERCISE 13 ▶ p. 70.

A: Are you going to come with us to the meeting?
B: No, I'm going to study. I have a test tomorrow.
A: I understand. I'll let you know what happens.

EXERCISE 14 ▶ p. 71.
Part II

A: Where are you going to move to?
B: We're going to look for something outside the city. We're going to spend the weekend apartment hunting.
A: What fees are you going to need to pay?
B: I think we are going to need to pay the first and last month's rent.
A: Are there going to be other fees?
B: There is probably going to be an application fee and a cleaning fee. Also, the landlord is probably going to check our credit, so we are going to need to pay for that.

EXERCISE 15 ▶ p. 72.
Before the Party

1. We'll need to get the house ready for the party tomorrow, but I'll be gone in the morning.
2. You'll need to fold the laundry and dust the furniture.
3. I talked to your sister. She'll clean the kitchen.
4. Your dad will be home. He'll vacuum the carpets.
5. Your brothers won't be home. They'll do the cleanup.
6. Some of the guests are going to come early. We'll need to be ready by 5:00.

EXERCISE 16 ▶ p. 72.
Part II
At the Pharmacy

1. Your prescription'll be ready in ten minutes.
2. The medicine'll make you feel a little tired.
3. The pharmacist'll call your doctor's office.
4. This cough syrup'll help your cough.
5. Two aspirin'll be enough.
6. The generic drug'll cost less.
7. This information'll explain all the side effects for this medicine.

EXERCISE 25 ▶ p. 78.
My Day Tomorrow

1. It's going to snow. I need to find my warm clothes.
2. I'll probably do a few errands.
3. I may stop at the post office.
4. I will probably pick up groceries at the store.
5. The roads are going to be icy.
6. Maybe I'll do my errands midday.

EXERCISE 37 ▶ p. 84.
Going on Vacation

A: I'm going on vacation tomorrow.
B: Where are you going?
A: To San Francisco.
B: How are you getting there? Are you flying or driving your car?
A: I'm flying. I want to be at the airport by 7:00 tomorrow morning.
B: Do you need a ride to the airport?
A: No, thanks. I'm taking a taxi. What about you? Are you planning to go somewhere over vacation?
B: No. I'm staying here.

EXERCISE 46 ▶ p. 89.
At a Chinese Restaurant

A: OK, let's all open our fortune cookies.
B: What does your cookie say?
A: Mine says, "You will receive an unexpected gift." Great! Are you planning to give me a gift soon?
B: Not that I know of. Mine says, "Your life will be long and happy." Good. I want a long life.
C: Mine says, "A smile solves all communication problems." Well, that's good! After this, when I don't understand someone, I'll just smile at them.
D: My fortune is this: "If you work hard, you will be successful."
A: Well, it looks like all of us will have good luck in the future!

Chapter 4: Present Perfect and Past Perfect

EXERCISE 12 ▶ p. 98.
At a Restaurant

1. My coffee's a little cold already.
2. My coffee's gotten a little cold already.
3. Your order's not ready yet.
4. Wow! Our order's here already.
5. Excuse me, I think our waiter's forgotten our order.
6. Actually, your waiter's just gone home sick. I'll take care of you.

EXERCISE 22 ▶ p. 104.
Part II

1. The cash machine's been out of service for two days.
2. I'm sorry. You credit card's expired.

3. My checking account fees've increased a lot.
4. Someone's withdrawn money from your account.
5. Our new debit cards've gotten lost in the mail.

EXERCISE 28 ▶ p. 107.

1. Every day, I spend some money. Yesterday, I spent some money. Since Friday, I have …
2. I usually make a big breakfast. Yesterday, I made a big breakfast. All week, I have …
3. Every day, I send emails. Yesterday I sent an email. Today I have already …
4. Every time I go to a restaurant, I leave a nice tip. Last night I left a nice tip. I just finished dinner, and I have …
5. Every weekend, I sleep in late. Last weekend, I slept in late. Since I was a teenager, I have …
6. I drive very carefully. On my last trip across the country, I drove very carefully. All my life, I have …
7. Every morning, I sing in the shower. Earlier today, I sang in the shower. Since I was little, I have …

EXERCISE 37 ▶ p. 112.

Today's Weather

The weather has certainly been changing today. Boy, what a day! We've already had rain, wind, hail, and sun. So, what's in store for tonight? As you have probably seen, dark clouds have been building. We have a weather system moving in that is going to bring colder temperatures and high winds. We've been saying all week that this system is coming, and it looks like tonight is it! We've even seen snow down south of us, and we could get some snow here too. So hang onto your hats! We may have a rough night ahead of us.

EXERCISE 39 ▶ p. 114.

1. A: What song is playing on the radio?
   B: I don't know, but it's good, isn't it?
2. A: How long have you lived in Dubai?
   B: About a year.
3. A: Where are the kids?
   B: I don't know. I've been calling them since I got home.
4. A: Who have you met tonight?
   B: Actually, I've met a few people from your office. How about you? Who have you met?
   A: I've met some interesting business people.

Chapter 5: Asking Questions

EXERCISE 6 ▶ p. 124.
Part II
At the Grocery Store

1. I need to see the manager. Is she available?
2. I need to see the manager. Is he in the store today?
3. Here is one bag of apples. Is that enough?
4. I need a drink of water. Is there a drinking fountain?
5. My credit card isn't working. Hmmm. Did it expire?
6. Where's Simon? Has he left?
7. The price seems high. Does it include the tax?

EXERCISE 11 ▶ p. 127.

A: Do you know Roberto and Isabelle?
B: Yes, I do. They live around the corner from me.
A: Have you seen them recently?
B: No, I haven't. They're out of town.
A: When are they going to be back? I'm having a party, and I can't reach them.
B: They're going to be back Monday. They are with Roberto's parents.
A: Oh, why are they there?
B: Because his dad is sick.
A: That's too bad.
B: Do you want Roberto's or Isabelle's cell number?
A: No, I don't, but thanks. I'll talk to them when they get back.
B: OK, sounds good.

EXERCISE 12 ▶ p. 127.

1. Do you want to go to the mall?
2. When are the Waltons coming?
3. Where will I meet you?
4. Why were you late?
5. What are you cleaning for?

EXERCISE 18 ▶ p. 130.

A Secret

A: John told me something.
B: What did he tell you?
A: It's confidential. I can't tell you.
B: Did he tell anyone else?
A: He told a few other people.
B: Who did he tell?
A: Some friends.
B: Then it's not a secret. What did he say?
A: I can't tell you.
B: Why can't you tell me?
A: Because it's about you. But don't worry. It's nothing bad.
B: Gee. Thanks a lot. That sure makes me feel better.

EXERCISE 29 ▶ p. 137.

1. A: How fresh are these eggs?
   B: I just bought them at the farmers' market, so they should be fine.
2. A: How cheap were the tickets?
   B: They were 50% off.
3. A: How hard was the driver's test?
   B: Well, I didn't pass, so that gives you an idea.
4. A: How clean is the car?
   B: There's dirt on the floor. We need to vacuum it inside.
5. A: How hot is the frying pan?
   B: Don't touch it! You'll burn yourself.
6. A: How noisy is the street you live on?
   B: There is a lot of traffic, so we keep the windows closed a lot.

7. A: How serious are you about interviewing for the job?
   B: Very. I already scheduled an interview with the company.

EXERCISE 33 ▶ p. 139.

Questions:

1. How old are you?
2. How tall are you?
3. How much do you weigh?
4. In general, how well do you sleep at night?
5. How quickly do you fall asleep?
6. How often do you wake up during the night?
7. How tired are you in the mornings?
8. How many times a week do you exercise?
9. How are you feeling right now?
10. How soon can you come in for an overnight appointment?

EXERCISE 41 ▶ p. 144.

1. Where's my key?
2. Where're my keys?
3. Who're those people?
4. What's in that box?
5. What're you doing?
6. Where'd Bob go last night?
7. Who'll be at the party?
8. Why's the teacher absent?
9. Who's that?
10. Why'd you say that?
11. Who'd you talk to at the party?
12. How're we going to get to work?
13. What'd you say?
14. How'll you do that?

EXERCISE 43 ▶ p. 145.

A Mother Talking to Her Teenage Daughter

1. Where're you going?
2. Who're you going with?
3. Who's that?
4. How long've you known him?
5. Where'd you meet him?
6. Where's he go to school?
7. Is he a good student?
8. What time'll you be back?
9. Why're you wearing that outfit?
10. Why're you giving me that look?
11. Why am I asking so many questions? Because I love you!

EXERCISE 44 ▶ p. 145.

1. What do you (*Whaddaya*) want to do?
2. What are you (*Whaddaya*) doing?
3. What are you (*Whaddaya*) having for dinner?
4. What are you (*Whaddaya*) doing that for?
5. What do you (*Whaddaya*) think about that?
6. What are you (*Whaddaya*) laughing for?
7. What do you (*Whaddaya*) need?
8. What do you (*Whaddaya*) have in your pocket?

EXERCISE 50 ▶ p. 148.

1. A: Did you like the movie?
   B: It was OK, I guess. How about you?
   A: I thought it was pretty good.
2. A: Are you going to the company party?
   B: I haven't decided yet. What about you?
   A: I think I will.
3. A: Do you like living in this city?
   B: Sort of. How about you?
   A: I'm not sure. It's pretty noisy.
4. A: What are you going to have?
   B: Well, I'm not really hungry. I think I might just order a salad. How about you?
   A: I'll have one too.

EXERCISE 54 ▶ p. 150.

1. Simple Present
   a. You like strong coffee, don't you?
   b. David goes to Ames High School, doesn't he?
   c. Leila and Sara live on Tree Road, don't they?
   d. Jane has the keys to the storeroom, doesn't she?
   e. Jane's in her office, isn't she?
   f. You're a member of this class, aren't you?
   g. Oleg doesn't have a car, does he?
   h. Lisa isn't from around here, is she?
   i. I'm in trouble, aren't I?
2. Simple Past
   a. Paul went to Indonesia, didn't he?
   b. You didn't talk to the boss, did you?
   c. Ted's parents weren't at home, were they?
   d. That was Pat's idea, wasn't it?
3. Present Progressive, *Be Going To*, and Past Progressive
   a. You're studying hard, aren't you?
   b. Greg isn't working at the bank, is he?
   c. It isn't going to rain today, is it?
   d. Michelle and Yoko were helping, weren't they?
   e. He wasn't listening, was he?
4. Present Perfect
   a. It has been warmer than usual, hasn't it?
   b. You've had a lot of homework, haven't you?
   c. We haven't spent much time together, have we?
   d. Fatima has started her new job, hasn't she?
   e. Bruno hasn't finished his sales report yet, has he?
   f. Steve's had to leave early, hasn't he?

EXERCISE 56, p. 151.

Checking in at a Hotel

1. You have our reservation, don't you?
2. We have a non-smoking room, don't we?
3. There's a view of the city, isn't there?
4. I didn't give you my credit card yet, did I?
5. The room rate doesn't include tax, does it?
6. The price includes breakfast, right?
7. Check-out time isn't until noon, is it?
8. There are hair dryers in the rooms, aren't there?
9. You don't have a pool, do you?
10. There isn't a hot tub, is there?

EXERCISE 58 ▶ p. 153.

Part I

Ordering at a Fast-Food Restaurant
CASHIER: So, what'll it be?
CUSTOMER: I'll have a burger.
CASHIER: Would you like fries or a salad with your burger?
CUSTOMER: I'll have fries.
CASHIER: What size?
CUSTOMER: Medium.
CASHIER: Anything to drink?
CUSTOMER: I'll have a vanilla shake.
CASHIER: Size?
CUSTOMER: Medium.
CASHIER: OK. So that's a burger, fries, vanilla shake.
CUSTOMER: About how long'll it take?
CASHIER: We're pretty crowded right now. Probably 10 minutes or so. That'll be $6.50. Your number's on the receipt. I'll call the number when your order's ready.
CUSTOMER: Thanks.

Chapter 6: Nouns and Pronouns

EXERCISE 5 ▶ p. 160.

1. hat
2. toys
3. pages
4. bridge
5. keys
6. dish

EXERCISE 7 ▶ p. 161.

1. prizes
2. lips
3. glasses
4. taxes
5. plates
6. toes
7. laws
8. lights

ways
pants
matches
shirts
stars
fingers
maps
places

EXERCISE 9 ▶ p, p. 161.

1. This shirt comes in three sizes: small, medium, and large.
2. How much will the sales tax be?
3. Taxes are low here.
4. I'm not going to buy this car. The price is too high.
5. I can't find my glasses anywhere. Have you seen them?
6. The prize for the contest is a new bike.

EXERCISE 27 ▶ p. 171.

How Some Animals Stay Cool

How do animals stay cool in hot weather? Many animals don't sweat like humans, so they have other ways to cool themselves.

Dogs, for example, have a lot of fur and can become very hot. They stay cool mainly by panting. If you don't know what *panting* means, this is the sound of panting.

Cats lick their paws and chests. When their fur is wet, they become cooler.

Elephants have very large ears. When they are hot, they can flap their huge ears. The flapping ear acts like a fan, and it cools them. Elephants also like to roll in the mud to stay cool.

EXERCISE 35 ▶ p. 174.

A: I'm looking for a new place to live.
B: How come?
A: My two roommates are moving out. I can't afford my apartment. I need a one-bedroom.
B: I just helped a friend find one. I can help you. What else do you want?
A: I want to be near the subway … within walking distance. But I want a quiet location. I don't want to be on a busy street.
B: Anything else?
A: A small balcony would be nice.
B: That's expensive.
A: Yeah. I guess I'm dreaming.

EXERCISE 47 ▶ p. 181.

1. Who's knocking on the door?
2. Whose coat is on the floor?
3. Whose glasses are those?
4. Who's sitting next to you?
5. Whose seat is next to yours?
6. Who's outside?

Chapter 7: Modal Auxiliaries, the Imperative, Making Suggestions, Stating Preferences

EXERCISE 3 ▶ p. 194.

A: Where do you and Joe have to go tomorrow?
B: I have to go downtown. Joe has to take the kids to buy school supplies. He couldn't do it today.
A: May I come with you?
B: You can if you want to get up early.
A: Would you wake me up? Sometimes I'm not able to hear my alarm.
B: Sure. I have a great way to wake people up. You definitely won't sleep in!
A: I can't wait!

EXERCISE 7 ▶ p. 197.

In the Classroom

A: I can't understand this math assignment.
B: I can help you with that.
A: Really? Can you explain this problem to me?
B: Well, we can't figure out the answer until we do this part.
A: OK. But it's so hard.
B: Yeah, but I know you can do it. Just go slowly.

A: I need to leave in a few minutes. Can you meet me after school today to finish this?
B: Well, I can't meet you right after school, but how about at 5:00?
A: Great!

EXERCISE 13 ▶ p. 199.

1. A: Mom, are these oranges sweet?
   B: I don't know. I can't tell if an orange is sweet just by looking at it.
2. A: What are you going to order?
   B: I'm not sure. I might have pasta, or I might have pizza.
3. A: Mom, can I have some candy?
   B: No, but you can have an apple.
4. A: What are you doing this weekend?
   B: I don't know yet. I may go snowboarding with friends, or I may try to fix my motorcycle.
5. May I have everyone's attention? The test is about to begin. If you need to leave the room during the examination, please raise your hand. You may not leave the room without asking. Are there any questions? No? Then you may open your test booklets and begin.

EXERCISE 17 ▶ p. 201.

In a Home Office

A: Look at this cord. Do you know what it's for?
B: I don't know. We have so many cables and cords around here with all our electronic equipment. It could be for our old printer.
A: No, that isn't a printer cord.
B: It might be for one of the kids' toys.
A: Yeah, I could ask. But they don't have many electronic toys.
B: I have an idea. It may be for an old cell phone. You know — the one I had before this one.
A: I bet that's it. We can probably throw this out.
B: Well, let's be sure before we do that.

EXERCISE 37 ▶ p. 212.

Filling out a Job Application

1. The application has to be complete. You shouldn't skip any parts. If a section doesn't fit your situation, you can write N/A (not applicable).
2. If you fill out the form by hand, your writing has to be easy to read.
3. You've got to use your full legal name, not your nickname.
4. You've got to list the names and places of your previous employers.
5. You have to list your education, beginning with either high school or college.
6. All spelling has to be correct.
7. A: Do I have to write the same thing twice, like a phone number?
   B: No, you can just write "same as above."
8. A: Do I have to apply in person?
   B: No, for a lot of companies, you can do it online.

EXERCISE 52 ▶ p. 220.

Puzzle steps:

1. Write down the number of the month you were born. For example, write the number 2 if you were born in February. Write 3 if you were born in March, etc.
2. Double the number.
3. Add 5 to it.
4. Multiply it by 50.
5. Add your age.
6. Subtract 250.

Chapter 8: Connecting Ideas: Punctuation and Meaning

EXERCISE 11 ▶ p. 233.

Paying It Forward

A few days ago, a friend and I were driving from Benton Harbor to Chicago. We didn't have any delays for the first hour, but we ran into some highway construction near Chicago. The traffic wasn't moving. My friend and I sat and waited. We talked about our jobs, our families, and the terrible traffic. Slowly it started to move.

We noticed a black sports car on the shoulder. Its blinker was on. The driver obviously wanted to get back into traffic. Car after car passed without letting him in. I decided to do a good deed, so I motioned for him to get in line ahead of me. He waved thanks, and I waved back at him.

All the cars had to stop at a toll booth a short way down the road. I held out my money to pay my toll, but the toll-taker just smiled and waved me on. She told me that the man in the black sports car had already paid my toll. Wasn't that a nice way of saying thank you?

EXERCISE 15 ▶ p. 235.

A Strong Storm

1. The noise lasted only a short time, but the wind and rain …
2. Some roads were under water, but ours …
3. Our neighbors didn't lose any trees, but we …
4. My son got scared, but my daughter …
5. My son couldn't sleep, but my daughter …
6. My daughter can sleep through anything, but my son …
7. We still need help cleaning up from the storm, but our neighbors …
8. We will be OK, but some people …

EXERCISE 28 ▶ p. 243.

Strange Allergies

Allergies make people sneeze, cough, itch, or turn red. Common causes of allergies are dust, flower pollen, animal fur, and nuts. There are other things that cause allergies, but they are not so well known. Dark chocolate can make some people sneeze. The metal in cell phones can cause some people's skin to turn red and itch. Cold weather and leather clothing can also cause redness and itching in some people.

EXERCISE 33 ▶ p. 246.

1. Even though I looked all over the house for my keys, ...
2. Although it was a hot summer night, we went inside and shut the windows because ...
3. My brother came to my graduation ceremony even though ...
4. Because the package cost so much to send, ...
5. Because gas is so expensive, ...
6. Although the soccer team won the game, ...

Chapter 9: Comparisons

EXERCISE 7 ▶ p. 254.

Opinions

1. Old shoes are more comfortable than new shoes.
2. Food from other countries is better than food from my country.
3. Winter is more enjoyable for me than summer.
4. Cooked vegetables are more delicious than raw vegetables.
5. Taking a bath is more relaxing than taking a shower.
6. Writing English is easier than speaking English.
7. Science is more interesting than history.
8. A math test is more stressful than an English test.

EXERCISE 13 ▶ p. 257.

My Family

1. My brothers are shorter than my sisters.
2. My mother is the tallest person in our family.
3. My father is a fun person to be around. He seems happy all the time.
4. My grandmother was happier when she was younger.
5. I have twin brothers. They are older than me.
6. I have another brother. He is the funniest person in our family.
7. My sister is a doctor. She is a wise person.
8. My grandfather is also a doctor. He is the wisest person I know.

EXERCISE 30 ▶ p. 267.

Part II

5. Tom has never told a funny joke.
6. Food has never tasted better.
7. I've never slept on a hard mattress.
8. I've never seen a scarier movie.

EXERCISE 37 ▶ p. 271.

1. Frank owns a coffee shop. Business is busier this year for him than last year.
2. I've know Steven for years. He's the friendliest person I know.
3. Sam expected a hard test, but it wasn't as hard as he expected.
4. The road ends here. This is as far as we can go.
5. Jon's decision to leave his job was the worst decision he has ever made.
6. I don't know if we'll get to the theater on time, but I'm driving as fast as I can.
7. When you do the next assignment, please be more careful.
8. Is dinner ready? I've never been hungrier.
9. It takes about an hour to drive to the airport, and my flight takes an hour. So the drive takes as long as my flight.

EXERCISE 41 ▶ p. 273.

1. a. A sidewalk is as wide as a road.
   b. A road is wider than a sidewalk.
2. a. A hill isn't as high as a mountain.
   b. A hill is higher than a mountain.
3. a. In general, hiking along a mountain path is more dangerous than climbing a mountain peak.
   b. In general, hiking along a mountain path is less dangerous than climbing a mountain peak.
4. a. Toes are longer than fingers.
   b. Fingers aren't as long as toes.
   c. Toes are shorter than fingers.
5. a. Basic math isn't as hard as algebra.
   b. Algebra is harder than basic math.
   c. Basic math is as confusing as algebra.
   d. Basic math is less confusing than algebra.

EXERCISE 48 ▶ p. 277.

Gold vs. Silver

Gold is similar to silver. They are both valuable metals that people use for jewelry, but they aren't the same. Gold is not the same color as silver. Gold is also different from silver in cost: gold is more expensive than silver.

Two Zebras

Look at the two zebras in the picture. Their names are Zee and Bee. Zee looks like Bee. Is Zee exactly the same as Bee? The pattern of the stripes on each zebra in the world is unique. No two zebras are exactly alike. Even though Zee and Bee are similar to each other, they are different from each other in the exact pattern of their stripes.

Chapter 10: The Passive

EXERCISE 24 ▶ p. 294.

A Bike Accident

A: Did you hear about the accident outside the dorm entrance?
B: No. What happened?
A: A guy on a bike was hit by a taxi.
B: Was he injured?
A: Yeah. Someone called an ambulance. He was taken to City Hospital and treated in the emergency room for cuts and bruises.
B: What happened to the taxi driver?
A: He was arrested for reckless driving.
B: He's lucky that the bicyclist wasn't killed.

EXERCISE 36 ▶ p. 301.

1. This fruit is spoiled. I think I'd better throw it out.
2. When we got to the post office, it was closed.
3. Oxford University is located in Oxford, England.
4. Haley doesn't like to ride in elevators. She's scared of small spaces.
5. What's the matter? Are you hurt?
6. Excuse me. Could you please tell me how to get to the bus station from here? I am lost.
7. Your name is Tom Hood? Are you related to Mary Hood?
8. Where's my wallet? It's gone! Did someone take it?
9. Oh, no! Look at my sunglasses. I sat on them, and now they are broken.
10. It's starting to rain. Are all of the windows shut?

EXERCISE 40 ▶ p. 304.

1. Jane doesn't like school because of the boring classes and assignments.
2. The store manager stole money from the cash register. His shocked employees couldn't believe it.
3. I bought a new camera. I read the directions twice, but I didn't understand them. They were too confusing for me.
4. I was out to dinner with a friend and spilled a glass of water on his pants. I felt very embarrassed, but he was very nice about it.
5. Every year for their anniversary, I surprise my parents with dinner at a different restaurant.
6. We didn't enjoy the movie. It was too scary for the kids.

EXERCISE 45 ▶ p. 306.

1. In winter, the weather gets …
2. In summer, the weather gets …
3. I think I'll stop working. I'm getting …
4. My brother is losing some of his hair. He's getting …
5. Could I have a glass of water? I'm getting really …
6. You don't look well. Are you getting …

Chapter 11: Count/Noncount Nouns and Articles

EXERCISE 11 ▶ p. 321.

1. At our school, teachers don't use chalk anymore.
2. Where is the soap? Did you use all of it?
3. The manager's suggestions were very helpful.
4. Which suggestion sounded best to you?
5. Is this ring made of real gold?
6. We have a lot of storms with thunder and lightning.
7. During the last storm, I found my daughter under her bed.
8. Please put the cap back on the toothpaste.
9. What do you want to do with all this stuff in the hall closet?
10. We have too much soccer and hockey equipment.

EXERCISE 31 ▶ p. 332.

1. We have a holiday next week.
2. What are you going to (*gonna*) do?
3. I don't know. Do you have a suggestion?
4. Let's go shopping at the new mall.
5. They're having a big sale.
6. Actually, I'm going there in an hour.
7. Do you want to (*wanna*) come?
8. I can't. I just got a message.
9. I need to call my boss.
10. Hmmm. That's unusual. He's on vacation.

EXERCISE 39 ▶ p. 336.

Ice-Cream Headaches

   Have you ever eaten something really cold like ice cream and suddenly gotten a headache? This is known as an "ice-cream headache." About 30 percent of the population gets this type of headache. Here is one theory about why ice-cream headaches occur. The roof of your mouth has a lot of nerves. When something cold touches these nerves, they want to warm up your brain. Your blood vessels swell up, and this causes pain. Ice-cream headaches generally go away after about 30–60 seconds. The best way to avoid these headaches is to keep cold food off the roof of your mouth.

Chapter 12: Adjective Clauses

EXERCISE 23 ▶ p. 356.

My Mother's Hospital Stay

1. The doctor who my mother saw first spent a lot of time with her.
2. The doctor I called for a second opinion was very patient and understanding.
3. The room that my mother had was private.
4. The medicine which she took worked better than she expected.
5. The hospital that my mom chose specializes in women's care.
6. The day my mom came home happened to be her birthday.
7. I thanked the people that helped my mom.
8. The staff whom I met were all excellent.

EXERCISE 32 ▶ p. 361.

1. The plane which I'm taking to Denver leaves at 7:00 a.m.
2. The store that has the best vegetables is also the most expensive.
3. The eggs my husband made me for breakfast were cold.
4. The person who sent me an email was trying to get my bank account number.
5. The hotel clerk my wife spoke with on the phone said he would give us a room with a view.

EXERCISE 37 ▶ p. 364.

1. I like the people whose house we went to.
2. The man whose daughter is a doctor is very proud.
3. The man who's standing by the window has a daughter at Oxford University.
4. I know a girl whose parents are both airline pilots.
5. I know a girl who's lonely because her parents travel a lot.
6. I met a 70-year-old woman who's planning to go to college.

EXERCISE 40 ▶ p. 365.

Friendly Advice

A: A magazine that I saw at the doctor's office had an article you ought to read. It's about the importance of exercise in dealing with stress.
B: Why do you think I should read an article which deals with exercise and stress?
A: If you stop and think for a minute, you can answer that question yourself. You're under a lot of stress, and you don't get any exercise.
B: The stress that I have at work doesn't bother me. It's just a normal part of my job. And I don't have time to exercise.
A: Well, you should make time. Anyone whose job is as stressful as yours should make physical exercise part of their daily routine.

Chapter 13: Gerunds and Infinitives

EXERCISE 4 ▶ p. 371.

1. A: Do you have any plans for this weekend?
   B: Henry and I talked about seeing the dinosaur exhibit at the museum.
2. A: When you finish doing your homework, could you help me in the kitchen?
   B: Sure.
3. A: I didn't understand the answer. Would you mind explaining it?
   B: I'd be happy to.
4. A: I'm thinking about not attending the meeting tomorrow.
   B: Really? Why? I hope you go. We need your input.
5. A: I've been working on this math problem for an hour, and I still don't understand it.
   B: Well, don't give up. Keep trying.

EXERCISE 23 ▶ p. 382.

A: Have you made any vacation plans?
B: Kind of. We're going to take a staycation.
A: You mean you're going to stay home and vacation?
B: Yeah. To be honest, I don't like traveling so much. I hate flying. It's so uncomfortable nowadays.
A: But your wife loves to travel, doesn't she?
B: Right. But we don't see our kids so much because they're in college. So we decided to spend time here so we can see them, and we can be tourists in our own town.
A: So, what are you planning to see?
B: Well, we haven't seen the new Museum of Space yet. There's also a new art exhibit downtown. And my wife would like to go sailing in the harbor. Actually, when we began talking about it, we discovered there were lots of things to do.
A: Sounds like a great solution!
B: Yeah, we're both really excited about seeing our kids and more of our own town.

Chapter 14: Noun Clauses

EXERCISE 22 ▶ p. 412.

1. WOMAN: My English teacher is really good. I like her a lot.
   MAN: That's great! I'm glad you're enjoying your class.
2. MOM: How do you feel, honey? You might have the flu.
   SON: I'm OK, Mom. Honest. I don't have the flu.
3. MAN: Did you really fail your chemistry course? How is that possible?
   WOMAN: I didn't study hard enough. Now I won't be able to graduate on time.
4. MAN: Rachel! Hello! It's nice to see you.
   WOMAN: Hi, it's nice to be here. Thank you for inviting me.
5. WOMAN: Carol has left. Look. Her closet is empty. Her suitcases are gone. She won't be back. I just know it!
   MAN: She'll be back.

EXERCISE 40 ▶ p. 424.

Angela called and asked me where Bill was. I told her he was in the lunchroom. She asked when he would be back. I said he would be back around 2:00. I asked her if I could do something for her.

She said that Bill had the information she needed, and only he could help her. I told her that I would leave him a message. She thanked me and hung up.

Trivia Answers

Chapter 1, Exercise 6, p. 6.
1. runs   T
2. run   T
3. live   F [According to a 1993 study: The death rate for right-handed people = 32.2 percent; for left-handed people = 33.8 percent, so the death rate is about the same.]
4. cover   T
5. has   F [The official Eiffel Tower website says 1,665.]
6. spoils   F [Honey never spoils.]
7. is   T
8. takes   T
9. beats   T
10. die   T

Chapter 5, Exercise 31, p. 138.
1. c   4. a
2. d   5. e
3. b

Chapter 6, Exercise 17, p. 165.
(*Some items have more than one answer.*)
1. Georgia, Azerbaijan, Kazakhstan, China, Mongolia
2. Denmark
3. The Thames
4. The Dominican Republic, Cuba, Jamaica
5. Laos, Thailand, Cambodia, China
6. (*Answers will vary.*)
7. Liechtenstein
8. Vatican City
9. (*Answers will vary.*)
10. Egypt, Sudan, Eritrea, Iran

Chapter 6, Exercise 42, p. 178.
1. earth's   T
2. elephant's   F [gray and wrinkled]
3. man's   T
4. woman's   T
5. women's   T
6. person's   T
7. People's   F [Men's voices have a higher pitch.]

Chapter 9, Exercise 4, p. 252.
1. larger   T
2. colder   T
3. bigger   F [Asia is bigger than Africa.]
4. hotter   T
5. wetter   T
6. deeper   F [The Pacific Ocean is deeper than the Atlantic Ocean.]
7. more humid   T
8. more crowded F [China is more crowded than Canada.]
9. longer   T
10. higher   F [The Himalayas are higher than the Andes.]

Chapter 9, Exercise 10, p. 256.
2. The coldest ocean is the Arctic. / The Arctic is the coldest ocean.
3. The biggest ocean is the Pacific. / The Pacific is the biggest ocean.
4. The windiest continent is Antarctica. / Antarctica is the windiest continent.
5. The hottest continent is Africa. / Africa is the hottest continent.
6. The most populated continent is Asia. / Asia is the most populated continent.
7. The largest country in Asia is China. / China is the largest country in Asia.
8. The smallest country in Asia is the Maldives. / The Maldives is the smallest country in Asia.
9. The tallest mountain is Denali. / Denali is the tallest mountain.
10. The lowest mountain is Mount Fuji. / Mount Fuji is the lowest mountain.
11. The heaviest animal is the whale. / The whale is the heaviest animal.
12. The fastest animal is the cheetah. / The cheetah is the fastest animal.

Chapter 9, Exercise 42, p. 273.
Seattle and Singapore have more rain than Manila in December.
[Manila: 58 mm. or 2.3 in.; Seattle: 161 mm. or 6.3 in.; Singapore: 306 mm. or 12 in.]

Chapter 9, Exercise 44, p. 275.
2. Indonesia has more volcanoes than Japan.
3. Saturn has more moons than Venus.
4. São Paulo, Brazil, has more people than New York City.
5. Finland has more islands than Greece.
6. Nepal has more mountains than Switzerland.
7. A banana has more sugar than an apple.
8. The dark meat of a chicken has more fat than the white meat of a chicken.

Chapter 10, Exercise 18, p. 291.

3. a. Princess Dianna was killed in a car crash in 1997.
4. j. Marie and Pierre Curie discovered radium.
5. f. Oil was discovered in Saudi Arabia in 1938.
6. i. Nelson Mandela was released from prison in 1990.
7. b. Michael Jackson died in 2009.
8. d. Leonardo da Vinci painted the *Mona Lisa*.
9. e. John F. Kennedy was elected president of the United States in 1960.
10. g. Romeo and Juliet were kept apart by their parents.

Chapter 10, Exercise 29, p. 298.

1. sand
2. whales
3. China and Mongolia
4. small spaces

Chapter 11, Exercise 42, p. 338.

1. Ø ... Ø   T
2. The ... Ø   T
3. Ø ... Ø   F [Austria]
4. The ... Ø   T
5. The ... the   F
6. The ... Ø ... the T
7. Ø   F [psychology / psychiatry]
8. Ø ... Ø   T [It also lies in Uganda and borders Kenya.]
9. Ø ... the   T
10. The   F [The Himalayas]

Index

A/an, 316, 317, 330 (Look on page 316 and also on pages 317 and 330.)	The numbers following the words listed in the index refer to page numbers in the text.
By hand, 383*fn.* (Look at the footnote on page 383.)	The letters *fn.* mean "footnote." Footnotes are at the bottom of a chart or the bottom of a page.

A

A/an, 316
    a vs. *an*, 316
    with count/noncount nouns, 317, 330
Ability, expressions of, 195, 200, 224
Accustomed to, 308
Active verbs, 283
Adjective clauses (*a man who lives*), 344–368
    vs. adjectives, 345
    defined, 345
    prepositions in, 359
    pronouns in, 346, 349, 353, 362
    singular and plural verbs in, 358
    after superlative adjectives, 258
    whose in, 362
Adjectives (*good, beautiful*), 171
    vs. adjective clauses, 345
    articles with, 332
    after *be*, 171
        in stative passive, 298
        with *that*-clause (*am sorry that*), 411
    comparative (*more/-er*), 251, 258
    defined, 171, 345
    demonstrative (*this*), 332
    after *get* (*get hungry*), 305
    modifying comparatives with, 266
    nouns as (*a flower garden*), 173
    participial (*interesting, interested*), 302
    past participles as (*be tired, be surprised*), 298, 302, 305
    possessive (*my, our*), 181, 332, 433
    superlative (*most/-est*), 255, 258
Adverb clauses:
    with *because*, 125*fn.*, 241, 244
    defined, 241
    with even *though/although*, 244
    with *if*, 80, 401, 406
    with *since*, 99
    of time, 57, 80, 81*fn.*, 99
Adverbs (*quickly*):
    comparative (*more/-er*), 262
    defined, 262
    of frequency (*always, sometimes*), 14
    midsentence (*usually, seldom*), 14, 77*fn.*
    modifying comparatives with, 266
    negative (*seldom, never*), 14
    superlative (*most/-est*), 262
Advice, expressions of, 207, 209, 209*fn.*, 224
A few, 322
After, 57, 80, 116
Alike, 276
A little, 322
A little (***bit***), 266
Almost, 268
A lot, 266
A lot of, 322
Already, 96
Although, 244
Always, 14
Am, is, are + ***-ing*** (*am eating*), 2 (SEE ALSO Present progressive)
An (SEE *A/an*)

And:
- auxiliary verbs after, 87, 236
- connecting ideas with, 229, 230*fn.*, 231
- contractions with pronouns after, 234*fn.*
- with parallel verbs, 87
- with personal pronouns, 175
- with *so, too, either, neither,* 236
- subject–verb agreement with, 169

Another, 184
Answer, 421
Answers (SEE Short answers to questions)
Apostrophes, in possessive nouns (*Tom's*), 178
   (SEE ALSO Contractions)
Articles (*the, a, an*), 332–333 (SEE ALSO *individual articles*)
- with adjectives, 332
- with count/noncount nouns, 317, 330
- in titles, 339

As:
- in *as ... as* comparisons, 268, 272
- in *as soon as,* 57, 80
- after *the same,* 276

Ask if, 421
At, as preposition of time, 167
Auxiliary (helping) verbs:
- after *and,* 87, 236
- after *but,* 234
- in contractions, 69*fn.*, 122
- modal (SEE Modal auxiliaries)
- with *probably,* 77
- in short answers to *yes/no* questions, 122
- in tag questions, 149

B

Be:
- adjectives after, 171
  - in stative passive, 298
  - with *that*-clause (*am sorry that*), 411
- in contractions:
  - with nouns, 178
  - with pronouns, 3, 21*fn.*
  - with question words, 143
- with *-ing* (*is/was eating*) (SEE Progressive verbs)
- with past participles (*be interested in*):
  - and noun clauses (*be worried that*), 411
  - in passive, 283, 296, 298
- in present progressive (*am, is, are + -ing*) (SEE Present progressive)
- in simple past (*was, were*), 32
- in simple present (*am, is, are*), 2
  - for future time, 85
  - in *yes/no* questions and answers, 21

Be able to, 194, 195, 224
Be about to, 86
Because, adverb clauses with, 125*fn.*, 241, 244
Before, 57, 80, 116
Be going to, 66
- for future time, 65, 66, 77
- pronunciation of, 71
- vs. *will,* 73

Believe so, 414
Best, 333
Be supposed to, 312
Be + there (*is there, there is*), 122, 169
Better:
- in double comparatives (*the sooner, the better*), 264
- *had better,* 209, 209*fn.*, 224
- *like ... better,* 222

Be used to/accustomed to, 308, 310, 310*fn.*
But:
- auxiliary verbs after, 234
- connecting ideas with, 229, 232
- contractions with pronouns after, 234*fn.*
- vs. *so,* 232

By:
- gerunds after (*by doing*), 383
- with passive (*by*-phrase), 283, 292
- with reflexive pronouns (*by myself*), 183
- vs. *with,* 383

By hand, 383*fn.*
By the time, 116

C

Can, 194, 224
- in expressions of ability, 195
- in expressions of permission, 198, 202
- negative of (*can't*), 195, 198
- in polite requests, 202, 205
- pronunciation of, 195
- in tag questions, 218

Capitalization, 229, 339, 416
Certainty, expressions of, 77, 224
Clauses:
- defined, 57*fn.*, 345*fn.*, 401*fn.*
- dependent, 345*fn.*
- *if-,* 80, 401, 406
- independent, 229, 230*fn.*, 231, 232, 345*fn.*
- main, 57, 241
- nonrestrictive, 353*fn.*
- *since-,* 99
- time, 57, 80, 81*fn.*, 99
- (SEE ALSO Adjective clauses; Adverb clauses; Noun clauses)

Commas:
:   with adverb clauses, 241
    with conjunctions, 229, 230*fn.*, 231, 232
    vs. periods, 229
    in quoted speech, 416
    in series of items, 229*fn.*, 231
    with time clauses, 57
Comparatives (*more/-er*):
:   adjectives as, 251, 258
    adverbs as, 262
    completions for, 258
    double (*the more ... the more*), 264
    with modifiers, 266
    with *never*, 267
    with nouns, 274
    repeated (*more and more*), 264
    spelling of, 251, 255*fn.*
Comparisons, 250–281
:   *as ... as*, 268
    with comparatives (SEE Comparatives)
    less ... than, 272
    negative, 267, 268, 272
    not as ... as, 268, 272
    same, similar, different, like, alike, 276
    with superlatives (*most/-est*), 255, 258, 262, 267
Conjunctions (*and, but, or, so*), 229, 230*fn.*, 231, 232
Consonants:
:   *a* before words beginning with, 316
    defined, 11*fn.*
Continuous verbs (SEE Progressive verbs)
Contractions of verbs:
:   with *not*:
    :   *can't*, 195
        couldn't, 195
        didn't, 32
        doesn't, don't, 3
        hasn't, haven't, 94
        isn't, aren't, 3
        mustn't, 214, 214*fn.*
        pronunciation of, 40, 195, 214*fn.*
        shouldn't, 207
        wasn't, weren't, 32
        won't, 69
    with nouns:
    :   *am, is, are*, 178
        will, 71
    with pronouns:
    :   *am, is, are*, 3, 21*fn.*
        after *but* and *and*, 234*fn.*
        had, 116, 209

have, has, 94
will, 69, 69*fn.*, 71, 122
would, 222
with question words, 143
who's vs. *whose*, 180, 362*fn.*
in short answers to *yes/no* questions, 21
Coordinating conjunctions, 231
Could, 194, 224
:   in expressions of ability, 195, 200
    in expressions of possibility, 200
    negative of (*He couldn't*), 195
    in polite requests, 202, 205
    in tag questions, 218
Count/noncount nouns, 315–343
:   *a lot of, some, several, many/much,* and *a few/a little* with, 322, 323*fn.*
    articles with, 317, 330
    defined, 317, 318
    lists of, 318, 320
    nouns used as either (*paper* vs. *a paper*), 325
    units of measure with (*two cups of tea*), 328

D

Demonstrative adjectives (*this*), 332
Dependent clauses, defined, 345*fn.* (SEE ALSO Adjective clauses; Adverb clauses; Noun clauses)
Different, 276, 276*fn.*
Different from, 276, 276*fn.*
Direct speech (SEE Quoted speech)
Distance, expressions of (*to ... from, how far*), 140
Does, do, did:
:   negative of (*I don't ...*):
    :   contractions of, 3, 32
        with *have to*, 214
        in imperative sentences, 219
        in simple past, 31, 32
        in simple present, 2–3
        with *used to*, 60, 60*fn.*
    in questions (*Did you ... ?*):
    :   contractions of, 143
        with *how come*, 125
        of necessity, 210, 214
        pronunciation of, 40
        in simple past, 31, 32
        in simple present, 2
        tag, 149, 218
        with *used to*, 60, 60*fn.*
        with *what*, 128, 131
        with *who*, 128
        yes/no, 21
Double comparatives (*the sooner, the better*), 264

E

-Ed (*asked, played*):
   in past participles (SEE Past participles)
   pronunciation of, 40, 310, 432
   in simple past (SEE Simple past)
   spelling with, 43
Either, 236
Enough, 394, 394*fn.*
-Er/more (SEE Comparatives)
-Es/-s (SEE -S/-es:)
-Est/most (SEE Superlatives)
Even though, 244
Ever, 14, 94
Ever since, 102*fn.*
Every, 169

F

Far, 266
Farther/further, 262
(*A*) *few*, 322
For:
   in expressions of purpose (*I went to the store for milk*), 391
   in expressions of time (*I stayed for two days*), 99, 104, 108
   in *for* (*someone*) to do (*something*), with *it* (*It is important for you to study*), 388
Frequency:
   adverbs of (*always, sometimes*), 14
   expressions of (*a lot, every day*), 138
   questions about, with *how often*, 138
From:
   after *different*, 276, 276*fn.*
   from ... to, to express distance, 140
Full stop (period), 229*fn.*
Future time, 64–90
   be going to for, 65, 66, 77
   if-clauses for, 80
   immediate (*be about to*), 86
   present progressive for, 83
   simple present for, 80, 85
   in time clauses (*Before he comes, we will ...*), 80
   will for, 65, 69, 77

G

Gerunds (*riding, working*), 369–399
   after *by* (*by doing*), 383
   defined, 370
   after *go* (*go shopping*), 372
   after prepositions (*about going*), 380, 383
   as subjects (*Riding horses is fun*), 386
   after verbs (*enjoy working*), 370, 375
Get + adjective/past participle (*get hungry, get tired*), 305
Get used to/accustomed to, 308
Glottal stop, 195*fn.*
Go + **-ing** (*go shopping*), 372
Gonna (*going to*), 71 (SEE ALSO *Be going to*)

H

Habitual past (*used to do something*), 60
Had:
   in contractions with pronouns (*I'd*), 116, 209
   in past perfect (*She had already eaten*), 116
Had better (*You'd better study*), 209, 209*fn.*, 224
Had to, 210, 218
Has to, 210, 218
Have/has:
   in present perfect (*They have eaten*), 94
   in present perfect progressive (*They have been driving*), 108
   in questions, contractions with, 143
Have got to, 210, 224
Have to, 194, 224
   in expressions of necessity, 210, 214
   negative of (*do not have to*), 214
   in tag questions, 218
Helping verbs (SEE Auxiliary verbs; *individual verbs*)
Hope so, 414
How:
   in noun clauses, 402
   in questions, 125, 135, 146
      contractions with, 143
      how about, 147
      how come, 125
      how do you do, 146, 146*fn.*
      how far, 140
      how long, 141
      how many, 141
      how many times, 138
      how often, 138

I

-Ied, 31*fn.*, 43
-Ies, 158
***If*-clauses**:
   defined, 80
   expressing future time in, 80
   as noun clauses, 401, 406
Immediate future (*be about to*), 86

Imperatives, in expressions of prohibition, 214
Imperative sentences (*Stop!*), 219
In, as preposition of time, 167
Independent clauses:
    commas between, 229, 230*fn.*, 231, 232
    connected with *and*, 229, 230*fn.*
    connected with *but* or *or*, 231
    connected with *so*, 232
    defined, 229, 345*fn.*
Indirect speech (SEE Reported speech)
Infinitives (*to eat*), 369–399
    in expressions of purpose (*in order to*), 391
    with *it* (*It is easy to cook eggs*), 386, 388
    with modals (*have to study*), 194
    as subjects (*To ride horses is fun*), 386*fn.*
    with *too* and *enough* (*too heavy to lift*), 394
    after verbs (*decided to buy*), 374, 375
Information questions, 125, 433 (SEE ALSO *individual question words*)
-Ing:
    be with (*is/was eating*) (SEE Progressive verbs)
    in gerunds (*Swimming is fun*) (SEE Gerunds)
    in present participles (*They are swimming*) (SEE Present participles)
    spelling with, 43
In order to, 391
Interested vs. *interesting*, 302
Intransitive verbs, 290, 290*fn.*
    phrasal, 434
Irregular adjectives (*good, bad*), 251, 255
Irregular adverbs (*well, badly*), 262
Irregular plural nouns (*tomatoes, fish*), 158, 178
Irregular verbs (*eat, ate, eaten*):
    lists of, 33, 92, 430
    past participles of, 92, 429, 430
    present participles of, 429
    in simple past, 32, 33, 92, 429, 430
It:
    to express distance (*It is two miles …*), 140
    infinitives with (*It is easy to do*), 386, 388
    its vs. *it's*, 181, 433
    with *take* (*length of time*), 141

J

Just:
    in *as … as* comparisons, 268
    in present perfect, 96

L

Least, 255
Less … than, 272

Let's, 221
Like:
    in comparisons, 276
    gerunds or infinitives after, 375*fn.*
    in *like … better*, 222
    in preferences, 222
(A) little, 322
Logical conclusions, 215, 224
(A) lot, 266
(A) lot of, 322
Love, 375*fn.*

M

Main clauses:
    with adverb clauses, 241
    defined, 241
    with time clauses, 57
Many, 322, 323*fn.*
    how many, 141
    how many times, 138
May, 194, 224
    in expressions of permission, 198, 202
    in expressions of possibility, 77, 198, 200
    in polite requests, 202, 205
Maybe, 77
    in expressions of advice, 207
    in expressions of possibility, 198
    vs. *may be*, 198
Measure, units of (*a cup of, a piece of*), 328
Midsentence adverbs (*usually, seldom*), 14, 77*fn.*
Might, 198, 200, 224
Modal auxiliaries, 193–227 (SEE ALSO *individual verbs*)
    defined, 194
    in expressions of ability, 195, 200
    in expressions of advice, 207, 209, 209*fn.*
    in expressions of necessity, 210, 214, 215
    in expressions of permission, 198, 202
    in expressions of possibility, 198, 200
    in expressions of prohibition, 214, 215
    in logical conclusions, 215
    in passive, 296
    in polite requests and questions, 202, 205, 222
    summary of, 224
    tag questions with, 218
More/-er (SEE Comparatives)
Most/-est (SEE Superlatives)
Much:
    modifying comparatives with, 266
    with noncount nouns, 322, 323*fn.*

Must, 224
- in expressions of necessity, 210, 215
- in expressions of prohibition, 214
- in logical conclusions, 215
- negative of (*must not*), 214, 214*fn*., 215

N

Names:
- capitalization of, 339
- *the* with, 337

Nearly, 268

Necessity, expressions of, 210, 214, 215, 224

Negatives:
- of adverbs (*seldom, never*), 14
- of *be* (*am/is/are not*), 2–3, 66
- of *can* (*cannot*), 195, 198
- in comparisons, 267, 268, 272
- contractions of (SEE Contractions)
- of *could* (*could not*), 195
- of *do* (*do not*):
  - contractions of, 3, 32
  - with *have to*, 214
  - in imperative sentences, 219
  - in simple past, 31, 32
  - in simple present, 2–3
  - with *used to*, 60, 60*fn*.
- of gerunds (*not going*), 370
- of *had better* (*had better not*), 209
- of *have to* (*do not have to*), 214
- of infinitives (*not to keep*), 374
- of *may* and *might* (*may/might not*), 198
- of *must* (*must not*), 214, 214*fn*., 215
- in past progressive (*was/were not*), 47
- in present perfect (*has/have not*), 94, 96
- in present progressive (*am/is/are not*), 2
- of *should* (*should not*), 207
- in simple past (*did not*), 31, 32
- in simple present (*does/do not*), 2, 21
- in tag questions, 149
- of *will* (*will not, won't*), 69

Neither, 236

Never, 14
- with *either, neither*, 236, 239*fn*.
- in negative comparisons, 267
- in present perfect, 94

Non-action verbs (SEE Stative verbs)

Noncount nouns (*furniture, mail*), 317, 318
- articles with, 330
- defined, 317, 318
- lists of, 318, 320
- *a lot of, some, several, many/much,* and *a few/a little* with, 322, 323*fn*.
- units of measure with (*two cups of tea*), 328
- used as count nouns (*paper* vs. *a paper*), 325

Non-progressive verbs (SEE Stative verbs)

Nonrestrictive clauses, 353*fn*.

Nonseparable phrasal verbs, 434

Not (SEE Negatives)

Not as ... as, 268, 272

Not so ... as, 268*fn*.

Noun clauses, 400–427
- defined, 401
- with *if/whether*, 401, 406
- with question words (*what he said*), 402
- in quoted speech, 416, 418, 419
- in reported speech, 418, 419, 421
- with *that* (*I think that ...*), 401, 410, 411, 414, 418

Nouns, 157–192
- as adjectives (*a flower garden*), 173
- comparatives (*more/-er*) with, 274
- in contractions:
  - with *am, is, are*, 178
  - with *will*, 71
- count/noncount (*chairs/furniture*) (SEE Count/noncount nouns)
- plural forms of, 9, 158
  - irregular, 158, 178
  - pronunciation of final *-s* in, 160, 432
  - subject–verb agreement with, 169
- possessive (*Tom's*), 178, 258
- as subjects and objects, 162, 164

O

Object pronouns (*him, them*), 175, 433
- in adjective clauses (*whom I met*), 349, 353, 359
- in comparatives (*than him*), 258
- defined, 175

Objects:
- of prepositions (*on the desk*), 164
- of verbs (*is reading a book*), 162
- transitive, 290

On, as preposition of time, 167

One of, 258

Or, 222, 231

Other, 184, 186, 188

Ought to, 207, 209, 209*fn*., 224

P

Parallel verbs (*walks and talks, is walking and talking*), 87

Participial adjectives (*interested* vs. *interesting*), 302

Particles, in phrasal verbs (*put away*), 434
Partitives (SEE Units of measure)
Passive (*It was mailed by Bob*), 282–314
    by-phrase in, 283, 292
    defined, 283
    get in, 305
    modal auxiliaries in (*should be mailed*), 296
    non-progressive (*stative*) forms of, 298
    progressive forms of, 287
    summary of, 283
    transitive verbs in, 290
Past habit (*I used to live in …*), 60
Past participles, 92
    as adjectives (*be tired, be surprised*), 298
        after *get* (*get tired*), 305
        vs. *-ing* (*interested* vs. *interesting*), 302
        with *be* (*be interested in*):
            and noun clauses (*be worried that*), 411
            in passive, 283, 296, 298
    defined, 92, 429
    of irregular verbs, 92, 429, 430
    list of, 92
Past perfect (*had left*), 116
    vs. past progressive, 431
    vs. present perfect, 431
Past progressive (*was eating*), 46–47
    passive, 287
    vs. past perfect, 431
    vs. present progressive, 46
    vs. simple past, 46, 50
Past time, 30–63 (SEE also *individual tenses*)
Periods, 229, 229*fn.*, 416
Permission, expressions of, 198, 202, 224
Personal pronouns (*she, him, they*), 9*fn.*
    subject vs. object, 175, 433
        in adjective clauses (*a man who is/a book that was*), 346, 349, 353, 359
        in comparatives (*than he is/than him*), 258
Phrasal verbs, 434–436
    defined, 434
    gerunds after, 370
    intransitive, 434
    list of, 435–436
    nonseparable, 434
    separable, 434
    three-word, 434
Phrases, defined, 401*fn.*
Place, prepositions of, 168
Please:
    in imperative sentences, 219
    in polite requests, 202, 205
Plurals (SEE Singular and plural)
Polite questions using modals (*May I? Would you?*), 202, 205, 222, 224
Possessive form:
    of adjectives (*my, our*), 181, 332, 433
    of nouns (*Tom's*), 178, 258
    of pronouns (*mine, theirs*), 181, 362, 433
Possibility, expressions of, 77, 198, 200, 224
Prefer, 222
Preferences, 222
Prepositional phrases (*on the desk*), 164
Prepositions (*at, from, under*), 437–438 (SEE also *individual prepositions*)
    in adjective clauses, 359
    in combinations with verbs and adjectives, 437
    gerunds after, 380, 383
    lists of, 164, 437–438
    objects of, 164
    as particle in phrasal verbs (*put off, put on*), 434
    of place, 168
    in questions, as first word, 129*fn.*
    in stative passive (*be married to*), 298
    of time, 167, 168
Present participles (*eating*), 429
    as adjective (*interesting*), 302
    defined, 429
Present perfect (*have eaten*), 91–120
    with *already, yet, just*, and *recently*, 96
    defined, 94
    with *ever* and *never*, 94
    vs. past perfect, 431
    vs. present perfect progressive, 110
    vs. simple past, 104
    with *since* and *for*, 99, 104, 108
    stative verbs in, 108
Present perfect progressive (*have been driving*), 108
    vs. present perfect, 110
    vs. present progressive, 108
Present progressive (*am working*), 2
    for future time, 83
    passive, 287
    vs. past progressive, 46
    vs. present perfect progressive, 108
    vs. simple present, 2, 18*fn.*
Present time, 1–29 (SEE also *individual tenses*)
Principal parts of a verb (*eat, ate, eaten, eating*), 429
Probably, 77, 77*fn.*

Progressive verbs (*be* + *-ing*):
   vs. non-progressive verbs (*I am thinking* vs. *I think*), 18, 108
   passive, 287
   past (*was doing*) (SEE Past progressive)
   present (*is doing*) (SEE Present progressive)
   present perfect (*has been doing*) (SEE Present perfect progressive)
Prohibition, expressions of, 214, 215
Pronouns, 157–192
   in adjective clauses (*who, that, which*), 346, 349, 353, 362
   after comparative adjectives, 258
   contractions with (SEE Contractions)
   personal (*I, them*) (SEE Personal pronouns)
   possessive (*mine, theirs*), 181, 362, 433
   reflexive (*myself, themselves*), 183
Pronunciation:
   be going to, 71
   can vs. *can't*, 195
   of contractions with *not* (*n't*), 40, 195, 214*fn.*
   -ed, 40, 310, 432
   have to, has to, have got to, 210
   'll, 71
   mustn't, 214*fn.*
   -s/-es, 11, 40, 160, 432
   of tag questions, 149
   their, they're, there, 181
   whose vs. *who's*, 180, 362*fn.*
Punctuation, 228–249
   apostrophes (*Tom's*), 178 (SEE ALSO Contractions)
   commas:
      with adverb clauses, 241
      with conjunctions, 229, 230*fn.*, 231, 232
      vs. periods, 229
      in quoted speech, 416
      in series of items, 229*fn.*, 231
      with time clauses, 57
   periods, 229, 229*fn.*, 416
   question marks, 402
   quotation marks, 416, 416*fn.*, 418
Purpose, expressions of, with *in order to* and *for*, 391

Q

Quantity, expressions of (*some*), 328
Question marks, 402
Questions, 121–156 (SEE ALSO *individual question words*)
   about advice (*what should I do?*), 207, 209*fn.*
   contractions with question words, 143, 180
   frequency adverbs in, 14
   information (*why, when*), 125, 433
   of necessity (*do I have to?*), 210
   in past progressive (*were you doing?*), 47
   polite (*would you please?*), 202, 205, 222, 224
   of possession (*whose car is this?*), 180
   prepositions as first word of, 129*fn.*
   in present perfect (*have you done?*), 94, 96
   in present perfect progressive (*have they been driving?*), 108
   in present progressive (*are you doing?*), 2
   in quoted speech, 416
   in reported speech, 421
   in simple past (*did you do?*), 31, 32
   in simple present (*do you do?*), 2
   tag (*You know Bob, don't you?*), 149, 218
   wh-, 125
   yes/no, 21, 31, 122, 406, 433
Quite, 268
Quotation marks, 416, 416*fn.*, 418
Quoted speech, 416, 418, 419

R

Recently, 96
Reflexive pronouns (*myself*), 183
Relative clauses (SEE Adjective clauses)
Reply, 421
Reported speech, 418, 419, 421
Reporting verbs, 419, 421

S

-S/-es:
   with plural nouns (*birds*), 9, 158, 317
   with possessive nouns (*Tom's*), 178
   pronunciation of, 11, 40, 160, 432
   with simple present verbs (*eat*), 2
   spelling with, 11, 158
Same, 276
   as after (*same as*), 276
   the before (*the same*), 276, 333
Say vs. **tell**, 421
-Self/-selves, 183
Separable phrasal verbs, 434
Several, 322
Shall, 65*fn.*
Short answers to questions, 122
   adverb clauses as, 241
   in past progressive, 47
   in simple past, 31, 32
   in simple present, 21
   tag, 149
   with *will*, 69

Should, 224
    in expressions of advice, 207, 209, 209*fn.*
    in tag questions, 218
Similar, 276
Simple form of verbs, 33, 429, 430
    after modal auxiliaries, 194
Simple past, 31
    defined, 31, 429
    irregular verbs in, 32, 33, 92, 429, 430
    vs. past progressive, 46, 50
    vs. present perfect, 104
    regular verbs in, 31, 429
Simple present, 2
    defined, 2
    for future time, 80, 85
    in future time clauses, 80
    vs. present progressive, 2, 18*fn.*
    spelling of, 11
    yes/no questions in, 21
Since:
    present perfect progressive with, 108
    present perfect with, 99, 104, 108
    in *since*-clauses, 99
Singular and plural:
    adjectives, 171, 173
    nouns (*a bird, birds*), 9, 158 (SEE ALSO Count/ noncount nouns)
        a and *an* before, 316
        irregular, 158, 178
        possessive (*student's, students'*), 178
        pronunciation of final *-s* in, 160, 432
        subject–verb agreement with, 169
    of *other*, 184, 186, 188
    personal pronouns (*I, we*), 175
    verbs
        in adjective clauses (*man who is, men who are*), 358
        in simple present, 9
        subject–verb agreement with, 169
So:
    with *and* (*and so do I*), 236
    in *believe so*, 414
    vs. *but*, 232
    connecting ideas with, 232
    in *hope so*, 414
    in *not so … as*, 268*fn.*
    in *so far*, 103*fn.*
    substituted for *that*-clause (*I think so*), 414
Some, 317, 322
Spelling:
    -ed, 43
    -er/-est, 251, 255, 255*fn.*, 262
    -ing, 43
    -s/-es, 11, 158
Stative (non-action/non-progressive) verbs (*know, want, belong*), 18
    defined, 18
    in passive (*is married*), 298
    in present perfect (*have known*), 108
Subject pronouns (*I, she, they*), 175, 433
    in adjective clauses (*a man who is, a book that was*), 346, 353
    in comparatives (*than he is*), 258
    defined, 175
Subjects, verbs, objects, 162
    with transitive vs. intransitive verbs, 290
Subject–verb agreement, 169
Suggestions, 221 (SEE ALSO Advice)
Superlatives (*-est/most*):
    adjectives as, 255, 258
    adverbs as, 262
    with *never*, 267
    spelling of, 255, 255*fn.*
Suppose, 414
Supposed to, 312
S-V-O-P-T, 168

T

Tag questions (*You know Bob, don't you?*), 149
    with modal auxiliaries, 218
Take, with ***it***, for length of time, 141
Tell vs. ***say, ask***, 421
Tenses (SEE *individual tenses*)
Than:
    in comparatives (*more/-er*), 251, 258, 274
    after *different*, 276*fn.*
    in *less … than*, 272
    after *like … better, would rather*, 222
That:
    in adjective clauses (*a book that I read*), 346, 349, 353, 359
    in noun clauses (*He said that …*), 401, 410, 411, 414, 418
    in reported speech, 418, 421*fn.*
The, 332–333
    common expressions without, 333
    with count/noncount nouns, 330
    with double comparatives, 264
    with people and places, 337
    with *same*, 276, 333
    with superlative adjectives, 255
There:
    with *be* (*is there, there is*), 122, 169
    vs. *their* and *they're*, 181

Think:
   as progressive and non-progressive verb, 18
   so after, 414
This, 332
This + morning/afternoon/evening, 65
Though, 244
Three-word phrasal verbs, 434
Till, 164*fn.*
Time:
   expressions of length of, 99, 104, 108, 141
   prepositions of, 167, 168
Time clauses, 57
   defined, 57
   future, 80
   past, 57
   placement of, 81*fn.*
   with *since*, 99
To:
   with auxiliary verbs and simple form of verbs, 194, 207
   with gerunds, 370, 372
   in *in order to*, to express purpose, 391
   after *similar*, 276
   with simple form of verb (SEE Infinitives)
   in *to ... from*, to express distance, 140
Today, 65
Tonight, 65
Too:
   with *and* (*and I do too*), 236
   infinitives with (*too heavy to lift*), 394
Transitive verbs, 290, 290*fn.*
Two-word phrasal verbs, 434

U

Units of measure (*a cup of, a piece of*), 328
Until:
   vs. *till*, 164*fn.*
   in time clauses, 57, 57*fn.*, 80, 81*fn.*
Used to (*past habit*), 60
   vs. *be used to*, 310, 310*fn.*

V

Verbs:
   active, 283
   irregular, 32, 33, 92, 429
   parallel, 87
   principal parts of, 429
   reporting, 419, 421
   simple form of, 33, 194, 429
   singular and plural:
      in adjective clauses, 358
   in simple present, 9
   subject–verb agreement with, 169
   vs. subjects and objects, 162
   transitive and intransitive, 290, 290*fn.*
   (SEE ALSO Auxiliary verbs; Modal auxiliaries; Passive; Phrasal verbs; *individual verbs*
Verb tenses (SEE *individual tenses*)
Very, 266
Vowels:
   an before words beginning with, 316
   defined, 11*fn.*

W

Was, were:
   in past progressive, 46–47
   in simple past, 32
What:
   in noun clauses, 402
   in questions, 125, 128
      contractions with, 143
      with forms of *do*, 131
      what about, 147
      what ... for, 125
      what kind of, 133
      what time, 125
   vs. *which*, 133
When:
   in noun clauses, 402
   in questions, 125
      contractions with, 143
   in time clauses, 57, 80
   vs. *while*, 50
Where:
   in noun clauses, 402
   in questions, 125
      contractions with, 143
Whether, in noun clauses, 401, 406
Which:
   in adjective clauses, 353, 359
   in nonrestrictive clauses, 353*fn.*
   in noun clauses, 402
   in questions, 133
   vs. *what*, 133
While:
   in time clauses, 57, 80
   vs. *when*, 50
Who/who(m):
   in adjective clauses, 346, 349, 353, 358, 359
   in noun clauses, 402
   in questions, 128
      contractions with, 143
   who's vs. *whose*, 180, 362*fn.*

***Whose*:**
   in adjective clauses, 362
   in noun clauses, 402
   in questions, 180
   vs. *who's,* 180, 362*fn.*
***Wh*-questions,** 125 (SEE ALSO *individual question words*)
***Why*:**
   negative of (*why don't*), 221
   in noun clauses, 402
   in questions, 125
      contractions with, 143
   why don't, 221
***Will*,** 194, 224
   vs. *be going to,* 73
   in contractions:
      with nouns, 71
      with pronouns, 69, 69*fn.,* 71
      with question words, 143
   forms with, 69
   for future time, 65, 69, 77
   in polite requests, 205
   with *probably,* 77
   in tag questions, 218

With vs. ***by*,** 383
Word order (S-V-O-P-T), 168
***Would*,** 194, 224
   in contractions with pronouns, 222
   in polite requests, 205
   in tag questions, 218
   in *would rather,* 222

Y

-*Y*:
   adjectives ending in, 251, 255
   nouns ending in, 158
   verbs ending in, 31*fn.,* 43
***Yes/no* questions,** 122
   defined, 122
   vs. information questions, 433
   noun clauses as answers to, 406
   in simple past, 31
   in simple present, 21
***Yet*,** 96

Credits

Photo Credits: Page **xv**: Mjth/Shutterstock; **1**: Eugenio Marongiu/Shutterstock; **3**: Mavo/Shutterstock; **4**: Frantic00/Shutterstock; **5** (top left): Sergey Nivens/Shutterstock; **5** (top right): Sergey Nivens/Shutterstock; **5** (A1): Motive56/Shutterstock; **5** (A2): Irina Schmidt/123RF; **5** (A3): Fesus/123RF; **5** (A4): Igor Goncharenko/123RF; **5** (A5): Nullplus/Shutterstock; **5** (A6): Margouillat photo/Shutterstock; **5** (B1): Maru1122maru/123RF; **5** (B2): Kzenon/123RF; **5** (B3): Sergey Nivens/123RF; **5** (B4): Prostock-studio/Shutterstock; **5** (B5): Nicoelnino/123RF; **5** (B6): Hannamariah/Shutterstock; **7**: Gorodenkoff/123RF; **8** (top): Andriy Popov/123RF; **8** (center): Anastasia Kazakova/123RF; **9**: Orla/Shutterstock; **10**: Welcomia/123RF; **11**: Amicabel/123RF; **12** (1): Believeinme33/123RF; **12** (2): Jozef Polc/123RF; **12** (3): Wavebreakmedia/Shutterstock; **12** (4): IM_photo/Shutterstock; **12** (5): Tetiana Kolinko/123RF; **12** (6): EpicStockMedia/Shutterstock; **16**: Ekaterina_Minaeva/Shutterstock; **17**: Leekris/123RF; **20**: Kiryl Lis/Shutterstock; **21**: Maxpro/Shutterstock; **22**: Ampyang/123RF; **23**: Zanna Bojarsinova/123RF; **24**: Shutterstock; **25** (gorilla): Andrey Gudkov/123RF; **25** (mosquito): Dimijana/Shutterstock; **26**: Nestor Rizhniak/Shutterstock; **27**: Syda Productions/Shutterstock; **28**: Andrey Guryanov/123RF; **30**: Funandrejss/123RF; **32**: Kylie Ellway/123RF; **34** (1): Ansis klucis/123RF; **34** (2): Nelson Marques/Shutterstock **34** (3): Kwangmoozaa/Shutterstock; **34** (4): Odua Images/Shutterstock; **34** (5): Brian Jackson/123RF; **34** (6): Viacheslav Muzyka/123RF; **35**: Donaveh/123RF; **36**: Space Chimp/Shutterstock; **37** (top): Ariwasabi/Shutterstock; **37** (center): Fizkes/Shutterstock; **39**: Joe Tabb/123RF: **40**: Castleski/Shutterstock; **42**: Shutterstock; **45** (top): Anna Kucherova/123RF; **45** (bottom): Mark benford/123RF; **48** (1): Andriy Popov/123RF; **48** (2): Anatoliy Sadovskiy/123RF; **48** (3): Danil Chepko/123RF; **48** (4): Andrey_Kuzmin/Shutterstock; **49**: Narongsak Nagadhana/Shutterstock; **50**: Pio3/Shutterstock; **52**: Richard Whitcombe/Shutterstock; **53** (ant): Iimages/123RF; **53** (toucan): Dazdraperma/123RF; **53** (lion): Chris Doehling/123RF; **53** (mouse): Blueringmedia/123RF; **55** (top): Maksym Chornii/123RF; **55** (bottom): Evgenyi Lastochkin/123RF; **56**: Carolyn Franks/Shutterstock; **59**: Pablo Hidalgo/123RF; **61**: Sabphoto/Shutterstock; **62**: Rondale/123RF; **64**: Sunny Forest/Shutterstock; **67**: Marina Troshenkova/123RF; **68**: Diane Garcia/Shutterstock; **69**: Leonard Zhukovsky/Shutterstock; **74**: Rockongkoy/Shutterstock; **77**: Ilfede/123RF; **79** (top): Antonio Guillem/123RF; **79** (bottom): IQoncept/Shutterstock; **81**: Tanya Puntti/Shutterstock; **82**: Wavebreak Media Ltd/123RF; **86** (top left): Digital Storm/Shutterstock; **86** (top right): Tyler Olson/123RF; **86** (1): Luckyraccoon/Shutterstock; **86** (2): Aleksandra Suzi/Shutterstock; **86** (3): Maru1122maru/123RF; **86** (4): Pressmaster/Shutterstock; **86** (5): Belozerova Daria/Shutterstock; **86** (6): Matushchak Anton/Shutterstock; **86** (7): Carballo/Shutterstock; **86** (8): Jaromir Chalabala/Shutterstock; **86** (9): Lan Iankovskii/123RF; **89** (top): Ekaterina Minaeva/123RF; **89** (bottom): Phase4Photography/Shutterstock; **90**: Tetyana Kulikova/Shutterstock; **91**: Ali osman pekoglu/123RF; **93**: Maria Dryfhout/123RF; **95** (muscle): Hobrath/123RF; **95** (cabin): Dvoevnore/Shutterstock; **96** (left): Odua Images/Shutterstock; **96** (right): Wavebreakmedia/Shutterstock; **97**: Jesadaphorn/Shutterstock; **101** (top): SpeedKingz/Shutterstock; **101** (bottom): Iryna Inshyna/Shutterstock; **102** (top): Sornwut tabtawee/123RF; **102** (bottom): Mona Makela/Shutterstock; **103**: Goldenjack/Shutterstock; **104**: Wavebreakmedia/Shutterstock; **105**: Kostenko Maxim/Shutterstock; **106**: Noppasin Wongchum/123RF; **108**: Shutterstock; **109**: Viacheslav Nikolaenko/Shutterstock; **110** (left): India Picture/Shutterstock; **110** (right): Imagedb.com/Shutterstock; **112**: Suti Stock Photo/Shutterstock; **113**: Diego vito cervo/123RF; **114**: PR Image Factory/Shutterstock; **115**: Alexander Raths/Shutterstock; **116** (left): George Rudy/Shutterstock; **116** (right) Wavebreakmedia/Shutterstock; **117**: Dean Drobot/Shutterstock; **119**: Leungchopan/Shutterstock; **121**: Wideonet/Shutterstock; **123**: Alex Popov/123RF; **124**: Duplass/Shutterstock; **125**: Creative Travel Projects/Shutterstock; **127**: Katarzyna

Białasiewicz/123RF; **128**: Iakov Kalinin/123RF; **130**: Asier Romero/Shutterstock; **131**: Albertus engbers/123RF; **132**: Foodandmore/123RF; **135**: Pearlphoto/123RF; **136**: Vadim Petrakov/Shutterstock; **137**: Shutterstock; **138**: Johan2011/123RF; **139**: Olegdudko/123RF; **143**: Ruth Black/123RF; **144**: Matej Kastelic/Shutterstock; **147**: Arena Creative/Shutterstock; **151**: Kamil Macniak/Shutterstock; **152**: Justmeyo/123RF; **153**: Olga Dogadina/Shutterstock; **157**: Elvira Koneva/123RF; **158**: Ymgerman/123RF; **159** (businesspeople): Mark Bowden/123RF; **159** (Mexican food): Tonobalaguer/123RF; **159** (butterfly): Tobkatrina/123RF; **159** (boy & dinosaur skeleton): Pavel L Photo and Video/Shutterstock; **162**: Jaysi/123RF; **163**: Vanessa van Rensburg/ Shutterstock; **164**: Freeograph/123RF; **165**: Elenathewise/123RF; **166**: Dracozlat/123RF; **167** (student in library): My Visuals/123RF; **167** (sad birthday): Dmitriy Shironosov/123RF; **167** (fashion designer): Elnur/ Shutterstock; **169**: Volodymyr Burdiak/Shutterstock; **170**: Angela Waye/Shutterstock; **171**: Five-Birds Photography/Shutterstock; **173** (roast chicken): Magone/123RF; **173** (brick wall): Sedat seven/123RF; **174**: Vicspacewalker/Shutterstock; **176** (carrot cake): Brent Hofacker/123RF; **176** (chocolate tart): Alexey Astakhov/123RF; **176** (ice cream sandwiches): Natasha Breen/123RF; **176** (bees): Diyana Dimitrova/ Shutterstock; **176** (ping pong table): Mark Vorobev/123RF; **177** (left): Ammentorp/123RF; **177** (right): Ammentorp/123RF; **179** (top): Eobrazy/123RF; **179** (bottom right): Shutterstock; **180** (woman and handbag): Akz/123RF; **180** (boy with apple): Parinya Binsuk/123RF; **180** (man getting into car): Andrey_Popov/ Shutterstock; **180** (dog): Jaromir Chalabala/123RF; **180** (ski vacation): ProStockStudio/Shutterstock; **182**: Gresei/Shutterstock; **183** (man and mirror): Dean Drobot/Shutterstock; **183** (woman and mirror): Katielittle/Shutterstock; **183** (cat and mirror): Rasulov/Shutterstock; **184**: Marina Lvova/123RF; **184**: Marina Lvova/123RF; **184**: Marina Lvova/123RF; **185** (washer & drier): Golf Money/Shutterstock; **185** (washer & drier): Golf Money/Shutterstock; **185** (stove): Neamov/Shutterstock; **185** (stove): Neamov/Shutterstock; **186** (microwave): Oleksandr_Delyk/Shutterstock; **186** (dishwasher): Moreno Soppelsa/Shutterstock; **186** (refrigerator): Ppart/Shutterstock; **186** (saw): Phrej/Shutterstock; **186** (hammer): Revers/Shutterstock; **186** (screwdriver): Gareth Boden/Pearson Education Ltd; **186** (wrench): Lotus_studio/Shutterstock; **186** (tulips left): Allegro7/123RF; **186** (tulips right): Liligraphie/123RF; **189**: Dolgachov/123RF; **191** (man): Blaj Gabriel/ Shutterstock; **191** (woman): Maridav/123RF; **193**: Germanskydiver/Shutterstock; **195**: 2xSamara.com/ Shutterstock; **196** (chess): Vetkit/Shutterstock; **196** (guitar player): Arieliona/Shutterstock; **198**: Kichigin/ Shutterstock; **199**: Sirtravelalot/Shutterstock; **200**: Dotshock/Shutterstock; **201**: Nadezda Ledyaeva/123RF; **202**: Eunika/123RF; **204**: Shutterstock; **207**: Image Point Fr/Shutterstock; **209**: Woodoo007/123RF; **213**: Stokkete/Shutterstock; **215**: Golubovy/123RF; **217**: Dolgachov/123RF; **219**: Belchonock/123RF; **220**: Dieter Hawlan/Shutterstock; **222**: Africa Studio/Shutterstock; **225**: StockLite/Shutterstock; **228**: Markus Mainka/Shutterstock; **229**: Laurent davoust/123RF; **230** (all images): Marina113/123RF; **231**: Lightspring/ Shutterstock; **232** (top): Thamkc/123RF; **232** (bottom): Arena Creative/Shutterstock; **233** (tarantula): Mirek Kijewski/Shutterstock; **233** (elephants): Claudia Paulussen/Shutterstock; **233** (dolphin): Christian Musat/ Shutterstock; **233** (toll booth): S-F/Shutterstock; **235**: Samuel Acosta/Shutterstock; **238**: Markus Pfaff/ Shutterstock; **241**: Larry Rains/123RF; **242**: G215/123RF; **243**: Alex Cofaru/Shutterstock; **244**: Xray Computer/Shutterstock; **245** (top): Ollyy/Shutterstock; **245** (bottom): Feruz Malik/Shutterstock; **247** (writing with pen): Sakkmesterke/Shutterstock; **247** (baseball): Gino Santa Maria/Shutterstock; **248**: Jordan Tan/ Shutterstock; **250**: Murali Nath/123RF; **250** (Daniel): Wang Tom/123RF; **250** (Taka): Arek_malang/ Shutterstock; **252**: Almoond/123RF; **253**: John McLaird/123RF; **256**: Ildogesto/Shuttertsock; **257**: Dolgachov/123RF; **261** (diamond): Alexander Maslennikov/Shutterstock; **261** (Great Wall): Songquan Deng/ Shutterstock; **261** (volcano): Orxy/Shutterstock; **263** (top): Stefanolunardi/Shutterstock; **263** (bottom): Sergey Novikov/Shutterstock; **265** (boy & balloon): Sabphoto/123RF; **265** (ambulance): Cheryl Casey/Shutterstock; **265** (globe): Serg64/Shutterstock; **267**: Serazetdinov/Shutterstock; **268** (Niki): Bruno135/123RF; **268** (Alex): Rido/123RF; **268** (Emilio): Auremar/123RF; **268** (Maya): 123RF; **270** (Tia): Sjenner13/123RF; **270** (Amira): Antonio Guillem/123RF; **270** (Jasmine): Michel Borges/Shutterstock; **270** (Sachi): Kenneth Man/Shutterstock; **270** (Emily): Jon Barlow/Pearson Education Ltd; **271** (ox): Prapass/Shutterstock; **271** (mule): Robynrg/ Shutterstock; **271** (hornet): Melinda Fawver/123RF; **273**: Thomas Dutour/123RF; **274**: Sam D Cruz/123RF; **276** (geese): E. O./Shutterstock; **276** (duck): Anatolii Tsekhmister/123RF; **277** (orange): Roman Samokhin/ Shutterstock; **277** (peach): Natika/123RF; **277** (silver & gold): Konstantin Inozemtcev/123RF; **278**: apoplexia/ RF123; **279**: Anek Suwannaphoom/123RF; **280**: Andreas G. Karelias/Shutterstock; **284**: Sergey Mironov/ Shutterstock; **285**: Oleksiy Mark/Shutterstock; **286**: Noviantoko Tri Arijanto/123RF; **287**: Elena Dijour/

Shutterstock; **288**: Peshkova/Shutterstock; **289**: Action Sports Photography/Shutterstock; **291**: Wdg Photo/Shutterstock; **292**: Travelview/Shutterstock; **293**: Bea Rue/Shutterstock; **294** (police officer): Paul Vasarhelyi/123RF; **294** (bicyclist): Szefei/Shutterstock; **295**: Alberto cervantes/Shutterstock; **296**: Karelnoppe/Shutterstock; **297**: Africa Studio/Shutterstock; **299** (anxious man): Kurhan/Shutterstock; **299** (confident woman): Iodrakon/Shutterstock; **302** (shark): Clay S. Turner/Shutterstock; **302** (swimmer): Pacter Gudella/123RF; **303** (top left): Neil Lang/Shutterstock; **303** (top right): Jacob Lund/Shutterstock; **303** (bottom): Kittipong Jirasukhanont/123RF; **304**: Vladimir Tarasov/123RF; **306**: Mark Bowden/123RF; **309**: Rawpixel.com/Shutterstock; **310**: Fejas/Shutterstock; **312**: Rob Wilson/Shutterstock; **313**: Nick Reynolds Photography/Shutterstock; **315**: Poznyakov/Shutterstock; **316**: Robyn Mackenzie/Shutterstock; **317** (blue chair): Photobac/Shutterstock; **317** (red chair): Photosync/Shutterstock; **317** (orange chair): Aleksandr Kurganov/Shutterstock; **322**: DOPhoto/Shutterstock; **325** (eye glasses): Aimy27feb/123RF; **325** (broken window): Maroon Studio/Shutterstock; **325** (drinking glass): Belchonock/123RF; **326** (brown chicken): Stockphoto mania/Shutterstock; **326** (chick): Anneka/Shutterstock; **326** (roast chicken): Dani Vincek/Shutterstock; **326** (fried chicken): Bigacis/Shutterstock; **326** (white chickens): Malcolm Harris/Pearson Education Ltd; **326** (free range chicken): Elenathewise/123RF; **327**: Miroslav Pesek/123RF; **328** (pasta with sauce): Subbotina/123RF; **328** (shopping basket): Cherries/Shutterstock; **329** (one dog): Wasitt Hemwarapornchai/Shutterstock; **329** (three dogs): Rybaltovskaya Marina/Shutterstock; **330** (red house): Pixel Embargo/Shutterstock; **330** (ice cream scoop): Olga Lyubkina/Shutterstock; **330** (ice cream bowl): M. Unal Ozmen/Shutterstock; **333** (prisoner): Liron Peer/Shutterstock; **333** (bottom): Peter Engstrom/123RF; **334**: Sari ONeal/Shutterstock; **335**: Africa Studio/Shutterstock; **336** (center): Primagefactory/123RF; **336** (bottom): kastianz/Shutterstock; **337**: Aetherial Images/Shutterstock; **338**: Scanrail/123RF; **341**: Tinseltown/Shutterstock; **342**: Olga Khelmitskaya/123RF; **344**: Andrey Armyagov/Shutterstock; **345**: Chris Noble/123RF; **346**: Wavebreak Media Ltd/123RF; **347** (top): 3quarks/Shutterstock; **347** (bottom): Budimir Jevtic/Shutterstock; **348**: Rido/Shutterstock; **349**: Suzanne Tucker/Shutterstock; **350**: Alexander Raths/Shutterstock; **351** (top): Kasto/123RF; **351** (bottom): Katarzyna Białasiewicz/123RF; **352**: Eric Isselee/123RF; **353**: Sirinapa/123RF; **354** (like symbol): Umarazak/Shutterstock; **355**: Flamingo Images/Shutterstock; **356**: Mark Bowden/123RF; **357**: V_E/Shutterstock; **361**: Ljansempoi/Shutterstock; **362**: Michaeljung/Shutterstock; **363**: Shutterstock; **365**: Focus and Blur/Shutterstock; **368**: Anna Shepulova/Shutterstock; **369**: Federico Rostagno/Shutterstock; **370** (bakery owners): Racorn/123RF; **370** (eating hamburger): Peter Albrektsen/Shutterstock; **370** (stressed woman): Voyagerix/Shutterstock; **371**: Chitsanupong Chuenthananont/123RF; **372**: Olga Khoroshunova/123RF; **373** (skier): Shutterstock; **373** (camping): Bozulek/Shutterstock; **373** (bowling): Africa Studio/Shutterstock; **373** (ice skating): Roman Babakin/Shutterstock; **373** (sailing): Ivan Smuk/Shutterstock; **373** (hiking): Maridav/Shutterstock; **373** (fishing): Mark Bowden/123RF; **373** (jogging): Fotokostic/Shutterstock; **373** (swimming): Jane September/Shutterstock; **373** (shopping): Zoriana Zaitseva/Shutterstock; **375**: Belchonock/123RF; **377** (top right): Anastasia Vish/123RF; **377** (bottom): Wang Tom/123RF; **380** (woman): Kinga/Shutterstock; Aaron Amat/Shutterstock; **382**: Alexei Novikov/123RF; **385** (scissors): Tsz-shan Kwok/Pearson Education Asia Ltd; **385** (thermometer): Kanchana Phikulthong/123RF; **385** (needle & thread): Konstantin Kirillov/123RF; **385** (broom): Jarp5/123RF; **385** (spoon) Pirtuss/Shutterstock; **385** (hammer): Sergiy Kuzmin/Shutterstock; **385** (shovel): Lostintrance/Shutterstock; **385** (saw): Gearstd/Shutterstock; **386**: Rido/123RF; **387**: Mark Brooks/123RF; **388**: Wavebreak Media Ltd/123RF; **389**: Wang Tom/123RF; **390**: Mangostock/Shutterstock; **391**: Mangostock/Shutterstock; **393** (top): Joao Virissimo/Shutterstock; **393** (bottom): Zapp2Photo/Shutterstock; **394**: Gleb TV/123RF; **395** (top): Angela Waye/Shutterstock; **395** (center): ChristianChan/Shutterstock; **398**: Rob Marmion/123RF; **400**: Voin_Sveta/Shutterstock; **402**: Michaeljung/Shutterstock; **404**: Oleksiy Mark/Shutterstock; **407**: Goodluz/Shutterstock; **408**: Ion Chiosea/123RF; **409**: Dolgachov/123RF; **410**: Rawpixel/123RF; **411** (capsule): Nirot Sriprasit/123RF; **411** (party): Wavebreakmedia/Shutterstock; **412**: Nicoelnino/Shutterstock; **413**: Olena Yakobchuk/Shutterstock; **414**: Andriy Popov/123RF; **415**: Elwynn/Shutterstock; **416**: Petr Podrouzek/123RF; **417**: Andreypopov/123RF; **418** (top): Jon Barlow/Pearson Education Ltd; **418** (bottom right): StockLite/Shutterstock; **421**: Vadim Guzhva/123RF; **422**: Ilic Nikola/123RF; **424**: Katja Heinemann/Cavan/Aurora Photos/Alamy Stock Photo; **429**: Igors Rusakovs/123RF.

Illustration credits: Aptara, page 188; Don Martinetti—70, 140, 187, 236, 237, 254, 268, 269, 277, 282, 283, 426; Chris Pavely—33, 43

NOTES